Additional Praise for *A Church Undone*

"Our temptation for seven decades has been to seek out and describe Christians in Germany who opposed the Nazi regime. The publication of these documents provides a very welcome corrective. It is not just that Christians in Nazi Germany lacked the courage to oppose Hitler. Too many also misconstrued what we would like to consider the appropriate Christian stance."

Robert P. Ericksen
Pacific Lutheran University

"English-language audiences have had extensive exposure to Holocaust studies. Thousands of works have investigated how a nation, then teacher to the world, could have descended to the depths of unspeakable evil. But English-language audiences have not had, until now, documentation and analysis of a significant movement in the Protestant churches that contributed to the theological and cultural production of that evil. Mary Solberg, in *A Church Undone*, provides previously untranslated documents for close-in contact with the German Christian Faith Movement. Until religious perversion of truth and humanity are ended, the cautionary tale of this volume remains relevant. I highly commend careful attention to it and thank Fortress Press for making it available."

Larry Rasmussen
Emeritus, Union Theological Seminary

A Church Undone

A Church Undone

Documents from the German Christian Faith Movement,
1932-1940

Selected, Translated, and Introduced by Mary
M. Solberg

Fortress Press
Minneapolis

A CHURCH UNDONE

Documents from the German Christian Faith Movement, 1932-1940

Cover image: Bundesarchiv Bild, Berlin/Wikimedia Commons

Cover design: Laurie Ingram

Library of Congress Cataloging-in-Publication Data

Print ISBN: 978-1-4514-6472-6

eBook ISBN: 978-1-4514-9666-6

The paper used in this publication meets the minimum requirements of American National Standard for Information Sciences — Permanence of Paper for Printed Library Materials, ANSI Z329.48-1984.

Manufactured in the U.S.A.

This book was produced using PressBooks.com, and PDF rendering was done by PrinceXML.

Contents

Preface and Acknowledgments

The material from which these translated excerpts were drawn is interesting, sometimes even fascinating, but very little of it could be described as edifying. As the bibliography of German Christian documents at the back of this volume indicates, much more could be translated. Whether even what appears here *deserves* to be translated and published is of course open to discussion. There is always a danger, when one engages in a project like this one, that one might be providing a platform—or be seen to be providing a platform—for views that are ignorant at the least and utterly repugnant at the worst. Other documents, including those expressing views sharply critical of the views presented here, may well have an equal or even a more urgent claim to be published. I took on this project because I believed that it was important for these documents to be accessible in English to those who study this period and either cannot access them or do not read German.

My engagement with this project has broadened my understanding of the challenges that faced the Protestant [Lutheran] church in Nazi Germany and intensified my sense of profound disappointment with its conduct during a period that cried out for ethical and religious courage and found very, very little of it. I am also chastened by the sobering realization that, had I lived through that period of history and faced those challenges, I might not have shown much courage either.

I have been encouraged in this project by a number of people who know much more about all of this than I do. Their conviction that this project is worthwhile has buoyed me often, and I will always be grateful. Among them are Victoria Barnett, Doris Bergen, Larry Rasmussen, and Lisa Dahill. In Germany I was privileged to interview Peter von der Osten-Sacken and Manfred Gailus, both of whom provided sharp insights into the conduct of the churches during 1930s Germany. Hartmut Ludwig helped me appreciate the considerable variety, and the tensions, that existed among German Christian groups.

Friends as well as colleagues who were kind enough to read and respond to various versions of the introduction have helped me improve it, chiefly by pointing out the need for more information here and there and by reminding me that an introduction needs to be an invitation and not so much a dissertation. I appreciate especially the constructive comments of Mary Beth Walsh, Marty Sozansky, Susan Sparks, Jeanne Gilbertson, John Cha, Thia Cooper, and Sarah Ruble. I am completely responsible for any shortcomings in the general introduction and the introductions to individual documents.

The commitment of Fortress Press to this project started with Michael West and Pamela Johnson; Will Bergkamp and Lisa Gruenisen have shepherded it through to its publication, patiently, attentively, and competently. Linda Maloney made sure my translation was publishable, and I thank her warmly!

My life partner and spouse, Sonia Ramirez, never doubted either the significance of this project or my ability to complete it. That is only a fraction of what I am grateful to her for!

I cannot leave my late parents, Richard and June Solberg, out of these prefatory reflections. Their work in helping to rebuild the church and church-related social services in Germany after World War II and during the Cold War shaped their lives and their children's lives (including mine) profoundly. Friendships born during those years were passed on to my generation. And we, their children, wrestle even today with what our parents must have known, lived through, and lived out. May God bless their memory.

Mary M. Solberg
St. Peter, MN
December 2014

List of Images

Figure 1. German text of "Guidelines of the German Christian Faith Movement." From Deutsche Christen (Nationalkirchliche Einung), *Handbuch der Deutschen Christen*, 2nd ed. (Berlin-Charlottenburg, 1933).

Figure 2. Hitler leaving the St. Mary's Church in Wilhelmshaven. From Constantin Grossmann, *Deutsche Christen: Ein Volksbuch: Wegweiser durch die Glaubensbewegung unserer Zeit* (Dresden: Verlag E. am Ende, 1934), between pp. 8 and 9.

Figure 3. Title page for *Theological Existence Today!* by Karl Barth. From Karl Barth, *Theologische Existenz heute!*, 9th ed. (Munich: Christian Kaiser Verlag, 1934). First published 1933.

Figure 4. Title page for *What the German Christians Want for the Church* by Emanuel Hirsch. From Emanuel Hirsch, *Das kirchliche Wollen der Deutschen Christen*, 2nd ed. (Berlin-Charlottenburg: Verlag Max Grevemeyer, 1933).

Figure 5. Cover of *Handbook of the German Christians*. From Deutsche Christen (Nationalkirchliche Einung), *Handbuch der Deutschen Christen*, 2nd ed. (Berlin-Charlottenburg, 1933).

Figure 6. Sketch of Martin Luther. From Constantin Grossmann, *Deutsche Christen: Ein Volksbuch: Wegweiser durch die Glaubensbewegung unserer Zeit* (Dresden: Verlag E. am Ende, 1934), between pp. 126 and 127.

Figure 7. Sketch of and quotation from Hitler. From Christian Kinder, ed., *Der Deutschen Christen Reichs-Kalender 1935* (Meissen: Schlimpert & Püschel Gmbh, 1935), frontispiece.

Figure 8. Title page for *Our Struggle* by Joachim Hossenfelder. From Joachim Hossenfelder, *Unser Kampf* (Berlin-Charlottenburg: Verlag Max Grevemeyer ["Deutsche Christen"], 1933).

Figure 9. Title page for *Outline of German Theology* by Friedrich Wieneke. From Friedrich Wieneke, *Deutsche Theologie im Umriss* (Soldin: H. Madrasch, 1933).

Figure 10. Title page for *German Christians: A People's Book: A Guide Through Today's Faith Movement,* by Constantin Grossman. From Constantin Grossmann, *Deutsche Christen: Ein Volksbuch: Wegweiser durch die Glaubensbewegung unserer Zeit* (Dresden: Verlag E. am Ende, 1934).

Figure 11. German Christian logo from the title page for *Der Deutschen Christen Reichs-Kalender 1935.* From Christian Kinder, ed. *Der Deutschen Christen Reichs-Kalender 1935.* Meissen: Schlimpert & Püschel, 1935.

Figure 12. Reich bishop Müller speaking to students at the University of Berlin about the responsibilities of the church. From Constantin Grossmann, *Deutsche Christen: Ein Volksbuch: Wegweiser durch die*

Introduction

Mary M. Solberg

This book lays before the reader a selection of texts published mainly during the 1930s by the German Christians, a minority movement within the Protestant church in Germany that enthusiastically supported Hitler and National Socialism and sought to make the church their instrument.[1] Scholars who write about this period and this movement have of course unearthed and pored over many such documents—flyers, pamphlets, and books. These documents have provided a basis for substantive historical and theological analyses of the Protestant church, the German Christian movement in particular, and their roles in the larger drama of the Third Reich. I am deeply indebted to these scholars, whose work has guided my own understanding of the German Christians and their context.[2] I have relied heavily on their insights.

---

1. Throughout this book the phrase "German Christian" and its variants refer not to German people who were Christians, but rather to members of the German Christian faith movement. The category "German Christian" included a wide variety of groups, all dedicated to nazifying the Christian church.
2. A bibliography at the end of this volume includes some of the most significant English-language books that deal with the German Christian faith movement.

In contrast to the books written by such scholars, however, the present project is less a book *about* the German Christians than an attempt to provide access *in their own words* to what the German Christians believed and thought. This book contains representative selections from these documents, making them available in English for the first time.

The documents in this volume represent one piece of a very complicated and much larger puzzle. Expressions of the ideological corruption of religion in Nazi Germany, they provide a unique, microcosmic view of a particular collection of groups. Responses to several German Christian documents from those who opposed them are also included in this volume. But many other incisive, critical reactions to German Christian positions and activities, reactions that came both from within Germany and from ecumenical groups outside of Germany, remain to be translated and published.[3] The addition of these materials to the resources available to scholars and students will surely both complicate the picture and help complete it.

In his study of the ideas that animated the German Christians, James A. Zabel articulates a view other scholars share:

> It is difficult to ascertain the precise importance of the German Christians to the rise and furtherance of Nazism, but one can be certain that theirs was no small contribution. . . . German Christians provided ideological briefs for the rise and maintenance of Nazism that encouraged almost total church support for the regime.[4]

---

3. One of the most important protest documents is the memorandum sent to Hitler in early June 1936 by the Provisional Church Government of the Confessing Church. See Victoria Barnett, *For the Soul of the People: Protestant Protest Against Hitler* (New York: Oxford University Press, 1992), 83-84, for a brief account of the contents of this memo, the circumstances surrounding its delivery, and the fallout that ensued.

4. James A. Zabel, *Nazism and the Pastors: A Study of the Ideas of Three Deutsche Christen Groups* (Missoula, MT: Scholars Press, 1976), xii.

With respect to the German Christians, "What were they *thinking?*" is not simply a rhetorical question, but a serious one, to which the translated texts offered here suggest elements of a response. Documents published by the German Christians, including those found in this volume, reveal that their authors played what they believed to be a consequential role in constructing elements of a powerful myth, both German and Christian, that complemented, strengthened, and served National Socialist goals. As Siegfried Leffler, an influential leader within the German Christian faith movement, wrote, "[S]triving for the kingdom [*Reich*] of God and striving for the German Reich, being a German and being a Christian—these notions are indissolubly linked with one another!"[5]

To Begin With

For many years, I knew next to nothing about the role of the churches in Nazi Germany in facilitating ignorance or tolerance in the face of evil. I knew of course about Dietrich Bonhoeffer, the young Lutheran pastor executed by the Nazis for his role in a plot to kill Hitler. If he was atypical in his heroic work in the resistance, I supposed, at least he must have had some numerically significant company among his fellow Christians in Germany. Surely others—theologians, pastors, laypeople—had spoken out or actively stood in the way of the Nazi juggernaut.

As it turned out, I had made some assumptions that I had not examined.

This I discovered when one of my students, Aaltje Baumgart, chose to write her thesis on the conduct of the German churches during the Third Reich. I urged her to try to locate whatever primary

---

5. From *Christ in Germany's Third Reich: The Nature, the Path, and the Goal of the German Christian Church Movement*, excerpted in this volume. See p. 337ff.

materials she could and to integrate them into her work. Instead of immediately recruiting Dietrich Bonhoeffer—a move my assumptions would have led me to make—my student had the pluck to scan a wider horizon. At a nearby college library, she was able to track down the *Handbook of the German Christians* [*Handbuch Der Deutsche Christen*], a 28-page pamphlet published in 1933 by a group associated with the German Christian Faith Movement. Bound together with a few others like it, the pamphlet had evidently been purchased by an American traveler in Germany during the mid-1930s and donated to the college library decades ago.

I was eager to examine the book. "German Christians," I wondered. "Who could they be?" As I pored over the fragile, yellowing pages, covered with old-fashioned Gothic German font, I was by turns fascinated and horrified, a bit as if I were watching an automobile accident. I read this: "The great experience from which radiates everything we think and do today is Adolf Hitler and the National Socialist revolution!"[6] What kind of Christian, I asked myself, had produced these paragraphs in praise of National Socialism? And this: "Just as . . . Martin Luther . . . freed the core of the German soul, just so Adolf Hitler . . . as the instrument of our God, became the framer of German destiny . . . !"[7] What kind of Christian had generated such a full-throated association of Adolf Hitler with the great reformer Martin Luther, the founder of the tradition I claimed as my own? And this: "The Jews are certainly not God's people."[8] What kind of Christian had declared this to an audience of thousands?

6. Constantine Grossmann, *German Christians: A People's Book: A Guide Through Today's Faith Movement* [*Deutsche Christen: Ein Volksbuch: Wegweiser durch die Glaubensbewegung unserer Zeit*] (Dresden: Verlag E. am Ende, 1934). See p. 299 in this volume.

7. Deutsche Christen (Nationalkirchliche Einung). *Handbuch der Deutschen Christen*. 2nd ed. [Berlin-Charlottenburg]: Deutsche Christen, 1933[?]. See p. 197 in this volume.

8. Reinhold Krause, *Speech of Dr. Krause, the regional district leader of the German Christian Faith Movement in Greater Berlin (according to two stenographic reports)* [*Rede des Gauobmannes der*

Had these materials really been written by Christians—for other Christians? If so, what kind of Christian had bought pamphlets like these for a few pennies, stuck them in a coat pocket, and walked off to find a quiet place to eat a sandwich and read all about it? What kind of Christian had absorbed these ideas, this language, and the attitudes they expressed?

The Journey from There to Here

I could read these pages because I knew German, a legacy of three sojourns in Germany: the first two—1949-50 and 1953-56—as a young child, when my parents had worked alongside German churches and social service agencies that were digging their way out of the spiritual and material rubble of the Second World War, and then, right after college (1968-69), as a student on a Fulbright fellowship at the University of Heidelberg. I was raised in the 1950s, mainly in Sioux Falls, South Dakota, where my college professor father taught U. S. history. At home, we said table grace in German and sang German rounds in the Advent and Christmas seasons; my parents, writing in English, corresponded regularly with several dozen families they'd befriended in Germany, who wrote back in German. In high school—my graduating class numbered just over 800—I knew only two Jewish students.

In the fall of 1964, I went off to college at Swarthmore. During my first week there, I met more Jews than I had ever known in my life. I recall having heated discussions with several of them about "the Germans" and Germany, which in those days I considered my "second home." The subject of the Holocaust, as nearly as I can recall, never arose, at least not explicitly. And although I majored in history,

Glaubensbewegung "Deutsche Christen" in Gross-Berlin Dr. Krause (nach doppeltem stenographischen Bericht] (n.p., n.d.). See p. 258 in this volume.

the Holocaust was not a subject our professors, or we students, spent much time on.

I came of age politically in the tumult of the 1960s—multiple political assassinations, the war in Vietnam, student protests on college and university campuses, the civil rights movement—and the early 1970s, when I entered wholeheartedly into the women's movement and the gay liberation movement, as well as my first full-time professional work, in book publishing. I returned to school in 1977, starting (but not completing) a Ph.D. program in sociology and, after two years, deciding to earn a masters degree in social work, which I received in 1981. To the best of my recollection, the subject of the Holocaust did not come up in either my first professional setting or even in the two academic settings I traversed.

Beginning in the summer of 1981, I found myself drawn into the struggle of undocumented Salvadoran refugees fleeing to the United States from the early stages of the civil war in their country. In late 1983, I accepted a position representing the Lutheran World Federation in Central America, based in El Salvador. It was a life-changing experience in the midst of the violence of war and of poverty, and my own nation's implication in both. When I returned to the U.S., my goal was to find conversation partners who could help me sort through what I had experienced there. I chose to return to school; theology seemed more likely than other disciplines to offer the intellectual resources I sought to meet this challenge. If it didn't, I sensed rather than knew, it would not be worth its salt—at least not to me.

First I attended Luther Seminary in Saint Paul, Minnesota. A year and a half later, I transferred to the Lutheran School of Theology at Chicago. There, having decided to pursue what I imagined would be my last career—as a theologian and perhaps a college professor—I transferred into a doctoral program. None of my teachers at either seminary turned the theological or ethical spotlight on the challenge I had made the centerpiece of my theological project. Remarkably, or so it seemed to me, few of my professors and fellow students were informed about or interested in what was happening in Central America, or how what was happening there could compel someone like me to want to interrogate theology with such intensity. Neither the Holocaust nor the conduct of the German churches in the years preceding it seemed to be on anyone's radar, either.

I transferred once again, in 1989, to Union Theological Seminary in New York City. In this intellectually vibrant community, both the curriculum and the faculty reflected the conviction that the study of theology *had* to have something to do with the seemingly intractable issues of the day, issues still knotted together for me in the civil war that continued to rage in El Salvador. At Union, I also encountered the intellectual, theological, and ethical challenge of the Holocaust. In one seminar I read Lucy S. Dawidowicz's *The War Against the Jews, 1933-1945*, and in another I studied the life and theology of Dietrich Bonhoeffer.[9]

But my intellectual passion was still focused on El Salvador. I finished my Ph.D. at Union in 1995. My dissertation, "in partial fulfillment of the requirements" for the degree I sought, was also a way of coming to terms with, though not resolving, the profound existential challenge my experience in El Salvador had raised. I wrote on what I argued was an unlikely but fruitful conversation between secular feminist philosophers focused on epistemology, on the one hand, and Martin Luther's *theologia crucis*, or "theology of the cross," on the other. The point of my project was to figure out *how* we

---

9. Since then I have become aware of considerable scholarly controversy surrounding Dawidowicz's book. Perhaps the most telling criticisms came from the great Holocaust historian Raul Hilberg, who wrote a scathing critique in his 1996 memoir *The Politics of Memory*.

(Christians) must know, *how we can come to know,* what we must know, to live lives that mean something. When I finished, I knew there was much more to it than what I had done to complete my degree, much more for me to "come to know." It was a start. It was also the beginning of this project, though I certainly did not know it then. . . .[10]

Today, my long period of relative ignorance about the Holocaust, and about the conduct of the churches during the Third Reich, may seem unbelievable. I hope so. If awareness of these matters is now so widespread that we can assume they are "common knowledge," I will happily tolerate the humbling experience of admitting how little I knew for how long.

Or perhaps I *had* learned—perhaps I *did* know—but did not *remember* that I knew. Perhaps I had salted away the information in my intellectual memory, but it had not "struck" me. As an intellectual, a Christian, a theologian, I had not (yet) been "conscience-stricken" by what I knew. Nor did I recall the German Christians having been held up as a crucial challenge to Christian believers or theology. I wish I could claim that I was aware and suggest that others were less or not at all aware. Looking back, though, it seems that we were carrying out our vocations as theologians and, later, as teachers, without giving all of this the attention it warranted.

Today, organizations dedicated to "Holocaust education" urgently continue to produce resources aimed at informing learners of all ages about events that took place many decades ago, as well as more recent genocides. And if it seems a foregone conclusion, at this point in our

10. What role, if any, did the German Christians play in making it easier for their compatriots to avoid coming to know what they had to know to recognize and confront the profound moral challenges Nazism presented to them as followers of Jesus Christ? With chagrin, I have also had to ask what has kept me and so many others from coming to know and confront the moral and theological challenges that period of the church's history clearly presents.

history, that reasonably well-educated individuals will surely have learned about the horrors of the Nazis' "Final Solution," this state of affairs owes much to these Holocaust educators, within and outside of public schools, and the centers from which they draw support. Books and films about the Holocaust are far more plentiful today than they were even a few decades ago.[11]

As far as the conduct of the churches in Hitler's Germany in the years preceding and during the Holocaust is concerned, far too few people in or out of the academy know far too little, despite the slowly growing body of scholarship focused on this subject.

How Could They Not Have Known . . . or *Did* They?

Bending over the German Christian pamphlets my student had found in the nearby college library, I marveled at their simple-minded theological slogans and overheated nationalism, their crass antisemitism and Hitler-worship. I thought about the people who had written these documents—and those for whom they had been written. As they cheered Hitler on, surely these people knew—didn't they?—or at least must have thought about, where they were headed. How could they have avoided hearing Hitler's speeches, in person or on the radio?[12] Had they not read *Mein Kampf,* or talked with someone who had?

11. For decades after the Holocaust, neither schools nor churches, neither scholars nor public intellectuals—with very few and remarkable exceptions—paid attention to the subject, and just a handful of individuals who had survived the horror of the camps wrote about it. Only relatively recently has education about the Holocaust become more widespread. Most Holocaust education materials take the form of resources for teachers at all levels who wish, or are mandated by state or local law, to tackle with their learners what is still an extraordinarily challenging subject. As for the complicity or participation of the churches in Nazi policies and practices leading up to the Holocaust, by and large this matter remains shrouded in ignorance.
12. Most German families had radios, thanks to the mass production of two cheap types of radios known as "People's Receivers." Josef Goebbels was convinced of the effectiveness of radio for disseminating Nazi propaganda.

As the dehumanizing and then murderous Nazi policies toward the Jews were being implemented—the April 1, 1933, boycott of Jewish businesses; shortly thereafter, the Aryan paragraph, expelling Jews from the civil service; the Nuremberg Laws of 1935, stripping Jews of citizenship; the pogrom that came to be known as the Night of Broken Glass [Kristallnacht] in November of 1938—how was it that millions of their non-Jewish neighbors looked the other way, literally and figuratively? Surely they saw, and many of them read, Der Stürmer, the vulgar antisemitic tabloid newspaper sold at countless kiosks on the street and in the train stations. And what about the road signs outside towns and villages all over Germany, saying, "Jews are not wanted here"? Had not the farmers and shop owners permitted these signs to be planted, one by one, in the soil on the edges of their towns? Or perhaps they themselves had helped plant them, then washed the dirt from their hands and gone on with their day's work.

One imagines that for most ordinary Germans, it would have been hard not to know of the active persecution of the Jews. Many must have looked on but not perceived what was happening as offensive. Much or most of this may even have passed for "normal" for the good Christian people of Germany. Should one not have expected different responses from parish pastors and church leaders? As disturbing as these expressions of antisemitism are in retrospect—speeches, laws, signs, print and broadcast propaganda—they seem not to have insulted the religious faith of most Germans. Historian Ian Kershaw suggests that popular opinion in this overwhelmingly Christian nation was "largely indifferent and infused with a latent anti-Jewish feeling."[13]

13. *Popular Opinion and Political Dissent in the Third Reich: Bavaria 1933-1945* (Oxford, U.K.: Clarendon Press, 1983), 277.

Pastors, theologians, and ordinary churchgoers alike appear to have understood their faith in terms that permitted or even encouraged attitudes and practices that now seem utterly to contradict the most basic ethical precepts of Christianity. Could faithful Christians have been oblivious to their complicity in the monstrous violence done against their neighbors?

Knowing and Not Knowing

Far more often than we care to acknowledge, knowing or failing to know are choices. Sometimes they are individual choices; sometimes, institutional or even societal. As is often true of choices, a host of factors—overt and covert, conscious and unconscious, implicit and explicit—impinge on the choice to know or not to know. Whatever factors bear on them, however, such choices have ethical implications. The ethical implications of knowing—or failing to know—were as critical during the Third Reich as they are today, as the twenty-first century unfolds. Today, as then, they drive us toward the question of how we are implicated in what we have come to know—what we have to do with it—and to the question of how we are to live with what we come to know.[14]

As a theologian, I continue to wrestle with these challenges, sparked for me in the first place by my Salvadoran experience in the 1980s. The longer I teach, the less surprised I am to discover that such questions provoke and frustrate many of my students too, as their education opens windows and doors, revealing a world in deep distress. It is a world in which most people hold on to life by their fingernails, a world that hungers and thirsts for food and water as much as for justice and peace, a world being transformed and de-formed by climate change and global capitalism, religious conflict

---

14. A more extensive treatment of this subject can be found in my book *Compelling Knowledge: A Feminist Proposal for an Epistemology of the Cross* (Albany: SUNY Press, 1997).

and acts of terrorism. As they move further and further beyond the boundaries of their "comfort zones," my students ask, how shall they live with what they are coming to know?

A crucial corollary question is this one: what *keeps us from knowing* (or choosing to know) what we must know to live rightly, responsibly, accountably? What keeps us from knowing about the large and small ways in which how we live, as individuals and as a nation, contributes to burgeoning economic inequality? What keeps us from knowing how what we do and fail to do accelerates the rate of climate change, imperiling this planet and everything that inhabits it? What keeps us from knowing the appalling history of Euro-American treatment of Native peoples in North and South America? What keeps us from knowing how profoundly our nation's history has been corrupted by slavery and lynching, Jim Crow and segregation?[15]

Perhaps it makes more sense to reiterate the language used above. What keeps us from *remembering that we know*? What keeps us from being "struck" by what we know?

Returning to the theme of this volume: what has kept so many of us, especially those of us who identify ourselves as Christians, from knowing about the complicity of the churches whose tradition we share in the rise and progress of Nazism and all its horrific sequelae, including the murder of millions of Jews? Why do we lift up the witness of a Dietrich Bonhoeffer and believe, without further examination, that he exemplified rather than defied the behavior of his, and our, co-religionists?

---

15. Documentaries commemorating the fiftieth anniversary of the events of 1964's "Freedom Summer" include newsreels that remind us how violently and unapologetically hatred has been expressed in our own land. News coverage of local responses to the arrival of undocumented immigrants frequently reveals our capacity to demonize and exclude other human beings who (we may say) "have no right to be here."

Little in our Christian theology as it is written, taught, or preached seems to require us to choose to know or remember that we know, to acknowledge ourselves as members of the same family with those who have perpetrated such crimes against others, human and nonhuman. Nor are we challenged to recognize that we are kin to those who suffer or live on the margins, and that we ought to live in response to that knowledge, that kinship. Far too much serious Christian theology lets us off the hook, by never raising the questions or explaining why we have little or no choice about our ignorance, both of the marginalization and the suffering of others and of our (possible or even likely) implication in it. Far too much serious Christian theology simply ignores—or chooses not to know about—these persistent realities.[16]

The Documents

Those who wrote and published most of the documents in this volume were true believers, not only in Jesus Christ, but also in Adolf Hitler and his Nazi revolution. These documents and many others like them functioned to help other Hitler-era Germans who read them, and who almost without exception identified themselves as Christian believers, comprehend what was happening around them as fully compatible with their Christian faith. In doing so, these documents helped them evade the troubling moral and ethical implications and imperatives they would otherwise have had to face. Reading the documents gives us access to ideas and language,

---

16. On reading this paragraph, a trusted colleague pointed out that we should neither overestimate the importance of theology in these respects nor underestimate the significance of the small betrayals of the Gospel both "in church" (preaching and worship and liturgy) and in the daily lives of "ordinary" Christians. Two recently-published books in theological ethics *do* take "these persistent realities" very seriously: Cynthia D. Moe-Lobeda's *Resisting Structural Evil: Love as Ecological-Economic Vocation* (Minneapolis: Fortress Press, 2013); and Larry L. Rasmussen's *Earth-honoring Faith: Religious Ethics in a New Key* (New York: Oxford University Press, 2012).

mixed together from both Christian and Nazi lexicons. This language permitted readers to ignore or dismiss what was happening, or deny its ethical significance and their own ethical agency—and, when necessary, even to justify themselves in the process.[17]

Commitments near and dear to German Christians—including a fierce nationalism, anti-Judaism, and the notion of the "people's church" [*Volkskirche*]—were deeply rooted in Germany's history. What became the German Christian faith movement—most scholars writing about the church struggle [*Kirchenkampf*] use the expression "German Christians" or "German Christian faith movement" to refer to any and all of its various expressions—emerged during the late 1920s and early 1930s out of a number of groups within German Protestantism, groups that were often distinguished by ideological differences and leadership styles.[18]

---

17. Dietrich Bonhoeffer's reflections "On Stupidity" seem apropos in this connection. They appear in his 1942 letter/essay for his co-conspirators, "After Ten Years," and are worth quoting at some length. ". . . This much is certain, that [stupidity] is in essence not an intellectual defect but a human one. . . . The impression one gains is not so much that stupidity is a congenital defect but that, under certain circumstances, people are *made* stupid or that they allow this to happen to them. . . . [E]very strong upsurge of power in the public sphere, be it of a political or a religious nature, infects a large part of humankind with stupidity. . . . The process at work here is not that particular human capacities . . . suddenly atrophy or fail. Instead, it seems that under the overwhelming impact of rising power, humans are deprived of their inner independence and, more or less consciously, give up establishing an autonomous position toward the emerging circumstances. . . . Having thus become a mindless tool, the stupid person will also be capable of any evil and at the same time incapable of seeing that it is evil." In Dietrich Bonhoeffer Works in English, Vol. 8, *Letters and Papers from Prison* (Minneapolis: Fortress, 2010), 43-44. "What keeps us ignorant" may be equivalent to "what makes us stupid" in Bonhoeffer's sense.

18. I am indebted to Hartmut Ludwig of the Theological Faculty at the Humboldt University in Berlin, who underscored for me the importance of appreciating the many distinct German Christian strands within the Protestant churches who organized in support of the Nazi project. In this connection, Prof. Ludwig also directed me to a chart in Gerhard Besier and Eckhard Lessing, *Die Geschichte der Evangelischen Kirche der Union, Vol. 3: Trennung von Staat und Kirche, Kirchlich-politische Krisen, Erneuerung kirchlicher Gemeinschaft (1918-1992)* (Leipzig: Evangelische Verlagsanstalt, 1999), 331, which sketches out the evolution of a variety of "German Christian movements" from the early 1920s through the late 1930s. With the gracious permission of Prof. Besier, I have translated and included this chart, which can be found at the end of this introduction.

The movement's earliest incarnation was arguably the League for a German Church [*Bund für Deutsche Kirche*], founded in Berlin in 1921.[19] In its emphasis on the centrality of the "heroic" (and Indo-European, not Jewish) Christ rather than the suffering Christ, its urgent call for the "dejudaizing" of Christianity (including discarding the Old Testament), and its claim on Martin Luther as the "German prophet," the League set the ideological stage. Twelve years later, in 1933, significant public figures in the emerging movement—among them Reinhold Krause, Friedrich Wieneke, and Arnold Dannenmann—all credited the League with having provided important early touchstones.

According to James A. Zabel, "An overview of German Christian development . . . resembles an hourglass figure with a mid-point reached in 1933," moving "from diversity to unity and back again to diversity."[20] Doris L. Bergen describes this development in terms of "five distinct stages . . . between 1932 and 1945: ascendancy, fragmentation, regrouping, ambiguous success, and postwar reintegration."[21] The first period, Bergen argues, dates from the founding of the German Christian Faith Movement [*Glaubensbewegung Deutsche Christen*] in 1932, which Dannenmann describes in his 1933 *History of the German Christian Faith Movement*, excerpted in this volume. It ends with the so-called Sports Palace scandal: Reinhold Krause's speech there on November 13, 1933, also included in this volume. During these months, German Christians

---

19. Zabel, 9ff. Zabel, who provides a very helpful "overall ideological picture of the German Christian movement in its wide variety" (xiii), references the extensive work of German historian Kurt Meier on the institutional development of the German Christians.
20. Zabel, 21.
21. Doris L. Bergen, *Twisted Cross: The German Christian Movement in the Third Reich* (Chapel Hill and London: University of North Carolina Press, 1996), 15. Bergen's is the best English-language book on this subject. The documents excerpted in this volume emerge from the first four of these "stages," with the lion's share clustered around the period of the German Christians' "ascendancy," which was also the period of their greatest influence.

received considerable support from the Nazi Party, both locally and nationally, for their grassroots organizing efforts. Thanks in no small measure to this support, they won an overwhelming victory in the July 1933 church elections, enabling them to bring about the unification of Germany's 29 regional Protestant churches [Landeskirchen] into one national church [Reichskirche], and to impose on this consolidated church the first and only national bishop [Reichsbischof], Ludwig Müller.[22]

Reinhold Krause, a high school teacher and an enthusiastic though undistinguished member of the Nazi Party, was the Berlin district leader of the German Christian Faith Movement. His speech before a fervent crowd of 20,000 German Christian loyalists was also published in newspapers all over Germany. "In crude, abusive language," Bergen writes, "[Krause] attacked the fundaments of Christianity as unacceptable marks of Jewish influence. [He] lambasted the Old Testament, the Apostle Paul, and the symbol of the cross as ridiculous, debilitating remnants of Judaism, unacceptable to National Socialists."[23] The speaker's extreme views, it seems—or perhaps it was his rhetoric and manner of speech—were not mainstream, even among movement members, at least not as early as 1933. During the following weeks and months, German Christian membership rolls declined dramatically. Pressured by more moderate colleagues, Reich Bishop Müller dissociated himself from the organization and publicly repudiated what Krause had said.[24] The

---

22. Several pieces by Müller are also excerpted in this volume.
23. Bergen, 17.
24. See Müller's "Declaration of the National Bishop Regarding the Events in the Sports Palace," ["Kundgebung des Reichsbischofs zu den Vorgängen im Sportpalast"], in Constantin Grossmann, German Christians: A People's Book: A Guide Through Today's Faith Movement [Deutsche Christen: Ein Volksbuch: Wegweiser durch die Glaubensbewegung unserer Zeit] (Dresden: Verlag E. am Ende, 1934). In this volume, see p. 263ff. Two months later, however, Müller made clear his ongoing loyalty to Nazi goals and his desire to curry favor with Hitler himself. He concluded an agreement with Baldur von Schirach, the head of the Hitler Youth, to incorporate all Protestant church youth—comprising 700,000 members—into the Hitler Youth

national leader of the organization, Pastor Joachim Hossenfelder, was forced to relinquish his post to a more moderate figure, Dr. Christian Kinder, and Krause lost his position, too.

The fragmentation of the movement after the Sports Palace speech also signaled disagreements among its protagonists about both political and theological matters, as well as sharp personal conflicts and differences in leadership styles. Like almost all of their fellow citizens, they certainly supported Hitler's National Socialist program for the "renewal of Germany," loved the Fatherland and the German people, and shared a centuries-old Christian anti-Judaism that morphed all too easily into the racial antisemitism preached and practiced by the Nazis. But German Christians disagreed, sometimes intensely, regarding their views on whether or how closely to work with the Nazi Party's organization, whether or how loyally to protect Protestant confessional traditions and texts, and not whether, but how passionately to pursue the exclusion of all things Jewish from the churches.

Of the panoply of German Christian groups that emerged (or re-emerged) in 1934 and 1935, perhaps the most notable, and certainly the most radical, was the one that had gathered around the Thuringian pastors Siegfried Leffler and Julius Leutheuser.[25] Founded by Leffler and Leutheuser in 1929 under the name the German Christian Church Movement [*Kirchenbewegung Deutsche Christen*], the Thuringian German Christian movement had maintained its independence throughout the tumultuous events of 1933 and early 1934. From the mid-1930s on, more moderate German Christians gravitated toward the Thuringians' organization, which "emerged . . . as the center of a new national German Christian organization."[26]

organization. For a detailed account, see Klaus Scholder, *The Churches and the Third Reich, Vol. 1: Preliminary History and the Time of Illusions, 1918-1934* (London: SCM Press, 1987), 573ff.

25. Excerpts of documents by both these men appear in this volume.

26. Zabel, 39.

Its name changed several times as its leadership made attempts to establish ideological as well as organizational unity with other German Christian groups. In 1937, Leffler and Leutheuser founded the German Christian Movement for a National Church [*Nationalkirchliche Bewegung Deutsche Christen*], which then became the National Church Union [*Nationalkirchliche Einung*].

Six years into the Third Reich, in April 1939, representatives of various German Christian groups, as well as some non-German Christian pastors and laypeople, came together to sign the so-called "Godesberg Declaration." Drafted largely by Siegfried Leffler, the document's contents manifested the radical pass to which the Thuringians had brought the broader movement.[27] The signatories pledged themselves to serve Adolf Hitler, "the man who has led our people out of servitude and misery to freedom and true greatness." National Socialism, they averred, had opened to the German people a "true understanding of Christian faith." Judaism and Christianity were characterized as "unbridgeable religious opposite[s]," and all forms of "international" and ecumenical Christianity were utterly rejected. The Declaration also provided the basis for the establishment of the Institute for the Study and Eradication of Jewish Influence in German Church Life in May 1939. The effort was spearheaded by Walter Grundmann of the University of Jena, by then a bastion of German Christianity.[28]

Those outside the German Christian movement, Ian Kershaw observes, may have worried about the Nazi Party's increasingly anti-church and anti-Christian character. Such reservations, however, did not dampen their "fervent support for the conservative-national goals

---

27. The text of the Godesberg Declaration and the response of the Confessing Church are included in this volume. See pp. 443.
28. Excerpts from Grundmann's *Who Is Jesus of Nazareth?* [*Wer ist Jesus von Nazareth?*] (Weimar: Verlag Deutsche Christen, 1940; published in connection with the Institute for the Study of Jewish Influence on German Religious Life), appear in this volume. See pp. 453.

and values which after the commencement of the war could only with . . . [great] difficulty be separated from the 'specifically Nazi' components of Nazism."[29] As for the German Christians themselves, their commitment to the realization of Hitler's vision of a vast, racially pure, thousand-year Reich only intensified. They were helping to refashion key elements of public moral discourse and spiritual and religious self-understanding at all levels of Germany society. Through various media, including the published materials from which the excerpts included here are taken, German Christians did work neither the Nazi Party nor Hitler's government *could* have done.

The Historical Context

The historical context for the documents in this volume was the rise of National Socialism and its *Machtergreifung*, or "seizure of power," in early 1933. (In January, the power of government was handed over to Hitler quite legally; within weeks, he had managed to consolidate virtually absolute power in himself.) Pastors within the German Protestant Church [*Deutsche Evangelische Kirche*, or *DEK*[30]] had already established several different groups that, with some others that emerged later, came to comprise the German Christian movement. They were already organizing energetically on both local and national levels, often in cooperation with and taking much the same structure as the National Socialist party.

---

29. Kershaw, 184.
30. The German word *evangelisch* can be translated "evangelical." While in the American context this word has come to connote a particular kind of Protestant, in the German context it usually means "Protestant" in contrast to "Catholic." In this volume, in all but a few cases, the German designation *Deutsche Evangelische Kirche* (literally, the German Evangelical Church) is translated "German Protestant Church," comprising regional Lutheran, Reformed, and United (Reformed and Lutheran) churches.

More specifically, the historical context for these documents was what came to be known, even as early as 1933, as the "church struggle" [*Kirchenkampf*]. The church struggle was not a battle between the German Protestant church and the Nazi state. Rather, it played out within and was a contest for administrative and theological control of the German Protestant Church and the hearts and minds of its members. The church struggle's two chief antagonists were the German Christians and what came to be known as the Confessing Church [*Bekennende Kirche*].[31] Most of the documents excerpted here—and others, including those listed in the bibliography at the end of this volume—would likely have been published even in the absence of the struggle. But the struggle surely generated some of them, as well as much of the intensity with which authors addressed a number of themes, particularly those having to do with the relationship of the church to the Nazi state.

The church struggle had very, very little to do with the Jews. It began early in 1933 in response to the efforts of those (chiefly, the German Christian faith movement) who sought to bring the Protestant church fully into Hitler's project of *Gleichschaltung* (literally, "shifting into the same gear")—legally, structurally, culturally, and theologically. The Nazis understood this coordination of all German institutions—all German life, really—to be essential to the "revolution" they envisioned. It was a revolution whose goals were *race* and *space*: Hitler's determination to "purify" what he believed to be the ancient, noble German "master race" and to ensure that this "race" would have the *Lebensraum*, or living space, to prosper and grow throughout Europe and beyond. The ideological, philosophical, and religious productions that accompanied the Nazi revolution wittingly or unwittingly served these goals. Much of the

31. For a compelling account of the story of the Confessing Church, and the church struggle, see Victoria Barnett's *For the Soul of the People*.

rhetoric they employed drew on, reflected, and intensified deeply-rooted prejudices, especially Christian antisemitism.

Players on both sides of the church struggle were passionately committed to what they and the Nazis called the "renewal of Germany." Whether they were members of the Party or not (and many were), most German Protestants—most Germans, in fact—were captivated by the promise of Hitler's revolution. Several well-known church leaders stated publicly that the date of Hitler's ascent to power was for Germany "an Easter moment." Even those who may have had reservations about one government measure or action or another were at pains to reiterate publicly their love for and loyalty to the German people, the Führer, and the Fatherland. Criticism of the Nazi state or party, or of positions taken in support of them, was exceptional; at least during the early years, the dearth of critical voices seems to have reflected both assent and nationalist fervor, rather than reservations or fear of reprisal. It is also clear that many highly intelligent and thoughtful people, including university professors with international reputations, believed in Hitler and his vision for Germany. And almost to a person, they identified themselves as Christians.[32] As Christians, they perceived no contradictions between their profession of faith and their commitment to Hitler's vision of a "new Germany."

The German Christian faith movement, whose earliest strands had been woven in the early 1920s, was perhaps the most articulate expression of this commitment.[33] Even before Hitler's ascent to

32. In 1933, the population of Germany was about 67,000,000. About sixty percent of the population was Protestant, mainly Lutheran; about forty percent was Roman Catholic. Less than one half of one percent was Jewish.

33. The German Christian faith movement, almost entirely Protestant Christian, is to be distinguished sharply from the German Faith Movement, a neo-pagan organization associated with Professor Jakob Wilhelm Hauer of the University of Tübingen. The similarity of the names—*Glaubensbewegung Deutsche Christen*, or German Christian Faith Movement, and *Deutsche Glaubensbewegung*, or German Faith Movement—led many to confuse them with each

power in January 1933, the movement's pastor-founders sought to wed Christianity to National Socialism. Once the "German Revolution" was underway, members of the movement saw themselves as essential to its accomplishment; they were spiritual and theological co-workers who apprehended the deep, even mystical affinities between what Hitler wanted and what they believed God wanted for their Germany.

The German Christians were convinced that Christians had critical roles to play in Germany. They were to play these roles, not simply as Germans who happened also to be Christians, but also as Christians who by God's grace, they would have said, were irreducibly *German* Christians. Germany was once the heart of Christendom, the land of the Reformation, and the home of some of the most influential theologians of the previous five centuries. And Hitler exploited the German Christians' passionate commitment to bring the Protestant churches into his grand *Gleichschaltung*.[34]

Within the context of the church struggle and the larger story of the Third Reich, what members of German Christian groups and their sympathizers had in common was much more important than what divided them.[35] And in the context of the church struggle, both sides claimed to represent the true church of Christ; neither the German Christians nor the Confessing Church formally broke with the established German Protestant Church. Members of both groups—and the vast majority of "neutral" Protestant Christians, who were members of neither—looked to make sense of the relationship

other. The former identified itself as Christian, while the latter was both neo-pagan and anti-Christian.

34. It was actually Hitler who suggested that the name "German Christians," with all its evocative ambiguity, would be more effective than "Protestant National Socialists," the name the movement's leaders originally proposed.

35. Despite the "bewildering array of splinter groups that divided and coalesced in countless constellations," Bergen writes, "various authorities [during and after the Third Reich] treated German Christianity as a recognizable whole" (7).

between their faith and their new political reality, the National Socialist revolution. Among German Christians the conviction ran deep that, as a German Christian chronicler wrote in 1933, "in their origins, Christianity and National Socialism both go back to God," and consequently, "Some kind of living relationship between the two must therefore also be possible in the present."[36]

The German Christians were numerically never more than a minority within the Protestant church in Germany. Doris Bergen cites the "generally accepted figure of six hundred thousand [members] as a reasonable estimate... in the mid-1930s."[37] Nonetheless, a complex set of forces, some profound and some pathetic, allowed them to wield considerable influence within both the church and the broader German society. Political hubris, personal ambition, fear of being left out or of suffering political reprisals, a desire for position in German society and access to political power, old personal feuds, and a variety of other factors, all worked in favor of, and sometimes also against, the German Christians' plans for Germany and especially for the churches.

Beginning in 1933, the German Christians sparked the church struggle over control of the Protestant church. During that same year, they forced what had been decentralized, individual regional churches to reorganize as a national church. Embracing the Nazis' Führer principle, they elected a national bishop to preside over this centralized national church. And throughout the 1930s and early 1940s, they played key roles in most university faculties of theology, training grounds for both academic theologians and pastors. Beyond its institutional influence, Bergen notes, "the movement was most significant in the intangible sphere of ideas."[38] In the words of

---

36. Arnold Dannenmann, *The History of the "German Christian" Faith Movement* [*Die Geschichte der Glaubensbewegung "Deutsche Christen"*] (Dresden: Oskar Günther Verlag, 1933). See pp. 121ff in this volume.

37. Bergen, 7.

German Christians themselves, the documents excerpted and translated in this volume provide illustrations and explications of some of these ideas.

The Documents' Audiences

To whom are German Christians' documents addressed? Some, like the 1932 "Original Guidelines of the German Christians," function to declare—unapologetically, one assumes—the foundational commitments of the leaders of the movement. This document, and a 1933 revision, seem to be addressed both to other Christians whom German Christians hoped to recruit into the movement and to members of the Nazi Party apparatus who might be surprised by, or even skeptical about, the depth and intensity of their commitment to National Socialist principles and goals. Others, like Arnold Dannenmann's 1933 *History of the "German Christian" Faith Movement*, seem to have several audiences in mind, among them Christians enthusiastic about Hitler and the National Socialist revolution in Germany but still unfamiliar with the historic, crucial role German Christians understand themselves and the church to be playing in that revolution, precisely *as* Christians.

The Jewish Question is a speech Gerhard Kittel gave in June of 1933 and then published very successfully. This internationally-respected scholar's intention, according to Robert P. Ericksen, is "to raise the discussion of the Jewish question above the level of slogans and vulgar racism and give it a moral, Christian basis."[39] Perhaps he believes there are fellow Christians who are seeking such a basis amidst the "slogans and vulgar racism" of radical Nazi propaganda. Kittel himself was not a member of the German Christian movement, though

---

38. Bergen, 8.
39. *Theologians Under Hitler: Gerhard Kittel, Paul Althaus, and Emanuel Hirsch* (New Haven, CT: Yale University Press, 1985), 32.

he certainly resonated with its agenda and provided professional underpinnings for some of its dearest priorities. Emanuel Hirsch—like Kittel, a theologian of considerable reputation—was a committed German Christian; his *What the German Christians Want for the Church,* excerpted here, is a direct response to Karl Barth's critique of the movement's claim that Germany's experience of the National Socialist revolution is an integral part of "salvation history," written by God and engaging the German people.[40] His audience would very likely be other convinced and theologically-literate German Christians, including those within the universities' theological faculties who surely would find exchanges like this intellectually exhilarating.

Some of the writings sampled here, including those by Kittel and Hirsch, qualify as theologically sophisticated; others, however, are aimed at "the choir," that is, those already on the German Christian bandwagon. The published version of Reinhold Krause's November 1933 speech at the Berlin Sports Palace, complete with the recording stenographers' notations of the applause and appreciative shouts from the audience, reached hundreds of thousands of readers through the newspapers. Outside the hall and after the event, the reaction was decidedly mixed. The enthusiasm Krause's speech inspired can be attributed to the extremity of Krause's attack, both on the church as a business-as-usual bystander in what was perceived as a seminal historical moment, and on the Old Testament as a "Jewish book" with no place in the Christian church. The chagrin—and among some, the revulsion—his speech inspired likely resulted from that same extremism, perceived with clarity perhaps for the first time by those who did perceive it.[41] That the same speech could inspire such

---

40. See Barth's *Theological Existence Today!,* excerpted in this volume on pp. 81ff.
41. Hundreds of pastors left the rolls of the German Christian movement, which began to splinter. The ranks of the Pastor's Emergency League, founded some months earlier by Pastor

diverse responses may itself be a sign of the ambivalence present within the churches, or at least among pastors, in this first year of Nazi ascendancy. One wonders if the same speech delivered four or five years later would have elicited the same expressions of excitement and of rejection.[42]

Reinhold Krause's published 1933 speech certainly represents German Christian propaganda in its most vulgar form; so does a 1936 pamphlet titled *Jesus and the Jews*, published by the radical German Christian group, the Organization for German Christianity [*Bund für deutsches Christentum*]. "Is Christianity, out of an inner bondage, forcing us to submit to Judaism?" the pamphlet's author asks—not entirely rhetorically, one assumes. "Listening carefully to what the people are saying, one perceives clashing viewpoints. . . . And because the Jewish question is so fundamental to the National Socialist worldview, we can neither skip over it nor resolve it in a cavalier manner."[43] The pamphlet proceeds to "prove" that Jesus was not Jewish.

The format of the pamphlet *What Do the German Christians Want?: 118 Questions and Answers,* compiled by Otto Brökelschen in 1937, suggests it is directed to a popular audience. The pamphlet's introduction explains the need to which it responds: "Despite five years of struggle and work, the question [What do the German Christians want?] continues to meet with astonishing ignorance, and responses to it are often mean-spirited misrepresentations." The pamphlet was published "to clear the air" and to give German

Martin Niemöller, swelled; within several months, the League gave rise to what became the Confessing Church.

42. Ian Kershaw writes, "The . . . attitude of the . . . leaders of both [Protestant and Catholic] denominations to racism was highly ambivalent. . . . Steeped in [the tradition of anti-Judaism], and also in the contemporary commonplaces of racial prejudice, many Church leaders were unable or unwilling to speak out forcefully and unambiguously against anti-Semitism" (247).

43. Bund für deutsches Christentum, *Jesus and the Jews!* [*Jesus und die Juden!*] (Weimar: Verlag Deutsche Christen, 1937). See p. 437 in this volume.

Christians "who are on the front lines the practical handle they need to provide urgently needed explanations . . . with respect to the matter of German Christianity, or who reject or oppose it."[44] Clearly, even well into the Third Reich, members of the German Christian faith movement felt they were still not getting through to, or were being misrepresented in, some quarters of German society.

German Christian publications had a variety of audiences and purposes. It is my hope that the documents excerpted in this volume represent some of the most significant among them.

Criteria for the Selection of Documents

A number of criteria guided the selection of documents excerpted and translated for this volume.[45]

1. *Chronology.* The German Christian movement is often thought to have been active and influential only in the early to mid-1930s. In fact, the movement persisted throughout the lifespan of the Third Reich—and beyond. As mentioned earlier, Doris Bergen frames its activity in terms of five periods: ascendancy, fragmentation, regrouping, ambiguous success, and postwar reintegration. About half the documents excerpted here were published during the movement's ascendancy; these were also the years during which German Christians published most widely.

The movement's period of most visible and consistent influence occurred during 1933-34, when it enjoyed Hitler's favor; he saw it as an instrument for accomplishing the *Gleichschaltung* of the Protestant church. Organized resistance to the German Christian agenda

---

44. Otto Brökelschen, *What Do the German Christians Want?: 118 Questions and Answers* [*Was wollen die Deutschen Christen: 118 Fragen und Antworten*] (Weimar: Verlag Deutsche Christen, 1937). See p. 397 in this volume.

45. In this regard I am especially grateful to Doris L. Bergen for her counsel at an early stage of this project.

emerged in the church, chiefly in the form of the Pastors' Emergency League and then the Confessing Church. At that point Hitler seems to have dropped his initial plan, and any pretense of favor toward the German Christians who favored his plan, as far more trouble than it was worth.

Remarkably, however, the German Christians' passion for the Führer's program did not abate. Unrequited, they continued to act to sustain and further it. As they did, the German Christians proclaimed and explained the irreplaceable spiritual, moral, and social contribution only (German) Christianity could make to the destiny of the Fatherland. The publications excerpted here, spanning the years between 1932 and 1940, reflect their persistent efforts to bend the church toward the trajectory dictated by National Socialism.

2. Key *issues*. From the beginning, antisemitism was as central to the German Christians' contribution as it was to their self-understanding. In pursuing their chief goal—to erase all signs of Judaism from Christianity—they both fomented and relied on anti-Jewish sentiments and scholarship that had circulated throughout Europe for centuries, sometimes dormant, sometimes virulent. The so-called Jewish question was also unavoidable because of the troubling but obvious matter of Christianity's origins in Judaism.

Closely-related issues included the authority of the Old Testament: Was it ineradicably and irredeemably Jewish, or was it actually anti-Jewish and prophetic of Jesus' coming and the supersession of Judaism by Christianity? The character and "race" of Jesus was under scrutiny: Was he really a Jew—or, as the German Christians set out to prove, "Aryan"? Martin Luther's vicious later writings on the Jews gave this sixteenth-century figure a supportive role in many German Christian discussions of the Jewish question. Luther was "the German prophet," the man who had called the German people [*Volk*] into being; they claimed he was also the forerunner and noble forbear of an all-but-messianic Adolf Hitler. According to the German Christians, Hitler and National Socialism were in fact completing the task Luther had begun some four centuries earlier.

The nature and function of the church within German society were also critical matters for the German Christians. The fact that the German government and the Nazi Party were for all practical purposes indistinguishable was for some a stumbling block. For others, it was entirely appropriate and even desirable. In the church struggle, the Confessing Church brought the issue of the relationship between the state and the church to center stage. The organizational independence of the church, rather than the question of what was happening to the Jews, was perhaps the issue most bitterly contested between the German Christians and the Confessing Church. Even the question of whether the church would adopt a version of the Aryan paragraph was principally an issue of the church's independence from state interference, rather than an issue of either its implications for the Jews more generally or of the efficacy of the sacrament of baptism. For the German Christians, all three matters were involved, in different ways and to different degrees.

3. *Authorship.* In print as well as on the speaking platform, German Christian groups had prolific and articulate leaders and spokesmen, including Friedrich Wieneke, Siegfried Leffler, Julius Leutheuser, Joachim Hossenfelder, Wolf Meyer-Erlach, and Walter Grundmann. Chroniclers and pamphleteers, among them Arnold Dannenmann and Friedrich Brökelschen, put pen to paper. The national bishop Ludwig Müller not only made pronouncements but also tried his hand at reworking some passages of Martin Luther's translation of the New Testament. Finally, Protestant theologians and university professors of international stature, including Paul Althaus,

Emanuel Hirsch, and Gerhard Kittel, contributed intellectual sheen to the movement's efforts.

4. *Contemporary critics.* Before the window of opportunity closed, several theologians, including Karl Barth and Dietrich Bonhoeffer, produced sharply-written and spoken public critiques of the German Christians. Their arguments, suggested in the excerpts included here, illustrate the struggle to shape, or reshape, the myth that undergirded the self-understanding of millions of German Protestants. Interestingly, Paul Althaus, an early sympathizer with the German Christians, found some of their claims went too far; perhaps he can be categorized as an "internal critic."

5. *Types of documents.* Pamphlets and tracts were, of course, easily produced, cheap, written in popular language, and portable: ideally suited to spread German Christian ideology.[46] Reaching into every corner of German life, the movement published posters, broadsides, and scholarly books, calendars and almanacs, "dejudaized" liturgies, hymns, and Bibles, and reprints of speeches and radio sermons. I have suggested that these publications became resources for the German public's moral frame of reference. In a place and at a historical moment where propaganda played a key role, German Christian publications offered language and logic that both permitted and taught Germans—university-educated and working-class, nominal or

---

46. The invention of the printing press and moveable type in the late fifteenth century made it possible to reproduce many copies of written materials. During the centuries since then, pamphlets and tracts—sometimes a few pages, sometimes many bound together and folded over—played a crucial role in communicating information, political and religious opinion, new and even revolutionary ideas. It is difficult to imagine that Martin Luther's theological protest in 1517 would have had the tumultuous impact it did have, absent the dissemination of his 95 Theses and subsequent writings throughout Germany and the rest of Europe. It is also difficult to imagine the American Revolution without the pamphlets and tracts written by men like Thomas Paine. Perhaps the best contemporary analogies to this medium of communication would be the "tweet" and the blog.

committed religionists—how to fuse their (German) Christian faith with faith in the Führer and the Fatherland.

Determining the influence on people's thinking or behavior of particular documents is, of course, impossible in almost all cases. However, several documents excerpted here record events that seem to have had considerable impact: among them are those that have to do with the introduction of the Aryan paragraph into the church; Barth's June 1933 "manifesto" *Theological Existence Today!*, and the transcript of the speech delivered by Dr. Reinhold Krause in November 1933 to a packed Sports Palace in Berlin. Other documents, judging from the multiple editions registered on the title pages of the original German publications, seem to have been widely distributed and probably widely-read. In any case, as Doris Bergen observes, while

> [t]he movement had a national profile and spread its views via widely circulated newspapers and well-known theologians . . . its persistence depended on local bases of support. Protestant church members in a Westphalian village may never have attended one of the movement's mass rallies or read its publications, but they may have listened to German Christian ideas from the mouth of their pastor every Sunday.[47]

Documents like those excerpted and translated in this volume were "carriers" of those ideas.

---

47. Bergen, 15. Several pages later, describing the "frenetic production of spin-off [German Christian] organizations throughout 1934 and 1935," after the Sports Palace scandal and the onset of the church struggle, Bergen writes, "Yet the movement persisted. German Christian pastors went on preaching in pulpits across the country; parish representatives, synodal officers, and regional bishops, elected or appointed in 1933, remained in office and continued to propagate the cause." The proliferation of German Christian groups that, according to Bergen, led to renewed efforts to "regroup," is evidence of "the intense energies generated" by the people and ideas associated with this movement (18).

What Can We Learn from Reading These Documents?

About the momentum of antisemitism. It is impossible to read these documents without awareness of their historical context; they are written, published, and read at a time and in a place heading toward the Holocaust. In his June 1933 lecture, world-renowned New Testament scholar Gerhard Kittel underscores the seriousness of "the Jewish question" and argues that "the fight against the Jews . . . must be carried out on the basis of conscious and clear Christian convictions," which he proposes to explore in the talk that follows.[48] There are four possible responses to the question, "What must happen to the Jews?" The first one is extermination.[49] Kittel makes short work of this possibility, devoting to it only a few sentences:

> The violent extermination of the Jews is not a serious option: if the systems of the Spanish Inquisition or the Russian pogroms did not succeed, it seems highly unlikely this will happen in the 20th century. Nor does the idea make any moral sense. A historical reality like this one may be resolved through the extermination of this people at most in demagogic slogans, but never in actual historical circumstances. The point of a particular historical situation is always that it presents us with a task that we must master. Killing all Jews is not mastering the task at hand.[50]

What is chilling about this 1933 statement is first that it was made at all—in a public lecture by a highly-regarded teacher-scholar on the theological faculty at Tübingen, then (and still) one of the most renowned universities in Germany. Furthermore, Kittel seems to dismiss the "option" of extermination chiefly on the grounds of expedience: if it has been tried before and has failed, it is unlikely to

---

48. Gerhard Kittel, *The Jewish Question* [*Die Judenfrage*] (Stuttgart: Verlag von W. Kohlhammer, 1933). See the excerpt from this document included in this volume, p. 201ff.
49. The other three are Zionism, assimilation, and "guest status," the last of which he favors as the only possible solution to the problem of what to do with the Jews in Germany.
50. Kittel, p. 207 in this volume.

work if it is tried again. With historical hindsight, Kittel's statement and the complete absence of any expressed moral compunction take our breath away. In the broader context of his lecture, and despite his dismissal of its likelihood, what he says seems to override any serious intellectual, moral, or theological objection to its implementation. How many Germans could or might have anticipated that this "option" would eventually be implemented is impossible to know.

Kittel's published lecture is exceptional in that it mentions Jews and extermination in the same breath. But many of the German Christian documents in this volume, however refined or vulgar their language, reflect, justify, and even nurture attitudes and actions, public and private, that denigrate, devalue, exclude, and attack Jews and Judaism. Some German Christian writers perpetuate the centuries-old Christian lie that the Jews crucified Jesus and that they continue to live under that curse. Others identify Judaism with "godless" Bolshevism, a threat the National Socialists successfully exploited with the German public before, during, and after their ascent to power.

About the power of public discourse. *Das Volk*, or "the people," is a perfectly ordinary German term. Like most Germans living in the Third Reich, however, those who generated these documents embraced this word (and its panoply of variants) in its nazified meaning, which excluded everyone and everything the Nazis considered "un-German," especially the Jews. In Nazi-German, *Volk* could mean "race" or "nation." One of the documents in this volume defines *Volk* as "the divinely willed community of German people based on the created orders of race, blood, and soil."[51] As this German

---

51. Otto Brökelschen, *What Do the German Christians Want?: 118 Questions and Answers* [*Was wollen die Deutschen Christen? 118 Fragen und Antworten*] (Weimar [Thüringen]: Verlag Deutsche Christen, 1937), p. 395ff in this volume.

Christian definition suggests, the word *Volk* and words compounded with it—there were scores of them—carried a meaning by turns mystical, ideological, and even theological. *Volksgemeinschaft,* for example—literally, "the people's community," or "the community of the people"—referred to "the mystical unity of the blood-race of the national-German-Aryan community," and, in Nazi thought, bound the Third Reich together.[52] *Völkisch*, an adjective made from *Volk*, may be best translated "ethno-national," or "ethnic," but it also carried race-related, exclusionary freight. *Volksgenossen* [literally, "comrades from among the people"] were all those within this community, and no one outside it. Widely-respected university theologians like Paul Althaus sanctified *Volkstum*, perhaps best translated as "ethnic culture," and often employed as the Nazi-German racial-ethnic replacement for "nationality." Like *Volk*, *Volkstum* was one of God's "orders of creation"[53]—part of the structure of all that God had made—that faithful Christians dare not undermine or disrespect, but rather should protect and seek to purify.

What we think, learn, know, and say, as well as what we "leave out," ignore, forget, or dismiss as irrelevant: all of it takes shape through the power of language. Language and thought are woven together, not least of all as children and young people grow into adults. In the Third Reich, fluency in this vocabulary of "race," "community," and "blood" developed quickly and organically. The nazified terms above were seen, read, and heard continuously all over the Third Reich. They became the building blocks of public

52. Robert Michael and Karin Doerr, *Nazi-Deutsch/Nazi German: An English Lexicon of the Language of the Third Reich* (Westport, CT: Greenwood Press, 2002), 423.

53. "Orders of creation" is a theological construct referring to certain structures or institutions God is said to have established in the earthly realm to order human life; marriage, family, the economy, the state, and the church might all be counted among them. For the German Christians, race—as they understood it—and *Volk* or *Volkstum* were "orders of creation," too, and, because they were established by God, were utterly sanctified.

discourse and were more and more easily applied to identify those who did and did not fit in. Philologist and linguist Victor Klemperer, who lived through the horrors of Nazism as a German Jew, "paid close attention to the language as it evolved . . . noting that words have the potential to be a small can of arsenic—they can be swallowed without being noticed, they seem not to have any effect, and yet after a period of time, the effect of the poison becomes apparent."[54]

It must have been exceptionally difficult—and dangerous—to think, let alone to converse with others, in any language that might have been considered "counter-cultural," not only by the Nazi state, but also by the neighbors. The published language out of which the documents in this book are crafted reflects German Christians' particular appropriation of the nazified German almost everyone in Germany heard, and likely spoke, every day. Those who want to explain, persuade, and announce what they believe to be good news must make themselves intelligible by speaking the language of those they want to reach; it will be no surprise, then, if they find themselves, intentionally or unintentionally, more and more fluent in that same language.

About being a "real" Christian. Those who are tempted to say that the people who wrote these documents or spoke the lectures and speeches that then appeared in print were not *real* Christians face several challenges. The first and vociferous objection would come from the German Christians themselves. One cannot spend very much time with these documents without recognizing how passionately their authors embrace their faith and their church, or how urgently they identify themselves as Christians. For them there

---

54. Leslie Morris, in the Foreword to Michael and Doerr, xiii. Klemperer's powerful linguistic and anthropological study of "Nazi-German," originally published in German in 1957, is *The Language of the Third Reich: LTI: Lingua Tertii Imperii: A Philologist's Notebook* (New York: Continuum, 2006).

is no contradiction between their commitment to Jesus Christ and their commitment to Adolf Hitler and his National Socialist program for Germany's renewal. They are far more concerned, on the one hand, about the Protestant "establishment," which they view as fearful, dogma-bound, and backward-looking, and, on the other hand, about the emerging neo-pagan, anti-Christian German Faith Movement. They are deeply concerned, too, about those surrounding Hitler who reject Christianity completely and would like to see it wither and die. The language and themes of the German Christian documents address and can be better grasped in light of these multiple concerns.

The German Christians' 1932 Guidelines call for "a vigorous people's church [*Volkskirche*] . . . that expresses the power of our faith." The movement has arisen because its members believe that "the church may not stand on the sidelines" in the fight for freedom.[55] Emanuel Hirsch, one of the theologians most closely allied to the movement, writes that the church must develop "a new and concrete teaching about a Christian way of life in the present situation . . . of the German people."[56] A renewal of the church must accompany the renewal of the nation: this theme crops up repeatedly. So does the urgency of combatting "godlessness," chiefly in the form of Bolshevism—what we would call Marxism or Communism. German Christians argued about the relative value of the Old Testament. While some from more radical circles sought to excise it from the Christian canon, they were in a minority. Admittedly, the Old Testament was of lesser value than the New Testament. However, the Old Testament did after all comprise the scripture that Jesus studied. Considered as a whole, it was also part of

---

55. Found in *Deutsche Christen (Nationalkirchliche Einung), Handbook of the German Christians* [*Handbuch der Deutschen Christen*], 2nd ed. (Berlin-Charlottenburg, 1933), pp. 163ff in this volume.

56. From Emanuel Hirsch, *What the German Christians Want for the Church*, p. 101ff in this volume.

"God's great story," leading to the fulfillment represented in Christ and Christianity. "[T]he Bible," writes Friedrich Wieneke, in his *Outline of German Theology*, "is the book of destiny for German Christians."[57]

About being "the church" here and now. For Germany, the years following World War I were characterized by upheaval, uncertainty, and a good deal of suffering. Trying, as we humans do, to make sense of it all, many German Christians—many Germans, period—interpreted these years as a kind of "Golgotha" experience. Hitler's ascent to power in early 1933 was the clearest possible evidence of God's blessing, long in coming and hence all the more welcome. "[T]he last 14 years," writes Joachim Hossenfelder, referring to the years leading up to 1933, "have been . . . about the faith and the soul of our nation."[58] The *Handbook of the German Christians* puts it this way: "On January 30, 1933, a new stage in the history of our people . . . [began] . . . Adolf Hitler believed in Germany, when there was nothing left to believe in." Comparing Hitler to Martin Luther, it continues, "with his faith in Germany, as the instrument of our God, [he] became the framer of German destiny."[59] Some even believed Hitler, "the most German man, is also the most faithful, a believing Christian. We know he begins and ends the course of his day with prayer, that he has found in the gospel the deepest source of his strength."[60] Perhaps it goes without saying that we humans are often tempted to project onto those who govern the qualities, character, and commitments we have and would like them to share.

---

57. Wieneke, *Outline of German Theology*, p. 283 in this volume.
58. From Hossenfelder, *Our Struggle*, p. 234 in this volume.
59. p. 197 in this volume.
60. From Constantin Grossmann, *German Christians: A People's Book: A Guide Through Today's Faith Movement*, p. 302 in this volume.

Several scholars with whom I have discussed this project at length have stressed how important religion was in Germany between 1933 and 1945, and not only in terms of faith movements like the German Christians, or denominations like Protestants and Catholics. One has only to view National Socialist rallies to get a sense of their quasi-religious fervor. The German Christian chronicler Arnold Dannenmann writes that adherents of the National Socialist movement, as they organized for change throughout Germany, "were carrying out a religious task." He goes on, "The Führer Adolf Hitler . . . was utterly aware of his divine mission," and "the thousands of gatherings that took place during the National Socialist movement's struggle to take power in Germany actually fulfilled a religious purpose."[61] From the German Christian viewpoint, the "experience of these times"—binding together the whole German people—was "God-given."[62]

Clearly, while people both within and outside the various German Christian groups all used terms like "religious," "church," and a host of others as if their meanings were plain, they often meant very different things. The renewal or revitalization of the church, including its responsiveness to the urgent needs of the world around it, is certainly something most Christians favor. Many German Christians would probably have agreed with Siegfried Leffler's analysis:

> Most Germans do not attend church these days. For this the churches, not the people, are to blame. The church must be renewed. But it doesn't allow itself to experiment, to risk anything. Hence it needs a free movement that is willing to risk starting something new . . . without being dogmatically harnessed.[63]

61. From Arnold Dannenmann, *History of the German Christian Faith Movement.* See p. 127 in this volume.
62. From Joachim Hossenfelder, *Our Struggle.* See p. 149 in this volume.
63. From Siegfried Leffler, *Christ in Germany's Third Reich,* p. 361 in this volume.

In their time and place, German Christians understood their mission *as* Christians to involve the cooperation of "the new church" (reformed from within by German Christians) with the National Socialist government, whose declared mission was the renewal of the whole German society. The German Christians' efforts to actualize this cooperation included, among other things, their proposal to implement within the church the Aryan paragraph, the law that excluded Jews from the German civil service. Those opposed to the German Christians argued that "the mission of the church is not political," and the German Christians' position on the Aryan paragraph "puts [pastors] in danger of subordinating their personal responsibility to the pressures of the subjective and time-bound political or church-political views of those in superior offices, church groups, or entities outside the church." Making "church members of non-Aryan descent into church members with fewer rights and less worth" was not acceptable, and even if the state limited the civil rights of Jews, the church would not accept such limitations—at least, not those the state imposed on baptized Jews.[64]

In this and almost every other case, the totalitarian claims of Nazism made neutrality impossible. For the German Christians, this was not a problem, since their dedication to the Nazi program, on the one hand, and their commitment to Christ, on the other, were both heartfelt and fully compatible. Their opponents were, for the most part, most deeply exercised by what they saw as the German Christians' eagerness to politicize the church, aligning the church's priorities with those of the government. In the process, few identified or condemned the ways in which a nazified Christianity—a Christianity that understood itself in terms of Germany's national

---

64. From the opinion of the University of Marburg theological faculty regarding the Aryan paragraph. See pp. 58ff in this volume.

priorities, defined by race and blood and soil—threatened the theological and spiritual foundations of the church itself.

Some Concluding Reflections

It is surely tempting to believe that if *we* had been there, things would have been different—that in 1933, *we* would have seen what Germans (almost all of them Christians) did not see, and that *we* would have made other choices, and things would not have turned out as terribly as they actually did. Or even to believe that if *they*—those Germans, who were after all Christians—had only seen through Hitler's demented plans for Germany's future, they would have stopped cheering and started resisting. But in the interest of humility and truthfulness, we must resist these temptations. And for the sake of the church—more than that, for the sake of the world—we must take quite seriously the likelihood that, Christians or no, we would have thought and spoken and acted in similar ways.

When I asked several of my German interlocutors what they thought we could learn from studying the conduct of the church during the 1930s, they responded, "*das Versagen der Kirche*": the failure of the church. Responding in 1933 to the German Christians, Karl Barth wrote that his deepest concern was the Protestant churches' failure to resist them. The church community is determined by the Holy Spirit and baptism, he wrote, not by blood and race, as the German Christians seemed to think; what was at stake was the crucial question of Christian truth. In 1935 the Nazis ran Barth out of Germany, forcing him to resign from his position as professor at the University of Bonn. Even theologian Paul Althaus, who in 1933 welcomed Hitler's accession to power and argued that the *Volk* was a divinely-given "order of creation," wrote in 1935 that the German Christians' identification of German history with salvation history was "an embarrassing piece of religious presumption," and "[t]he attempt to appoint the German people as the people of God of the new covenant is a bald-faced theological heresy."[65] These were surely not the only public expressions of distress coming from Christian churchmen, but such statements were very few and far-between, and increasingly rare as the decade advanced.

Most egregious of all, of course, was the church's failure to act on behalf of the Jews. Ideologically, the German Christians outdid the Nazis. They married the racial antisemitism of the Nazis to the religious and theological anti-Judaism that had threaded its way through the Christian tradition for centuries. In this overwhelmingly Lutheran land, recruiting "the German prophet" Martin Luther for their purposes was not difficult; his 1543 tract *On the Jews and Their Lies*, with its hateful and violent suggestions for how to treat the Jews in sixteenth-century Germany, seemed tailor-made for Nazi purposes in twentieth-century Germany.[66] Perusing the documents in this volume, it appears that German Christians found it both convenient and compelling to embrace Luther, even to bracket him with Hitler as the two greatest Germans who ever lived.

German church historian Kurt Scholder argues that the church, in claiming the "divine order of *Volkstum*"—which excluded and devalued the Jews—made antisemitism a respectable topic. In doing so, he observes, "the church lost its claim to speak for the simple truth of the Christian command to love."[67] After chiding the German Christians because they conflated the eternal kingdom [*Reich*] of God with the German *Reich*, Paul Althaus could write that "the kingdom

---

65. From Paul Althaus, *Political Christianity: On the Thuringian "German Christians."* See p. 378 in this volume.
66. See *Luther's Works, Volume 47: The Christian in Society IV* (Philadelphia: Fortress Press, 1971). In 1994 the Evangelical Lutheran Church in America repudiated Luther's anti-Jewish writings in a "Declaration to the Jewish Community."
67. Scholder, 115.

[of God] that is already here is present in our national, political history *to the extent that people serve their brothers, their people*, in the peace of Jesus Christ. . . ."[68] One could hardly imagine, however, that he would have included the Jews among "their brothers" or "their people," or that he would even have given the matter a second thought. German Christian leader Julius Leutheuser could write in 1935, "Our love for our fellow Germans is the confirmation of our faith in the fact that we are all children of God."[69] No self-respecting Christian would object. To declare that Jews are no longer "fellow Germans"—after the Nuremberg Laws were promulgated (in 1935), they were no longer German citizens—is only a short step away from excluding them in thought, word, and deed, from the larger circle formed by all of us "children of God." Once that happens, all moral and ethical bets are off.

Several of the questions suggested here continue to challenge us, both as we look back to the German churches in the 1930s and as we consider our commitments as Christians in our own time. Among them, I would underscore these:

- What *is* the church, and what should be its role within society?
- What should the relationship be between Christian people and their governing authorities?
- How should one weigh one's commitments as a Christian in relation to one's commitments as a citizen and a member of civil society?
- How should one engage with, even embrace, the present reality, even as one nurtures the capacity to consider that reality critically?
- Perhaps most poignantly, who is the neighbor—and what does it mean to love that neighbor as myself?

68. See Althaus, p. 380 in this volume. Emphasis added.
69. In Julius Leutheuser, *The German Community of Christ*. See p. 335 in this volume.

Other important issues have to do with the subtle and not-so-subtle ways in which an institution's or a government's public discourse functions to obfuscate rather than clarify. Nationalism, for example, generates a great deal of such discourse. The obfuscation it creates is not always intentional. But it is pernicious when a people must navigate through circumstances that require moral discernment and informed engagement. For example, to conflate love of country, a perfectly noble sentiment, with a religious commitment is to undermine the capacity, and sometimes even the will, to think critically about either one. The German Christians were quite sincere in identifying the Nazi cause with the cause of Jesus Christ. The language they used to propagate their sincerely-held conviction may or may not have convinced ordinary Germans who were Christians that the two causes were identical. But it surely made it easier to imagine that they were and did nothing to alert anyone to the possibility that they were not.

Implicitly, questions about knowing and not knowing—about what allows us to remain ignorant in the face of evil and what might help us avoid being "made stupid" (to use Bonhoeffer's words, quoted earlier in this introduction)—thread their way through all of this. These matters resonate deeply in today's world. Resolving them today is no simpler than it was in Hitler's Germany. For all people of good will—among whom I believe many Christians can be counted—engaging them is an urgent task. My hope is that the documents assembled here will bring them into high relief for students of history and for those who care about what the church may have to say today.

German Christian Movements

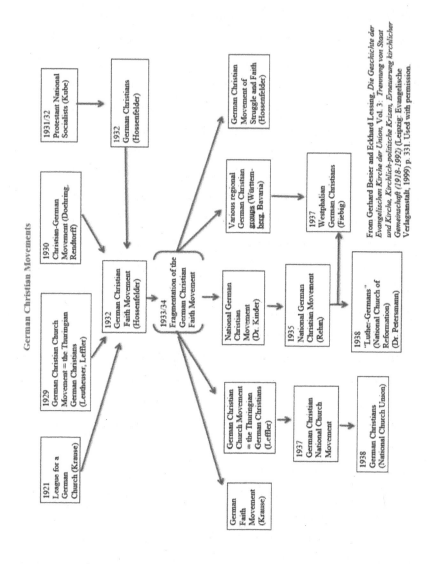

German Christian Movements

1921
League for a German Church (Krause)

1929
German Christian Church Movement = the Thuringian German Christians (Leutheuser, Leffler)

1930
Christian-German Movement (Doehring, Rendtorff)

1931/32
Protestant National Socialists (Kube)

1932
German Christians (Hossenfelder)

1932
German Christian Faith Movement (Hossenfelder)

1933/34
Fragmentation of the German Christian Faith Movement

German Faith Movement (Krause)

National German Christian Movement (Dr. Kinder)

German Christian Church Movement = the Thuringian German Christians (Leffler)

German Christian Movement of Struggle and Faith (Hossenfelder)

Various regional German Christian groups (Württemberg, Bavaria)

1935
National German Christian Movement (Rehm)

1937
German Christian National Church Movement

1937
Westphalian German Christians (Fiebig)

1938
"Luther-Germans" (National Church of Reformation) (Dr. Petersmann)

1938
German Christians (National Church Union)

From Gerhard Besier and Eckhard Lessing, *Die Geschichte der Evangelischen Kirche der Union*, Vol. 3: *Trennung von Staat und Kirche, Kirchlich-politische Krisen, Erneuerung kirchlicher Gemeinschaft (1918-1992)* (Leipzig: Evangelische Verlagsanstalt, 1999) p. 331. Used with permission.

1

The Original Guidelines of the German Christian Faith Movement

Joachim Hossenfelder

Introduction

These ten guidelines were written by Pastor Joachim Hossenfelder and published in June 1932. Key words and phrases point to some of the movement's preoccupations. "Positive Christianity" refers directly to the same phrase in Point 24 of the 1920 platform of the National Socialist German Workers (Nazi) Party.[1] The German Christians favor a "heroic piety," reject both the "weak" leadership and the

---

1. A "positive Christianity" was understood to be beyond denominations and emphasized an "active," heroic Christ. That Hitler included this in the platform signaled his sense that he would need the support of the churches as he embarked on his National Socialist project.

"parliamentarianism" of the church as it is presently configured, and dedicate themselves to the battle against Marxism. The guidelines spell out the movement's conviction that "race, ethnicity [*Volkstum*], and nation" are "orders of life given and entrusted to us by God." The movement opposes "race-mixing," the "mission to the Jews," and both pacifism and "internationalism." In every important respect this self-identified Christian movement resonates with and reflects all the important commitments favored by the National Socialists.

The following year the movement's guidelines were revised; a slightly muted text left out all references to Jews and Judaism.[2]

---

2. Find the revised guidelines translated as part of Arnold Dannenmann's *The History of the German Christian Faith Movement*, pp. 121ff in this volume.

Richtlinien
der Glaubensbewegung „Deutsche Christen"

1. Diese Richtlinien wollen allen gläubigen deutschen Menschen Wege und Ziele zeigen, wie sie zu einer Neuordnung der Kirche kommen. Diese Richtlinien wollen weder ein Glaubensbekenntnis sein oder ersehen, noch an den Bekenntnisgrundlagen der evangelischen Kirche rütteln. Sie sind ein Lebensbekenntnis.

2. Wir kämpfen für einen Zusammenschluß der im „Deutschen Evangelischen Kirchenbund" zusammengeschlossen 29 Kirchen zu einer evangelischen Reichskirche und marschieren unter dem Ruf und Ziel:

   Nach außen eins und geschlagkräftig.
   Um Christus und sein Wort geschart,
   Nach innen reich und vielgestaltig,
   Ein jeder Christi nach Ruf und Art!"

   (Nach Beibel.)

3. Die alte „Deutsche Christen" will keine kirchenpolitische Partei in dem bisher üblichen Sinne sein. Sie wendet sich an alle evangelischen Christen deutscher Art. Die Zeit des Parlamentarismus hat sich überlebt, auch in der Kirche. Kirchenpolitische Parteien haben keinen religiösen Ausweis, das Kirchenvolk zu vertreten und stehen dem hohen Ziel entgegen, ein Kirchenvolk zu werden. Wir wollen eine lebendige Volkskirche, die Ausbruch aller Glaubenskräfte unseres Volkes ist.

4. Wir stehen auf dem Boden des positiven Christentums. Wir bekennen uns zu einem bejahenden artgemäßen Christusglauben, wie er deutschem Luthergeist und heldischer Frömmigkeit entspricht.

5. Wir wollen das wiedererwachte deutsche Lebensgefühl in unserer Kirche zur Geltung bringen und unsere Kirche lebenskräftig machen. In dem Schicksalskampf um die deutsche Freiheit und Zukunft hat sich die Kirche in ihrer Leitung sich als zu schwach erwiesen. Die Kirche hat bisher nicht zum entschiedenen Kampf gegen den gottesfeindlichen Marxismus und das gottfremde Zentrum aufgerufen, sondern mit den politischen Parteien dieser Mächte einen Kirchenvertrag geschlossen. Wir wollen, daß unsere Kirche in dem Entscheidungskampf um Sein oder Nichtsein unseres Volkes an der Spitze kämpft. Sie darf nicht abseits stehen oder gar den Befreiungskämpfern abrücken.

6. Wir verlangen eine Änderung des Kirchenvertrags (politische Klausel) und Kampf gegen den religiös- und volksfeindlichen Marxismus und seine christlich-sozialen Schlepventräger aller Schattierungen. Wir vermissen bei diesem Kirchenvertrag das treumste Bagnis auf Gott und die Sendung der Kirche. Der Weg ins Reich Gottes geht durch Kampf, Kreuz und Opfer, nicht durch falschen Frieden.

7. Wir sehen in Rasse, Volkstum und Nation uns von Gott geschenkte und anvertraute Lebensordnungen, für deren Erhaltung zu sorgen uns Gottes Gesetz ist. Daher ist der Rassenvermischung entgegenzutreten. Die deutsche äußere Mission ruft auf Grund ihrer Erfahrung dem deutschen Volke seit langem zu: „Halte deine Rasse rein" und sagt uns, daß der Christusglaube die Rasse nicht zerstört, sondern vertieft und heiligt.

8. Wir sehen in der recht verstandenen Inneren Mission das lebendige Tat-Christentum, das aber nach unserer Auffassung nicht im bloßen Mitleid, sondern im Gehorsam gegen Gottes Willen und im Dank gegen Christi Kreuzestod wurzelt. Bloßes Mitleid ist „Wohltätigkeit" und wird zur Überheblichkeit, gepaart mit schlechtem Gewissen, und verweichlicht ein Volk. Wir wissen etwas von der christlichen Pflicht und Liebe den Hilflosen gegenüber, wir fordern aber auch Schutz des Volkes vor den Untüchtigen und Minderwertigen. Die Innere Mission darf keinesfalls zur Entartung unseres Volkes beitragen. Sie hat sich im übrigen von wirtschaftlichen Abenteuern fernzuhalten und darf nicht zum Krämer werden.

9. In der Judenmission sehen wir eine schwere Gefahr für unser Volkstum. Sie ist das Eingangstor fremden Blutes in unsern Volkskörper. Sie hat neben der äußeren Mission keine Daseinsberechtigung. Wir lehnen die Judenmission in Deutschland ab, solange die Juden das Staatsbürgerrecht besitzen und damit die Gefahr der Rassenverschleierung und Bastardierung besteht. Die Heilige Schrift weiß auch etwas zu sagen von heiligem Zorn und sich versagender Liebe. Insbesondere ist die Eheschließung zwischen Deutschen und Juden zu verbieten.

10. Wir wollen eine evangelische Kirche, die im Volkstum wurzelt, und lehnen den Geist eines christlichen Weltbürgertums ab. Wir wollen die aus diesem Geist entspringenden verderblichen Erscheinungen wie Pazifismus, Internationale, Freimaurertum usw. durch den Glauben an unsere von Gott befohlene völkische Sendung überwinden. Die Zugehörigkeit eines evangelischen Geistlichen zur Freimaurerloge ist nicht statthaft.

Diese zehn Punkte der Glaubensbewegung „Deutsche Christen" rufen zum Sammeln und bilden in großen Linien die Richtung für eine kommende evangelische Reichskirche, die unter Wahrung konfessionellen Friedens die Kräfte unseres reformatorischen Glaubens zum Besten des deutschen Volkes entwickeln wird.

                                                                Hossenfelder, Pfarrer.

Figure 1. German text of "Guidelines of the German Christian Faith Movement"

The Original Guidelines of the German Christian Faith Movement (1932)[3]

Joachim Hossenfelder

1. These principles are intended to show all faithful Germans the path and the goals that will lead them to a new church order. These principles are not intended to be or to replace a confession of faith, nor are they meant to undermine the confessional foundations of the Protestant [evangelische] Church.[4] They are a confession of life.

2. We are fighting to achieve an integration of the twenty-nine constituent churches of the "German Evangelical Church Association" into one National Protestant Church [evangelische Reichskirche], and we march under the slogan and goal:

> Externally, one and strong in spirit,
> gathered around Christ and his Word,
> internally, rich and diverse,
> each Christian according to individual calling and style.

3. The name "German Christians" does not connote an ecclesiastical political party as known heretofore. It addresses itself to all Protestant Christians who are Germans. The era of parliamentarianism is over, in the church as well. The parties associated with various churches do not have the religious credentials to represent the people of the church; in fact, they

---

3. From Deutsche Christen (Nationalkirchliche Einung), *Handbook of the German Christians* [*Handbuch der Deutschen Christen*], 2nd ed. (Berlin-Charlottenburg, 1933). The *Handbook* in its entirety appears on pp. 163ff in this volume.

4. The German word *evangelisch* can be translated "evangelical." While in the American context this word has come to connote a particular kind of Protestant, in the German context it usually means "Protestant" in contrast to "Catholic." The German Protestant Church [*Deutsche Evangelische Kirche*] would have comprised regional Lutheran, Reformed, and United (Reformed and Lutheran) churches.

stand in the way of the noble goal of our becoming a churchly people. We want a vigorous people's church [*Volkskirche*], one that expresses the power of our faith.

4. We stand on the ground of positive Christianity.[5] We confess an affirmative faith in Christ, one suited to a truly German Lutheran spirit and heroic piety.

5. We want to bring to our church the reawakened German sense of life and to revitalize our church. In the fateful struggle for German freedom and our future, the leadership of the church has proven to be too weak. Up to this point the church has not risen to the challenge of a determined struggle against godless Marxism and the Center Party, so alien to our spirit [*geistfremd*[6]]; instead, it has made a compact with the political parties of these powers. We want our church to be front and center in the battle that will decide the life or death of our people. The church may not stand on the sidelines or dissociate itself from those who are fighting for freedom.

6. We demand a revision of the political clauses of this church compact, as well as a battle against irreligious and anti-*Volk* Marxism and its Christian-Socialist minions of every stripe. We do not see in this present church compact a daring confidence in God and in the church's mission. The path to the Kingdom of God leads through struggle, cross, and sacrifice, not through a false peace.

7. We recognize in race, ethnicity [*Volkstum*], and nation orders of life given and entrusted to us by God, who has commanded us

---

5. A phrase that appears in the 1920 platform of the NSDAP, written by Hitler. The phrase means more or less, and with intentional vagueness, "an affirmative faith in Christ, one suited to [*gemäss*] the German Lutheran spirit and heroic piety."

6. In its National Socialist usage the common German word *fremd* [strange, foreign, peculiar, alien to]—together with whatever other word it was attached to (in this case *Geist*, having to do with the spiritual dimension)—generally meant "un-German," hostile, or inferior, connotations not ordinarily associated with the word itself.

to preserve them. For this reason race-mixing must be opposed. Based on its experience, the German foreign mission has long admonished the German people: "Keep your race pure!" and tells us that faith in Christ does not destroy race, but rather deepens and sanctifies it.

8. We see in Home Mission, rightly conceived, a living, active Christianity that, in our view, is rooted not in mere compassion but rather in obedience to God's will and gratitude for Christ's death on the cross. Mere compassion is charity, which leads to arrogance coupled with a guilty conscience that makes a people soft. We are conscious of Christian duty toward and love for the helpless, but we also demand that the people be protected from those who are inept and inferior. The Home Mission must in no way contribute to the degeneration of our people. Furthermore, it should avoid economic adventures and must not become a shopkeeper.[7]

9. In the mission to the Jews we see great danger to our people. It is the point at which foreign blood enters the body of our people. There is no justification for its existing alongside the foreign mission. We reject the mission to the Jews as long as Jews have citizenship, which brings with it the danger of race-blurring and race-bastardizing. Holy Scripture speaks both of holy wrath and of self-denying love. It is especially important to prohibit marriages between Germans and Jews.

10. We want a Protestant church with its roots in the people, and we reject the spirit of a Christian cosmopolitanism. Through our faith in the ethno-national [völkisch] mission God has commanded us to carry out, we want to overcome all the

---

7. The admonition not to become "shopkeepers" [Krämer] as it is used here is a not-very-subtle reminder to avoid the appearance of any socio-economic association with Jews, who were often categorized disparagingly as "shopkeepers."

destructive phenomena that emerge from this spirit, such as pacifism, internationalism, Freemasonry, and so forth. No Protestant clergy may belong to a Masonic lodge.

These ten points of the "German Christian" movement are a call for us to come together; they form in broad outline a direction for a future **Protestant National Church** [*Reichskirche*] that, while safeguarding peace among denominations, will develop the strengths of our Reformation faith for the good of the German people.

2

The Aryan Paragraph in the Church and Responses

Various Authors

Introduction

On April 7, 1933, two months after Adolf Hitler's appointment as chancellor, the National Socialist government passed the Law for the Restoration of the Professional Civil Service. The legislation allowed for the removal of tenured members of the civil service, specifically those who could not document their "Aryan" descent and those "who given their previous activities offer no guarantee that they will act at all times and without reservation in the interests of the national state," that is, opponents of the Nazi regime. Jews were the clearest targets. President Hindenburg insisted on several exceptions, which were incorporated into the new law: exemptions were granted to

World War I veterans who had served at the front, to those who had served in the civil service since 1914 (the beginning of the war), and to those who had lost fathers or sons in the war. Although variations on an Aryan paragraph had been part of the founding documents of many cultural, social, and political organizations in Germany (and elsewhere) since the mid-nineteenth century, this was the first anti-Jewish national legislation since 1871. The April 7 law applied to teachers, professors, and judges, among other civil servants. Technically, pastors and higher church officials were considered civil servants; the Nazi regime, however, not wanting to antagonize the churches at this juncture, did not press enforcement, and the third ordinance (issued on May 6, 1933) on the implementation of the law made it clear that it did not apply to "officials, employees and workers of religious societies recognized by public law." Later legislation extended the reach of the Aryan paragraph to lawyers, doctors, tax consultants, musicians, and notaries.

Discussion within the churches about whether the Aryan paragraph should be implemented there began as soon as the Reich law was enacted. In early September of 1933 the General Synod of the Protestant Church of the Old Prussian Union, by far the largest of the autonomous regional churches [Landeskirchen], and dominated by German Christians, adopted the measure, tailored specifically to apply to pastors and other church officials, as did the synods of several other German regional churches. Its adoption generated concern in some church circles; regional church governments sought the advice of theological faculties at several universities, notably Marburg and Erlangen, as to whether the Aryan paragraph was consistent with the Bible and Christian confessions. The faculties' respective responses, professional opinions called Gutachten, were contradictory. The Marburg professors rejected the Aryan paragraph while the Erlangen professors were equivocal but generally favorable.

When the national synod of the German Protestant Church met late in September of 1933 there was no attempt to enact the Aryan paragraph within the church nationally. The archbishop of Sweden had made it known publicly that he would be bound to separate himself from the German Protestant Church if such a measure were adopted, and the Reich Foreign Office—demonstrating the sensitivity of the Nazi regime to international opinion—sent a letter to officials of the national synod advising them not to force passage of the Aryan paragraph at the synod meeting.

Mobilized by the Prussian synod's acceptance of the Aryan paragraph, pastors who opposed it, led by Martin Niemöller of Berlin, founded the Pastors' Emergency League [*Pfarrernotbund*]. Those who joined the League were asked to sign a four-point pledge that committed each pastor "as a servant of the Word [to be] bound only by Holy Scripture and by the confessions of the Reformation." The pledge's fourth point read: ". . . I bear witness that the application of the Aryan paragraph in the area of the church of Christ is an infringement upon such a confessional position."[1] The Pastors' Emergency League was the forerunner of the Confessing Church, which emerged in May 1934.

The documents that follow are (1) the text of the Aryan paragraph in the church document; (2) the opinion of the theological faculty at the University of Marburg; (3) the opinion of the theological faculty at the University of Erlangen; and (4) Dietrich Bonhoeffer's theses on "The Aryan Paragraph in the Church," written by the end of August 1933 and discussed during preparations for the Old Prussian General Synod of September 5–6, 1933, by those who opposed the introduction of the Aryan paragraph in the church.

---

1. As quoted in Ernst Christian Helmreich, *The German Churches Under Hitler: Background, Struggle, and Epilogue* (Detroit: Wayne State University Press, 1979), 147.

Eine photographische Zufälligkeit wird zum Symbol
Adolf Hitler beim Verlassen der Marinekirche in Wilhelmshaven

Figure 2. A chance photo becomes a symbol. Adolf Hitler leaving St. Mary's Church in Wilhelmshaven. [Original caption.]

Aryan Paragraph in the Church and Responses[2]

Paragraph 1.

(1) Only those persons may be called as clergy or officials in the general church administration who have the requisite educational training and enter into their office in unconditional support of the national state and the German Protestant Church.[3]

(2) Those of non-Aryan descent or married to someone of non-Aryan descent may not be called as clergy or officials in the general church administration. Clergy or officials who marry a person of non-Aryan descent are to be dismissed. Who counts as a person of non-Aryan descent is to be determined by the regulations accompanying the laws of the Reich.

Paragraph 3.

(1) Clergy or officials who given their previous activities offer no guarantee that they will act at all times and without reservation in the interests of the national state and the German Protestant Church [may] be retired.

(2) Clergy or officials of non-Aryan descent or married to someone of non-Aryan descent are to be retired.

Paragraph 8.

(1) The regional church government shall make the final decisions on matters of retirement or dismissal, without the right of appeal.

Paragraph 11.

Correspondingly, paragraphs 1 and 3 shall apply also to members of church bodies as well as those in volunteer church positions.

2. From *The Protestant Church in Germany and the Jewish Question: Selected Documents from the Years of the Church Struggle 1933 to 1943* [*Die Evangelische Kirche in Deutschland und die Judenfrage: Ausgewählte Dokumente aus den Jahren des Kirchenkampfes 1933 bis 1943*], compiled and edited by order of the Refugee Service of the Ecumenical Council of Churches (Geneva: Verlag Oikumene, 1945), 35–36. Only excerpts from the Aryan Paragraph are provided.
3. The German Protestant Church [*Deutsche Evangelische Kirche*] would have comprised regional Lutheran, Reformed, and United (Reformed and Lutheran) churches.

The Marburg Statement[4]

A professional opinion from the theological faculty of the University of Marburg with regard to the Aryan paragraph in the church.

The theological faculty received the following petition:

Pastors and both ordained and lay delegates of the Church Convention of Kur-Hesse from the three Upper-Hessian church regions of the regional Protestant Church in Hesse-Kassel send this petition to the esteemed theological faculty of [the universities at] Marburg and Erlangen. We request a serious and responsible instruction directed to German Protestant Christians regarding the measure recently adopted by the General Synod of the Old Prussian Union and proposed for the whole German Protestant Church. This measure, which contains the Aryan paragraph, has to do with the conditions of employment of pastors and church administrators. We wish to know whether this measure is in conformity with or contradicts the teaching of Holy Scripture, the gospel of Jesus Christ and the teachings of the apostles, the essence of the sacraments, baptism and the Lord's Supper, the ecumenical creeds, and the Reformation doctrines regarding salvation through Jesus Christ, the church and its place, and baptism and the Lord's Supper, as well as the preamble of the constitution of the German Protestant Church.

Marburg, on September 11, 1933

The faculty, after meeting to discuss this matter on September 19, decided unanimously to provide the following response . . .

---

4. From *The Protestant Church in Germany and the Jewish Question: Selected Documents from the Years of the Church Struggle 1933–1943* [*Die Evangelische Kirche in Deutschland und die Judenfrage: Ausgewählte Dokumente aus den Jahren des Kirchenkampfes 1933 bis 1943*], compiled and edited by order of the Refugee Service of the Ecumenical Council of Churches (Geneva: Verlag Oikumene, 1945), 47–55.

The law having to do with the legal status of pastors and church officials . . . contains the following basic provisions corresponding to the new law pertaining to officials of the Reich:[5]

The possible exceptions provided for in paragraph 3, sections 3 and 4[6] . . . need not be taken into consideration . . . even though they make it clear that the legislators are unsure about their own basic principles and at the same time demonstrate the political origins of these measures and their basic incompatibility with the nature of the church.

The faculty considers that neither of the fundamental provisions in paragraphs 1 and 3, as well as 11, can be reconciled with the nature of the Christian church as it is determined by the sole decisive authority of the Holy Scripture and the Gospel of Jesus Christ and attested to by the confessions of the Reformation. The faculty notes at the same time that the Concordat that has just been concluded between the German Reich and the Holy See contains nothing that corresponds to these legal regulations.

The first of the above-mentioned regulations threatens the independence of the clergy, bound only by God's Word and the faithful conscience, in their proclamation and their pastoral work, and the officials of the church in the administration of their office, and puts them in danger of subordinating their personal responsibility to the pressures of the subjective and time-bound political or church-political views of those in superior offices, church groups, or entities outside the church. The danger is all the greater since the mandate of the law is formulated vaguely and very elastically, thereby explicitly

5. For the text, see p. 57 above.
6. (3) The application of section 2 can be set aside in cases where there have been special meritorious contributions to the development of the church in the German spirit. (4) The prohibitions in section 2 do not apply to pastors and officials who have been pastors or officials . . . since August 1, 1914, or who during the World War fought on the front for the German Reich or its allies, or whose father or son(s) were killed in the war. (Ed./trans.: footnote in the original German text)

ruling out a legally regulated procedure for establishing proof in the application of this law. It goes without saying that Protestant clergy and church officials as Christians will support their church and the government of their nation; the duty to do so is part and parcel of their obedience to God's Word. This duty, however, carries the proviso that is inalienably grounded in this same obedience, namely, that the mission of the church is not political and that in certain cases this mission may require that the church take a critical stance, appropriately expressed, regarding events in the life of the state and the church. A law in the church of the Reformation can only protect the freedom of the church to perform its mission in a pure and untrammeled manner precisely by preventing the politicization of its pastors. Cases of apparently intolerable conflict require proceeding in a way that is protected against false accusations and arbitrary decisions. Well-known historical experiences caution us most forcefully—for the sake of the state as well—against binding the church's proclamation or service to any political obligation.

The second of the above-mentioned basic regulations makes church members of non-Aryan descent into members with fewer rights and less worth, inasmuch as it fundamentally denies them—and those church members of Aryan descent who are married to them—eligibility to hold office in the Christian congregation.

It is undisputed that the message of Jesus Christ as the Savior of the World is directed to all peoples and therefore to all races, and in keeping with this that everyone who believes and is baptized into this message belongs to the church of Christ. The members of the church are brothers to one another. The concept of brotherhood precludes any inequality before the law as well as any avoidable segregation in secular relations. It makes no particular difference whether this dissolution or inequality of rights is realized in such a way that special Jewish Christian congregations are established or that Jewish

Christians are barred from holding office in a Christian congregation. The Christian church recognizes no other form of organization than that of inter-Christian confessions on the one hand and of regions and peoples on the other. The latter applies only in the sense that people who speak the same language will naturally come together and form a congregation, as will people who are citizens of the same country, for political-legal reasons. But in neither case will people who speak a different language or are citizens of a different country be excluded. Even the relevant civil law applying to churches, as well as international law, requires that clergy be citizens only as a rule, with exceptions permissible. All of church history, as well as the civil and church law of all peoples, has treated the concept of the Jew not as a racial one, but rather exclusively in a confessional sense, that is, that the Jew does not recognize Jesus as the Christ of God. The Jew who recognizes in the law and the prophets of his ancestors that Christ is the one prophesied, who converts and is baptized, is for the church no longer a Jew, and the church has never advocated limits on the civil rights of baptized Jews. It may be that the state, out of national-political considerations, will find that such limitations are called for, based on an assessment of racial factors previously not considered, but it cannot require from the churches as such any acceptance of these limits, since the church is nothing more or less than a fellowship of those who believe in Christ and have been baptized in his name. The church would cease to be this in its fullest sense if it permitted distinctions within its fellowship to be based upon some other attribute. The church cannot surrender its unity as the unity of the Body of Christ, into which all believers, in his Spirit, are baptized. The church recognizes no other grounds for separation [of any members] than unbelief and heresy, if and so long as these cannot be overcome by the power and proof of the Holy Spirit.

One cannot say that this unity exists only with respect to the invisible church, while in the visible church categories that divide people are to be respected and protected. To the degree that it is humanly possible, the visible church is to shape itself in conformity with the invisible, if it truly believes in its reality. "Spots and wrinkles" may appear on its body as ineradicable signs of its temporal weakness (Eph. 5:27). But to mutilate this body consciously is a sin against the Holy Spirit that is given to it. To put up with any imperfection within the church other than those caused by [human] weakness—and we do not argue that depriving Christians of Jewish descent of their rights within the German Protestant Church is intended in this way—is to make a virtue out of a lack of faith and love, and invalidates the gospel of God's Lordship and the justification of the sinner by grace through faith.

Nor can the objection be made that race and ethnicity [*Volkstum*] should not be ignored but are to be respected by the church as orders of creation.[7] Certainly the fact that the church in its entire history up to now would have been mistaken on this point would give no grounds not to follow better awareness all the more decisively now. However, the reference to the orders of creation in this connection is wrong. Perhaps the church has not always done justice in its preaching and pastoral work to the serious question and obligation that race and ethnicity present to it; perhaps the church has often given way to these natural-historical forces as the easier course, and from time to time has found it unnecessary [to do otherwise]. The fact that the church constitution has granted them no special rights corresponds to what is recognized in faith as the true order of

---

7. "Orders of creation" is a theological construct referring to certain structures or institutions God is said to have established in the earthly realm to order human life; marriage, family, the economy, the state, and the church might all be counted among them. For the German Christians, race—as they understood it—and *Volk* or *Volkstum* were "orders of creation," too, and, because they were established by God, were utterly sanctified.

creation, which is nothing other than God's unified Lordship over everything that he has created, and his redeeming judgment of sin, in which all are included. The church would surrender the essential character of its message to race and ethnicity, both of which it is bound to serve, if it were to recognize race and ethnicity as circumstances that include or exclude from membership or rights in the congregation. To treat race and ethnicity as properties of creation is only possible for the church to the degree that it incorporates them and proclaims to each person the vocation of his particularity as well as the blame for his segregation. Otherwise reverence for what is created takes the place of reverence for the Creator.

The very isolated examples of non-European church cultures characterized by racial restrictions on church membership, as they are found in Asia, Africa, and America (where, by the way, no distinctions are made between Jews and Aryans), should be judged to be underdeveloped or relapsed cultures, in which the Christian message and its demands have been violated. It is just as inappropriate here to point to the Jewish Christian congregations of the ancient Christian church. For one thing, these cases did not have to do with racially defined communities, but rather with Christians who believed they had to link their faith in Jesus as the Christ with the observance of the Old Testament law; moreover, this did not come about because Christian Jews were excluded from Christian congregations in the Greco-Roman world, but rather because some of the Christian Jews separated themselves. If one recognizes in the apostle Paul "the chosen instrument" of the Lord Jesus Christ (Acts 9:15), then it wounds his gospel, which is also the gospel of Luther, to acknowledge or to introduce that sort of division. It would also be worth noting at this point that Christians of Jewish descent have in our own Fatherland, as they have at many times and among many peoples, until recently been called to provide faithful service in Christian congregations. Here we mention only the theologian August Neander, the composer of hymns Philipp Spitta, and the painter Wilhelm Steinhausen. In the theological work of Neander, the spiritual hymn texts of Spitta, and the art of Steinhausen one detects nothing un-German. Rather, they all represent the genuinely German expression of Protestant piety and prove that the particular talents they were given, which they were also obliged to use, are not compromised by the preservation of Christian unity in faith and love.

Those who do not recognize full unity between Jewish and non-Jewish Christians in the church, as it is most impressively developed in the New Testament in the letter to the Ephesians—a unity recognized by the apostles and the Reformers—and do not want to realize this unity comprehensively in the constitution of the church, deceive themselves if they confess that the Holy Scripture is the Word of God and that Jesus Christ is the Son of God and the Lord of all people. It is indisputable that God proclaims his word in the world not only in the Old, but also in the New Testament through Jews, and chose his Son from among the Jews. Attempts to see in Jesus an Aryan have absolutely no historical basis and are pointless, not least because his message assumes that the law and the prophets of the Jews were God's revelations, and in any case his apostles were Jews. To deny the salvation-historical meaning of his birth from David's line, with its signal of his divine Sonship, is to misunderstand completely what faith in the divine Sonship means. To turn Jesus' crucifixion at the hands of the Jewish people into a reason to take away the rights of Christians of Jewish descent is Pharisaic error. Insofar as this occurs, the salvation history that God has brought about has been condemned by people who are ashamed of it, and service to the spirits of this world has been placed on a par with service to Christ.

The first article of the constitution of the German Protestant Church of July 11, 1933, says:

The inviolable foundation of the German Protestant Church is the gospel of Jesus Christ as it is attested to in the Holy Scripture and as it was further illuminated in the confessions of the Reformation. By it the authority that the church requires for its mission is determined and defined.

If these sentences are taken seriously, then neither a political or church-political shackling of the church's proclamation nor a diminution of the rights of non-Aryan Christians in the church is compatible with them.

The theological faculty of the University of Marburg.
[Signed by] The dean: Dr. von Soden

The Erlangen Statement[8]

A professional theological opinion [by members of the theological faculty of the University of Erlangen] on permitting Christians of Jewish descent to hold office in the German Protestant Church.

The theological faculty, after extensive consultation that resulted in complete agreement on matters of substance, asked their representatives to respond to the request . . . [The faculty's] opinion is as follows . . .

. . . With these regulations the Prussian General Synod is formally following a custom common to Christian churches of all times, which is to make the admission of persons to office in the church contingent on whether applicants fulfill certain personal criteria (1

---

8. From *The Protestant Church in Germany and the Jewish Question: Selected Documents from the Years of the Church Struggle 1933 to 1943* [*Die Evangelische Kirche in Deutschland und die Judenfrage: Ausgewählte Dokumente aus den Jahren des Kirchenkampfes 1933 bis 1943*], compiled and edited by order of the Refugee Service of the Ecumenical of Churches (Geneva: Verlag Oikumene, 1945), 55-62.

Tim. 3:1-13). Among the German regional churches, the criteria for spiritual office, for example, already include, besides German citizenship, certain biological characteristics relating to age, gender, and physical ability. The cited regulations add the new requirement of Aryan descent. In order to make a theological evaluation of this requirement, it is necessary to examine the attitude of the Christian churches to ethno-national [*völkische*] distinctions, especially the effect of this attitude on approval to serve in church offices.

1. According to the witness of the New Testament, Jesus Christ our Lord, in his death and resurrection, fulfilled the will of God to come to the aid of all people. No one—let alone a whole people—may be excluded from the universal validity of this gospel. All who have come to faith are, according to the witness of the apostle, one in Christ. In the bond with Christ there is before God neither Jew nor non-Jew. But the fact that all Christians are children of God does not dissolve their biological and social differences, but rather binds each person to the condition to which he is called (1 Cor. 7:20). Christians must also recognize with conviction and in deed their biological attachment to a particular people, which we cannot escape.

2. According to Reformation teaching, and in contrast to the Roman Catholic Church, the external order of the Christian church must conform not only to the universality of the gospel but also to the historical-*völkisch* classification of Christian people. According to the seventh article of the Augsburg Confession, the requirement of unity is limited to the purity of teaching and the administration of the sacraments. The Apology[9] deals with the possible diversity in other questions of

---

9. Philipp Melanchthon wrote the Apology to the Augsburg Confession in 1530. The Apology was a defense of the Confession that replied to the imperially-commissioned, official Roman Catholic response to the Augsburg Confession of June 25, 1530. Both the Apology and the

church order by noting that in the ancient church the Jewish Christians had a different church organization than the gentile Christians. Being one in Christ is for the Lutheran Confessions not a question of external organization but of faith.

In keeping with these principles, the churches that emerged from the Wittenberg Reformation have designated the boundaries of various peoples, and, in their church vocabulary, in their worship, and their constitutions they have not only protected particular national characteristics, but have substantially contributed to their cultivation and preservation. In the foreign mission of the Lutheran church, too, increasing consideration has been given to accomplishing the proclamation of the gospel among foreign peoples through the organization of new "people's churches" [*Volkskirchen*] that would be especially suited to their ethno-national characteristics [*völkische Art*].

3. If it is in fact the case that the ethno-national diversity of the church's external organization is a necessary consequence of an ethno-national structure that we must acknowledge as destined and ethically correct, then must also be taken into account with respect to the authorization to enter into church offices the point in time when a mission church has become a people's church. The one who exercises the ministry should be so bound to his congregation in its earthly existence that the commitments that grow out of it are also his. These include the commitment to the same ethnic culture. In practice the Reformation churches have followed this principle, even before it was articulated theoretically.

4. Whether and to what degree this principle should also apply to Christians of Jewish descent who live among us requires

Confession itself can be found in *The Book of Concord: The Confessions of the Evangelical Lutheran Church*, Robert Kolb and Timothy J. Wengert, eds. (Minneapolis: Fortress Press, 2000).

particular discussion. First the question must be raised whether Jews who reside in Germany belong in the fullest sense to the German people or constitute their own ethnic culture and are therefore a people who are resident aliens. The church as such cannot decide this. Certainly, for the church even today the Jewish people is not a people like any other: in election and in curse it remains the people of salvation history, the people of Jesus and the apostles according to the flesh, a people preserved for an ultimate history with Jesus Christ (Matt. 23:39, Romans 11). In its landless dispersion among the peoples it reminds us of the limits of all cultural unity, the provisional nature of the divisions among people, of the one kingdom of God that comes through the Christ promised to Israel. However, this knowledge of the church regarding the salvation-historical uniqueness and the mystery of the Jewish people does not equip it to decide the question as to whether the Jews who live among us belong fully to the German people or rather constitute an alien or guest-people. The church cannot even decide this question comprehensively for Jewish Christians, perhaps by pointing to the sacrament of baptism. The church's confession regarding the salvific significance of baptism as such yields no judgment, for example, as to whether marriages between Germans and baptized Jews who believe in Christ are generally to be welcomed or counseled against. The question of the ethnic relationship between Germanness and Jewishness is a biological-historical one. Our people, like any other people, can respond to it only within its particular biological-historical context.

5. Today more than ever the German people experiences the Jews in its midst as an alien ethnic body. It has become aware of the threat to its own life from emancipated Jewry and protects itself from this danger through exceptional regulations. As part of the

struggle for the renewal of our people, the new government has excluded men of Jewish or half-Jewish descent from holding important offices. The church must recognize the state's fundamental right to implement lawful measures. In the present circumstances the church knows that it is called to a new awareness of its task, namely, to be the church of the German people [*Volkskirche der Deutschen*]. As part of that, the church must renew the fundamental principle of the ethnic bond between the officeholder and his congregation and apply it as well to Christians of Jewish descent. In the present situation the church's position in the life of the people and the fulfillment of its duties would be hindered and severely impeded were its offices occupied, in general, by those of Jewish descent. The church must therefore require that Jewish Christians be restrained from assuming church office. This in no way disputes or limits their full membership in the German Protestant Church, any more than it does for any other members of our church who may not fulfill the conditions that would allow them to occupy church office.

6. This fundamental posture is in no sense an inflexible law, but rather leaves room for exceptions to the rule. The civil "Law for the Restoration of the Civil Service" recognizes in the establishment of exceptions from its regulations that Jews, for example, may be integrated into the German people by their readiness to offer their lives for Germany. This acknowledges that the boundary between the Jews and the German people in individual cases is not rigid but flexible. The church itself knows that genuine conversion to Jesus Christ can also and as such lead a Jew, as he becomes rooted in the church, from alien status to membership in the German people.

In accordance with all of this, the church definitely leaves room in its structure for exceptions that permit those of Jewish or half-Jewish descent to be admitted to office. Placing people of Jewish descent in church positions has always been rare in our churches, and in the future it should continue to be exceptional, but as such it must remain possible under particular circumstances.

7. This exception chiefly concerns the clergy and officers of Jewish or half-Jewish descent who are already in office. It would damage the nature, especially of the ministry, ordination, and calling if the church were generally to dismiss proven clergy of Jewish or half-Jewish descent, simply because of their background. Not—as in paragraph 3 of the Prussian church law—leaving them in office, but rather dismissing them from office requires special justification on a case-by-case basis. In those cases in which, because of the Jewish descent of the pastor, insurmountable difficulties arise between the pastor and the congregation, matters should be dealt with according to church rules that cover all cases pertaining to the destruction of the relationship of trust between the pastor and the congregation. Here the church cannot simply appropriate the regulations of the civil law, but rather must conduct itself according to rules that arise from its own nature as church.

8. Finally, respecting future cases that have to do with authorizing men of Jewish descent to hold church office, the church will have to develop its own principles by which to justify and limit these exceptions. The church would be well advised to refer this matter to its bishops.

Erlangen, September 25, 1933

[Signed by] Dr. Paul Althaus and Dr. Werner Elert,

Professors of Theology

Theses on "The Aryan paragraph in the Church"[10]

Dietrich Bonhoeffer

1. Radical version of the Aryan Paragraph:

Non-Aryans are not members of the German Reich Church and are to be excluded through the establishment of their own Jewish Christian congregations.

2. Second version of the Aryan Paragraph:

The law governing state officials is to be applied to church officials; thus employment of Jewish Christians as pastors should be discontinued, and none should be accepted for new employment.

3. Third version of the Aryan Paragraph:

Although the Reich Church constitution has not adopted the Aryan paragraph, it has made clear by its silence that it recognizes the regulations affecting students, which are designed to exclude Jewish Christians from theological study, as binding on the church. Thus it accepts the future exclusion of Jewish Christians from the ministry of the church.

Re: version 1. The exclusion of Jewish Christians from the church community destroys the substance of Christ's church, because

first: it reverses the work of Paul, who assumed that through the cross of Christ the dividing wall between Jews and Gentiles had been broken down, that Christ has "made both groups into one" (Eph. 2), that here (in Christ's church) there should be neither Jew nor Gentile... but rather all should be one.

second: if the church excludes the Jewish Christians, it is setting up a law with which one must comply in order to be a member of the church community, namely, the racial law. It means that Jews can be asked at the door, before they can enter Christ's church in

---

10. From *Dietrich Bonhoeffer Works: 1932-1933*, ed. Larry L. Rasmussen, trans. Isabel Best and David Higgins (Minneapolis: Fortress Press, 2009), 425-432.

Germany, "Are you Aryan?" Only when they have complied with this law can I go to church with them, pray, listen, and celebrate the Lord's Supper together with them. But by putting up this racial law at the door to the church community, the church is doing exactly what the Jewish Christian church was doing until Paul came, and in defiance of him; it was requiring people to become Jews in order to join the church community. A church today that excludes Jewish Christians has itself become a Jewish Christian church and has fallen away from the gospel, back to the law.

The German Christians say:

The church is not allowed to undo or to disregard God's orders, and race is one of them, so the church must be racially constituted.

We answer:

The given order of race is misjudged just as little as that of gender, status in society, etc.... In the church, a Jew is still a Jew, a Gentile a Gentile, a man a man, a capitalist a capitalist, etc., etc. But God calls and gathers them all together into one people, the people of God, the church, and they all belong to it in the same way, one with another. The church is not a community of people who are all the same but precisely one of people foreign to one another who are called by God's Word. The people of God is an order over and above all other orders. "Who is my mother, and who are my brothers?... whoever does the will of my Father in heaven is my brother and sister and mother." [Matt. 12:48 and 50] Race and blood are one order among those who enter into the church, but it must never become a criterion for belonging to the church; the only criterion is the Word of God and faith.

The German Christians say:

We don't want to take away from Jewish Christians the right to be Christians, but they should organize their own churches. It is only a matter of the outward form of the church.

We answer:

(1) The issue of belonging to the Christian community is never an outward, organizational matter, but is of the very substance of the church. Church is the congregation that is called together by the Word. Membership in a congregation is a question not of organization but of the essence of the church.

(2) To make such a basic distinction between Christianity and the church, or between Christ and the church, is wrong. There is no such thing as the idea of the church, on one hand, and its outward appearance, on the other, but rather the empirically experienced church is the church of Christ itself. Thus to exclude people forcibly from the church community at the empirical level means excluding them from Christ's church itself. That part of the church that excludes another is, of course, the one that is truly shut out—that is the particular danger of the German Christians' undertaking.

(3) When the church's organizers exclude anyone, they are interfering with the authority of the sacraments. Here in our church, Jewish Christians have been accepted, by the will of God, through the sacrament of baptism. Through baptism they are joined together with our church, and our church with them, by indissoluble ties. If the church that has baptized Jewish Christians now throws them out, it makes baptism into a ceremony, which implies no obligation on its part.

The German Christians say:

We are not so much concerned with these thousand Jewish Christians as with the millions of our fellow citizens who are estranged from God. For their sake, these others might in certain cases have to be sacrificed.

We answer:

We too are concerned for those outside the church, but the church does not sacrifice a single one of its members. It may even be that the church, for the sake of a thousand believing Jewish Christians that it is not allowed to sacrifice, might fail to win over those millions. But what good would it do to gain millions of people at the price of the truth and of love for even a single one? This could represent not gain but only loss, for the church would no longer be the church.

The German Christians say:

The German church people [Kirchenvolk] can no longer endure communion with Jews, who have done them so much harm politically.

We answer:

This is the very point where it must be made crystal clear: here is where we are tested as to whether we know what the church is. Here, where the Jewish Christian whom I don't like is sitting next to me among the faithful, this is precisely where the church is. If that is not understood, then those who think they cannot bear it should themselves go and form their own church, but never, ever, can they be allowed to exclude someone else. The continuity of the church is in the church where the Jewish Christians remain.

In summary:

The church is the congregation of those who are called, where the gospel is rightly taught, and the sacraments are rightly administered,[11] and it does not establish any law for membership therein. The Aryan paragraph is therefore a false doctrine for the church and destroys its substance. Therefore, there is only one way to serve the truth in a church that implements the Aryan paragraph in this radical form, and that is to withdraw. This is the ultimate act of solidarity with my church. I can never serve my church in any other way than by adhering to the whole truth and all its consequences.

Re: version 2. Removal of Jewish Christians from the pastorate contradicts the nature of the ministry. Luther taught that through baptism all Christians are made priests, they all have the same rights, and each has the right and the duty to obey and to teach the word of God.[12] The office of the ministry is conferred by the Christian community on a Christian who has already been consecrated a priest through baptism, and demands right teaching, Christian living, and spiritual gifts of the pastor. The pastor takes up this office as the call of Christ, and only an offense against one of these requirements can be grounds for the congregation to revoke this ministry.

If Jewish Christians are barred in principle from the pastorate, they become church members with lesser rights. To cite the biblical admonition, "Women should be silent in the churches" [1 Cor. 14:34], does not lead to any conclusion with regard to Jewish Christians as such. Either we consider this admonition as legally binding, in which case it still does not say anything about Jewish Christians' keeping silent in the churches, or we do not consider it legally binding, that is, women also are allowed to speak in the churches, in which case there is no possibility of forbidding Jewish Christians to speak as a matter of principle. As soon as Jewish Christians are excluded, moreover, the meaning of the ministry itself

---

11. See the Augsburg Confession VII, Book of Concord, 42.
12. Cf., for example, Luther, "That a Christian assembly or congregation has the right and power to judge all teaching...," 1523 (LW, 39).

is destroyed, since it is subjected to the whim of the congregation. Ordination itself is then revoked and made invalid; the ordinatio is placed, in a disorderly way, at the mercy of the congregation.

The German Christians say:

For the sake of the patriotic sentiments of German church people, a leader in the church must be Aryan.

We answer:

Church people must learn to pay attention not to the person of the pastor but rather to the pastor's proclamation. "What does it matter? Just this, that Christ is proclaimed in every way..."[13] If Paul, a Jew, had not proclaimed Christ to the heathen world, without worrying about any patriotic sentiment, there would never have been a German church.

This demand for the gospel to be preached by Aryans is a typical demand of those who are weak in the faith, so they want to set up legal restrictions in matters where, in truth, only faith and the Word of God has a say. This demand from the weaker members of the congregation might possibly be considered in exceptional individual cases, for pastoral reasons, to avoid giving serious offense. But in each such case the most earnest thought should be given to whether, for the sake of what church is about, the congregation should be asked to tolerate an offense to its sensibilities. It is totally impossible, however, to allow the demands of the weak in the faith to rule the church, because that means turning the freedom of the gospel into its opposite, a law.

The German Christians say:

---

13. See Phil. 1:18.

The laws that apply to state officials must also apply to church officials; otherwise the church is placed in opposition to the will of the state.

We answer:

This is precisely where the completely political character of all the German Christians' arguments about the Aryan paragraph is revealed. Seen in connection with current political events, they can appear only as the church emulating whatever the state does. However, the true service and loyalty that the church must render to the state consists never in blindly emulating its methods but only in the freedom of its own preaching and in displaying the form and character that properly belong to it as the church.

In summary:

The German Christians' demands destroy the substance of the ministry by making certain members of the Christian community into members with lesser rights, second-class Christians. The rest, those not affected by this demand, who remain privileged members, should prefer to stand by those with lesser rights rather than to benefit from a privileged status in the church. They must see their own true service, which they can still perform for their church, in resigning from this office of pastor as a privilege, which is what it has now become.

Re: version 3. If regulation of the right to university study makes it impossible for Jewish Christians to become pastors, the church, for its part, must open new doors to the ministry for Jewish Christians and thereby protest, through its proclamation, against such measures that attack the substance of the ministry. If the church does not do so, it is guilty of responsibility for the entire Aryan paragraph.

The German Christians say:

The Aryan paragraph is an *adiaphoron*,[14] which doesn't affect the confession of the church.

We answer:

1. All that we have said above is evidence that the church and the ministry have been attacked in their substance, that is, the confession has been attacked.
2. Even if this were not the case, the following judgment on the part of the confessional writings would be true. "Thus, Paul submits and gives in to the weak in matters of food or days (Rom. 14:6). But he does not want to submit to false apostles, who wanted to impose such things upon consciences as necessary even in matters that were in themselves free and indifferent. Col. 2:16: 'Do not let anyone make matters of food or drink or the observation of festivals a matter of conscience for you.' And when in such a case Peter and Barnabas did give in to a certain degree, Paul criticized them publicly, as those 'who were not acting consistently with the truth of the gospel' (Gal. 2[:14]).

"For in such a case it is no longer a matter of external matters of indifference, which in their nature and essence are and remain in and of themselves free, which accordingly are not subject to either a command or a prohibition regarding their use or discontinuance. Instead, here it is above all a matter of the chief article of our Christian faith, as the Apostle testifies, 'so that the truth of the gospel might always remain' (Gal. 2:5). Such coercion and command obscure and pervert the truth of the gospel, because either these opponents will

---

14. The Greek *adiaphoron* means a "matter of indifference."

publicly demand such indifferent things as a confirmation of false teaching, superstition, and idolatry for the purpose of suppressing pure teaching and Christian freedom or they will misuse them and as a result falsely reinstate them....

"Thus, submission and compromise in external things where Christian agreement in doctrine has not already been achieved strengthens idolaters in their idolatry."

3

———

Theological Existence Today!

Karl Barth

Introduction

Karl Barth (1886–1968) was a member of the theology faculty at the University of Bonn when he wrote *Theological Existence Today!* He wrote it quickly, at the urging of friends and in response to the increasing intensity of German Christian efforts to nazify the German Protestant Church. Published in July 1933, it has the character of a manifesto and is directed chiefly to pastors and theologians. Whether by Barth's intention or not, it came to have a much broader audience; before it was confiscated by the Nazi government in 1934, the Kaiser Verlag had published 37,000 copies. To those who were already opposed to the German Christians, it gave a voice; for those who were still on the fence, it helped them articulate their unease. It infuriated the German Christians. Barth personally sent a copy of the piece to Hitler.

Barth makes a number of key points in these excerpts. Within the Protestant churches, the German Christians were greeting the "German Revolution" led by the Nazis as a turning point in world history, a new beginning for the German nation and people, a sign of God's providential engagement in earthly events. "For them," Barth writes, "the recognition of the 'glory of the National Socialist State' is not only a civic duty . . . but instead a matter of faith . . . ." Barth's sharp response is that the attention, loyalty, and passion of theological existence—the church's vocation—must be utterly focused on the Word of God. No other claim may be permitted to deflect the church from its vocation or insinuate itself in place of that calling. Even worse than the theology of the German Christians, Barth avers, is "the way the Protestant church has up until now dealt with them. . . . [There has been] a puzzling lack of resistance . . . to the assault of this movement." He calls for a "*spiritual* center of resistance," a church that will carry out its responsibility, namely, "to serve the Word of God in the midst of this people."

Barth's strong claim to the independence of the church from the state and from the politicized agenda of the German Christians in support of that state was surely an implicit attack on the totalitarian claims of the Nazi state. In this sense Barth was a threat to the Nazi state and to the German Christians who supported it.

Theologische Existenz heute
Schriftenreihe, herausgegeben von Karl Barth und Ed. Thurneysen
Heft I

KARL BARTH

Theologische Existenz heute!

9. Auflage

29. bis 32. Tausend

1 9 3 4

Chr. Kaiser Verlag / München

Figure 3. Title page of Barth's *Theological Existence Today!* (Ninth edition, published in 1934).

Theological Existence Today![1]

Karl Barth

. . . [I]f I should nevertheless allow myself to be persuaded to say "something about the situation," my dear theological friends, far and near, then in terms of content I can really only put it as a question: "Would it not be better for the church and for us all if we did not at this point speak 'about the situation,' but rather, and above all, that each one spoke—considering and working through the necessary requirements for speaking, day after day, within the limits of one's own calling, 'about the thing itself'—as we are called to do, not only today, but today also?"

What must not happen under any circumstances is that, in our enthusiasm for something we believe is a good thing, we abandon our theological existence. Our theological existence is our existence in the church, as those who have been called to be the church's preachers and teachers.

Within the church there is agreement that in all the world there is no more urgent claim on us than the one made by the Word of God, that it be proclaimed and heard. We must comply with this demand, whatever the cost, whatever becomes of the world and the church itself. Within the church there is agreement that the Word of God banishes from the field everything and anything that may stand against it, that it will therefore triumph over us and over all its other enemies, because—"crucified, dead, buried, on the third day raised again, seated at the right hand of the Father"[2]—it has once and forever triumphed over us and for us and all its other enemies. Within the church there is agreement that God, precisely through this Word,

---

1. From Karl Barth, *Theological Existence Today!* [*Theologische Existenz heute!*], 9th ed. (Munich: Christian Kaiser Verlag, 1934), 3–7, 21–28, 34–40. First published 1933.
2. Phrases from the Apostles Creed.

sustains all things (Heb. 1:3), answers all questions, answers every request justly, preserves all that he has made and guides it to its truest purpose; that nothing in the world can endure or flourish without his Word. In the church there is agreement that it is good for the human being—and through time and eternity only this can be good for him—to cling to the Word of God with his whole heart, his whole soul, his whole mind, and his whole strength. Within the church there is agreement that in the world, in our space and our time, God is for us nowhere other than in his Word; that this Word has for us no other name and content than Jesus Christ; and that Jesus Christ is to be found nowhere in our world but every day anew in the Holy Scriptures of the Old and New Testaments. Either the church is in agreement on this, or one is not in the church.

And we as preachers and teachers of the church in particular are in agreement, both in fear and in joy, that we are called to serve the Word of God in the church and in the world through our preaching and teaching; that in the fulfillment of this calling we ourselves not only stand or fall, but we also see utterly everything in this world that may be important, dear, and significant to us stand or fall; that therefore no concern can be more urgent, no hope more moving, than the concern and hope we apply to our service, no friend more beloved than the one who helps us in this service and no enemy more hated than the one who wants to hinder us in this service. We agree that next to this first [commitment], which is the very meaning of our work and our rest, our grave focus and our composure, our love and our anger, there is no second; anything that may be second or third among those things that may or must move us is embraced and lifted up in the first, is judged and blessed by it. We agree about these things, or we are not preachers and teachers of the church. And this is what I call our "theological existence": that in the midst of the rest of our existence (for example, as men, as fathers and sons, as Germans, as citizens, as thinkers, as possessors of ever-restless hearts, and so on), the Word of God is to be simply what it is and what it alone can be to us, and in particular that our calling as preachers and teachers lays claim to us in a way that it alone can and may do.

This, our theological existence—that is, our attachment to the Word of God and the validity of our particular calling to serve the Word of God—can be lost to us. To put it another way: Today we can neglect to lay claim to this existence, now above all and more than ever before. To put it another and still better way: it may be that it will no longer be given to us, as it should be given each day anew, because we forget to pray for it and reach out for it, as we should now more than ever, so that it will be given to us. For that is the powerful temptation of our time, and it appears in every possible form: that we no longer understand the intensity and exclusivity of the demand of the Word of God as such over the power of other demands and thus immediately fail to understand this Word at all. That in our anxiety in the face of all kinds of dangers we no longer trust fully in the power of the Word of God, but rather believe that we must come to its aid with all sorts of organizations, and doing so we utterly cast aside our confidence in its triumph. That we think we can find answers, solutions, and achievements better elsewhere than in and through the Word of God, thereby proving that in fact we do not know how to honor it in anything as Creator, Reconciler, and Redeemer. That we divide our heart between the Word of God and everything else that we explicitly or implicitly costume, alongside it, with the glory of the divine, thus showing that the Word of God is not at all present in our hearts. That under the stormy influence of certain "principalities, powers, and rulers of this world's darkness"[3] we seek God elsewhere than in his Word, and his Word elsewhere than in Jesus Christ, and Jesus Christ elsewhere than in the Holy

3. See Ephesians 6:12.

86

Scriptures of the Old and New Testament, and thereby are actually those who do not seek God at all. All this, despite the fact that within the church we all affirm the opposite! How, then, can we be in the church? And this is the particular form of this temptation for us as preachers and teachers of the church: that it occurs to us that there could really be a competition between our calling in the church and this or that other calling, such that we could feel ourselves pushed and pulled to carry out this or that other calling in competition with our churchly calling or next to it, or to interpret or to shape our churchly calling from the perspective of this or that other calling. That we see ourselves and those to whom we are sent as standing and falling by standards completely different from the sole rule: that we fulfill our ministry rightly. That the secondary or tertiary thing that we know should be taken up in the first thing for all practical purposes becomes itself the first thing, mixes in with it, and in the end takes the place of what is first. Whereupon the real first thing and our calling itself are hopelessly lost to us. This, despite the fact that as preachers and teachers of the church we agreed on something quite different! At that point we are no longer the church's preachers and teachers. We are then politicians and church-politicians. It is not a disgrace, but rather a particular honor, to be a politician or even a church-politician. But to be a theologian is something different. For a theologian to become a politician or a church-politician can well mean the loss of his theological existence. Today it appears to mean that in a very particular way. Now, then, it is time to say this: that we should under no circumstances lose our theological existence, exchanging our birthright for a mess of pottage.[4] Or to say it positively: that we should remain, every one of us, in the church as it has borne us through the Word of God, and in the incomparable place of our calling, or return to the church and to this place of our

4. The reference is to Gen. 27:1-40.

calling, in all circumstances and at all costs, setting aside all other considerations and concerns.

I am writing this on the evening of the critical 24 June 1933. I will try to clarify what I mean in terms of three examples, questions that concern us at the present time.

[Barth writes about these issues: calls for church reform, the struggle over the question of a national bishop, and the German Christians. The translation picks up at the discussion of the German Christians.]

. . . The dubious renown of having set in motion the German church reforms of 1933, and not least the question of the [national] bishop, belongs to the so-called "German Christian Faith Movement." I have been asked specifically why I have never yet said anything publicly against this movement. I have not done so because until now I have believed that whatever I had to say in this matter would be so self-evident that anyone who knows me even a little could probably say it just as well. But doubts have arisen about this because certain members of the Reformed tradition with whom I have been working during these months, and others who have more or less counted as my students, have shown up in the ranks of the German Christians. So what is self-evident needs to be stated clearly. Explicitly and emphatically, but still only in passing, I say it simply because it is apparently unavoidable if I am to lay the groundwork for what I want to say about the "German Christians."

According to the guidelines of the German Christians in the two definitive documents published on May 5 and May 19, 1933, the position and purpose of those who so call themselves is as follows, in the theologically important points: "It appears," they say, "that the German people, reflecting on the deepest sources of its life and strength, wants also to find its way back to the church. The German churches have therefore to do everything they can to make this happen." The church has to prove itself the church for the German people by "helping them to be able to recognize and fulfill the calling that God has given them," which is also "the ultimate goal of the present government." The German churches must take on a form "that will enable them to serve the German people as the Gospel of Jesus Christ requires." This is what the German Christians are striving to do. But what is it that distinguishes these German Christians and their claims from other groups that may sound quite similar? This is what distinguishes them: For them the recognition of the "supremacy of the National Socialist state" is not only a civic duty, not only a matter of political conviction, but a matter of faith, and they demand a church that agrees with them on this. According to them the Gospel must in future be proclaimed as "the Gospel in the Third Reich."[5] The creed is to be retained, but it must be developed further to emphasize a "sharp rejection" of mammonism, Bolshevism, and "unchristian pacifism." In the future the church must be "the church of German Christians, that is, of Germans of the Aryan race." The national bishop, as "spiritual leader [Führer], who personally makes and takes responsibility for authoritative decisions," is to be chosen through a primary election by electors selected "by the recommendation and from the ranks of the German Christians," in which election Christians of non-Aryan descent are not eligible to vote. (In a later announcement a third criterion for the future bishop is specified: that he must be a man especially trusted by the Chancellor of the Reich.) What shall the church do with her confession? It shall "supply us with the weapons for the battle against everything unchristian and everything that may corrupt the people." How is this to occur? "The formation and guidance of pastors requires a

5. *The Gospel in the Third Reich* was the title of the German Christians' weekly church newspaper.

fundamental transformation that will bring them closer to daily life and solidarity with the community," and so forth!

What I have to say to this is simple: I say, unconditionally and without reservation, No! to the spirit and the letter of this doctrine. I am of the opinion that this doctrine has no right of domicile in the Protestant church. I am of the opinion that if such teaching were to become the autocrat of the Protestant church, as is the desire of the German Christians, it would be the end of the Protestant church. I am of the opinion that the Protestant church should rather shrink to the tiniest little pile of people and go into the catacombs than to make peace with this doctrine even at arm's length. I consider that those who have embraced these teachings are either seducers or seduced, and I can recognize the church in this "movement" only as I must recognize the church in the Roman papacy. I can only plead with my various theologian friends who—having been hypnotized or persuaded by some kind of sophism—have found themselves in a position to accept this doctrine that they take it from me that I consider them utterly and decisively divorced from me, unless, by some fortunate inconsistency, they have retained some otherwise Christian, ecclesiastical, and theological substance alongside this heresy. I offer as grounds for my rejection [of this doctrine] the following points:

1. The church does not have to "do everything," in order that the German people "find its way back to the church," but instead must do everything so that the German people may find *in* the church the commandment and the promise of the free and pure Word of God.

2. The German people receives its calling from Christ and to Christ through the Word of God, to be proclaimed according to the Holy Scriptures. This proclamation is the task of the church. It is not the church's task to help the German people along the road

to recognizing and fulfilling a "calling" different from the one from and to Christ.

3. The church is absolutely not there to serve human beings, and not the German people, either. The German Protestant church is the church for the German Protestant people, but it serves the Word of God alone. It is God's will and his work if through his Word humanity and thus also the German people are served.

4. The church believes that God has established the state as the agent and guardian of the public order among the people. But the church does not believe in a particular state, and thus not in the German state, nor in a particular kind of state, hence not the National Socialist kind. The church preaches the Gospel in all the kingdoms [Reiche] of this world. It also proclaims it *in the* Third Reich, but not *under* it, nor in *its* spirit.

5. The creed of the church, if it is to be further developed, must be so developed according to the standards of Holy Scripture and in no case according to standards set by the positions or negations of a particular worldview, whether political or other—not even the National Socialist worldview—that may be regnant at a particular time. It does not have to supply either "us" or anyone else with "weapons."

6. The community of those who belong to the church is not determined by blood and so also not by race, but rather by the Holy Spirit and by baptism. If the German Protestant church were to exclude Jewish Christians or treat them as second-class Christians, it would have ceased to be a Christian church.

7. If the office of national bishop [Reichsbischof] in the Protestant church were even possible, then, like every church office, it would be filled not according to political viewpoints or methods (primary election, party membership, etc.), but rather by official

representatives of the appropriate offices of the congregations from the point of view of what is suitable for the church.

8. The formation and guidance of pastors is not to be transformed in the interest of "bringing them closer to daily life and greater solidarity with the community," but instead in the interest of greater discipline and substance in the carrying out of the task that has been commanded and entrusted to them, namely, the proclamation of the Word according to the Scriptures.

9. . . . .

Though I make no claim to have covered everything, these are some of the points of opposition to the German Christians. But as emphatically as I would like to advocate them, just as little do I want them emphasized in connection with what really matters to me. I would not have spoken out simply for the sake of rejecting the "German Christians," and I expect absolutely nothing from a discussion with their spokesmen. Certainly their appearance and growth raises concerns, but not because they have come up with a heresy that has never appeared before: anyone who knows theology even a little knows that their teaching, with the exception of only a few original ideas—to use a nice phrase that is not original with me—consists of a small collection of specimens from the great theological garbage can of the now widely disparaged eighteenth and nineteenth centuries. And most certainly not because they know how to put forward their arguments with particularly dangerous intellectual artistry and power!! In the end, the concern arises only because they have shown and continue to show that it is possible to give form and influence to a "faith movement" simply by using violent methods like political mass demonstrations and protest marches. That a scholarly preachers' conference at which a purely scholarly paper was to be presented could not proceed because a crowd of pastors not politically sympathetic with the speaker threatens to disrupt the proceedings—that is, to be sure, both new and astonishing. That "A mighty fortress is our God" can be sung to the accompaniment of drums, that one can hear the battle cry, "Farmers, seize the churches!"—that is also new and very dangerous. . . . When it appears that it is in the nature of this faith movement to function at this level, then it is so dangerous that it is certainly more prudent not to get into an argument with it, but rather to give it, or at least its leaders, a wide berth and speak to other audiences.

I think we have more pressing and more serious things to be concerned about than countering the theology of the "German Christians" and instructing them. As bad as they may be, what is much worse, it seems to me, is the way the Protestant church has dealt with them up to now. If the Protestant church were healthy, something else would have happened than has happened. What, then, has occurred?

On the one hand we have the reality of a very puzzling lack of resistance on the part of pastors and members of congregations and leaders of the church, professors and students of theology, educated and uneducated people, old and young people, liberals, fundamentalists, and pietists, Lutherans and Reformed, who have succumbed in droves to the assault of this movement—succumbed as if to a real, serious psychosis. One group surrenders in the honest belief that they have finally received a positively messianic message, others with some deep philosophical justification or other, the kind we find most reliable when we let "reality" take us by storm. A third group capitulates with the simplistic reflection that whatever makes sense in the political arena will also be easiest in the ecclesiastical; a fourth with anxious judiciousness, fearful that it will be "shut out," its valuable gifts left unexploited, because everything is heading in the same direction, anyway; a fifth with the wise caveat that they affirm only what is "good" in this movement; a sixth goes along, somewhat hesitantly, thinking that, when the time is right, they will become the "loyal opposition" and "overcome the one-sidedness" of the movement "from the inside out." But one and all capitulate to a cause that bears the stamp of error so clearly on its forehead . . .

As all this became possible, where was the straightforward but decisive question as to the Christian *truth*? Or can this question no longer be asked in today's Protestant church? Has it been completely drowned out in shouts of jubilation or groaning at the new departure, reality, life, the historical moment, and all sorts of other slogans intended to suffocate all Christian critique? Is one an ossified old churchman or a scholar buried in the library if one allows oneself to refuse to accept even the loudest drumbeats, as such, as an argument in this matter? Is this what is so wonderful about this movement, that in face of it thousands have not even raised the question of Christian truth? . . .

. . . [I]n the church—today more than ever—the definitive thinking must be of the most serious nature. The protection now to be accorded freedom of proclamation and theology cannot consist primarily in safeguarding it against what is to be expected: an external technical assault by the "German Christians." The freedom that must be protected is the freedom—that is, in fact, the sovereignty—of the Word of God in proclamation and theology. We cannot be too clear about the fact that, in the wake of the last two centuries of the church's history, which is our own history, *this* freedom or sovereignty is by no means self-evident; that on this side we are by no means secure, even if we had long been fully secure against attack and from the external threats of the "German Christians." This invasion could itself be just a last clear sign of how endangered the freedom, that is, the sovereignty, of the Word of God is and has been for a long time and universally in the whole German Protestant Church. The threat of the technical mutilation of the church could be a reminder that, if we are indifferent, God is free to take the lampstand of the Gospel away from the church in Germany just as it was taken from the church of North Africa, which was as much Augustine's church as the German church is the church of Luther. It would then be foolish and fruitless, in the face of the sign given to us, to fight what might be a last-minute battle with the resources of church politics, in which case, given this terrible sign, our only hope would be to cry out to God that, despite the great faithlessness of the modern German Christian and ecclesial spirit, he would not tire of reigning over us, that he might, by means of his Word, make us more faithful to his Word than we or our ancestors have been. Then it could turn out that we would fear less the threatening technical rape by the "German Christians," together with the resulting danger of spiritual famine and poisoning, and dread all the more that the Word of God would be taken away from us altogether—we ourselves, and precisely we who are not "German Christians"—if we do not repent immediately. It could turn out that a completely different battle would lay claim to us, a battle that has nothing to do with elections and proclamations and protests, with movements and fronts, a battle not *for* the church but rather *within* the church, not in order to protect it but rather to *practice* proclamation and theology, not *against* the "German Christians," but rather both implicitly and explicitly *for* them, a battle in which we could want, not to win, but to be compelled to submit, and in so doing, like Jacob, to *be* an evangelical church. . . .

. . . What we need more than anything today is surely a *spiritual* center of resistance that would give sense and substance to a corresponding church-political center. Whoever understands this will not choose just any fight, but will place a sober admonition to "pray and work!" on his program.

Let us not be too quick to say "this is no help at all in the midst of the worries and tumults of the summer of 1933." Theologians who have so often preached fine sermons on God's help as the only true aid should be a little ashamed to say this so quickly. They should let themselves be persuaded by the Word: God's help really is the only help, indeed the only real and current church-political help, that we can seek at the moment and evidently must at present learn to seek with new seriousness.

Let us not say too quickly, either, that in the concrete situation of the congregations something must be done—in fact, something quite different from what has been suggested here—in order to get control of the evil. Certainly something must be done—actually, a great deal must be done—but certainly nothing other than this: that congregations be gathered together again, rightly and anew, in fear and great joy, by means of the Word, to the Word. All the shouting about and concerning the church will not save the church. Where the church is truly the church, it *is* already saved. No matter how powerful the assault, it will not move the church. *Nevertheless*, it is written, *nevertheless*, the city of God will be made glad by its little stream! (Ps. 46:5) Nor should we be too quick to say that with this advice the whole church, so perilously called into question today, has been forgotten. The whole church is always present where two or three are gathered in his name. Let us repeat and reaffirm the church's creed through word and deed, wherever it is necessary, that is to say, wherever the enemy comes concretely into view! Let us repeat and reaffirm it, too, in the fellowship of the congregations, where this fellowship is truly a community of faith and not a community dedicated only to church-political business! Where the creed is, there the one holy church does battle with error, and in that battle the church will never be laid low. On the other hand, where there are "movements," even with the best intentions and goals, there error and sectarianism are, at the very least, nearby. The Holy Spirit needs no "movements," and by far most of the "movements" are probably inventions of the devil. . . .

. . . I am not interested, God knows, in calming down anyone who is presently upset. I would, however, like to be able to ask many of those who are now upset whether they are seriously upset: *so* upset that that they can no longer be calmed by an upset church-political situation; *so* upset that there is really nothing left for them to do except at last simply to *be* the church . . . the church that is the congregation of those who are called, who listen, who obey, who watch and pray . . . .

. . . I return to where I began . . . . but I want to and must say to Protestant theologians, in direct reference to these questions that are troubling us all, quite simply: We must guard our theological existence, today better than yesterday; we must plainly, directly, unconcerned, and tirelessly walk the path we have been commanded to walk. . . . Now if someone responds: "In light of the great movement sweeping through the people, in light of the great task that it sees before it, in light of the great hope in which it now lives, isn't this too petty, too particular, even a self-seeking business, to say that we have to protect our theological existence no matter what the cost?"—Then I would say once again in conclusion: Friend, let us think spiritually and thereby in *real* terms! You're right, theological existence does not exist for its own sake, just as God himself was not satisfied to be simply for himself, who on the contrary "did not withhold his own Son, but gave him up for all of us, will he not with him also give us everything else?" (Rom. 8:32) If God in Jesus Christ is wholly and completely for us human beings, so then the church, where his glory dwells, must also be the place that is wholly and completely for humankind, and therefore the German Protestant church for the German Protestant people, and therefore too we German theologians truly and honorably, wholly and completely, for this people. But we must be for them as who *we* are, and we must also do what *we* have been called to do. And what we are called to do is to serve the Word of God in the midst of this people. We sin not only against God, but also against this people, if we pursue other ideals and tasks to which we are *not* called. But it is in the nature of the task we have that it can be ranked neither below nor alongside any other issue that might move us. Again, we sin not only against God but against our people if we allow this order of priority to be disturbed to the smallest degree. And this task must be carried out, . irrespective of whether the people itself wants it to be carried out or not, understands it or does not understand it, approves of it or does not approve of it. We must expect neither thanks nor honor as we carry it out. We should not be surprised if we receive the contrary. Under some circumstances we must take it upon ourselves to be quite lonely, precisely for the sake of being together with the people. In this as well we would be sinning not only against God but also against the people if we chose to go *with* the people rather than stand *for* the people. The people, including and especially the German people of 1933, needs and cannot do without this: that the duty laid upon us be carried out. Today the prospect of something extraordinary is being held out to it: that of itself it go forth, united and free, on a path that its leaders have said they know and have determined to go with them. But the German people will need the admonition and the comfort of the Word of God, even if that goal is reached, and today more than ever, as they stand at the beginning of the path. . . . What has become of all that, even a year ago and also for a hundred years before that, was called freedom, justice, and spirit? Now, these are temporal and earthly goods. All flesh is like grass . . . . No doubt about it: there have been peoples in both ancient and recent times that have had to do without these goods and have also been able to do without them, when the audacious project of the "total State" has required it of them. "But the Word of our God remains forever." And that is why, every day—for each day hastens toward eternity—it is true and indispensible. This is why, in a totalitarian state, neither the church nor theology can hibernate, nor can they put up with a moratorium or being forced into line [*Gleichschaltung*].[6] [The church] is by its nature the limit of any state, even the totalitarian state. For even in a totalitarian state the people live from the Word of God, whose content is "the forgiveness of sins, the resurrection of the body, and life everlasting." The church and theology must serve this Word, for the sake of the people. In so doing they are the limit of the state. This they are for the health and salvation [*Heil*] of the people, which neither the state nor the church can create but which the church is called to proclaim. The church must be allowed to remain true to its unique function, and desire to do so. Faced with the special concern that is laid upon him, the theologian must stay *awake*, a lonely bird on the roof, that is, on the earth, but under the open—wide and unconditionally open—sky. Oh, that the German Protestant theologian would stay awake! or, if he happens to have fallen asleep, that today, today, he would awaken!

Completed: Sunday, June 25, 1933

---

6. Refers to the National Socialist plan to coordinate all German institutions.

4

What the German Christians Want
for the Church

Emanuel Hirsch

Introduction

Emanuel Hirsch (1888–1972), "a major figure in twentieth-century German theology,"[1] was a Lutheran pastor, theologian, and professor. He taught church history and then systematic theology at the University of Göttingen, where he also became dean of the theological faculty. He was a recognized authority on both Martin Luther and Søren Kierkegaard, and was known for his translations of the latter's work from Danish to German. Early in the history of the German Christian movement he became one of its leading

1. Ericksen, 123.

theological advisors, and personally counseled Ludwig Müller, who became national bishop [*Reichsbischof*]. Hirsch, a close friend of theologian Paul Tillich during their student days, parted political and theological ways both with him and with Karl Barth after the National Socialists came to power. He joined the Nazi Party in 1937 and also became a supporting member of the S.S. Hirsch identified himself as a committed Christian and a dedicated National Socialist; he never wavered in his support for the Nazi project.

The excerpts that follow are from his response to Karl Barth's attack on the German Christians in *Theological Existence Today!* but Hirsch has a larger audience in view. Declaring that Barth himself "has closed his ears," Hirsch states that the best way to answer the points Barth has raised is to provide an account of what he believes the German Christians want for the church. In his account Hirsch elucidates some of the key assumptions of German Christian theological reflection. For example, he argues that while Scripture may be the "best vehicle of [the] living Word," it is not the only one; God speaks also in and to the particular historical situation in which people find themselves—in this case, National Socialist Germany—and the church must be fully engaged in its particular historical reality. Barth, Hirsch contends, is isolating theology from what God is doing in Germany's present moment, which is precisely where and how God is now speaking to the German people.

Hirsch also argues that "Germanness and Christianity must encounter each other in a deeply spiritual manner." Echoing Nazi principles, he writes that the German "spirit" resides in "good, old, and pure German blood." In the German Protestant church, which must reflect and contribute to the drive for racial "purity," there is no room for Jewish Christians.

Das kirchliche Wollen der Deutschen Christen

D. Emanuel Hirsch
o. Professor an der Universität Göttingen

2. Auflage
4. — 8. Tausend

Verlag: Max Grevemeyer, Berlin-Charlottenburg

1933

Figure 4. Title page of *What the German Christians Want for the Church* by Emanuel Hirsch.

What the German Christians Want for the Church:
An Assessment of Karl Barth's Attack
(in *Theological Existence Today*, Munich 1933)[2]

Emanuel Hirsch

For us German Christians there is no talking with Karl Barth. He calls us "openly wild heretics" . . . . He calls German Christians the "bad guys," warning that the church must withstand the temptation they represent. For us there is no talking with Karl Barth. Though aware of his responsibility to the church, he has closed his ears.

To speak with others—those before whom he makes such an effort to blacken our good Christian name—is difficult. Reading what he has written, one is seized by a longing for the conscientiousness and thoroughness with which the sixteenth- and seventeenth-century theologians of our church fought against heresy. There, every judgment was grounded in hard, clean work. There it was possible to seek clarification of the disputed questions. Karl Barth makes his condemnation of us "explicitly and emphatically, but still only in passing." It suits his ecclesiastical sense of responsibility to dispense in this way with a church movement to which a whole host of people confess they have committed themselves, for God's sake and the sake of the gospel.

In this situation, what is to be done? The simplest and most obvious answer is to give an account of what one desires for the church, of the faith out of which the willingness to take this risk emerges. That is what I hope to do in what follows . . . .

---

2. From Emanuel Hirsch, *What the German Christians Want for the Church* [*Das kirchliche Wollen der Deutschen Christen*], 2nd ed. (Berlin-Charlottenburg: Verlag Max Grevemeyer, 1933), 5, 8–14, 17–20.

2. Christian Belief in God

At one point [in *Theological Existence Today!*] Karl Barth offers an opening for a theological reflection beyond the question of the church itself. He says:

> Within the church there is agreement that in the world, in our space and our time, God is for us nowhere other than in his Word; that this Word has for us no other name and content than Jesus Christ; and that Jesus Christ is to be found nowhere in our world but every day anew in the Holy Scriptures of the Old and New Testaments. Either the church is in agreement on this, or one is not in the church.

These sentences apparently claim to express a dogma, a basic teaching. If they truly are meant to be taken as a basic doctrine of the Protestant church, then it seems I do not belong in that church. . . .

This new dogma is indeed quite strange. I can find Jesus Christ "nowhere in our world but every day anew in the Holy Scriptures"? So if a tyrant threw me in jail and took away my Bible—then would Jesus Christ simply be gone for me? Or he would be there for me only insofar as I happened to know individual passages of the Bible from memory? But let us leave aside the extreme case and look at something more ordinary. If I talk to a friend who has not found Christ, and I want to give him an account of my faith in the gospel, and in the process I do not use biblical expressions, but do so in my own words, words that God gives me—then is Christ not there for my friend or for me, and can he not encounter him in that way? And something else. I have read in the Apostle Paul the following: "It is no longer I who live, but Christ who lives in me." [Gal. 2:20] So am I not permitted to repeat what Paul says, not permitted to confess, that in faith I have a living Lord who is present to me and comforts and guides and knows me? Whoever says such a thing doesn't belong to the Christian church? It's a good thing that I have reason to believe that God has not handed over the keys to his church to any human being.

But Barth's statement says more. In fact, he says that God himself is present for me nowhere in the whole world except in the Holy Scriptures, the Old and New Testaments. I think that on the basis of his new dogma Barth would belatedly lock Calvin[3] out of the Christian church. For I read in Calvin just the opposite of what Barth says. In the Geneva Catechism we read, "Why do you go on to call God 'Creator of heaven and earth'? Because he has revealed himself in his works (Rom. 1:20), he is also to be sought in them. For his nature is not accessible to our spirit. So the world itself is likewise a mirror in which we can see God, as far as we are able to recognize him." And on the first pages of the *Institutes*[4] I read, "Every individual will not only be driven by knowledge of himself to seek God, but also led by the hand to find him." In this context it is clear that self-knowledge means the conscience that is given to us. In it is knowledge of God. But leaving Calvin aside, I am afraid that not even the Apostle Paul belongs to the Christian church in which Barth says everyone agrees with his new dogma. Speaking to the Athenians about God, did not Paul presume to say, "He is not far from each one of us, for 'In him we live, and move, and have our being'; as even some of your poets have said, 'For we too are his offspring.'" (Acts 17:27-28). Does Barth think that Paul here has fallen into an unfortunate concession to Greek idealism?

These statements by Barth rest on a twofold confusion. It is indeed an inalienable element of the heart of Christian proclamation that only in faith in the living Word of the gospel, which is Jesus Christ himself, can we know God truly as our Father, so that we may live

---

3. John Calvin (1509–1564), Geneva reformer and founder of the Reformed tradition (of which Barth is a successor).

4. *Institutes of the Christian Religion*, written by John Calvin and first published in 1536.

before him as his children and have peace with him. But to begin with, this knowledge of God as our Father in Christ Jesus, knowledge that brings us life and blessing, is not the first or the only evidence we have of God. If he did not bear witness every day in the reality of our lives, around us and in us, the word of the gospel would never reach us, and we would never be able to live from the word of the gospel. The Christian's concrete, living knowledge of God comes about only in this way: that, observing the signs of God's presence in the historical reality in and around him, he receives faith in the gospel, and in turn, out of his faith in the gospel he hears and understands anew God's presence in the reality of life in and around him. *Faith in Christ must become concrete as a believing reception and framing of the particular historical situation, and the acceptance and framing in faith of the particular historical situation must be realized through faith in Christ.*[5] That is the first point. The other is this, that Barth is not clear about the Reformation—or at least the Lutheran—analysis of the relationship between Christ, the living Word of God, and the book that is the Bible. *Which is the Word of God through which Christ rules his church, in which he is present? Only what is written in the book that is the Bible? No—rather, every living word of the gospel witness that goes from mouth to ear and, in the miracle of the Spirit, from heart to heart.*[6] In this living Word we find Christ, and find him in such a way that in the Spirit he himself becomes for us a living Word. Sacred Scripture is surely the principal bearer of this living Word, and it is the guideline and the measure for all preaching and all other speaking in the church. But it does not hold Christ and his Gospel captive, so that he is not to be found anywhere but there.

Now on these two points depends a great deal in any evaluation of the ecclesiastical character of the German Christians. For, if there

5. Emphasis in original.
6. Emphasis in original.

is anything distinctive about them as regards their theology, it is that they take the two statements I have emphasized above with the utmost seriousness, and that they want to thoroughly re-educate the church on that basis. With respect to the first, they demand a new and more concrete teaching about the Christian way of life in the situation in which people really find themselves today, that is, for us, a new and concrete teaching about a Christian way of life in the present situation and responsibility of the German people. It is my honest opinion that the re-formation of the ethos of our people that is underway in Germany needs to be deepened and clarified by Protestant teaching on justification, and that we are wasting one of the opportunities for service laid upon us by God if we do not help here with new thinking and guidance from the gospel. How does the teaching on justification become a concrete way of life for a National Socialist German today? This is a question that we must answer if we want to guide today's National Socialist German into Protestant Christianity. He will never embrace faith in Christ if we cannot demonstrate, in the church's preparatory instruction, how Protestant and National Socialist morality and way of life merge. As regards the second statement, the German Christians believe that the gospel witness is life-giving only if the one truth of the gospel according to God's will can be told and retold by every generation in its own new words and its own new way of speaking. Living in new historical circumstances always renews the language with images, parables, and experiences, and everything that is renewed in this way may and must, for love's sake, for the sake of the accessibility of the message, be put at the service of the proclamation of the gospel, as God's grace allows it.

But of course, if a theologian believes that outside of the Bible he is in a wilderness where there is no God and no evidence of God, no testimony to or for him, he will not understand us. In today's

Germany, whoever is in the world without God cannot have any sense of the divine action and initiative that call us in the church to dare anew.

3. Germanness [Deutschtum] and Christianity

It seems that Barth sees only paganism in the fact that the German Christians have dared to ask the Protestant church the question of the relationship between Christianity and the German character, [and] the question of whether men of non-German blood may lead the church. Whoever wants to understand us on this point must first appreciate fully a profound ecclesiastical failure of the last generation.

Every human accomplishment and design is limited and bound by the natural character we bring with us into life. *If the blood is tainted, the spirit also dies*; for the spirit of both peoples and individuals arises from the blood. Only an intellectualistic generation so arrogant that it no longer recognizes any limits to human ability within the mystery of creatureliness could forget this. Forgetting, they have done infinite damage. Our people's blood-bond was nearly undone. Had this process gone on fifty years more, the bearers of good, old, pure German blood would have become a minority among the leading sectors of our people. In its doctrine of creation, the church had the opportunity to keep holy the mystery of how strength and character are received through the blood. This it has not done.

Despite all its resistance to birth control, the church has not been able to impress upon the leading strata of the people their duty to give back to the people, by bearing German children, the blood-inheritance they have received. It has looked with indifference on mixed marriages (as it has on the proliferation of inferior persons), not realizing that such things can be justified only as rare exceptions justified by special divine guidance. And why not? There was nothing about it in the catechism, and it has never been the particular strength of the church's leadership to see beyond the catechism and find, in a moment of emerging historical urgency, the sting that provokes to new and beneficial ways [of thinking and acting].

This change has now come without the church's support. It has come with the naturalness and abandon, with the instinct for self-preservation of a people that senses that it is threatened at the root. It is a tribute to the good-heartedness of our people [*Volk*] that so many see in this change only the nameless suffering that the foolishness and carelessness of their ancestors has brought down on the heads of their descendants, who want so much to be German but are just not recognized as such. But it will be no tribute to the Protestant Church if it sees the change that is in progress only from the viewpoint of what happens to individuals.

The church must open its eyes to what is healthy in this change, in line with the will of God. It must help the state in its difficult work, rekindling the sense of awe and loyalty to our blood and the willingness to bear children in all members of our people—even and especially the educated classes that are most resistant. Otherwise it is renouncing its role as teacher and shaper of our people, and will become for the people and its life an alien and bloodless shell. If, on the other hand, it takes up this task, then in the selection of its next generation of leaders it will not close itself to the new ethos that the state is seeking to realize.

Should the church expose itself to the danger that in future its offices will be flooded with the half-Germans whom the state excludes from its positions of leadership? How will it then be able to help with the correct formation and deepening of the German spirit and the German character? The questions are there, and however one responds to them, we have German Christians to thank that they have spoken them aloud, so that they cannot be ignored. None of them thought of suspending Eucharistic fellowship with Jewish Christians.

Something else emerges from this line of thought: namely, that the question regarding those among us who are not German Christians by blood is just a part of a far deeper and more urgent question. It follows from the obligation of Protestant Christianity to be a church of the people that *in a German Protestant church Germanness and Christianity must encounter each other in a deep intimacy that will determine the historical shape of both.* Here are the real obstacles. In our German Protestant church we have had no Grundtvig[7] who could have taken on this task for our church and our people with a lively popular sense and at the same time a deep, churchly seriousness. A great deal of what we northern Germanic Lutherans take for granted has therefore remained at issue. But if we do not learn here what is necessary, then either the German Church [*Deutschkirche*] or the German Faith Movement [*Deutsche Glaubensbewegung*][8] will gobble up the liveliest carriers of our ethno-national [*völkisch*] development. As I see it, we German Christians have never been hated as much by anyone as we are in the circles of the German Church and the German Faith Movement. Those groups know that the kind of theology Barth represents scares young German people away from Protestant Christianity and drives them into the arms of these groups. But it is clear that a German Protestant church with a sense of the people will easily do away with any half-pagan movements.

---

7. N. F. S. Grundtvig (1783–1872) was a Danish pastor, hymn writer, author, poet, philosopher, historian, and politician, who with his followers is credited with having deeply influenced the development of Danish national consciousness.

8. The *Bund für Deutsche Kirche* [League for a German Church], or [*Bund für*] *Deutschkirche*, founded in 1921 and fiercely anti-Jewish, actively sought to exclude the Old Testament from Christian theology and worship. The neo-pagan *Deutschreligion* [literally, German religion] professed by the *Deutsche Glaubensbewegung* [German Faith Movement] led by Jakob Wilhelm Hauer, had nothing to do with Christianity—except to attack it.

The resistance to saying an honest ecclesial "yes" to a truly German Protestant Christianity can be traced to a lack of theological work. I see here two still unresolved issues.

First, we have not worked hard enough on the concept of what is "natural." The "natural man," the "natural law," the "natural knowledge of God"—these have all remained for us general notions, notions that can be applied equally to any person, any historical type, any governmental and economic order, any form of society. What the field of law learned a long time ago—that "the natural" exists always and only as ethnic, historical individuality—this theology has not yet learned. Certainly we see in the natural man, the natural law, the natural experience of God—wherever we look—that we human beings are all creatures of the one God, who reigns over all of our lives with the same self-revealing goodness, the same stringency, and the same discipline. We all have something in common. But within all that is common, the ethnic and historical differences reveal themselves clearly. Stapel created a concept for this phenomenon, namely, that each people has its own national *Nomos*.[9] The natural man, the natural law, the natural experience of God—concretely, these mean something different for Germans than for the people of India.

Second, differences in what is "natural" have thus far been treated in theology, for the most part, as matters of indifference where Christianity is concerned. Only the missionaries realize that these differences mean something for the shape of Christian life and thought. What becomes of "the natural" when a person, born anew in faith, submits to the lordship of the Spirit of God? "The natural" is then drawn into the service of God. The form of Christian life is

9. Wilhelm Stapel (1882–1954), publicist and editor, from 1919 to 1938, of the monthly *Deutsche Volkstum*; author of *Der christliche Staatsmann: Eine Theologie des Nationalismus* [The Christian Statesman: A Theology of Nationalism], the 1932 book in which this idea is explicated. .

always a natural form of life that is at the service of and suffused by the Spirit. Our Christian way of thinking, speaking, and acting is always imprinted by the fact that we use our natural humanness to do these things, and this is God's will. According to God's will, then, there are varieties of Christian thinking, speaking, and acting that are adapted to a particular people at a particular time in history. This is not only a fate we must endure as a sign of earthly fragility—though it is certainly that; it is also something commanded that must be dared, in love and freedom, if Christ is truly to come to a people. When the Saxon troubadour sang the "Heliand," he was proclaiming the German Christ.[10] Even today the Christian concept of being the Lord's disciples has for us Germans a particular tonality that comes from its having been melded together with the Germanic idea of fealty. This found its first powerful expression in the [Heliand]. The brief sentence spoken by Thomas in John 11:16[11] prompts the bard of the "Heliand" to create the following verses (3993-4004):

> But one of the twelve,
> Thomas—the solid man,
> The dear knight, said—"We should not rebuke his deeds,
> Nor resist his will, but instead persevere with him,
> And stand fast with our master. This is the warrior's fame,
> That he stands fast with his lord,
> And dies with him. If we all alike do this,
> Following his path, letting our lives
> Be of little worth to us, if we also
> Perish with him, then our fame
> Will live long after us." And this is how the loyal disciples,
> The noble-born, of one accord,
> Came to do the Lord's bidding.

---

10. An anonymously composed, early-ninth-century epic poem in Old Saxon, 6,000 lines long, that recounts the life of Jesus, in the style of a Germanic saga, to non-Christian Germans during the period of European conversion to Christianity.

11. "Thomas, who was called the Twin, said to his fellow disciples, 'Let us also go, that we may die with him.'" (NRSV)

No one was more aware of our need to give birth anew in German to this word bestowed upon us, to actualize it concretely in a distinctively German way, in German life, than Martin Luther. His translation of the Bible into German testifies to the courage and the audacity with which he tackled this task. He strips Moses of his Hebrewisms, he lets the poet of the Psalms speak in German terms, even crying to God at solemn moments with German alliteration. He even dares to interpret Paul from the perspective of the Germanic understanding of freedom. "Were you a slave when called? Do not be concerned about it; but if you can gain your freedom, seize the opportunity," he has Paul say (1 Cor 7:21); what Paul really meant was, "Even if you can be free, remain instead a slave." This is not a difference in the gospel, but it is the imbuing of the gospel with a different natural-historical character.

If the purity of the gospel was not endangered because of what Luther dared to do, then God's mercy will surely also protect us under the Lordship of Jesus Christ if we imitate him, wherever it is necessary to do so for love's sake. The guarantee he gave us for the preservation of the gospel is the exuberant, life-liberating force of the biblical word itself. That is what is so wonderful about this word: that, under its lordship, the natural-historical *Volkstum*, the living and creative power of a *Volkstum*, is not destroyed but heightened and refined. We Germans, and likewise other European peoples, would never have become what we have become, if the gospel, with its guiding majesty, had not come to us. And we will not remain what we are if we forget to bow to this majesty, even when it breaks and judges us, even when it seems strange to us.

A Short Lesson on the Christian Religion (May 1933)

Preliminary remarks: I wrote down the main points of this short lesson in the Christian religion as my own confessional statement before I began my collaboration with the German Christians. I became a German Christian only because I know that collaboration in this spirit is welcomed.

1. The visible world of things and humans is not the ultimate, true reality. Imperceptible to our senses, incomprehensible to our reason, this reality belongs to the holy, almighty will of the Lord God. He calls into being everything that comes to be and lives. He creates and sustains and guides nations and human beings. Nothing can resist His will; He is Lord over life and death. To serve Him, to worship Him with all the faculties he has given us: this is our reason for being.

2. The Lord God makes Himself known in our hearts without any effort or thought on our part and in spite of all the questions and doubts of our brooding minds. He makes Himself known to us in the all the inexhaustible depth and richness of life around us; in the wonderful history of nations and humanity; in the unfathomable mystery of our living bodies and spirits with their nobility and their vulnerability; in the particular form and task He has given to each individual nation and to each individual man. He makes himself known to us in that we find ourselves called to unconditional obedience and unconditional service, to complete sacrifice and complete surrender; in that we are able to live only in the truth and are corrupted by lies; in that we must ask what is good and what is evil. He makes himself known to us in our yearning and seeking what is eternal, in our protest against the riddle of death, in the anxiety and torment of our hearts that have fallen out with Him; in the turmoil and misery that guilt brings into our lives. If we can be still and see these manifold signs of God within us, then we sense that

He surrounds us and moves all around us, our inescapable destiny that must be either a curse or a blessing to us. This is how we recognize that in truth He is the Lord.

3. Because the Lord God lives in light that blinds our eyes, all our thinking and reflecting about Him is entangled in folly and delusion. Because the Lord God is the Holy One who requires complete surrender, our half-heartedness and our selfishness keep us from ever worshiping him in wholehearted joy. He is our Father, but we are not able in our heart of hearts to believe that he is our Father. We experience Him as strange, powerful, One from whom we remain separated. That He makes himself known to us creates a judgmental terror in our hearts.

Therefore He sent the gospel of Jesus Christ to be proclaimed among us. In Jesus Christ's call to repentance our Lord and God speaks to us and reveals to us our sin and guilt even to the most profound depths of our lives. In the words of forgiveness spoken by Jesus Christ our Lord and God speaks to us and gives us the gift that, despite our sinfulness, we may stand before God and trust Him. In the promise of his kingdom, God brings us Jesus Christ and the hope of a life that cannot be overcome by any worldly power, any sin or any death—a life that beyond and through death and judgment will finally reveal to us His full glory. We confess Jesus Christ as God's eternal Word come to us, as the Father's only-begotten Son.

4. Through God's wondrous election, Jesus Christ, the Father's only begotten Son, became a human being like us. Temptation and struggle, distress and death, all the estrangement from God and the guilt of the whole of humanity tried their power against him. In the miracle of his divine Sonship he suffered them willingly; in obedience to his Father in heaven he offered himself on the cross for our sake. Therefore the power of sin and death were broken on him. God delivered him, raised him, and exalted him to His right hand, so that

with divine power and majesty he may be with us as the eternally Living One. We bend the knee before him in thanksgiving and worship as our God-given Savior and Lord.

5. The faith through which we confess Jesus Christ as our Lord and God as our Father is an incomprehensible miracle bestowed on us by the Holy Spirit of God. Despite the sin and infirmity that cling to us, this faith enables us to rise above ourselves and to transform us self-seeking and self-absorbed people into servants and instruments of God. It ignites within us the love of sacrifice and surrender, and noble courage in the struggle against sin, death, and the Devil. It makes us joyful and free in God, so that as God's children we willingly bear all temptation, sorrow, and anxiety, and in the end overcome them. It helps us to pass through death in a spirit of consolation, and into eternal life.

6. All of us who become Jesus' disciples in spirit and faith are bound in our Lord to a community [*Gemeinde*] of brothers and sisters that transcends all times and all places. In this community we petition and thank God with one heart and tongue, whatever earthly strife may divide us. In this community we are called to help one another freely and lovingly on our journey through the darkness of life to our heavenly Father.

7. As the community of Jesus Christ we are called by God to proclaim the gospel, which is life and blessing for believers, to everyone, both believers and non-believers, with words of witness and deeds of love. We baptize our children according to the word of the Lord with confidence in the Father's divine love, which also calls them to faith and repentance. We sanctify our community by celebrating the sacred Lord's Supper of the love of our Savior and Lord, who has promised that He will be our souls' food and drink.

8. God has given us the Holy Scripture of the Old and New Testaments as testimony to Jesus Christ, through which he awakens

and sustains and nourishes our faith. It is our guiding principle and help in our proclamation and our service. To interpret Scripture correctly and through it to help overcome all the power of human error and foolishness in our community, is the greatest and loveliest task of our theology. To read Scripture attentively each day and to be able to learn from it is the privilege of every Christian.

9. God has bound us together in natural community and order, as marriage partners, parents, and children, as coworkers, as comrades-in-arms, in the blood-bond of our nation, in the common destiny of our state. We accept these bonds with thanks to God our Father, as the joy and the treasure of our life, and with obedience to God our Father as the great opportunity, blessed by him, to serve and to sacrifice. But to the extent that the earthly community burdens us because of the harshness of life's struggles and oppresses us because of all our sins, we accept it as divine assistance and grace, which in the midst of earthly struggles reminds us of the peace of God that passes all understanding.

10. Our service to the gospel requires that we construct for ourselves, out of the community of faith, an embodied church order. God has given his Christians the freedom, in a judicious obedience of faith and love, to discern the appropriate forms for this organized church with its statutes, its institutions, and its unity, in accordance with the particularity of its historical context and the *völkisch* and spiritual life that surrounds it. We embrace this freedom with thanksgiving for the inheritance that our church fathers have left to us, and in readiness to create order and rules as God requires it of us.

11. Our constituted church with its worship services and in all its work is, even when God's grace lies upon it, only one of the instruments God uses to teach and prepare our people for the gospel. Those who work in worldly affairs, those who build and guide our government, those who seek to aid in the appropriate building and

shaping of the spiritual life of our people, should and may be God's coworkers and instruments in this service. Whenever circumstances call for it, our church will always work with them in fraternity and trust. Only in this union of our common will can the freedom we claim for our church and its service become a blessing for our people and our church. In this unity will we recognize our duty to remain true to the prayerful and helpful nature of our work, and without official government orders, out of a sense of our own responsibility before God, to serve the gospel for our people with all our church's faculties and facilities.

12. We want to go gladly on our way, [even] in the uncertainty of what is to come, which teaches us that not we, but rather God, guides human history, that the history of our people, too, is in his hands. With boldness grounded in unfathomable trust in God, we want to let ourselves, our activities, and our sorrows be woven into the great hidden plan of God's rule. We are, however, always certain in faith of the eternal future, the kingdom of glory, where God will be all in all.

Appendix: Confession for the Celebration of the Reformation

Preliminary note: When we commemorate the Reformation, the confession we say in the worship service should express the particular character of Reformation faith. This kind of confession is not easy to find today. What follows is an attempt whose every expression adheres closely to Luther. It is a purely personal attempt; the German Christians have absolutely no responsibility for it.

We believe in the invisible, eternal, incomprehensible God,

who created heaven and earth, and with His almighty Word guides and sustains,

who calls nations and people into being, so that they might serve him, each in his or her own way, who is Father of us all and deals with us strictly and graciously every day.

We believe in Jesus Christ, God's only begotten Son,

who became a human being like us, according to God's wondrous counsel,

who as our Redeemer sacrificed himself for us sinners on the cross and has bestowed on us God's mercy,

who as our Lord was raised by God from death, so that we may believe in Him and become children of God and heirs of eternal life.

We believe in God's Holy Spirit,

who brings God our Father to us in His holy Word and each day gives anew the faith that sanctifies us,

who in Jesus Christ our Lord binds us together in a holy congregation, which in worship comes before God with petitions and with thanks,

who in spite of all our guilt preserves us, as those whom God has sanctified, in the hope of the eternal kingdom that is promised us in the gospel at the end of all things.

Amen.

5

The History of the "German Christian" Faith Movement

Arnold Dannenmann

Introduction

Arnold Dannenmann (1907–1993), a Lutheran youth pastor, was a member of the German Christian Faith Movement. In addition to the book that is excerpted here, in 1933 he also published a book entitled *Youth Commits Itself to Christ and to National Socialism [Jugend bekennt sich zu Christus und Nationalsozialismus].*[1]

---

1. Dannenmann seems to have had second thoughts about National Socialism; during the war, as pastor of the Garrison Church in Berlin, he provided help to a number of people persecuted by the Nazis. After the war he founded what became a large and successful organization for youth.

Dannenmann begins by declaring boldly that every National Socialist is "bound to Adolf Hitler," not as a slave but voluntarily, because Hitler has revealed something entirely new: that the German people can become one, "a community of the same blood." From the beginning, then, the author is emphatic about the significance of National Socialism for Christian believers. His account reaches back to 1921 and the establishment of an early precursor of the movement, taking pains to distinguish it from neo-pagan and anti-Christian groups, but he focuses mainly on 1933. "For the German Christians," he writes, "January 30, 1933 was what it was to become for many Christians in the months to come, that is, God's day." The work concludes with a long excerpt from the radio address Hitler gave on July 22, 1933, the night before the church elections in which the German Christians gained an overwhelming victory and considerable administrative power throughout the German Protestant Church.

In terms of style, the work is clearly meant for a broad popular audience. Dannenmann's enthusiastic treatment of movement leaders like Friedrich Wieneke and Joachim Hossenfeld is almost hagiographic. Key German Christian ideas, among them race as an "order of creation" and the utter affinity of Christianity and National Socialism, are woven into the story, as are the revised [1933] guidelines of the German Christian Faith Movement.

Figure 5. Cross and swastika, symbol of German Christian faith movement, on the front cover of the *Handbook of the German Christians* (1933).

The History of the "German Christian" Faith Movement[2]

Arnold Dannenmann

Preface

How did a Faith Movement called "German Christians" arise within the Protestant church on German soil? The present book aims to answer this question. The question is before us; about that there can be no doubt. It is raised by those who, as old comrades-in-arms, would themselves like to give an account of the men and principles they once followed, obedient and brave, true to their hearts and consciences. It is raised by those who have only recently been deeply touched by this movement, who did not experience its beginnings. It is raised by those who are still seeking, distinguishing, and critiquing,

---

2. Arnold Dannenmann, *The History of the "German Christian" Faith Movement* [*Die Geschichte der Glaubensbewegung "Deutsche Christen"*] (Dresden: Oskar Günther Verlag, 1933).

and by those for whom this movement still looks like a sphinx in a room of familiar, comfortable old church relationships.

It is high time that all those who are asking receive an answer. Arnold Dannenmann provides it here with great skill, in a language that can penetrate into every ear and every heart. I would like nothing better than that the images, struggles, and the battle of ideas that are here placed before the soul of the reader, may delight the awakened German people with their unparalleled and endless power. I would like nothing better than that this look at the beginning of so grace-filled a movement would awaken in everyone a sense of holy duty to keep it going. I would like nothing better than that, as a result of all these things, the great Third Reich of the Führer would sink indestructible roots in a Christian community made up of all our fellow Germans [*Volksgenosse*], one that promises a new harvest.

Friedrich Peter

Church Administrator, Berlin

The National Socialist

Every National Socialist is unconditionally bound to the Führer Adolf Hitler. This is not a slavish bond, but a voluntary one. This bond is not accidental. It exists because the Führer has brought a new awareness to every real National Socialist.

The year was 1925! In Munich, huge red party posters invited everyone to a mass meeting in the *Hofbräuhaus*.

The whole legislative delegation, under the leadership of Dr. Buttmann,[3] was supposed to be there, and the Führer as well.

As young students, we were drawn to the gathering. The Führer himself did not speak once. But within a few minutes we were all

---

3. Rudolf Buttmann (1885–1947) was caucus leader of the Nazi Party in the Bavarian state parliament. Later he became head of the Cultural Division of the Reich Interior Ministry under Wilhelm Frick.

in the grip of a boundless enthusiasm. This was not just a mood that came over us. A new awareness had empowered us! Above all, we knew one thing: that *this same consciousness filled the whole assembly and turned it into one unified action group.*

It was not simply the awareness that we were German, that we had to become a single German people [*Volk*] again; it was the awareness that this German people could only exist if it consisted *not of a group of individuals but rather of a community of the same blood and the same history!*

Only race creates a people! The scales fell from our eyes. Those who oppose the movement have miscalculated and continue to do so because they simply have not recognized the deepest source of the National Socialist movement, because they continue to think that it is a "nationalist" and also a "socialist" movement, even though the contrary has been said a thousand times.

We modern people have far too little faith that we will ever experience something unbelievably great in the midst of all the important trivia that surround us.

And when today we assert—no, we know—that with Adolf Hitler and National Socialism an epoch in German history has begun that is at least as decisive for the German people as, for example, the epoch of Martin Luther, some may chuckle, and some will shake their heads, but the National Socialist knows that this really is a fact.

It is clear that the one who in his heart believes in Christ, and who has been gripped by the National Socialist vision, is faced with something new.

It's true that as youngsters we Christians were always taught by the church that people and faith belong together. It's true that it was not possible for a Christian who knew the articles of his faith, to fall into internationalist fantasies. It's true that it was even less possible that any Christian could become a traitor to his people. No!—No!—

But one thing we did not know, nor could we know: the immense significance for a people of its basis in blood and soil [*Blut und Boden*].

National Socialism has taught us that. Perhaps we young people sense this much more powerfully than the older generation possibly can. Today we know that it isn't enough simply to be German in name only, or through some patriotic act; rather, we know that Germany's future or fall depend on how it goes with the blood and soil of this people.

The Law of God

We see in this the holy laws of God!

We have always confessed: I believe that God has made me and all creatures, has given me body and soul, eyes, ears, and all my limbs, my reason and all my senses, and still preserves them; along with these also clothing and shoes, food and drink, house and homestead, wife and children, fields, cattle, and all my goods; that He provides me richly and daily with all that I need to support this body and life, protects me from all danger, and guards and preserves me from all evil; and all this out of pure, fatherly, divine goodness and mercy.[4]

But this statement of faith has been interpreted for us in countless gatherings of the National Socialist movement—in a way that it has rarely been interpreted for any people.

Many speakers from the movement were not even aware of the religious duty they were fulfilling. *The Führer Adolf Hitler, however, knew it and was utterly aware of his divine mission.*

---

4. From the explanation to the First Article of the Apostle's Creed in Martin Luther's *Small Catechism*.

The thousands of gatherings that roared through Germany during the National Socialist movement's struggle to take power actually fulfilled a religious purpose.

The masses listened breathlessly, not just for one hour, but sometimes for two, three, and four hours to the National Socialist speakers, not only because the speakers were rhetorically brilliant and skilled and able to strike a popular chord as they said what needed to be said, but because their speeches were actually filled with a new awareness. And this new awareness arose from the depths of this article of the Christian creed.

I repeat: The speakers may have been completely unaware of this, and the listeners likewise. It is simply a fact that it is only in retrospect that one can give a clear account of what one has experienced in such tumultuous times.

The Christian who dismisses this interpretation is bypassing one of the most significant divine facts in the history of his people.

German Christians!

It could not have happened otherwise than that a handful of men whose lives had been seized by Christ, and also by the consciousness of our times, gathered together to make sure this powerful current did not flow right past the church.

Nor did they want to incorporate it into the church "politically." By the very nature of the thing a church-political movement could never be the moving force behind such a profound discovery. Only the church as a whole, insofar as it wanted to be a German church, could become that moving force. This handful of men called themselves "German Christians."

The Führer Adolf Hitler himself suggested this name, "German Christians." Originally some in the group wanted to call themselves "Protestant Nationalists," but Hitler himself rejected this appellation.

With the exceptional gift that Adolf Hitler has for naming things in a way that shapes the future, he has created a concept that will have extraordinary significance throughout the entire history of the church. It already does!

Precursors!

Even at the beginning of the century the fragmented ethnic [*völkisch*] groups in Germany were raising the question of "German Christianity." . . .

. . . [A]fter the collapse brought about by the November revolution of 1918, the idea of renewing the Christian church on the basis of a conscious *völkisch* experience increasingly demanded action.

The League for a German Church [*Bund für Deutsche Kirche*] emerged as a church-political group. It is unquestionable that it represented a serious determination to make a species-specific Germanness the agent of the biblical Gospel.

But the League soon took some nasty detours. It relied on the findings of liberal religious-historical research and so took the field against the ancient creeds.

The League has unquestionably done a great service in popularizing German fairytales and heroic sagas. But for believing Christians, the League's approach had the effect of driving awareness of their people away, rather than bringing it nearer. They felt threatened in the depths of their faith-life in Christ, the Savior and Redeemer. So the League had to fail. *This is a clear warning to all those who don't want to know that the völkisch disposition must never lead to a fragmentation and dissection of the Word of God!*

Nevertheless, the League shook up people's thinking and brought the question of the "*völkisch* attitude and the Christian faith" to public attention. A host of texts, countless gatherings and debates were the result of their questioning. We remember them all.

But behind all this lurked all too clearly the ghost of the worldview of [Erich] Ludendorff and Artur Dinter.[5]

They fashioned their faith stance exclusively out of the *völkisch* experience—something that is impossible for us as Christians!

With their extremist agitation against Christianity, Ludendorff and Dinter effected equally extreme damage to the Christian community.

The fact that even today many faithful church people are prejudiced against the German Christians is the fault of Ludendorff and Dinter. They tore *völkisch* knowledge away from the original sources of divine reality.

As a consequence, they have imbued faithful believers with aversion to *völkisch* knowledge. It will take many years to banish this heresy from the hearts of the German people.

Ludendorff and Dinter have also made it more difficult for National Socialism to move forward.

Ludendorff and Dinter are to blame for the fact that for a very long time Christians resisted National Socialism.

Christians who did not see things clearly could easily be under the impression that any *völkisch* disposition must contradict the Christian

---

5. Erich Ludendorff (1865–1937) was one of the most important military commanders of the German forces in World War I. He was an early member of the Nazi Party (though he was later expelled from it by Hitler), which he tried to turn into a religious movement. With his wife Mathilde he founded the Tannenberg League [*Tannenbergbund*], a pagan, anti-Christian mystical religious sect that embraced what they called German faith in God. Artur Dinter (1876–1948), the author of *Sin Against the Blood* [*Die Sünde Wider das Blut*], a deeply antisemitic, best-selling novel published in 1917, was also an early Nazi (and was also expelled by Hitler). He, too, tried to turn Nazism into a religious movement, which Hitler utterly opposed. Dinter founded an organization in the 1920s that in 1934 became known as the German People's Church [*Deutsche Volkskirche*], which aimed to de-judaize Christianity. For more information on both these men, see, among other sources, Richard Steigmann-Gall, *The Holy Reich: Nazi Conceptions of Christianity, 1919–1945* (Cambridge, U.K.: Cambridge University Press, 2003).

faith, just as Ludendorff and Dinter repeatedly maintained in their writings.

There is even a third matter of which Ludendorff and Dinter are guilty. They are to blame for the fact that even today some groups within the National Socialist movement believe that a total *völkisch* surrender is in profound opposition to Christianity, that faith in Christ is a barrier to racial progress.

German Christians have here an enormous task before them, one that fell to them even before they stepped onto the historical stage.

The Earliest Beginnings!

But still, completely out of the public eye, something new began to stir in individual men.

The First Man!

The first person we must mention is a man whose name is already widely known in German churches: Dr. Friedrich Wieneke.[6]

Some stroke of destiny willed it that in the year 1929 the NSDAP[7] approached him, the pastor of the Soldin cathedral, to head their ticket as a candidate for city council.

In keeping with Dr. Wieneke's characteristic sense of duty, this matter could be for him nothing less than a decision based on his theological convictions and his faith. He could not simply say "Yes" without being clear about the path on which he was about to enter.

Through a difficult inner struggle it became clear to Dr. Wieneke that in their beginnings, Christianity and National Socialism both go back to God, that is, they have parallel origins. Some kind of living relationship between the two must therefore also be possible in the

---

6. See information on Wieneke that accompanies excerpts of his *Outline of German Theology* (1933), also in this volume.

7. *Nationalsozialistische Deutsche Arbeiterpartei*, or National Socialist German Workers Party.

present. At a gathering of German Christians, Dr. Wieneke once expressed it this way:

> The theology of the German Christians is by its nature the work of the eternal Father. The differences between races are willed by Him. A human being may never set his political commitments above the guidelines the Almighty has established. Even though the creation is fallen, God still permits us to perceive the traces of his plan again and ever again. For us German Christians this generates a new theological attitude vis-à-vis history, according to which Christ functions as the eternal King of truth who embraced the cross as the sign of militant heroism and a joyful willingness to sacrifice himself.

At that time Dr. Wieneke became the first pastor in Germany to take a public position on the issue of "National Socialism and Christianity," [which he did] in a series of [newspaper] articles. These articles retain their sweeping significance, so much so that they ought to be referenced even today in theological discussions about how the Protestant church should be organized for the sake of its inner development.

. . .

This brave fighter had to face many accusations. It could not have been otherwise. At the time National Socialism as a whole was being misjudged, hated, and stigmatized by the German public. It could only be the case that a pastor who discovered in the fundamental ideas of National Socialism something that would be deeply meaningful even for the church was himself ostracized.

But with his characteristic intelligence and thoughtfulness, Dr. Wieneke skillfully carried the battle forward.

The "Christian-German" Movement

In Berlin, in the meantime, regional youth pastor [Werner] Wilm, in association with the *Stahlhelm*,[8] established the Christian-German

Movement [*Christlich-deutsche Bewegung*]. Court Chaplain [Bruno] Döhring and Bishop [Heinrich] Rendtorff were its best-known leaders. Within this movement there also emerged a working group of German pastors that gathered under the leadership of Court Chaplain Döhring.

A short time later Professors [Paul] Althaus and [Emanuel] Hirsch[9] also joined the movement. At the time it was just a small group of men who gathered, but little by little—building on a sense of German nationalism—the movement began to grow. It did not yet possess the special character of what had been discovered by National Socialism. The movement had not fully thought through the notion of "people" [*Volk*] in the sense of race.

The discoveries of a Möller van den Bruck[10] and a Paul de Lagarde[11] were not the building blocks of their *völkisch* thinking. For the moment they understood "people" [*Volk*] in an older German way of thinking: as far as the hand can reach, as far as power reaches, as far as history reaches—all these together determine what Germany is. Dr. Wieneke was also part of this movement at first. He was the only National Socialist in the group. But given the fundamental differences in their ways of thinking, sooner or later a separation had to occur.

---

8. The *Stahlhelm, Bund der Frontsoldaten* ("Steel Helmet, League of Frontline Soldiers") was one of many paramilitary organizations that arose after Germany's defeat in World War I. With 500,000 members in 1930, the league was the largest paramilitary organization of Weimar Germany.

9. Publications by these two men are excerpted in this volume. See the introductions to these documents for biographical information about each of them.

10. Arthur Möller van den Bruck (1876-1925) was a German cultural historian and writer, author of *Das Dritte Reich* (1923), which promoted German nationalism and influenced the National Socialist German Workers Party.

11. Paul Anton Lagarde (1827–1891), German biblical scholar and orientalist, was probably the best-known nineteenth-century scholar of the Septuagint, and a violent antisemite whose views underpinned National Socialist ideology, particularly that of Alfred Rosenberg.

Dr. Wieneke's writings and articles hastened the course of things. A group of militants from across the Reich gathered around Dr. Wieneke, warriors who until then had been working on their own.

Guida Diehl,[12] the well-known leader of the New Land League [*Neulandbund*] in Eisenach, during the long years after the war did a great deal of faithful, painstaking work within her league, thinking through and discussing all these issues.

[Julius] Kuptsch,[13] the former Latvian Minister of Culture, at the same time published a series of excellent pamphlets in which he laid out clearly the only way in which the battle against cultural Bolshevism could be conducted. These were all preliminary to the truly decisive encounter of Dr. Wieneke with the man *who, as the history of the German Christians unfolded, would be of critical significance: Pastor [Joachim] Hossenfelder.*[14]

Pastor Hossenfelder

A domestic relationship brought these two personalities together. At the time of their meeting, Pastor Hossenfelder was already in Berlin. He had become a National Socialist in 1929, and by a stroke of luck these two pastors, both captivated by the same genuine National-Socialist purpose and having an equally strong sense of church matters, found each other.

---

12. Diehl (1868–1961) founded the nationalist New Land League in 1919 to help mobilize Christian energies in the war effort. She became a prominent leader among Protestant women; after joining the Nazi Party in 1930, she played an important role in the National Socialist Women's Organization. In the early 1930s she endorsed the German Christian cause, calling for a "renewal of faith" based on race, family, people [*Volk*], and Fatherland.

13. Kuptsch, a pastor from Riesenburg in East Prussia, was the author of a number of books, including *Christentum im Nationalsozialismus* [*Christianity in National Socialism*] (Munich: Eher, 1932) and *Nationalsozialismus und positives Christentum* [*National Socialism and Positive Christianity*] (Weimar: Verlag Deutsche Christen, 1937). In 1927 he had also published a book critical of biblical scholars.

14. For more on Joachim Hossenfelder, see the introduction to and excerpts from his *Our Struggle*, pp. 229ff in this volume.

Pastor Hossenfelder is the most controversial but also the most beloved leader of the German Christians. He was born on April 29, 1899, in Kottbus. His father, who came from a Silesian farm family, was director of the commercial school belonging to the city of Kiel.

In 1917, right after finishing high school with the academic diploma [*Abitur*], he volunteered for the army. After a brief period of training, he was sent to the front. He fought at the Somme and at Verdun, where he became a non-commissioned officer. The story of what Hossenfelder did during the war is in and of itself a testimony to this man, whose unique character is unsurpassable. All his heroic convictions are best understood in the context of what happened in the World War, where he showed himself among the bravest of those on the front lines.

When the war ended, Hossenfelder was one of those who, as soon as they had laid down the sword, immediately took up theology. At this time it was quite risky to become a theologian. No one knew how the church's history would unfold. In those days only committed warriors were brave enough to choose theology. . . .

For Hossenfelder it was quite clear that to be a theologian did not mean to live in an isolated world and to preach the Gospel only from the pulpit. For him a pastor was in the deepest sense of the word a man who shared everything with the people. He could never be indifferent to what concerned his people. If he was going to preach, he was obligated at the same time to be a fighter for the rights and duties of the German people.

This is why his studies were often interrupted. He could not bear to sit at a desk while his comrades were bleeding on the borders. In the summer of 1919 he joined a *Freikorps*[15] unit as a border guard in Grenzmark.[16]

Two years later he interrupted his studies once again and joined the combat on the borders at Posen and in Upper Silesia. He fought in the front lines at the storming of the Annaberg. *The leader of the "German Christians" is a man who truly invested his blood and his very life in the battalions of the freedom fighters to defend the borders of his beloved homeland.* This in itself characterizes the man.

But anyone who thinks that in those days when young Germans fought on the borders he was only a man of the sword is profoundly mistaken. Those who fought beside him tell how in the evenings, dog-tired, he would often speak intently to his comrades about his deepest spiritual experiences. He not only wanted to be a fellow warrior; he also wanted to be a pastor to them. He simply had to testify to his fellow soldiers about the strength he derived from the Gospel of his Savior. Here we can see what drives the Christian: "We cannot keep from testifying to that which burns in our hearts."[17]

The people who today still doubt Hossenfelder's inner disposition should listen to the accounts of his comrades—how during this time of conflict he was their most profound support. . . . The cross is for him the symbol of the inner freedom of a person, the sword rather [a symbol] of the external freedom of a people, each completing the other. If one is missing, some element of servitude is present, and that is unbearable.

After the conflict he took up his studies again and devoted himself totally to his work. But during his studies he never lost contact with

---

15. These were paramilitary organizations formed after World War I, when Germany was forbidden by the Versailles Treaty to have an army of more than 100,000. *Freikorps* units formed the vanguard of the Nazi movement.

16. After World War I ended, this name designated a disputed land area on the border between Germany/East Prussia, on the one hand, and a re-established Polish state, on the other.

17. An allusion to the words of Peter and Paul in Acts 4:20.

his brothers among the people. He took three months off from his studies to work in the gas works in Kiel. Here again he maintained the same friendly attitude he had practiced in his stint in the *Freikorps*. He took his first and second theological examinations in 1922 and 1923. September 13, 1923, the day of his ordination in the Church of the Magdalene in Breslau, is for him unforgettable. Now the way was clear for him to become a preacher of the Gospel.

After a period as an assistant, he entered on his own pastorate in Siemenau in Upper Silesia. There he experienced once again the difficulties and miseries of the border region. One part of his parish even lay on the other side of the border, in Polish territory. He got a very practical lesson in the meaning of "the people!" [*Volk*] and also how external boundaries cannot divide a people that is bound together inwardly. He also learned there how difficult it is to preach the Word of God among a people that no longer knows God's orders of creation,[18] as they are lived out in race and blood. . . .

After three years of happy marriage his wife contracted a lung ailment and died, leaving him with a little daughter. But perhaps this difficult personal blow of fate clarified for him what the German family means. It is well known that Hossenfelder has a special sympathy for the German mother and that in many of his works he repeatedly emphasizes the responsibilities of the German woman.

In October of 1927 he was called to Alt-Reichenau. He found a second marital partner in Agnes Maas, a gynecologist in Berlin, and was given two more children, a son and a daughter.

---

18. "Orders of creation" is a theological construct referring to certain structures or institutions God is said to have established in the earthly realm to order human life; marriage, family, the economy, the state, and the church might all be counted among them. For the German Christians, race—as they understood it—and *Volk* or *Volkstum* were "orders of creation," too, and, because they were established by God, were utterly sanctified.

Shortly after Pastor Hossenfelder joined the [Nazi] Party in 1929 he became the advisor on church issues to the national NSDAP leadership in Munich. . . .

Pastor Hossenfelder's lasting contribution is the creation, in the true sense of the word, of the "German Christians," which is in no wise to denigrate the contributions of all his coworkers. Those coworkers acknowledge the fact.

Pastor Hossenfelder is a deeply pious man who personally knows his Savior as the Son of God, who gave himself for us on the cross. Only out of exceptional ignorance could anyone judge him otherwise. Whoever has observed Pastor Hossenfelder even once in his own milieu knows that it is only his deep faith that could make him such an uncompromising fighter for a new church.

He is surely a fighter, and what is more, he is a man who can speak his mind in popular language. He is a born speaker.

No one has captured the hearts of the men of the S.A. and the S.S. like Pastor Hossenfelder. They listen to him; they follow him; and all those in the brown battalions,[19] once they have heard him speak, cannot forget this man's testimony. He is a witness sent by God. He is still young. And this is why some people find fault with his all-too-earthy and vehement manner. This is uncalled-for. None but such a man could lead a young movement like the "German Christians" to victory. The leader must combine two elements: a deep, pious faith and a lively, warrior spirit.

Certainly Hossenfelder can be sharp-tongued! But this is a good thing; on occasion it has been altogether necessary. He has laid out the uncompromising, straight path that the German Christian movement has taken over the last few years. Those who are in the know recognize that at several moments when the movement was

---

19. That is, the "Brown Shirts" of the S.A. [*Sturmabteilung*], the paramilitary arm of the Nazi Party.

threatened his tough, ruthless style showed the movement the only way it could go, and that it continues to follow to this day.

You can make your own judgment, but we say: *Pastor Hossenfelder is the man whose name can never be struck from the pages of the history of the German church.* He has made history, not of his own volition or by his own shaping, but rather driven by the Holy Spirit. Men like him are always controversial. That is their destiny—and their honor. The faithful Christian folds his hands and thanks God for continuing to send men who build His kingdom and proclaim His Gospel so that it is truly heard.

In Pastor Hossenfelder we see above all the consummation of one thing: within himself he unites knowledge of the people and of the Christian faith as few other leaders of the faith movement do. He has actually stood in the midst of raging battles, not only within the faith movement but also within the experience of the whole German people. As a young man, he grew up within the people's struggles, and yet in his heart he knew his divine mission: to speak the Gospel of the crucified and risen Savior. He is fully a leader.

We believe that the man Hossenfelder, who now stands at the beginning of his life, has a great deal to say to the German church. The story of his life is nowhere near its end; it has just begun.

One cannot really understand the story of the German Christians if one has not studied the life of Pastor Hossenfelder. Only by coming to know Pastor Hossenfelder can one truly understand the story of the German Christians. But then one will also find much to be thankful for in the German Christians' story—much, perhaps, that one may previously have misunderstood from a distance.

We had to tell the story of this life in this way because it really is of such endless significance for the whole history of the German Christians, and we also want it to be clearly understood and remembered.

The First Coworkers

All the coworkers Hossenfelder has brought together over the years agree on one thing: The first impression one has is that this man has a special gift for bringing people together in a common purpose. Hossenfelder has proved this without a doubt. Pastor Eckert from Zossen near Berlin was already among those in the circle around Dr. Wieneke; he was one of those who entered into the new struggle with particular passion. ... He was the one who pointed out to Hossenfelder the man who has since become one of the most remarkable personalities in the history of the faith movement, namely, *Pastor* [Friedrich] *Peter* of Berlin.

Friedrich Peter

In 1930 Pastor Peter had already written his book *When the Dice Fall: A Book About Gospel and Politics* [*Wenn die Würfel fallen: ein Buch von Evangelium und Politik*]. It was published in 1931. *This book is the first major theological statement* to come from the leaders of the faith movement. At the time he wrote the book Pastor Peter was not yet within the movement, but he had been a National Socialist for a long time; his book testifies on every page to an extremely keen theological analysis. It contains a host of clarifications for the Christian. All the issues that have emerged are here treated for the first time in a way that is intelligible to the general public. To this day this book, *When the Dice Fall*, is of decisive importance for the faith movement. One can only advise doubters to plunge into this book. It is probably not an exaggeration to say that with this book Pastor Peter provided the faith movement with its first recruiting tool. It came into Pastor Eckert's hands and he urged Hossenfelder to approach Pastor Peter. The first encounter between the two men was a telephone conversation in January of 1932. From that time on

Pastor Peter became as militant a coworker with Hossenfelder as he was an intelligent analyst. If one asks him how he ended up taking this path, he says simply this:

> I couldn't do anything else. What was unique about that moment—in fact, about the whole time we have worked together—has always been that what is objective has always overcome what is subjective. We have never really thought about whether we agree theologically. We have never bickered theologically. The one thing that bound us inseparably was the goal we were pursuing. That provided us with a powerful commitment to action. Every endless theological refinement of minutiae was for us a crime against the task we both felt so strongly about. It was a sense of being called to the same activity. It was a unity of spirit.

. . .

Here we must again repeat in general terms what we said earlier about Pastor Hossenfelder. One cannot understand the faith movement if one does not know its men.

This man Friedrich Peter has a life of struggle behind him. . . . He fought through the whole world war on the front lines. He belongs to those frontline fighters who truly, with all the passion of their lives, knew from the first to the last day that the world war was not just any war Germany was engaged in, but rather that it was the struggle that would establish Germany's destiny for years to come.

Returning from the front, he at first wanted to follow his inclinations and study art and philosophy. But it was clear to him from the first that a passionate struggle over matters of faith would inevitably take place in that November-Germany. It was in this spirit that he undertook his studies. He felt that his whole life up to that day was an adventure in faith. He worked in the [church's] social services programs in Magdeburg-Cracow. In Jessen near Wittenberg he had his earliest contacts with the National Socialist movement. Then came the call to Berlin. He took over the leadership of the work with young men in the East and, as a passionate warrior among the youth of eastern Germany, fought with word and pen for the cause of Protestant youth. . . . *Pastor Peter is an excellent speaker, one of the best the German church has.*

He demonstrates a fine sense of how to communicate. Pastor Peter has the gift to be able to carry the masses with him. But in his deeply penetrating lectures he can also engage learned listeners in his theme.

Pastor Peter engages passionately in everything he does. He never takes up an issue casually. Either he ignores it altogether or he throws himself into it fully.

He never yields weakly to any antagonist. He knows that an opponent has the right to receive a loving, forgiving hand only when he has truly had a change of heart. He is as generous in forgiving as he is passionate in fighting.

Pastor Peter's family life is heart-warming. A quiet observer in the house on Sophienstrasse in Berlin, where for years Pastor Peter has made his home . . . can find there a shining example of German family life.

He is a man who seizes life with both hands, who hates every rejection of life, who receives the Creator's gifts with thankfulness, who takes only one adage seriously: One must make of life all that one can make. A profoundly faithful man, he hates hypocrisy.

One can only understand the profundity of the force that held together the men of the faith movement if one reflects on the fact that Pastor Peter, who was quite a bit older than Pastor Hossenfelder, unhesitatingly joined him in joyful fidelity throughout all his struggles. It never occurred to either of these men—no matter how difficult the way became—to betray their loyalty and go their own ways. Hand in hand with Pastor Hossenfelder, Pastor Peter in particular is one of our most fearless warriors. *These two men have to a large extent determined the trajectory of the faith movement.* Pastor Peter was also the one who, in the first debates held within the then-small circle [of the faith movement], most keenly insisted that *the German Christians would never think of laying a hand on the confession of the church or the whole of the Gospel*, no matter where such an initiative came from.

Whoever has read Pastor Peter's book *When the Dice Fall* clearly understands that here stands a man who speaks the whole content of the Gospel and is determined to find the path from the life of the people to the Gospel without omitting any of it.

Here are some quotations from Pastor Peter:

> This notion of how the world should come to fulfillment is completely alien to Protestant faith and life. —What path does Protestant faith show us? — We believe that certain orders of earthly life, though they are of this world, nevertheless do not exist without God. This has to do with orders and institutions that in the second eon will no longer exist, but that in this eon God has not only permitted, but has himself willed, established, and through his word endorsed. To these orders belongs the State.

And in a lecture that he gave in connection with the great national gathering of the German Christian Faith Movement in Berlin at the beginning of 1933 on the topic "church and people," he expands on this when he says:

> And even if, in the coming Kingdom of Christ, this saying applies—"Here is neither Jew nor Greek, here is neither man nor woman"[20]—we must say that these words of the apostle emphasize the spiritual and at the same time the otherworldly character of the community of Christ. For according to creation it is a fact that there are men, there are women, there are Jews, there are Greeks. We are grateful [that] the Berlin Mission Society . . . has shown the church the way in relation to the question of race by explaining that the Gospel brings life for the soul, and it brings salvation through forgiveness and regeneration. But this is salvation from the powers of sin and death,

20. Galatians 3:28.

not from the God's ordering of things. To this divine order belong the divisions of humankind into peoples and races.

He also says: "I can only be a German Christian. This does not dig a chasm between us and those who live out their Christian lives as other peoples. They must recognize their place as we do ours. They, too, can obey God only within the order that he has established for them."

These are such foundational lines of thought that everything else is built upon them. We need not say much more. We have already succeeded in educating the wider public. We have already succeeded in clarifying for the common man, in his life of faith, what people and race mean on the one hand, and the proclamation of the crucified and risen Savior on the other.

A future theology will have to deal again and again with these two questions. We stand at a decisive theological point of departure for the whole way of thinking theologically in the next generation.

. . .

Chaplain Ludwig Müller

While most of the events we have described took place in the nation's capital [Berlin] or its surroundings, *Chaplain Ludwig Müller*[21] in Königsberg had been connected with National Socialism since 1926. He was already a National Socialist at heart when the Führer Adolf Hitler spoke in Königsberg in that year, and Müller met him at that time.

The meeting of these two men was of crucial significance for Germany. They very likely sensed this, for the conversation they had during those hours dealt with decisive questions about the future

---

21. For more on Ludwig Müller, see the introductions to several other documents by him that are included in this volume.

organization of the church. Even today both men refuse to talk about that first conversation; mere fragments of it are known. Only a future historical account will be able to provide a clear sense of what was discussed.

One thing is clear: after this first encounter Chaplain Müller became an uncompromising fighter for the National Socialist idea. . . . Even today [he] describes this first meeting with the Führer Adolf Hitler as a turning point in his life.

. . .

March 1932!

March 1932! A memorable meeting in the Behrenstrasse in Berlin! At that meeting Hossenfelder, Müller, Peter, Eckert, Dr. Wieneke, and a series of other persons joined together to adopt guidelines for the German Christians.[22] They had been drafted by Hossenfelder . . . [who] wrote in his pamphlet, *Our Struggle* [*Unser Kampf*]: "Struggle is the father of life. That is the law of God that our time bears on its brow. The new Germany and the people of the new Germany have learned together that struggle is part of their life. Wherever people live who are no longer willing to struggle and then, ultimately, are no longer capable of fighting, life fades, and with it the good of the nation."[23]

April 1932

Pastor Hossenfelder becomes the national leader of the "German Christians." Immediately he develops a comprehensive plan of action . . . He demonstrated right away that he is a first-rate organizer.

---

22. The Guidelines can be found in Hossenfelder's *Our Struggle*, pp. 229ff in this volume.
23. See p. 233 in this volume.

He created the press apparatus of the faith movement: the newspaper "The Gospel in the Third Reich" [*Evangelium im Dritten Reich*]. To this day he is its publisher. The paper is not only a battle sheet; it is above all a Sunday newsletter for the Christian home.

His gift for organizing was demonstrated with special clarity in the conduct of the church elections at the end of 1932. These elections were the first great test of Pastor Hossenfelder's abilities and his capacity for work.[24]

A Reproach

Today one occasionally hears the reproachful question: Why didn't the efforts to unify the church begin earlier, rather than only now when the victorious National Socialists support these efforts? Such a reproach is based on complete ignorance of the facts. Before the aims of the German Christians could be implemented, there first had to be a unified people under National Socialist leadership. In the old liberal State *a national church could not come into being*. It could be built only in a National Socialist state. So it was completely justified that the very first effort had to be to assemble all possible forces that favored the victory of National Socialism.

But no one could welcome January 30, 1933, more profoundly or more joyfully than the German Christian leadership. For them this triumph was, as it was for every *German*, the culmination of an intense political struggle over the course of the previous year. What they had fought and struggled for, what they had been jeered at and ridiculed for, had now become reality: a people stood upright and took its own measure. Hossenfelder later put it this way: "God said, 'Let there be a people, and there was a people.'"

24. Editor/Translator's note: Here follows a list of the divisional responsibilities within the German Christian movement and their respective leaders, with a note on the movement's signal success in the church election.

For the "German Christians," January 30, 1933 was what it became for many Christians over the following months, that is, God's day. Many perceived how important January 30, 1933, was only as the events of March unfolded, and they finally saw the abyss over which Germany's destiny, and with it that of the German church, were poised. *German Christians made a lasting contribution in that they recognized the magnitude of the danger of Bolshevism for the German church before anyone else did. And to their eternal honor they recognized before anyone else in the church that this danger could not be turned back by the will of the church alone, but rather that it had to be turned back by means of a political struggle.* But now the way was clear. On January 30 a people under a unified leadership emerged. There could be no more hesitation. *In a unified State, a unified church had to be built.*

At first the old church was speechless at the events of January 30. Silence. The people of the church waited. Silence. The National Socialists, who were loyal to the church, had no idea what was happening in this church. Silence. It seemed as if [the church] would stand completely apart from this powerful experience of the whole people. It appeared as if the Word of God had nothing to say to such a momentous hour. During these months and weeks even many faithful Christians who were not German Christians were shaken by the church's silence. They waited and waited. Nothing happened. No one moved. There could be only two reasons for this silence: one did not understand what had happened, or one was opposed to it. But both were equally impossible. Either one would allow an "hour of God" for the German church to pass it by. Clearly not every divine hour originates within a church; some are born instead in entirely different venues. This hour of God was the work of a political movement.

On February 3, 1933, the German Christians gathered in the Marienkirche in Berlin for a service of thanksgiving. Hossenfelder preached on the text from 1 Corinthians 15:57: "But thanks be to God, who gives us the victory through our Lord Jesus Christ." He continued:

In the lives of nations there are times to sow and times to reap.[25] Sixty-two years ago such times of sowing and reaping arrived for us Germans, times that could not have been prouder and brighter. A statesmanlike genius, the likes of which arise only now and then in the history of all nations and times, raised this will aloft. Christ was the Lord of this history. He is the Lord of all history.

We remember another moment in our German history: It was in late summer of 1914 that a murmur went through the forests of East Prussia: a nation in crisis, a people in need.

Then God sent the man who became East Prussia's champion. For ten days the superhuman struggle went on. In inexpressible anticipation the heart of East Prussia waited. But after ten days the jubilant news rang out: the Russian army had been defeated at Tannenberg.

From this remembered picture, our gaze turns to the last fourteen years. One word says everything there is to say about these years: from the empire that Bismarck forged, for which Hindenburg wielded his sword for four long years, all glory has faded and been brought low.

Faith in death has conquered us, and the united international powers that up to now have ruled in Prussia and in Germany have proclaimed it, since they themselves can live only as long as Germany is ill. Faith in death has created godlessness, dishonor, unemployment.

In this time of need, in which more than bare existence is at stake but far more, the soul of the German people, God fashioned for himself a man, one of the millions who fought in the world war, and gave him the greatest mission in our history: to pull the German people up out of despair and to restore their faith in life.

Unheard-of victories lie behind us. Superhuman feats have been accomplished. With iron discipline and rock-solid confidence, we endured. Even just a few days ago one could hear the anxious question, "When will Germany's time of trial be over? When will God intervene?" Then at last, on January 30, the hour arrived. Old Field Marshal

25. The complete text of Hossenfelder's sermon appears on pp. 243-247 of this volume.

Hindenburg called the Führer of the young Germany to head the Reich government.

It was a day of fulfillment, an auspicious hour, as the battalions of the brown army marched together with the old frontline soldiers through the Brandenburg Gate to greet the Marshal of the world war and the man who forged the Third Reich.

Once again God gives us the opportunity to build a stately house. Once again God calls the German people to its history. God grant that we all hear his call and obey it! We have lost a great deal—everything, really; but we still have three things: "ourselves, the future, and God."

The First National Conference

The further development of the German Christians received a very special stimulus from the first national conference of the German Christian Faith Movement, April 3–5, 1933, in Berlin.

The movement of German Christians now bore the name "Faith Movement." The name was never voted on or established in a [formal] meeting. [It] shows up for the first time in a publication by Dr. Wieneke: *The German Christian Faith Movement* [*Die Glaubensbewegung der Deutschen Christen*] . . . in July 1932. . . .

This national conference brought the movement to the attention of all German church people. If up until this point the Faith Movement had had a foothold only in northern Germany, [with this conference] the wave surged remarkably toward southern Germany, too.

The speeches at this conference will be of programmatic significance for the whole history of the German church. In his introductory remarks Pastor Hossenfelder made this classic statement: "The chief goal of the German Christian Faith Movement is that Christ and *Volkstum* encounter one another, that church and people harmonize with each other."

The entire conference was well attended. A whole series of leading public figures came. [Wilhelm] Kube,[26] who has been deeply sympathetic to the Faith Movement from its earliest days, spoke at the conference. Perhaps the most significant lectures were given by Pastor Peter of Berlin: "Church and People," and Dr. Wieneke of Soldin: "Theology and Higher Education."

The official reports about the first national conference and the two speeches have this to say:

> The discussion led by Pastor D. Freitag of Berlin, despite the presence of around 150 different theologians, produced an astonishing degree of consensus. Contrary to the opinion of General Superintendent Dr. [Otto] Dibelius that they had no theological leadership, the German Christians had in fact responded to God's powerful call to our times by joining their wills in one.
>
> Familiar and infamous religious proposals offered by certain ethno-national enthusiasts were not even mentioned, allowing the conference to maintain a positive tone, one that honors the old confessions and also responds to current events.
>
> Members of the Lutheran and Reformed groups clashed over the question of a national church. Here, too, those who had gathered gained the impression that our common, God-given experience in these times binds together and balances a great many things.

Ludwig Müller, the Chancellor's Plenipotentiary

By the time of the conference, *Chaplain Ludwig Müller* had already come into the limelight. For those who saw things only from afar, the effect of the conference was immense. National Socialists, who were wholeheartedly Christian, insofar as they were not already members of the faith movement, became acutely aware of it!

Everywhere, in the East and the South and the West and the North, people began to discuss the ideas of the German

---

26. Wilhelm Kube (1887–1943) was an active Christian and a zealous Nazi, National Socialist district leader [*Gauleiter*] of Brandenburg and chairman of the National Socialist group in the Prussian state parliament. He initiated one of the key efforts to "capture the energies of Germany's Protestant churches for the National Socialist cause." See Bergen, 5.

Christians—not only the theological issues, but also questions about those involved became the focus of discussion.

Who are these men, anyway? The German church public still did not know them! Opponents likewise threw themselves into the fray against the more and more swiftly growing movement with increasing fervor. They go on the attack. They complain to the Chancellor.

The Chancellor himself senses that a difficult struggle over the church is taking shape here, a struggle that in the end can only be resolved within the church itself. He appoints an advisor; he empowers this man, with whom he has had a relationship of trust for many years: Military Chaplain Ludwig Müller. As this news traveled rapidly throughout Germany those in the opponents' camp at first held their breath. Then, however, the most scurrilous intrigues began to be played out.

Attempts were made to sow seeds of division within the leadership of the faith movement and to divide it, to drive a wedge between Hossenfelder and Müller. By mid-May the tensions had reached a high point. The wildest rumors flew through Germany.

It could not have been otherwise!

Everything that had been accomplished during the previous weeks and months, the hard work and building, had to find expression somehow, and in stormy fashion, at the highest levels. The diverse elements that had come together in the faith movement had to be strengthened and the movement had to be constantly sifted.

Finally, on May 16, 1933, the die was cast. Ludwig Müller, in agreement with Pastor Hossenfelder, was given co-leadership of the German Christian Faith Movement as plenipotentiary of the Führer and Chancellor Adolf Hitler.

The idea was, first, to consolidate a unified front in the battle for the renovation of the church and in the struggle of the faith movement. A few days later Ludwig Müller became the patron of the movement.

In the meantime several important professors of theology had joined the faith movement: first among them Professor [Emanuel] Hirsch, the well-known Lutheran from Göttingen.[27]

Building a New Church!

As far as the faith movement was concerned, the full weight of responsibility here fell upon the shoulders of Chaplain Müller. His intention was first to take care of the matter of the church's constitution and then, by means of a three-man church committee—Dr. Kapler, Dr. Marahrens, and Dr. Hesse[28]—to complete and publicize the creation of the new church. Only then would the matter of who the national bishop would be come under discussion.

The idea was first of all to clarify, down to the last man in the church, what was actually going on, so that even that last man could truly feel as if he were also participating. Every Christian needed to understand why it was important to name a new national bishop and why the unification of the church was important.

A whole host of events, false reports, and obvious partisan lies doomed this plan. A detailed presentation belongs to another chapter of church history. At the very beginning of the discussions, significant difficulties arose between the leadership of the faith movement and the committee that had been named—Dr. Kapler, Dr. Marahrens, and Hesse. At this point Dr. Kapler requested that the faith movement provide a written version of the guidelines for

---

27. For more on Emanuel Hirsch, see the introduction to his *What the German Christians Want for the Church*, also in this volume.

28. Hermann Kapler (1867–1941) was a jurist and lay leader in the Protestant church; August Marahrens (1875–1950) was the Lutheran bishop of Hannover; Hermann Albert Hesse (1877–1957) was a pastor and a Reformed theologian.

further discussion. This request was promptly complied with, and at the beginning of May the faith movement proposed the following guidelines for the national church:

The Faith Movement's Guidelines for the National Church![29]

1. We want the National Protestant Church [*evangelische Reichskirche*] [to be] of Lutheran character [and] to be integrated with Reformed congregations, whose special character is to be safeguarded.

2. We want a state church, but not a church that is a state within the state; rather it should be a National Protestant Church that from the perspective of its faith recognizes the sovereignty of the National Socialist state and that proclaims the Gospel in the Third Reich.

3. The National Protestant Church is the church of German Christians, that is, of Christians of the Aryan race. To this extent it is also bound together with German Christians abroad. The proclamation of the Gospel among those who are not German is the business of the department of Foreign Missions.

4. The church so constituted can be neither the refuge of reaction nor a democratic-parliamentary forum.

5. The National Protestant Church will be sustained by the people's trust and led by the national bishop [*Reichsbischof*].

6. The National Protestant Church will be organized in not more than ten church provinces, each headed by a provincial bishop.

7. The national bishop will be Lutheran, given that the vast majority of church members are Lutheran; he will have a Reformed assistant.

---

29. These guidelines have been revised from the original ones issued in 1932, which appear on pp. 48-51 in this volume. In contrast to the earlier text, this one does not mention Jews or Judaism. Nonetheless, the concern about race remains.

8. The national bishop will have his seat in Luther's city, Wittenberg. The Schlosskirche [Castle church] will be his church.

9. On October 31, 1933, the entire Protestant church population shall vote in a primary election to decide on the guidelines offered here and, for the first time, on the person to be national bishop among those nominated from among the ranks of the German Christian Faith Movement. All members of Protestant congregations who also meet the requirements for civil eligibility are eligible to vote. Non-Aryan Christians are prohibited from voting.

10. The national bishop shall carry out the further organization of the National Protestant Church according to the above guidelines.

These theses created an uproar in German churches. Half the people took them up with enthusiasm, while the other half attacked them with equal zeal. The theses were written in very ordinary language; every common man understands them. All theological jargon has been set aside. And so it happened that this declaration took root among the people as few other things ever have.

But the widest variety of opponents now prepared a counterattack: on the one hand, the church authorities, and on the other, the Young Reformation Movement.

One thing is clear: Chaplain Müller and with him the German Christian Faith Movement behaved with great intelligence and self-control; never can the accusation be made that he bears any responsibility for the deplorable fights that flared up on Ascension Day 1933 in relation to the question of the national bishop.

In any case one thing was clear to the objective observer: Without the German Christian Faith Movement the issue of the renewal of the church, and with it the issue of the national bishop, would never have been discussed. Without the Faith Movement the German church would, by human measure, have been a complete bystander to the experience of National Socialism.

With years of hard work, [the church] might have come around, but it would never have accomplished what in these few short months the Faith Movement has produced:

a passionate struggle for the unity of church and people.

The Issue of the National Bishop!

On Wednesday, May 24, in an executive session, the German Christians made clear their position on the issue of the national bishop. It was:

1. The new national bishop must be chosen from the ranks of the German Christian Faith Movement.
2. He must have the utter confidence of the Führer.
3. He must also be trusted by the people of the church.

These points were decided in a non-public meeting.

In the meantime, on the evening of the same day, the other side had *publicly* announced their candidate [for national bishop]. It thus became clear that the German Christian Faith Movement had entered a new arena of struggle.

Now they had to carry the field in the battle over the national bishop.

This battle was clearly forced upon the Faith Movement.

Historically, it is clear to everyone that [the Faith Movement] had the right—no—the duty before God to place a man from its own ranks at the head of the new church. If it had not taken up the fight—if it had refused to carry the drama to the people of the church in this crucial hour—no one knows what might have happened.

The Protestant church would assuredly have been placed in an untenable stance in opposition to the National Socialist state. Surely those fighting for the National Socialist cause would never have been able to rely on such a church. They would always have seen it as a refuge of reaction; at best it would have taken years of work to win back their confidence, if that had even been possible.

Even God the Lord acts beyond the history of a church.

Even God the Lord can extinguish the history of a church that does not recognize its historical moment.

The circles around Ludendorff and Dinter would have been right in saying that Christianity must always be a stab in the back[30] of all that is truly German [*Germanentum*].

So the fight over the bishop became another struggle equal to those at the very beginning of the faith movement: a struggle carried on by men who knew that the historical moment had come for the people and the German church to unite, and that this unity would be possible only if both were bound by the common experience of National Socialism, in order to establish a trustworthy basis for the proclamation of the Gospel.

Unquestionably, these were difficult days, especially for Chaplain Müller. The bitterest accusations were made against him; people did not hesitate to attribute personal ambition to him, and yet there is no man more modest in relation to his own person, and yet more proud of the cause he represents, than Ludwig Müller.

He fought the whole way with remarkable dignity and purposefulness.

In any case, at every expression of hostility the movement surrounded him with an abundance of loyalty and support.

---

30. This evocative metaphor was widely used by Nazis and others to blame the civilian population, especially Communists, Socialists, and Jews, for Germany's defeat in World War I.

On the first day of the fight over the bishop, Protestant students sent him a telegram containing the following message:

> The students in the Protestant Youth of Germany demand a national bishop who is fully rooted in an understanding of the new Germany and who embodies in his person the deep, vital confessional faith of the Protestant church. This can be none other than Chaplain Müller, the confidante of the Reich Chancellor.

Organized Protestant Youth followed the leadership of its national director, Dr. [Erich] Stange, under the aegis of Ludwig Müller.

It is self-evident that the Hitler Youth and the S.A., insofar as they participated in any way in this struggle, stood completely behind Chaplain Ludwig Müller.

This was strong support indeed!

A continuous stream of information began to flow. Pastor Hossenfelder and his staff traveled swiftly throughout Germany, and he spoke to the people at huge mass gatherings. It had been a very long time since such masses of people had rushed to listen to church speakers as they did in those weeks. It is wrong to assume that the only subject of discussion was church infighting. Besides the explanation of what was going on [in the church], it was possible on dozens of occasions to bring the joy of the message of the Gospel to these broad masses of people.

. . .

Understandably, in the midst of this whole struggle, exaggerations and obfuscations occurred here and there. That probably had to happen! It would have been difficult to avoid it. But we must assert, here again, that terrorist tactics were used by a wide range of groups. In fact, this happened to me: I was on my way to preach in a city in northern Germany when the Superintendent [there] abruptly barred me from the pulpit because it was known that I had declared myself in support of Chaplain Müller. I was able to reclaim the pulpit only because I threatened to use the harshest terror tactics.

This is but a single instance, but it illuminates the situation like a flash of lightning. And still, I repeat: *it was necessary!* Decades from now these things will be judged very differently from what we can see at present.

. . .

The Harshest Judgment!

The Faith Movement has often been accused of irreligious acts. It may be that this accusation degrades those theologians it applies to more than any other charge. Perhaps the accusers will one day understand how painful it is for a good Christian to be accused of irreligion by another Christian who in fact is not fully engaged in what is unfolding among his people.

For a Christian there is no other stronger defamation than to say that he is not really a Christian, that he is a teacher of false doctrine. These accusations have been made dozens, even hundreds, of times against German Christians. Such attacks could be the result of misunderstanding, but they could also come from a malicious heart.

We know one thing: during these times, the leaders of the Faith Movement have not only struggled [in public]; they have also been on their knees, wrestling with their God.

. . .

Among all the theological statements made by the other side during the church struggle [*Kirchenstreit*], one thing is constantly evident: total misjudgment and wrong-headed intervention. [Our accusers] scent some pagan ideas, or they think they are seeing a shattering of Christianity and a Germanization of the Bible.

What is unfortunate in all of this is that to a great extent a non-German—Karl Barth—has been made the leading spokesman for the opposition.[31]

We believe that Prof. Hirsch[32] is right when he writes:

[When] the German Christians have dared to ask the Protestant church the question of the relationship between Christianity and the German character, [and] the question of whether men of non-German blood may lead the church, they [the opposition] seem to see only sheer paganism. Whoever wants to understand us on this point must first appreciate fully a profound ecclesiastical failure of the last generation.

Every human accomplishment and design is limited and bound by the natural character we bring with us into life. *If the blood is tainted, the spirit also dies.* . . . Our people's blood-bond was nearly undone. Had this process gone on fifty years more, the bearers of good, old, pure German blood would have become a minority . . . . In its doctrine of [hope], the church had the opportunity to keep holy the mystery of how strength and character are received through the blood. This it has not done.

. . .

This change has now come without the church's support. It has come with the naturalness and abandon, with the instinct for self-preservation of a people that senses that it is threatened at the root. . . .

. . . If . . . [the church] takes up this task, then in the selection of its next generation of leaders it will not close itself to the new ethos that the state is seeking to realize. Should [it] expose itself to the danger that in future its offices will be flooded with the half-Germans whom the state excludes from its positions of leadership?[33]

. . .

The resistance to saying an honest ecclesial "yes" to a truly German Protestant Christianity can be traced to a [change in] theological work.[34]

---

31. Karl Barth (1886–1968) was a citizen of Switzerland. For more on Barth, see his *Theological Existence Today!* excerpted on pp. 81 of this volume.
32. This quotation can be found in Emanuel Hirsch's *What the German Christians Want for the Church,* excerpted on p. 101 of in this volume.
33. Reference to the Aryan paragraph, whose text appears on p. 57 of this volume.
34. The quoted text draws on Hirsch's essay, but some subtle changes have been introduced, as a comparison with the text on p. 109 of this volume in this book will show.

Something Müller said after the resolution of the battle over the church's bishop—namely, "We will go straight to the people and keep fighting; the victory must be ours!"—has become the slogan of the Faith Movement. In the end, [the movement] won; it could not have be otherwise.

The battle became so intense that it expanded to include more than the church; it appeared that it might divide the people into two camps. Resistance grew not just against the German Christians but above all against the government. At this point the regime could no longer simply watch what was happening. The Prussian Minister of Culture[35] intervened with his well-known decree installing church commissars.[36]

At last, on July 11, 1933, the constitution of the German Protestant Church [*Deutsche Evangelische Kirche*] was adopted. The posting of the commissars was a temporary measure. It was the desire of the Führer and Chancellor that the people themselves should decide. In the brief period—fourteen days—before the elections there was scarcely enough time to conduct individual campaigns. In spite of this, the German Christians did a tremendous job of distributing information and advertising. A few days before the election rumors spread throughout Germany that the Chancellor had distanced himself from his representative [for church affairs].

Adolf Hitler and the "German Christians"!

Anyone who might have believed such rumors did not know the Chancellor well. Adolf Hitler never lets one of his associates down. He repays the loyalty shown toward him with even greater loyalty.

---

35. Bernhard Rust.
36. August Jäger was appointed by Rust on June 24, 1933; Jäger in turn appointed deputy commissars who served until July 14.

In his radio talk, broadcast the day before the elections, he took an unequivocal and clear position on the church elections. Without pressuring anyone, the Chancellor nonetheless expressed his opinion. He said:

If I take a position on the Protestant church elections, I am doing so solely as a political leader, that is, I am not motivated by questions of faith, dogma, or church teachings. These are purely internal church matters. Beyond these matters, however, there are problems that compel a politician and responsible leader of a nation to take a position. *These include völkisch and governmental interests related to the churches.* National Socialism has always made it clear that it is determined to extend the state's protection to the Christian churches. The churches for their part cannot doubt for even a second that they need this protection and that only thereby are they in a position to carry out their religious mission. *The state protects the church; the church supports the state.* Yes, the churches demand this protection from the state. In return the state must also require that [the churches] provide whatever support the state requires for its survival.

Churches that cannot demonstrate to the state any positive achievement in this sense are as worthless for the state as the state is for a church that is unable to fulfill its duties toward the state.

What is decisive for the right of church and state to exist is the maintenance of the spiritual and physical health of the people, because their destruction would mean the end of the state and of the church. For this reason it is as impossible for the state to be indifferent to the religious events of its time as it is for the church to be indifferent to ethno-national [*völkisch*]-political events and changes. Just as *Christendom* or later the *Reformation* had their tremendous political impact, so also every *political-völkisch upheaval* will affect the fate of the church. Only a dullard could imagine that, for example, the triumph of Bolshevism would have no impact on the Catholic or the Protestant church and thus would not disturb or hinder bishops or superintendents in carrying on their work. The claim that such dangers have been overcome because of the activities of the churches alone is unsustainable and is not supported by reality! Neither the Catholic, nor the Protestant, nor the Russian-United church has been or would be able to put a stop to Bolshevism.

Wherever no concrete *völkisch*-political resistance has been developed, the triumph of Communism has occurred, or at the least the battle remains undecided. It is therefore clear that the churches themselves must take a position with regard to such *völkisch*-political, revolutionary upheavals. In the Lateran Treaties the Roman Church has for the first time done so in a clear and unequivocal way in relation to fascism. The recently signed German Concordat[37] is the second equally clear step in this direction. It is my sincere hope that these steps have also produced for Germany a decisive clarification, through mutual agreement, regarding the respective areas of responsibility of the state and that one church.

A clear set of guidelines with the Protestant church also desired.

As a National Socialist I also wish with all my heart to be able to reach no less clear an agreement with the Protestant church. *This, however, presupposes that, instead of a multiplicity of Protestant churches, if at all possible there be one national church.* The state is not interested in dealing with twenty-five or thirty churches, especially since it is convinced that the only way we can effectively approach the formidable tasks we face today is by effectively *gathering* all our forces together. A strong state can only hope to provide its protection to those religious institutions that for their part are also disposed to be of use to the state.

In fact, a movement has emerged within the Protestant denominations, the "German Christians," who, filled with the desire to respond appropriately to the great tasks of our time, have sought the unification of the Protestant regional churches [*Landeskirchen*] and denominations. If this idea is really in circulation, then there will be no denying, in the face of history, through false or stupid objections, that this was a *service to the völkisch-political revolution* in Germany, and [rendered by] this movement within the Protestant confessions, which identified itself unequivocally and clearly with this nationalist and *völkisch* movement at a time when, unfortunately, just as in the Roman church, a great many pastors and superintendents have, often in the harshest and most fanatical ways, groundlessly taken positions against the national revolution.

---

37. The Concordat, a treaty signed on July 20, 1933, between the Vatican and the German Reich, was meant to regulate the relationship between them. In return for confessional freedom and self-administration, the Catholic Church agreed to withdraw from all political activities. Signing this treaty brought international prestige to the relatively new government of Adolf Hitler.

The strengths of a vital movement

In the interest of the renewed ascendancy of the German nation, which I see as inseparably bound up with the National Socialist movement, I would like—understandably—*for the results of the next church elections to support our new popular and state-political policies.* For since the state is prepared to guarantee the inner freedom of religious life, it has the right to hope that the churches themselves will give ear to those forces that have decided and are determined to commit themselves also to the *freedom of the nation.* This will not be accomplished, however, by the forces of religious petrification that turn away from the world and attach no importance to the signs and events of the times, but rather by the strength of a vital movement. This strength I see first and foremost among those Protestant church people who in the German Christian Movement have consciously taken a stand with the National Socialist state. Not with forced tolerance, but with living affirmation! The internal religious issues of the individual confessions are not in the least affected by all of this. It is not my job to take a position on those.

After the election the Faith Movement enjoyed overwhelming majorities in nearly all the church governing bodies. *The Faith Movement had become the church.*

. . .

As Christians we know how to be thankful for the turning point that was given to our people during 1933. We know that the destiny of the German people is also the destiny of the German Protestant Church! But we also know that the destiny of the German Protestant Church is the destiny of the German people! They are woven into each other! Both must be vital and strong!

6

The Handbook of the German Christians (1933)

German Christian National Church Union

Introduction

This "handbook" was published late in 1933, very likely for a popular audience. Its preface briefly recounts a version of the history of the German Christians that begins in 1932 and ends after the November 13, 1933, Sports Palace speech delivered by Reinhold Krause,[1] and the subsequent changes in German Christian leadership. The handbook includes several documents important to the movement: the 1932 Guiding Principles and the Twenty-eight Theses of the Church of Saxony. It also includes a membership application form that could

---

1. See p. 249 in this volume.

be torn out, filled in, and submitted. The German original includes pictures of virtually all the men mentioned in the preface, many of them in the uniforms of the S.A., or *Sturmabteilung*, the brown-shirted storm troopers who comprised the private army of the Nazi Party.

More than half the *Handbook* is devoted to a biography of "The German Prophet" Martin Luther (1483–1546), whom the German Christians claimed as a nationalist, the embodiment of their brand of "German Christianity." Clearly alluding to Hitler, the biography of Luther begins breathlessly, "The German people . . . look for a Führer. . . . [They] are ready to follow anyone who has the strength and the gifts to lead. . . . [W]ill it be a Führer called by God Himself . . . ?" As Luther's story unfolds, German Christian commitments appear: a disparaging reference to Charles V, the Holy Roman Emperor, as a "mixed-blood" [*Mischblut*]; Luther's translation of the New Testament (no mention is made of his translation of the Old Testament); a parallel drawn between the Diet, or imperial parliament, of Worms and the League of Nations, despised by the Nazis; a reference to Luther's honoring "God's orders for humanity" by marrying Katherine von Bora; linkage of Luther's burning books of canon law with the establishment of a new ethno-national [*völkisch*] system of laws. The biography ends by drawing parallels between the Reformer and Hitler, who—like Luther, the author declares—"with his faith in Germany, as the instrument of our God, became the framer of German destiny and the liberator of our people from their spiritual misery and contradictions."

The *Handbook* closes with some quotations from Luther and Hitler and a German Christian prayer loosely based on the Lord's Prayer. In the German original the prayer is followed by half a dozen pages of advertisements like those found in a guide to community resources or a program for a local sports event. The advertisers range from bakeries to furniture shops, from lawyers to sewing machine manufacturers; very likely the fees they paid to advertise underwrote the cost of producing the publication. The cover of the German original indicates multiple editions and a cumulative total printing of ten thousand copies.

The Handbook of the German Christians (1933)[2]

German Christian National Church Union

Preface!

In the days when godless propaganda had reached its zenith in Germany; when a bourgeois, more or less centrist government looked on passively as everything Christian was dragged through the mud; as churches were smeared with red[3]—in those days, Pastor Fuchs from Kray and Pastor Wagner from Homberg received from their respective district leaders [Gauleiter[4]] the assignment to represent the concerns of the Christian church within National Socialism in their districts. At the same time, the national leader of the German Christians, Pastor [Joachim] Hossenfelder of Berlin, gave them the task of calling the German Christian Faith Movement into existence in their districts. This began early in 1932; the movement's first guidelines were discussed and the work was undertaken with National Socialist thoroughness and conscientiousness. The goal was to support Hitler's work by creating a large, strong Protestant church, to sow new faith among those alienated from God, those who needed to be wrested from the grip of Marxism so that they might become

---

2. From Deutsche Christen (Nationalkirchliche Einung), *Handbook of the German Christians* [*Handbuch der Deutschen Christen*], 2nd ed. (Berlin-Charlottenburg, 1933).

3. Associated with the Communist Party.

4. A *Gauleiter* was the head of a regional administrative district (*Gau*) of the Nazi Party. In 1939 there were more than forty *Gaue*, or administrative districts, in Germany. The German Christians used the same nomenclature.

coworkers in the building up of the Third Reich. Local groups were established everywhere. The following were especially faithful fellow fighters: *Pg.*[5] Buschard of Kray; *Pg.* Rector (ret.) Hermann of Essen-West; *Pg.* Gerzmann of Oberhausen; *Pg.* Bysang of Dinslaken. The troop was small at the beginning, but it grew and grew. And when the first assault was undertaken in the church elections on November 13, 1932, despite all the difficulties placed its way, the new movement achieved great success. At this point it was crucial not to rest, but rather to really struggle, to penetrate the front lines of the enemy so as to break it apart bit by bit. In many places this was accomplished. As the National Socialist revolution was carried through, many came over to our side. The crush was so powerful at times that barriers had to be set up. During this time of rapid expansion it was unfortunately not always possible to tell whether people were driven to join by an honest desire to be part of the work of constructing [the movement], or whether they were opportunists who got wind of something they could take advantage of. While at first one had had to go looking for pastors with a lantern, all at once too many showed up. And yet it is a good thing that difficulties arise in such a situation, because then it becomes clear what is genuine. That is how it was with the "German Christians." One success followed another. Nearly everywhere the church, with all its offices, fell almost completely into our hands.[6] A "German Christian" was chosen National Bishop [*Reichsbischof*]: [Military] Chaplain Ludwig Müller.[7] With the goal in view, the work of unifying all the Protestant churches in Germany began. But, given the multitude of tasks, there were great difficulties, and when the state left the church to get its own house in order, these defectors needed only a lame excuse, like the "Krause-speech"[8] in Berlin, to withdraw,

---

5. *Pg.* = *Parteigenosse* = party comrade.

6. With the church elections of July 23, 1933, when German Christian candidates won two-thirds of the vote.

7. Elected at the national synod in September 1933.

with all flags flying, some of them directly into the enemy camp. We are delighted to be rid of them; they will give no lasting joy to our enemies either. The "German Christians," especially their leaders, were bombarded with calumnies and provocations; their detractors even managed to sow seeds of dissension [within the movement]. Nevertheless, the Essen and Düsseldorf districts stood firm, even when the rest of the Rhineland went its own way. We kept faith with the one to whom we vowed loyalty, Bishop Hossenfelder, until the day he turned over his leadership responsibilities to the present national leader [Reichsleiter], Dr. [Christian] Kinder.[9] We will not forget [Hossenfelder's] faithful, honest work and conduct, and will always be grateful to him.

The new national leader had taken over a difficult office. Everywhere the struggle raged, but he too led the movement with confidence and firmness. In order to avoid being confused with the "German Faith Movement," which stands on pagan ground, he renamed the movement simply "German Christians." He steadily drew the "German Christians" together into a tight, powerful unit. For the sake of unity, he organized the administrative areas according to the church provinces. So the districts of Koblenz, Trier, Cologne, Aachen, Düsseldorf, and Essen were abolished and formed into a single "Rhineland" district under the leadership of Pastor [Werner] Wilm of Cologne. This merger seemed necessary in order to carry out a more effective, unified struggle within each church province. As Protestant National Socialists responsible to the Führer and the national leader [of the German Christians], we continue on our path in the former districts of Düsseldorf and Essen, undisturbed by the

---

8. On November 13, 1933, in the Sports Palace in Berlin. See translation of this speech on p. 251 of this volume.

9. Hossenfelder announced his resignation on December 21, 1933. Kinder was a thirty-seven-year-old lawyer—not a theologian—and vice president of the Schleswig-Holstein state church, a member of the German Christian movement from its beginnings.

difficulties we encounter, oblivious to the favor or disfavor of all those who think they know or understand better, for we are certain: *Loyalty is first and last in heaven and on earth. Therefore, for the sake of the Third Reich,* [we stand] *with Hitler and those true to him, and with our national bishop and national leader and their companions in the struggle for a great, strong, German Protestant Church!*[10]

. . .

The Guiding Principles of the German Christian Faith Movement

The Original Guidelines of the German Christian Faith Movement (1932)

1. These principles are intended to show all faithful Germans the path and the goals that will lead them to a new church order. These principles are not intended to be or to replace a confession of faith, nor are they meant to undermine the confessional foundations of the Protestant [*evangelische*] Church.[11] They are a confession of life.

2. We are fighting to achieve an integration of the twenty-nine constituent churches of the "German Evangelical Church Association" into one National Protestant Church [*evangelische Reichskirche*], and we march under the slogan and goal:

> Externally, one and strong in spirit,
> gathered around Christ and his Word,
> internally, rich and diverse,
> each Christian according to individual calling and style.

10. Editor/Translator's note: A section on "How the German Christians Are Organized" follows. It describes the group's geographical organization and lists the names and occupations of the individuals responsible for various aspects of its work (legal questions, theological matters, community work, public information, etc.).

11. The German word *evangelisch* can be translated "evangelical." While in the American context this word has come to connote a particular kind of Protestant, in the German context it usually means "Protestant" in contrast to "Catholic." The German Protestant Church [*Deutsche Evangelische Kirche*] would have comprised regional Lutheran, Reformed, and United (Reformed and Lutheran) churches.

3. The name "German Christians" does not connote an ecclesiastical political party as known heretofore. It addresses itself to all Protestant Christians who are Germans. The era of parliamentarianism is over, in the church as well. The parties associated with various churches do not have the religious credentials to represent the people of the church; in fact, they stand in the way of the noble goal of our becoming a churchly people. We want a vigorous people's church [*Volkskirche*], one that expresses the power of our faith.

4. We stand on the ground of positive Christianity.[12] We confess an affirmative faith in Christ, one suited to a truly German Lutheran spirit and heroic piety.

5. We want to bring to our church the reawakened German sense of life and to revitalize our church. In the fateful struggle for German freedom and our future, the leadership of the church has proven to be too weak. Up to this point the church has not risen to the challenge of a determined struggle against godless Marxism and the Center Party, so alien to our spirit [*geistfremd*[13]]; instead, it has made a compact with the political parties of these powers. We want our church to be front and center in the battle that will decide the life or death of our people. The church may not stand on the sidelines or dissociate itself from those who are fighting for freedom.

6. We demand a revision of the political clauses of this church compact, as well as a battle against irreligious and anti-*Volk* Marxism and its Christian-Socialist minions of every stripe. We

---

12. A phrase that appears in the 1920 platform of the NSDAP, written by Hitler. The phrase means more or less, and with intentional vagueness, "an affirmative faith in Christ, one suited to [*gemäss*] the German Lutheran spirit and heroic piety."

13. In its National Socialist usage the common German word *fremd* [strange, foreign, peculiar, alien to]—together with whatever other word it was attached to (in this case *Geist*, having to do with the spiritual dimension)—generally meant "un-German," hostile, or inferior, connotations not ordinarily associated with the word itself.

do not see in this present church compact a daring confidence in God and in the church's mission. The path to the Kingdom of God leads through struggle, cross, and sacrifice, not through a false peace.

7. We recognize in race, ethnic culture, and nation orders of life given and entrusted to us by God, who has commanded us to preserve them. For this reason race-mixing must be opposed. Based on its experience, the German foreign mission has long admonished the German people: "Keep your race pure!" and tells us that faith in Christ does not destroy race, but rather deepens and sanctifies it.

8. We see in Home Mission, rightly conceived, a living, active Christianity that, in our view, is rooted not in mere compassion but rather in obedience to God's will and gratitude for Christ's death on the cross. Mere compassion is charity, which leads to arrogance coupled with a guilty conscience that makes a people soft. We are conscious of Christian duty toward and love for the helpless, but we also demand that the people be protected from those who are inept and inferior. The Home Mission must in no way contribute to the degeneration of our people. Furthermore, it should avoid economic adventures and must not become a shopkeeper.[14]

9. In the mission to the Jews we see great danger to our people. It is the point at which foreign blood enters the body of our people. There is no justification for its existing alongside the foreign mission. We reject the mission to the Jews as long as Jews have citizenship, which brings with it the danger of race-blurring and race-bastardizing. Holy Scripture speaks both of

---

14. The admonition not to become "shopkeepers" [Krämer] as it is used here is a not-very-subtle reminder to avoid the appearance of any socio-economic association with Jews, who were often categorized disparagingly as "shopkeepers."

holy wrath and of self-denying love. It is especially important to prohibit marriages between Germans and Jews.

10. We want a Protestant church with its roots in the people, and we reject the spirit of a Christian cosmopolitanism. Through our faith in the ethno-national [*völkisch*] mission God has commanded us to carry out, we want to overcome all the destructive phenomena that emerge from this spirit, such as pacifism, internationalism, Freemasonry, and so forth. No Protestant clergy may belong to a Masonic lodge.

These ten points of the "German Christian" movement are a call for us to come together; they form in broad outline a direction for a future **Protestant National Church** [*Reichskirche*] that, while safeguarding peace among denominations, will develop the strengths of our Reformation faith for the good of the German people.

The Twenty-eight Theses of the Church of Saxony, Generally Recognized by the German Christian Faith Movement[15]

I. Church and State

1. The German Protestant Church [*Deutsche Evangelische Kirche*] exists within the state. It cannot exist alongside the state in a little corner somewhere, which is what the anti-Christian movements would like. Nor can it remain in a neutral stance in relation to the state, which is what those circles want that mistrust the National Socialist state. It cannot be a church above the state, which would correspond to the Catholic stance. Nor can it be a church subject to the state, as in the old days of established state churches. **It can be**

---

15. These theses were drawn up chiefly by Walter Grundmann (see his *Who Is Jesus of Nazareth?* on p. 453 of this volume) and endorsed by the Saxon state church synod in December 1933. The new National Leader of the German Christians, Dr. Christian Kinder, announced that these would serve as the new guidelines for the German Christians (he dropped the words "Faith Movement").

a *Volkskirche* [the church of the German people] **only as a church within the state.** This is how Luther originally thought about state and church.

2. For the sake of its bond with the people, the church cannot stand apart by making a concordat with the state. As the church of the people it has full confidence in this state. Only those who possess the confidence of the state leadership can be leaders in the church. The state grants the church support and freedom to act, for the state and the church are for the people the two great forces for order. Their relationship is one of trust, not negotiation.

3. The church commits itself to [the doctrines of] blood and race, for our people are a community based on blood and nature [*Bluts- und Wesensgemeinschaft*]. Only those who are fellow Germans according to the law of the state can be members of the *Volkskirche*. Only those permitted by civil law to occupy official positions (the so-called Aryan paragraph) are permitted to hold office in the *Volkskirche*.

4. Being a *Volkskirche* does not mean excluding Christians of other races from Word and Sacrament and from the larger Christian community of faith. A Christian of another race is not a Christian of lesser rank, but of another kind. The *Volkskirche* takes seriously the fact that the Christian Church is not yet living in its eternal fulfillment, but rather is bound by the ordering[16] God has established for this life.

5. Because the German *Volkskirche* regards race as God's creation, it also regards the command to keep the race pure and healthy as a law of God. It considers marriage between members of different races an offense against God's will.

---

16. See #9 below for more about "orders of life."

II. The Church's Message

6. God claims the whole person. The goal of the church's preaching is to make all humanity subject to God's will.

7. As the church of Jesus Christ, the church has as its chief task the proclamation of the Gospel of Jesus Christ to the German individual, created by God as a German.

8. The Gospel of Jesus Christ means that God is our Lord and Father, that this God reveals Himself in Jesus Christ, and that we human beings find the way to the Father only through Jesus Christ. The church is bound to this proclamation.

9. God places people in the orders of life, which are family, *Volk* [people], and state. The *Volkskirche* therefore recognizes in the total claim [*Totalitätsanspruch*] of the National Socialist state the call of God to family, *Volk*, and state.

III. The Foundations of the Church

10. The foundations of the church remain the Bible and the creed. The Bible contains the message of Christ; the creed bears witness to this message.

11. The decisive revelation of God is Jesus Christ, and the New Testament is the documentation of this revelation. For this reason it has normative significance for all of the church's proclamation.

12. The Old Testament does not have the same value. The specifics of Jewish popular morality and popular religion have been superseded. The Old Testament remains important because it hands down the history and the decline of a people that, despite God's revelation, repeatedly turned away from Him. The prophets who were faithful to God show all of us, through this people, that a nation's attitude toward God is decisive for its historical destiny.

13. We therefore recognize in the Old Testament the apostasy of the Jews from God and in that apostasy, their sin. Their sinfulness is revealed to the whole world in the crucifixion of Jesus. From that day to this the curse of God rests on this people. At the same time we also recognize in the Old Testament the first rays of God's love, definitively revealed in Jesus Christ. Because of this perception the *Volkskirche* cannot relinquish the Old Testament.

14. The Augsburg Confession[17] and the other confessional writings of the German Reformation witness to the content of the Christian proclamation. Through these confessions we are bound to our forbears in faith. A church without creeds would be like a state without a constitution or law.

15. A creed is always bound to a particular time and its concerns. Certain questions to which the forebears' confessions of faith respond no longer exist for us. At the same time, we are faced with certain questions that these confessions could not have responded to. We are striving, therefore, to find in the confessions of our forebears a confessional response that the *Volkskirche* can give to the questions of our time: This does not mean going back to the faith of our forebears, but going forward in that faith!

IV. The Church's Path

16. The *Volkskirche* opposes liberalism. Liberalism undermines faith in Jesus Christ because it sees Him only as a human being. It knows Jesus only as a teacher of a higher morality or as a heroic person. It places human reason above God. For us Jesus Christ is God's Son, and his appearance is the miracle of human history.

---

17. One of the most important documents to come out of the Protestant Reformation and the primary confession of faith of the Lutheran church, the Augsburg Confession was presented by a number of German rulers and free cities to the Holy Roman Emperor Charles V at the Diet of Augsburg on June 25, 1530. The Augsburg Confession, like the present document, has twenty-eight theses.

17. The *Volkskirche* also opposes a new orthodoxy. This orthodoxy, through its dogmatic rigidity, blocks the way to Christ for those who are wrestling and searching, and hinders the lively proclamation of the Gospel.

18. The *Volkskirche*, however, also opposes attempts to replace faith in Christ with a religion that is based on racial experience. All religion, as a seeking and inquiring about God, differs from race to race. But Jesus Christ is in His miraculous person the fulfillment of every longing, question, and intuition in the human soul. The argument about whether Jesus was a Jew or an Aryan does not touch Jesus' essence. Jesus is not an exemplar of the human way of being, but rather in his person reveals God's ways to us.

19. The religion of the German people can therefore only be Christian. Christianity has various expressions, depending on race and ethnic character. This is exactly why we struggle to realize a German Christianity.

20. This German Christianity we find embodied in Martin Luther. In Luther's Reformation we glimpse the breakthrough of a truly German faith in Christ. German Christianity is Lutheranism. As German Lutherans we are completely German and completely Christian.

21. Nowadays all kinds of deceptive things are said about humanity, for example: that human beings have no responsibility before God and therefore no guilt before Him either; that humans can overcome destiny and death by their own strength; that human beings can save themselves.

22. Bondage to sin, the force of destiny, and the power of death are overcome only through faith in Jesus Christ. Through Him we gain forgiveness of sin, a bond with God, eternal life.

23. To say this is not to diminish humanity but simply to make a sober judgment about it. The nobility of humanity is the bond with God that is given anew through Christ.

24. This is the Christian message of salvation, which people of every time and nation need. Salvation is firmly grounded in the cross and resurrection of Jesus.

25. This message, which takes both the true God and true humanity seriously, prevents materialism and liberalism from making their return indirectly through religion.

26. In a *Volkskirche*, faith in Christ that is not acted on is of no value. The act of believing in Christ is decisively expressed in opposition to all that is evil and in courageous determination to serve and to sacrifice.

27. For this reason the people's church recognizes as positive Christianity (Point 24 of the Party Platform): Faith in Christ, Salvation through Christ, Acting out of Christ.

28. This German Christianity is the only foundation on which German people will be able to unite in faith as well.

Application for Membership

Herewith I declare that I desire to join the "German Christian" Faith Movement, whose principles I am familiar with and whose leadership I submit to.

I am of German–Aryan descent.

I do not belong to a Masonic lodge or to any other secret association, and I will not become a member of any such association for as long as I am a member of the "German Christians."

I do not belong to any other church group.

I pledge a monthly contribution of ____ Marks.

NSDAP membership number _____. Date joined

_____.

Write legibly!

First and last names _____

Status or profession _____

Place of residence _____

Street number _____

Date of birth _____ Baptized? _____

Confirmed? _____

Date _____ Signature_____

Membership Fee (Marks) ___ Contribution (Marks) ____

Für meine Deutschen bin ich geboren,
denen will ich dienen

(Luther)

Figure 6. "I was born to serve my Germans, and them I will serve." (Luther).

The German Prophet

By Anna Ilgenstein-Ratterfeld

Of all the conditions in life, that of a farmer is closest to creation. Through its rootedness in the earth, farming is bound to the order of creation; the farmer is dependent on the One who commands the sun and the rain, the cold and the heat, and yet free as a king, the earthly deputy of the Lord of Creation! This is the state in life that receives the Creator's gifts in order to hand them on to fellow residents of the earth. Wellspring of the people's [*Volk*] strength in body and soul. Where the condition of farmers suffers, there the people suffer. Healing the farmer's life means healing the people!

Germany was sick. Fever's heat wracked the body of the people. The foundations of the civic and church orders of the Middle Ages threatened to collapse. A new science, a new economic order, a new worldview arose.

Ferment and buzzing, seeking and questioning surge through the German people. They look for a leader [*Führer*]. The age holds within itself the most consequential decisions: The people are ready to follow anyone with the strength and the gifts to lead. Germany's future depends on who will be its leader—one from below who will lead the way into the abyss, or one called by God Himself, one who will lead the people upward toward the light, toward life?

Who, indeed, will this be? . . . Who is he, where does he come from—the one everyone is looking for? . . . Is he seated on an imperial or a princely throne? . . . Is he dressed in a Cardinal's purple; does he carry a bishop's crook? . . . Does he come from the world of scholarship, or is he a disciple of the fine arts?

The times provided an answer no one expected. The son of a farmer was to become Germany's leader. A farmer's son was to speak the saving word the world awaited. A farmer's son would return to the German people the earth and the heaven they had lost.

Farmer Hans Luther and his young wife Grete travel through the forests of Thuringia. He comes from a family of free farmers, one of the few who has preserved his freedom in this troubled time. But he was not the heir to the farm, and he was too proud to work as an indentured servant. So he exchanged his farmer's tools for the miner's pick, descended from the sunny fields into the darkness of the earth, and remained there, as he had been before, true to the earth and its order.

At around midnight on November 10, 1483, in the mining town of Eisleben, the expected child was born, the child the young mother had been carrying under her heart even on their journey. He was named Martin, for the saint's day on which he was born—Martin, the Lord's brave warrior, a man willing to sacrifice for the sake of his brothers in need.

And the child grew. . . . He grew up in a difficult time. . . . His upbringing at home and in school was hard, almost too strict for the tender disposition of a child, for the delicate body of a child. But austerity did not stunt his growth. His parents' hard demands became the demands of the child's conscience. This was the source of this future leader's sacred sensitivity of conscience; he would not rest until he had found the way to the forgiving grace of God, both for himself and for his people, who were longing for God.

Even greater than his parents' strictness were their love and fidelity. "They were angry [at me] for [my] own good." This was the underlying note of what the man remembered from his childhood. German family life, parental upbringing, and parental love were the healthy soil in which the Reformer grew up.

And the child grew. He became a young boy. Difficult years followed. In Magdeburg and Eisenach he went from door to door, singing for his meager existence, often attacking his schoolwork with a growling stomach and going to bed hungry. Not only his parents and his education—life, too, taught him hard lessons. Deep furrows were dug for God to sow seeds.

In Erfurt he began his advanced education. His father's diligence had paid off. Through tenacious work and iron thrift he had advanced from poor miner to well-placed foreman. His son could study at the university. The hungry little schoolboy became a well-turned-out student, "a lively, happy young fellow."

The Great Question

But the murmuring spring has its source deep in the darkness of the earth, and behind the joy and cheerfulness of the young student Martinus Luther slumbered unfathomable depths. The God-question, the great question, arose in his life: "*How can you find a gracious God? What will you say to God, when you must stand before his judgment seat?*"

External forces, suffering, and death had awakened these questions. And when such questions have awakened in the soul of an upright person, that soul cannot rest again until it has found answers. They become a bell that tolls day and night. They become a fire that burns in the conscience, one that only God himself can extinguish.

Martinus' path led to the monastery. In his day this seemed to be the most secure way.

Has there ever been, in any German monastery, a hotter and more serious struggle unleashed than the one that began on July 17, 1505, when the Thuringian miner's son and Master of Arts Martinus Luther entered the Augustinian monastery in Erfurt?

A human being of utterly unblemished integrity and an uncompromising passion for the truth stood here before his God, seeking an answer to the question of the path to peace with God.

He wanted the truth, only the truth; therefore no contemporary answer would do. No confession of sins, no prescribed prayer, no self-flagellation nor any other mortification of the flesh could quiet his tortured conscience. He felt that God claimed all of him and yet he could not give himself entirely to God; he sensed deep within himself the natural human resistance to God, saw in front of him the Judge and could not find his way to the Merciful One. "My good works did not count, they spoiled everything; my free will hated God's judgment but was completely dead to the good; anguish drove me to such despair that there was nothing left for me but to die and sink into hell."[18]

The Decision

Misery and fear of hell—if one has tasted these in the deepest recesses of one's own physical body—that is how it was for Brother Martinus in the Erfurt monastery.

Time went by. When it was time for him to be ordained a priest, his father visited and reminded his son that God commands filial obedience rather than a self-chosen monastic life. Like an arrow the words of the pious farmer pierced the heart of the young priest, remaining there like a thorn in his conscience.

Then came the short period of study and teaching in Wittenberg. Next came the trip to Rome on business for his order. Hope arose that here he would finally find release and forgiveness. The disappointment was all the more bitter, for here too God's grace remained distant, even as human sin and vice drew closer.

Then came the final move from Erfurt to the professorship at the University of Wittenberg, the poor little Saxon town in which God had prepared a cradle for the Reformation, just as once He

---

18. From Luther's hymn text, "Dear Christians, One and All, Rejoice."

had prepared one for the Savior of the world in a poor stable in Bethlehem. Then came close contact and friendship with Dr. Staupitz, the noble vicar general of the order, who had already been a wise guide to the struggling monk in Erfurt.

After painful refusal and a hard struggle he earned his doctorate, on which occasion the Wittenberg professor vowed "to preach and to teach the Holy Scriptures."

And finally came the great turning point: he was granted the answer to his life's question, the answer that turned the despairing, conscience-stricken monk into a hero and a conqueror.

> But God had seen my wretched state
> Before the world's foundation,
> And mindful of His mercies great,
> He planned for my salvation.[19]

Dr. Luther was supposed to preach the Scripture, and it was through the Scripture that help came.

"The righteousness of God," the phrase that had often nearly brought him to despair, appeared in a new light in the context of Scripture. He recognized that *God's righteousness was His compassionate grace.* For three days and three nights he wrestled with his new knowledge. For three days and three nights the darkness of the old heresy struggled in his soul with the emerging light of the Gospel. He paced restlessly back and forth in his little room. He threw himself to his knees in prayer. He knew that now everything was at stake. *It was an incomparable, decisive struggle equaled, in its significance for human history, by scarcely any struggle of nations on a bloody battlefield.*

At last, at last the victory was won! The triumphant song of Romans rang out in this liberated human soul: "The one who is

---

19. From the fourth stanza of the hymn cited above.

righteous shall live by faith," and "a person is justified by faith apart from works prescribed by the law"![20]

The gates to the kingdom of grace were thrown open. A freed prisoner strode through these opened gates into paradise. The man who had been struggling on shifting terrain had found the solid ground on which he could stand, the grace of his God. The leader who was to take on God's mission for his time had been called by God. The church had received its Reformer.

The church was sick to its roots, possessed by the spirit of Mammon. Obsession with money and profit had overpowered what is deepest and holiest on earth and in heaven, the relationship between human beings and their God. Because the penalties the church imposed could be paid off with money, liberation from purgatory and even the remission of sins became a matter of vile money. This disgraceful fraud was called absolution, the sleaziest deception of diabolical greed. Consciences were seized by wanton recklessness; God's grace became a commodity, and Rome's coffers bled Germany white.

In this awful situation the man who had felt in himself the terrible weight of sin could not remain silent. His concern for members of his congregation who had bought indulgences from Tetzel, the shameless indulgence peddler, and then went merrily forth to sin, compelled him to act.

On All Saints eve, October 31, 1517, he nailed the 95 theses on the door of the Wittenberg castle church. In essence, they declared that *forgiveness cannot be gained through external works, and certainly not through indulgences, solely and alone through repentance and faith.* The hammer blows with which they were nailed to the church door heralded a new era. The word that the times had been waiting for

---

20. Romans 1:17; 3:28.

had been spoken. The theses flew across Germany "as if the angels themselves had been the couriers." An electric spark flashed out. The German people began to pay attention, held its breath.

A bright ray of hope glowed in German hearts. *The German people had recognized its leader*: "It is he! The one we have waited for is here! He'll get the job done!" But a challenge means struggle. In this world nothing great is ever accomplished without a struggle.

Rome Intervenes

The struggle was not long in coming. Rome smelled danger. The German monk who had the nerve to attack the Pope on his throne and in his purse would disappear into Rome's dungeons. But this monk was the German people's man. He was their divinely chosen leader. Whoever laid hands on him would drag the people into the fray. His sovereign, Prince Frederick the Wise, held his hand protectively over him. His people stood behind him, ready for battle, ready to defend him.

When the papal bull finally arrived in Germany, its appearance having been long delayed by all kinds of political considerations, it was an impotent piece of paper. On December 10, 1520, the German hero carried it to the gates of Wittenberg, where he tossed it into the flames of the funeral pyre, together with books of canon law and other documents that supported the Pope's claims to power.

A shout of amazement rippled through the German people [*Volk*]. Even to the farthest village, everyone understood what he had done. It was a call to freedom, out of bondage to Rome. The great German painter Albrecht Dürer praised this man of God through whom God had awakened the German people, and soon after, in Nürnberg, Master Hans Sachs sang his song about the Wittenberg nightingale whose voice announces the sunrise.

The German leader had become the "German prophet." In powerful writings he showed the German people the path it should take. They were all like rousing fanfares, exposing age-old wrongs and signaling new pathways.

He writes the stunning piece "To the Christian Nobility of the German Nation." With a powerful grip he tears down the walls of the "papist Jericho," the bases of the papacy's claims to power, and points out new German pathways for building the life of the people in church and school, in economic and social realms.

Here the "German prophet" speaks to our time, too, as we are challenged to turn his proposals into realities.

And in his essay "On the Babylonian Captivity of the Church," he proposes a new understanding of piety. He shifts the emphasis from the "magical" effects of the sacraments to the promise of God and the faith of humanity.

And within this wealth of writings, which point the way to a new faith and a new morality, the short piece on the "Freedom of a Christian" shines like a bright star. It resolves into a wonderful harmony the two apparently contradictory statements: "A Christian man is the most free lord of all, and subject to none; a Christian man is the most dutiful servant of all, and subject to everyone." Faith and love are the key to freedom and service in a Christian life.

The German people had been awakened. Helping hands reached out toward the German prophet. The German knights came forward. Among his friends were names such as Ulrich von Hutten and Franz von Sickingen. They wanted to establish a militia, to spread the Gospel with sword in hand. The German prophet declined their help. He had an even stronger ally. "I do not despise such protection, but I intend instead to rely only on Christ," was his reply. And in this ally lay the deepest secret of his strength. With this ally he headed for Worms to testify before emperor and empire. The way was dangerous. One hundred years earlier [Jan] Hus had set out on a similar road and had ended at the stake.

A German Man

But the "German prophet" showed a holy defiance. Having won the victory over the power of Satan, he had no fear of imperial or papal power. "Even if they started a fire that blazed from Wittenberg to Worms and reached to the heavens, I would still appear in the name of the Lord and confess Christ and let him have his way." That is how this German hero spoke and how he acted.

His trip in April 1521 to the old city of the Nibelungen [Worms] on the Rhine was like a triumphant procession. Never before had a German man become so beloved by his people; never before had anyone so shown his love for them.

And then he stood before emperor and empire: the German leader and prophet before the German emperor.

It was a *turning point in the history of the world*. How different would Germany's destiny have been, if the German emperor had stood with the German prophet, and both of them, hand in hand, as the agents of civic and spiritual power, had led the German people toward freedom!

The German emperor did not comprehend that this was a world-historical moment. He could not, for he was a foreigner, a Spaniard, in spite of his German Hapsburg name, and what it meant to be German would always remain alien to him. So it was with the mixed-blood [*Mischblut*] who sat upon the imperial throne in that fateful hour of Germany's history. The emperor did not understand the language of the German soul in the words of the "German prophet" who stood before the assembled parliament on that fateful 18th of April. He saw in him only a stubborn monk who was rebelling against the ancient rule and order. In his heart he turned away from him, becoming his enemy, and thereby the enemy of the German people as well.

But the German hero gave his testimony. *"I neither can nor will recant anything, since it is neither safe nor prudent to do something against one's conscience. Here I stand; I can do no other. God help me! Amen."*

Outside, he smiled and raised his arms in victory. "I made it through!" he cried. "I made it through!"

The Emperor had his eye on Luther. He made him an outlaw, whom anyone could seize or kill at will. Among his German people he was safe. But there were still plenty of enemies.

His prince came to the rescue. Temporary concealment seemed the only way. The hiding place was quickly found: above Eisenach in the Wartburg [castle], where once Saint Elizabeth had done her service of love: that was the right place. There . . . Luther could take refuge for a while from his duplicitous enemies and his enthusiastic friends.

Luther's Gift

This is how the German prophet came to the Wartburg. Kidnapped late one evening on the road from Reisingen, he was brought there willingly. The quiet after the storm: how he needed it for body and soul. The farmer's son, monk, and professor became a country squire. It was important for him to become familiar with every station in German life, so that he could speak to them all and help all his fellow Germans [*Volksgenossen*].

Up there in the quiet of the lonely castle, surrounded by the rustling of the German forest, he gave his German people the sublimest of all his gifts—the New Testament in their German mother-tongue. Now the German mother could tell her child the wondrous secret of the Christmas message in the German language;

now the words of the Savior could really become seeds sown in German hearts; now the holy song of love could ring throughout the German land.

Solitude of the Wartburg—how rich you made our German people!

From Wittenberg came cries for help. The pure reformation of faith, the great revolution of life from the inside out threatened to become a revolt, a purely external coup. [Luther's] great and holy work appeared to be in danger. Iconoclasts and agitators were destroying old treasures of German culture. Heretics and sectarians wanted to turn the denial of the Pope's authority into the denial of any and all authority. *Thomas Münzer wanted to take Martin Luther's place.*

He couldn't stay in the Wartburg any longer.

"I do not intend to plead for protection from your Grace. In fact, I think I wanted more to protect your Grace than to accept the protection you could offer me. . . . What holds true here is, whoever has the most faith will be able to protect best," he wrote to his anxious prince.

By the beginning of March 1522 he was back among his timid friends in Wittenberg. With his unerring weapon, "the Word that created the heavens and the Earth and all things," he won a mighty victory over the preachers of error.

He had saved the Reformation. But it had even more difficult trials ahead of it. The enthusiasts' movement had been brought under control in Wittenberg, but it was not yet defunct, only glowing under the ashes. The political situation was also in ferment. The social sins that had been committed against the peasant class, the foundation of the life of the people itself, cried out for revenge. The enthusiasts made a pact with the social revolution of the peasants. The bloody uprising surged through Germany, using the Reformation as cover.

A human–diabolical thirst for revenge and cruelty raged under the guise of Luther's teaching on the freedom of the Christian.

God's work of reformation was in extreme danger. In all probability, never before has a spiritual movement had to withstand such a difficult trial! . . . *The fact that it did pass the test demonstrates the depth of its foundations, rooted as they were in God's truth.*

The "German prophet" was on the scene. He traveled to the region where the uprising was in progress. He hoped to change the minds of the raging peasants by the power of the Word. It was no use. A spirit of darkness had possessed them. Hate and animosity encircled the Reformer. He nearly became their victim.

Then he picked up the pen. He wrote sharp words, words born out of a difficult time and out of trembling fear for the work of God whose architect he had been called to be. He appealed to the authorities to take up their swords and exercise their office. Sharply and mercilessly that sword must reestablish God's order of authority and obedience over the human disorder of disobedience, libertinism, and rebellion.

Luther's Life-Work

Luther wanted to affirm God's order in his own life, too. God had established the human race on the basis of marriage, the holiest of God's orders for humanity. Rome had stripped it of its holiness and attached a stigma to it. "To honor the estate of marriage," to obey the Father as His child, to defy his scoffing enemies, Luther took a wife. On June 13, 1525, he married Katharine von Bora, the daughter of an old Saxon family, who as a child had taken Rome's wrong turn into the cloister.

This is how the "German prophet" gave his people the gift of the Protestant parsonage, which became a wellspring of strength for the people [*Volkskraft*], a place to cultivate Christian living and German traditions. The German prophet had become a *head of household* and a *teacher of the people*, someone who in his own home modeled the cultivation of a healthy, Christian, German family life.

As a head of his household and a teacher of his people, he gave that people rich gifts. He gave them the German hymn. When, in Brussels in July of 1523, the first two Protestant martyrs gave their young lives at the stake for the sake of the Gospel,[21] "By help of God I fain would tell a new and wondrous story," burst forth from his heart. From that time on, hymns poured out in a stream. "Dear Christians, One and All, Rejoice"[22] and "Out of the depths I cry unto Thee," "From heaven above to earth I come," "Christ lay in death's strong bands," and "Come, Holy Ghost, God and Lord": all the moods of the Christian life were accessible to him. The misery of sin and the joy of salvation, the festive joy of Christmas, Easter, and Pentecost—all served to "sing the Gospel" into the hearts of his German people with words and music. And at last he gave the church its victory song: "A mighty fortress is our God" sounded out like booming battle cry throughout the German land.

By giving the catechism to the German home and the German school he established himself as the teacher of the people.

He had been deeply shaken by the ignorance and superstition he had found on his visitations. "So help me God, with great pity I have seen that the ordinary man really knows nothing about Christian doctrine," he cried. And then he sat down and wrote, in question-and-answer form, in crystal-clear and pithy sentences, a short

21. At the Diet of Worms in 1521, Charles V, the Holy Roman Emperor, issued the first of a series of declarations to eradicate the Lutheran heresy in the Netherlands. In Brussels in 1523 two Augustinian monks, Henry Voes and John Esch, adherents of Luther, were publicly burned at the stake. Luther's hymn text recounts the story of their martyrdom.
22. This and the following hymns can be found in the hymnals of many churches, Lutheran and others.

summary of Christian doctrine. And so it was that the German people received its precious jewel, Luther's *Small Catechism*.

And he completed the work he had begun at the Wartburg. The whole Bible had to speak to the German people, from a German spirit, in its own language. It was difficult work. There were few resources. The study of languages was almost nonexistent. He took his work very seriously. Some words he tracked for days, seeking their meaning in the market and in the shops. And yet he could not have made this translation had he not united within himself these two elements: a capacity to feel his way first into the spirit of Bible, and then into that of the German language. So it was that in his translation of the Bible he also gave the German people back its language and created a bond of unity for all German tribes. The German we speak today is the language Luther opened up for us anew in his translation of the Bible.

Struggle for the Gospel

And the struggle for the Gospel? It went on even in the midst of the construction work. "Trowel and sword"—the German prophet had to work with both all his life.

The parliament met at Speyer. Luther was not present. But in his spirit, [his followers] rejected the council's dismissal. They were derided as "Protestants." The label became a badge of honor.

Then came Marburg. Zwingli, the Swiss reformer and popular leader, was also preaching the Gospel in the south. Philip, the Landgrave of Hesse, wanted him to join with the Wittenberg Reformation. Divergent understandings of Holy Communion stood in the way.

Luther and Zwingli faced off. Neither could in good conscience compromise his position. "This is my body," said Luther, placing his whole emphasis on God's act and the unmediated communion

He grants us. "This symbolizes my body," said Zwingli, by which he meant that we must make Jesus' sacrificial death present through our devout remembrance. So they went their separate ways. And the churches remained divided.

Then came the parliament at Augsburg, exactly nine years after Worms. Once again emperor and empire were to deal with the Gospel as Luther preached it. In Worms it had been just the one man who had triumphantly and defiantly confessed his faith. Now it was the majority of the German people; now princes and city magistrates stood by him.

The prince of Saxony traveled to Augsburg. Professors and counselors traveled with him. Even Luther took to the road. However, he went only as far as Coburg. Luther the outlaw was not permitted to appear before the emperor. But he supported the confessors in Augsburg with his consolation, his counsel, and his prayers. The battle they had to fight, he fought with them; he defeated the opposition in the invisible realm.

So the Augsburg Confession is no less his work than it is that of the men who stood there before the parliament on June 25, 1530, ready to abandon property and life for the sake of confessing the Gospel in the version crafted by Melanchthon, which they asked be read aloud to the emperor and the imperial court. So it was that in Augsburg was done "the most powerful work of one man that has ever been done on earth," according to a contemporary witness. *A single confessor became a confessing church.*

Luther and Us

The "German prophet" had done his duty and longed to return home. But his German people thought they could not get along without his leadership. The horizon was filled with dark clouds. It was no secret that the Spanish Hapsburg who sat on the German imperial throne was preparing to make war on the Protestants. They saw Luther as their surest earthly protection. "He was a prophet who could even stay God's wrath with his prayers." Such was the confidence the German people had in him.

But he was battle-weary. "God help me and give me a blessed little hour [of rest]," he was heard to sigh. "I have no wish to live longer." And the "blessed little hour" came.

In the middle of winter he traveled to Eisleben, his birthplace, to try to bring some peace to the family of his sovereign, the Count of Mansfeld, which was divided by a struggle over inheritances. There, where a little more than sixty-two years earlier he had begun his earthly pilgrimage, he would also begin his great journey into eternity. Birth and death, the two poles of human life, were here drawn close together. His task, one last battle with human sin and selfishness, took three weeks. Patience, love, and intercession were his weapons. In the end he again came away victorious. The estranged brothers were reconciled. Now he could fold his hands and rest.

For years one serious illness or another had already presaged that last "little hour." But when it came in the early morning hours of February 18, 1546, it was still unexpected. As his heart failed, he slipped away, a prayer on his lips. The friends who stood around his bed saw that this was his final sleep. But they longed for a last sign, the seal of his prophet's calling.

Bending over the dying man, his friend Dr. Jonas asked, "Honorable Father, is it your desire to die in Christ and in the doctrine you have preached?"

And once more his lips opened—the lips from which the Word had poured that had transformed the church so powerfully—and said, loudly and clearly, "Yes!"

This "Yes!" was the last earthly word of the dying Reformer. Even to this day it has not died away. To this day there is no other Gospel than the one Luther preaches to us. To this day this must be the foundation on which our people builds its life anew. To this day the ideas he drew from the Gospel and from his knowledge of the God-given orders of creation[23] show us how to heal the harm that has been done to our people. *To this day he is the "German prophet," even in the Third Reich, which will blossom even more beautifully the more it listens to the voice of this German prophet.*

Luther and Hitler

On October 31, 1517, Luther nailed his Ninety-Five Theses to the [door of] the Schlosskirche at Wittenberg. The hammer blows echoed like the strokes of a bell ringing in the beginning of a new era. The German soul had freed itself from the Roman straitjacket. A new stage in the history of our people was beginning. The German eagle stretched out its wings and the powerful swish of its beating wings awakened the German people. The message, "We have a gracious God," and the message about the freedom of a Christian became the confession of this Germany, now so rudely awakened.

Wary and suspicious, the international world power Rome waited to see what would happen. At the beginning Rome did not take the emerging Reformation seriously; in fact, they thought that if they offered the angry monk a bishop's hat they would win him back for the Roman world power. "I was born for my Germans, and them will I serve," was the response of this German Christian who after a

---

23. "Orders of creation" is a theological construct referring to certain structures or institutions God is said to have established in the earthly realm to order human life; marriage, family, the economy, the state, and the church might all be counted among them. For the German Christians, race—as they understood it—and *Volk* [people] or *Volkstum* [roughly, ethnicity] were "orders of creation," too, and, because they were established by God, were utterly sanctified.

difficult struggle had found his connection with God and who now would lead his German people on the same path, even if it meant the breakup of the church. The papal bull was drawn up and sent out, and when on December 10, 1521, Luther consigned the papal bull [excommunicating him] and the canonical Roman law of the pope to the pyre at the Elster Gate in Wittenberg, he believed he had cleared the way for a new *völkisch* system of laws that would emerge out of the ancient law of blood and soil. Justification by faith, the wonderful message of the German Reformation, would show the way.

But the [Holy] Roman Empire of the German nation was too closely coupled with the world power, Rome. The time had not yet come; only a few German princes understood the German prophet and, with him, the voice of the people. The Diet [parliament] at Worms witnessed a brilliant assembly of spiritual and worldly worthies, before whom the German reformer was to give an account of himself. Driven by his conscience, he had done nothing more than seek a relationship with God, and he felt compelled to establish this relationship for his people, too. The Diet at Worms, much like a "League of Nations," did not understand this German man who was fighting for the freedom of his German people. The guardian of the Roman system of law, the German emperor, declared him an outlaw. But the seed that Luther, as God's instrument, sowed among the German people germinated and bore fruit. Four hundred years have passed since then. Once again we stand at a turning point in history.

On January 30, 1933, a new stage in the history of our people and Fatherland began. Starting with a small group of determined men who carry their Fatherland in their hearts as a sacred trust, a movement grew here in Germany that is today the movement of the entire German people. And if we ask ourselves today, how this was possible and where the strength came from, after the terrible misery our land has experienced, to bring about this rebirth of our nation, we must with astonished but faithful hearts recognize the overwhelming strength of an idea that can move the world and transform it: the idea of National Socialism. The agent of the National Socialist idea is Adolf Hitler.

Adolf Hitler believed in Germany when there was nothing left to believe in. Just as our Dr. Martin Luther, with his "nevertheless" ["*Dennoch*"], and "even if the world were filled with devils," fashioned the German Reformation and with it freed the core of the German soul, just so Adolf Hitler, with his faith in Germany, as the instrument of our God became the framer of German destiny and the liberator of our people from their spiritual misery and division.

National Socialism and German Christianity belong together. They are two sides of one and the same thing, just as prayer and work belong together, or inner, invisible strength belongs with outer, visible structure. Just as a tree without roots must wither, so there is no such thing as Christianity without a people. But a people can only live and survive if it is ruled and sustained by an idea formed from the creative power of blood and soil, and only if this idea is suffused with the redemptive content of the Gospel.

In these times we see how more and more people are being caught up in a blaze of excitement, and how the German people, seized by the radical change in progress, are waking up, as if from a bad dream, from a terrible delusion, and are seeing their Germany with different eyes because the idea of National Socialism has made it possible for them to experience their Fatherland in a new way.

This renewal has sparked again in these people a burning love for their *Volk* and their Fatherland, and their hearts beat faster again when they think of Germany, because this thinking is once again being shaped by the voice of the blood, and this blood is once again bound up with the eternal law of blood and soil, of Mother Earth and the human *Volk* that she has brought into being and that lives upon her. During the last decades the laws of the divine order of creation have been disregarded far too often. This is why a new foundation has had to be laid for future generations. But the foundation of the German people's life is inextricably bound up with God, *Volk*, and Fatherland. This is why God, *Volk*, and Fatherland must be a sacred experience—for the will to be a community is born out of this experience, and the spirit of sacrifice grows out of the will to be a community. And high above stands the bright banner: "I serve."

Oh, may our whole *Volk* be caught up in this experience! Then, despite the League of Nations and the intrigues of our enemies, there will be one Germany whose strong framework will be able to serve as a foundation for generations to come.

"And be the world with devils filled . . ."[24]

Quotations from Luther; Quotations from Hitler

No one should relinquish the belief that God wants to use him to do something great. (Luther)

The freedom of a people is not something fate hands over easily; it is the result of a hard-won spiritual struggle. (Hitler)

On prayer

One should pray briefly, but often and urgently.

♦♦♦

Whenever any pious Christian petitions, "Father, may your will be done!" God above says, "Yes, beloved child, it will be and will be done, in spite of the Devil and all the world!" (Luther)

---

24. A line from Luther's great Reformation hymn, "A Mighty Fortress Is Our God."

Our Father

By Fritz Buschard

Worlds may go under, peoples may pass away,

But you remain forever!

Our Father, who art in Heaven.

You who from your heavenly tent guide the fates of mankind,

And write with unyielding strokes the story of the nations,

Give us also the strength to do Your will,

Give us the knowledge to understand Your Word!

Hallowed be Thy name.

You who gave our people its place,

And taught us to love this land,

Grant that this love may become both great and pure,

So that it becomes worthy of being Your instrument.

Thy Kingdom come to us.

You strengthen our love through struggle and affection,

The truest sons of our *Volk* gave their lives for this love.

May the blood of these heroes become the seed of a new freedom.

Seed to fruit, fruit to harvest! Sacrifice to freedom, freedom to life.

Thy will be done on earth as it is in heaven.

Just as the strength of your sun turns the seed into fruit,

So the strength of this sacrifice of love will win the freedom of this land,

So that each receives his due,

And our children as free people, pray:

Give us this day our daily bread.

You separated the light from the darkness,
And the light of the day heralded the triumph of your creation.
When we charge forward because of the suffering of our land,
And encounter our enemies, to put an end to our ruin
Forgive us our trespasses, as we forgive those who trespass against us.

Let them recognize that the night of bondage
Must give way to the light of freedom.
Our desire is sincere.
Therefore take our hands and lead us.
And lead us not into temptation, but deliver us from evil.

Now you turn a page in the book of your history.
In blazing letters the words appear:
Out of struggle and love and sacrifice to freedom, to life, to light,
And though worlds go under and nations pass away,
Your Word remains!
For Thine is the Kingdom and the power and the glory forever and ever.
Amen.

7

The Jewish Question

Gerhard Kittel

Introduction

Prior to 1933, Gerhard Kittel (1888–1948), professor of New Testament theology at the University of Tübingen, had established himself as an internationally recognized authority on Judaism and its relation to early Christianity. Kittel joined the Nazi Party in May 1933. "The Jewish Question" is a speech he gave in Tübingen a month later, on June 1, 1933. The seventy-eight-page print version published shortly thereafter went through three editions and nine thousand copies. That same year Kittel became a charter member of the National Institute for History of the New Germany (*Reichsinstitut für Geschichte des neuen Deutschlands*), which pursued and funded pseudo-scientific, racial-political studies aimed at underpinning the anti-Jewish policies of the National Socialist state. Beginning in 1936 he became a key resource person for that institution's new Research Section on the Jewish Question. Gerhard Kittel is perhaps best known in theological and academic circles as one of the founders and editor of the multi-volume *Theological Dictionary of the New Testament*, whose first volume was also published in 1933. The work is still a standard reference for New Testament scholars.

The Jewish question—What should be done with the Jews in Germany?—was as central to German Christians, with whom Kittel deeply sympathized, as it was to the Nazi state. In this speech, according to Robert P. Ericksen, Kittel intended "to raise the discussion of the Jewish question above the level of slogans and vulgar racism and give it a moral, Christian basis."[1] He begins by acknowledging the seriousness of the question, then argues that there are four possible answers: extermination; Zionism; assimilation; and guest-status. He discusses each option in turn and settles finally on guest-status as the only viable, morally acceptable resolution. It is a resolution he hopes will get Jews to return to what he argues is their own separate, inimitable religious culture and tradition, which he believes they have lost in the process of assimilation. Kittel's proposed "resolution" also leaves Jews legally unprotected in the context of Nazi Germany.

---

1. *Theologians Under Hitler: Gerhard Kittel, Paul Althaus, and Emanuel Hirsch* (New Haven, CT: Yale University Press, 1985), 32.

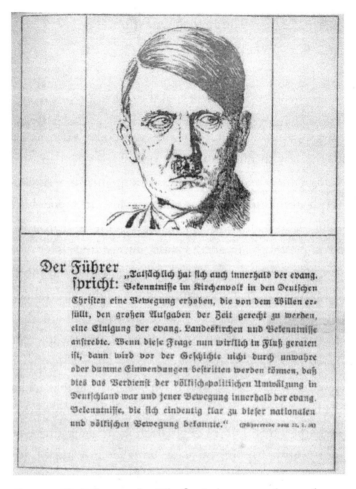

Figure 7. The Führer speaks: "The fact is that among the members of the Protestant denominations a movement has arisen, the German Christians, who are determined to do justice to the great challenges of this time, among them, to seek the unification of the Protestant churches. If this matter has truly been set in motion, then as history unfolds, no one will be able to gainsay that this has been a service to the *völkisch*-political revolution taking place in Germany, and that that movement within the Protestant churches has committed itself unequivocally to this national-*völkisch* movement." (Speech of the Führer, July 22, 1934).

The Jewish Question[2]

Gerhard Kittel

The Seriousness of the Question

Among the questions currently arising from today's German political situation, the Jewish question is the one that engenders an intense sense of insecurity and helplessness among many serious-minded people, both domestically and internationally. It is widely felt that there is much about antisemitism that is legitimate, that in fact there has been something about the situation of the Jews and their influence in Germany that has not been quite right. But most people simply acknowledge that something is not right, and remain stuck on certain details . . . but as to what are the roots of the Jewish question as an *issue*, not many people have a clear insight into that. It thus becomes a serious question whether such radical legislation against Jews is really necessary and fair—legislation that will after all inevitably have a severe impact on a very great number of honest people—whether this sort of legislation can be justified from an ethical or a Christian point of view; whether it is not really, as the whole world is saying about us, a piece of barbaric brutality.

For Christians generally a very hard question arises out of the polemic against the Old Testament and certainly from the antisemitic attacks on the Jewish aspects of New Testament religion. Is this sort of thing a requisite and substantive component of antisemitism, or is it only exaggeration, the outgrowth of a movement that is in itself justified? Many wrestle unsuccessfully over this point, trying to balance the ethno-national [*völkisch*] ideal and the Christian-ethical claim. Many a person—particularly among the serious-minded—has,

2. From Gerhard Kittel, *The Jewish Question* [*Die Judenfrage*] (Stuttgart: Verlag von W. Kohlhammer, 1933), 7–25, 68–76.

one would almost have to say, a bad conscience when thinking about the Jewish question.

And yet it is vital to the life of the young *völkisch* state that this problem of balance be made clear. The National Socialist German Workers Party represents a positive Christianity,[3] and the men of the German revolution have repeatedly professed this. This carries with it the unconditional claim that the fight against Judaism must also be carried out on the basis of a conscious and clear Christian conviction. It is not enough, then, to base this struggle solely on racialist views or popular religion. *The true and complete answer can only be found if the Jewish question is successfully supported in religious terms and the fight against Judaism is given a Christian frame of reference.* On this point we must also find a clear path, one that allows us to think and to act in a way *that is at the same time both German and Christian*, and thus to reach a decision characterized by integrity.

With respect to the Jewish question, the paucity of clear, basic information has significant consequences. For many, for example, antisemitism is just an emotion, out of which no purposeful behavior can come. For others, lack of knowledge takes them in the direction of slogans. No one can deny that, on the antisemitic side, slogans abound, taking the place of clear, substantive reasoning. . . . For most people, though, the lack of clear knowledge generates sentimentalism, and that is an even greater evil. God does not want us to be sentimental, but rather to see what is actually there and to take it into account. The Jewish question cannot be resolved with either slogans or sentimentalism; it can be resolved only to the extent that we draw the necessary implications from the actual

---

3. A "positive Christianity" was understood to be beyond denominations and emphasized an "active," heroic Christ. That Hitler included this as Point 24 in the Nazi Party platform of 1920 signaled his sense that he would need the support of the churches as he embarked on his National Socialist project.

circumstances. The National Socialist leadership is correct when it repeatedly emphasizes that "only those who completely master the Jewish question are in a position to make it the subject of public pronouncements."[4]

. . .

. . . [T]he Jewish question is not, in the first instance, a question about the destiny of individuals, but rather of a people. If I want to resolve it, or if I want to evaluate a proposed resolution to it, I may not look first at individual Jews. It is not about whether individual Jews are or are not upstanding Jews; nor is it about whether individual Jews suffer unjustly or whether for some this [suffering] is in fact just. The Jewish question is absolutely not a question of individual Jews, but rather a question of all Jews, of the Jewish people as a whole . . .

The question of what must happen to the Jews has four possible responses:

1. One can seek to exterminate the Jews (pogrom);
2. One can re-establish the Jewish state in Palestine or somewhere else and attempt to gather the Jews of the world there (Zionism);
3. One can allow the Jews to merge into other peoples (assimilation);
4. One can definitively and conscientiously maintain the historically grounded givenness of their status as aliens among all peoples.

---

4. Editor/Translator's note: The next few sections deal with what Kittel calls "two historical actualities" that have given shape to the Jewish question in its present form: the Jewish diaspora, which is the circumstance in which Jews have been living for nearly two thousand years; and the seventeenth- and eighteenth-century "emancipation" of the Jews, associated with the Enlightenment.

Extermination of the Jews?

The violent extermination of the Jews is not a serious option: if the systems of the Spanish Inquisition or the Russian pogroms did not succeed, it seems highly unlikely this will happen in the twentieth century. Nor does the idea make any moral sense. A historical reality like this one may be resolved through the extermination of this people at most in demagogic slogans, but never in actual historical circumstances. The point of a particular historical situation is always that it presents us with a task that we must master. Killing all Jews is not mastering the task at hand.

Zionism

That today's Zionism is no solution to the Jewish question has been proved as thoroughly as it can possibly be by the experiment that has been conducted in Palestine since 1919.

First, the Palestinian political system was neither established through the efforts of the Jews themselves nor created for the sake of the Jews. No one can doubt that it was established in the first instance as a means through which European super-powers could accomplish certain goals. They used the romantic attitudes and plans that had arisen among the Jews in a multitude of ways in the course of the nineteenth and twentieth centuries to expand what were for them above all purely political objectives.

Second, the establishment of Jewish colonies has led to a terrible social violation of the Fellahin,[5] who had settled in Palestine hundreds of years before. The ancient Mohammedan [Muslim] farmers were summarily driven from their land and uprooted; today they are

---

5. "Fellahin" was the term used throughout the Middle East in the Ottoman period and later to refer to Muslims, Christians, or Druze who might be tenant farmers, smallholders, inhabitants of a village that owned the land communally, or even landless workers.

largely either day laborers or in poverty. This turn of events produced a passionate hatred of and occasionally bloody attacks on Jews living in Palestine. If English military might were not standing behind Palestinian Jews, the Arabs would probably have made short work of them. An important lesson emerges here, namely, that one cannot simply shove the Jews onto any part of the world—even if it is an uninhabited piece of desert—without giving rise to conflict with the population of that land and injustice against that population.

Third, the question arises as to whether and to what degree the Jewish colonies in Palestine are even viable. Even the Zionists report substantial economic difficulties. Unemployment and misery reign in today's Palestine, too.

Out of this emerges—fourth—a very alarming political-ideological structure of this Zionist polity. Since the colonists streaming to Palestine came for the most part from socialist circles, even its beginnings were accompanied by socialist-communist tendencies. Economic calamity only strengthens this tendency, and the Zionist state becomes increasingly a nucleus of socialist ideas. One should not rule out the danger that these ideas will stream back into the developed societies, poisoning them in turn.

Fifth, since at most only a small percentage of the world's Jews will be able to be accommodated in Palestine, practically speaking, Zionism is not a real solution to the Jewish question. Even now strict migration laws are in force. It is significant that, after the German boycott of Jewish merchants,[6] the Palestinian authorities announced measures to help by issuing immigration visas; however, the number of those permitted to migrate was so small that the measures were virtually meaningless.

Most important, however, is a sixth point: the fact that the Jews themselves object passionately to Palestinian Zionism. This objection

---

6. Decreed April 1, 1933.

arises, on the one hand, from assimilated Jews, those who want to merge with the [non-Jewish] population. But pious, anti-assimilationist Jews are also opposed to it. These pious Jews surely long fervently for their holy land; they also feel the religious hope for that day on which their community will be restored to Zion. But that day is eschatological; it is a day that God himself will bring to pass at the end of days. To bring it about by political means and to make it a cultural act, as Zionism does, is, for pious Jews, to turn this hope into its opposite. The genuine religious, eschatological hope is politicized, secularized, made into something worldly. This correlates with the unarguable fact that contemporary Zionism has nothing at all to do with the Jewish religious movement. Far more substantively, Zionism unites enlightened, not to mention atheistic, Jews. The ardent efforts of Martin Buber and others to pump religious content into Zionism simply underscore the fundamental hopelessness of such attempts. It is indicative of the situation that even today pious Jews in Zionist Jerusalem gather at the ancient Wailing Wall to weep over the fall of Jerusalem. Of course, they are not "Zionists," but representatives of a genuine Judaism for which modern Zionism is a heresy at odds with religion and representing its dissolution.

I do not want to argue that the plan for a "Jewish state" is fundamentally and utterly impossible. The plan conceived by Theodore Herzl [1860–1904], the founder of Zionism, was not even in the first instance focused on Palestine, and in that sense was not inherently "Zionist." There was thought of Jewish colonies in the Crimea, in Argentina, in New Zealand, in British East Africa. Such solutions would have had the advantage that they could not have become pseudo-eschatological, something the Palestinian–Zionist solution cannot avoid.

Whether such solutions could be realized remains to be seen. But in any case none of these attempts could ever take care of more than a fraction of all the Jews. The problem of other groups of the world's Jews would remain. Both parties, Jews and Germans, must understand clearly that the problem will never be resolved with the slogan "all the Jews should go to Palestine." Even in the best of circumstances such a solution would never be more than a halfway measure that would in its own turn only produce a host of new questions and difficulties.

The Old Ghetto

It seems that only two alternatives can be considered as solutions to the Jewish question: *assimilation or guest-status [Fremdlingschaft]*.[7]

For centuries the peoples of the Western world had instinctively operated on the assumption that the Jews were to be seen as a guest-people who could pursue an existence in the Jewish section of town that, though subject to certain limitations—they were, after all, guests—was in general fairly peaceful. Until the eighteenth century the Jewish question was completely different from the Jewish question of the present day. Unrest and persecution, when they arose, had causes entirely different from contemporary antisemitism. They were a defense against indecent behavior on the part of the guests, or they were eruptions of an instinctive aversion to those of an alien race; if the latter, they arose very much the way they often do because of a sense of strangeness, various superstitious motives, legends about all sorts of weird things that Jews, as aliens, were accused of doing.

As much as this sort of thing may still function today, the actual roots of today's antisemitism lie elsewhere. Very likely there was some relationship with what is at stake today, for example, when popular fury lashed out at those Jews who managed through flattery to gain privileges from the princes or became "court Jews," Jews

---

7. Literally, the state of being an alien.

who gained and abused public influence that was not appropriate to them as guests.[8] In ancient times such Jews were the predecessors of assimilationist Jews, and the princes who encouraged this were even in those days out of touch with the true instinct of the people [*Volksinstinkt*], just like the governments of the nineteenth and twentieth centuries that have continued the process of assimilation.

The most severe persecution of the Jews during the Middle Ages, the Inquisition, does not really even belong with the Jewish question. It was not persecution of Jews as Jews, but rather as unbelievers who refused to convert. For the Inquisition the Jews were the same as the Waldensian heretics or the Mexican Incas [sic].

The Beginning of Jewish Emancipation

The ideas of the Renaissance and the French Revolution created a wholly new situation for the Jews. The concepts of "humanity" and "human rights" necessarily came to apply also to them. The liberal idea of "tolerance" led, in its classic interpretation, to the ideal type portrayed in *Nathan the Wise*. The catchphrase "emancipation of the Jews" led to the dissolution of the ghettos and of the restrictions on foreigners that had been considered a matter of course. Societal and civic equality for Jews followed, and then assimilation.

Alienation from Religion

From the time of the Vienna Congress onward, the so-called Christian states once again gave preferential treatment to the Christian churches. This may explain why Jews found it easier to convert. Having done so, they became unconditionally "Germans." Almost without exception, conversion to Christianity improved their

---

8. Kittel cites as his source for this statement Adolf Hitler's *Mein Kampf*, the 13th edition, pages 340ff. He provides no other publication information.

social standing. Conversion out of conviction was improbable and happened seldom. That this led to a complete alienation from religion should not surprise anyone—nor should the fact that as a consequence, religion was more and more despised and considered less and less relevant. For this reason the prevailing Judaism of the twentieth century has come to represent the putative cultural and political progress of atheist dissidents, especially since in the Weimar regime belonging to a Christian "confession" no longer brought with it any advantage. Because at the same time the liberal synagogues increasingly became simply institutions dedicated to a "rational" religion, ultimately nothing stood in the way of "modern" Jews' remaining members of these synagogues. Under certain circumstances [a Jew] even had an advantage in that they appeared to represent an especially modern religion, indeed, the true "religion of humanity," in contrast to the Christian churches with their "backward dogmatic beliefs"—something that was made much easier as a result of certain tendencies within so-called "Christianity."[9]

Connubium[10]

The emancipation of the Jews also meant *the nearly unrestricted possibility of mixed marriages [Mischehe] between Germans and Jews.* At the beginning of the nineteenth century, marriage between Jews and Germans was absolutely impossible, but within a few decades the true instincts of the people [*Volk*][11] had been so completely uprooted that the door stood open to unlimited mixing of the races. Two

---

9. Practically every modern Jewish religious teaching seeks to ground and support its claim of superiority by quoting Protestant liberal theology. [Footnote in the original text.]

10. Editor/Translator: Marriage. Among the Romans, a lawful marriage as distinguished from "concubinage," which was an inferior marriage. Kittel seems to be using the term to mean intermarriage between Jews and non-Jews in Germany.

11. Here the author again cites the 13th edition of Hitler's *Mein Kampf,* p. 311, as his source, without further publication information.

motives drove this development. One was money; as is well known, the old aristocratic families were especially likely to connect with wealthy Jewish families through marriage. The other was the strange but indisputable fact that the exotic can exercise a particular sexual appeal to which a passionate young person easily falls victim unless instinctual or legal precautions are in place. Nineteenth-century thinking had set such measures aside; one spoke of "human beings" [*Menschen*] or "citizens" rather than of comrades [*Volksgenossen*]. Such theories expanded to an almost unimaginable degree—and under their guise sexual desire or addiction to material gain overcame the true instincts of the German people.

Countless mixed-bloods [*Mischlinge*] pervaded the body of the German people. Because in many cases they bore strongly Jewish features, they strengthened the influence of the Jewish element on the body of the people. More important, however, over the last hundred years there has been increasing mixing of the races.

Race Mixing

The resulting problem for today is in no way mitigated by the fact that Germany already has racial elements of many types from earlier centuries. As we say, hardly a one of us is still of a racially pure Germanic type. Whether or not this last is the case is something racial hygiene researchers will have to determine; the layperson can make no definitive judgment in that field. In any event, however, the historical circumstances surrounding the present state of things are quite different. The one case has to do with historically complete processes of racial mixing that took place in the distant past. For example, in eastern Germany there are doubtless Slavic elements that entered German blood at particular periods in German history. But in the first place Slavs and Germans, both Aryan, are undoubtedly closer to one another than Semites and Germans. And in the second place, this mixing of the blood ended after a certain period of intermarriage. Thereafter peoples and races separated and established boundaries; after a certain period of time the element of Slavic blood could be considered to have been Germanized. But in the case of the Jewish question we are dealing with an ongoing mixing of blood and race that began in the early nineteenth century. Its historical development began at a particular historical point in time: for Germany, it was about a hundred years ago. At the beginning of 1933, before the new laws[12] were passed, this development was altogether unregulated and had no foreseeable end. Quite the contrary: over the last fourteen years it had gathered enormous strength and intensity. If this historical development has come to a definitive and radical end because of the laws passed in 1933, then it may be that future historians, looking back, will be able to evaluate the influence of this period of assimilation of German Jews on the body of the German people similarly to that of the Slavic epoch. Today, however, that would be a disastrous misjudgment, a minimalization of the situation.

The Jewish Problem in Other Nations

It would also be wrong to compare our Jewish problem in Germany with the Jewish problem of other nations, for example, the Italians, the English, the Swedes, etc. Naturally, they also must face the question of the assimilation of Jews; one day they too will surely find themselves facing the same consequences we face today. But for them, for a simple geographical reason, the problem is much less serious, or at least not as visible: they do not have the eastern border that Germany has. That is to say, unlike us, they do not have to deal

12. The reference is to the "Aryan paragraph."

with the broad exodus of assimilation-hungry Jews from the eastern ghettos.

The Jewish Question as a Problem of Decadence

As we have indicated, only a biologist can speak about the biological consequences of race mixing. His judgment, if it is based on sober scientific research, will have to be taken much more seriously than has generally been the case. But besides the fatal matter of intermarriage and the race mixing that occurs because of it, there is a spiritual reality of the most profound significance: namely, that *the assimilating Jew becomes uprooted from the culture of his own people*. He has lost his home within Judaism, but he cannot sink roots in any culturally appropriate way into the German culture [*Volkstum*]. This is his tragedy and his curse, for from it comes his decadence. *This decadence, and nothing else, is the real problem besetting the Jewish question today. Compared to today's situation, the Jewish question of the Middle Ages and its ghettos was insignificant and harmless*, because it was not a question of decadence. In its alien nature and its homelessness, that ghetto-Judaism was a burden to the nations. But the poison that is eating its way like a monstrous sickness through the body of the *Volk* is this uprooted, homeless, decadent Judaism. *This* is the Judaism that is subverting all the genuine religious, cultural, and national ideas that emerge from the *Volkstum*, because its rootlessness renders it separate by nature. This is the Judaism that connotes subversion. This subversion can appear in different guises. It can appear as a tired, sensitive, and yet—because it saps energy and infects—a dangerous resignation that eats away at the marrow of a people; it can be a cold, calculating, even self-tormenting and self-lacerating relativism; it can be a wild agitation and demagoguery that holds nothing sacred. Always, it is a spiritual homelessness, and therefore poison and dissolution.[13]

215

. . .

Judaism as a Religious Problem

The most severe spiritual crisis for liberal and modern Jews, of course, will be the ending of assimilation and the reversal of their emancipation *from their own Judaism*, because that Judaism has largely lost its meaning for them and it seems almost impossible for them to repossess that meaning. This is the problem within the Jewish question that is of more profound significance than any political or organizational measures on behalf of or against Judaism.

The problem consists in two circumstances: first, that *without the Jewish religion there is no such thing as Judaism*. The received religion of the ancestors is the essence of Judaism. A Jewish race, a Jewish culture without the religion of Judaism is a Judaism without a soul. Therefore when I say to an assimilated Jew "go back to being a Jew!" it can only mean "be a devout Jew again; return to the God of your ancestors; listen to the call of the ancient prophets of your people for repentance!"

But the result is a second fatal circumstance. It is the bitterest of all accusations against Jews that anyone must raise, and it must

13. The next several pages deal with the dangers of "internationalism" allegedly associated with Judaism. On p. 33 the author boasts [!] that the University of Tübingen, to whose faculty he belonged, is the "only German university where there is no Jewish question [i.e., no Jews], either among the professors or in the student body." Kittel then argues that the "scattering" of Israel is God's will, and therefore real Jews should be content to remain "guests/strangers" wherever they live, and not seek assimilation. The state should therefore restore the Jews to "guest status." Jews are to be barred from journalism and their works are to have no part in "German literature." (He mentions in particular Franz Werfel, the author of *The Song of Bernadette*, as someone to be excluded from the canon.) Jews are not to teach German youth, and in particular are not to be university professors. German physicians, lawyers, and merchants are likewise suspect (not least because the professions are overrun with Jews). All this ought to be a matter of course! In future, Jews who choose to be intellectuals or not to resign themselves to "guest" status are to be deported; those who remain are to comport themselves as inferiors in the occupations permitted them. Mixed marriages are, of course, to be forbidden; Germans who persist in marrying Jews are thereby to become Jews themselves, with all the associated limitations.

be uttered by one who knows not only the weakness but also the greatness of Judaism. And in uttering it I know that on this point more than all the others I am at one with the best representatives of Judaism itself. That accusation is that *the major part of present-day Judaism no longer has a living religious faith!*

The situation is as follows: two almost mutually exclusive extremes, the orthodox and the liberal, are at war within the synagogue. This opposition has existed throughout the whole history of Judaism since the Exile. Orthodoxy is always in danger of shriveling up into ritualism and a religion of law. I have adequately demonstrated that I do not despise the extreme rectitude of a ritual Judaism;[14] a Judaism that holds sacred the Sabbath and circumcision, sacrifice and the purity laws is truly worth more than the other kind that despises all these things. But when Sabbath and purity laws and fasting and prayer customs are made an external, orthodox law and no longer possess their internal anchor, *real religion sinks into sterility* and has nothing more to say to people living within the currents of their time.

As always in the history of Judaism, a counter-movement has arisen, the liberal synagogue, which seeks a balance with the cultural elements of the times and flattens out the deepest and best of its own, the living religion and faith in God. We can safely say that its members, on average, are as good as indifferent to religion. This Judaism flees increasingly into generalities: that Judaism is the spirit of freedom of the nations and their reconciliation, the spirit of justice, of progress, of freedom, of social thought, advocating the equality of all, or, in the end, an abstract ethicism or moralism. All that is a substitute for religion, but it is no longer the ancient, living religion of the ancestors of Judaism.

14. Kittel refers here to his *Jesus und die Juden* (Berlin, 1926).

Genuine Judaism cannot be constructed by joining this modern philosophical babble with the idea of a nationalist Judaism. That is in large part the program of modern Zionism, and therein lies its most profound sterility. The result is an almost atheistic Judaism for which a national Jewish state, a national Jewish culture, a Hebrew literature takes the place of religion. Achad Haam, one of the spiritual leaders of Palestinian Zionism, has, for example, developed a comprehensive theory in which religion and ethics are two separate spheres; in which it is not religion, but the national ethic constitutes the core of Judaism; in which the religion of Judaism is merely a symbol and an external embodiment of the national ideal; and in which the religion of Judaism may ultimately be dissolved into modern spiritual development.

The majority of Jews have, during the past century, taken no account of the seriousness of this religious question. Jokes have been made about religion; its forms have been seen at best as national symbols. In the last few weeks there has come from the Jews themselves a lament and an accusation that Judaism, since it left the ghetto, has wholeheartedly adopted the role of a satisfied, materially well-off, intellectualistic and self-satisfied bourgeoisie. "And now that bourgeoisie stands here empty-handed. It is no use rubbing our eyes. We have to reclaim ourselves at last."[15] But "reclaiming ourselves" can never be anything else for Judaism than *returning to God*. Therefore I say that for Judaism the response to present events must be, more than ever, having the courage to be and want to be Jews again and rejecting the fatal dream of assimilation. To be a Jew again can ultimately mean only having the courage to turn back to the sources

15. Kittel refers to an article in the *Jüdische Rundschau* of April-May 1933. This widely read monthly German-language Jewish publication, published in Berlin, appeared from 1902 through 1938, when it was shut down by the Nazi regime.

of Jewish religion—not to modern philosophical babble, but to the living God proclaimed by Moses and the prophets and the Psalms.

But this means something still more, and here I return to the core of the current Jewish question. For Jews, returning to the God of the ancestors also always means coming back to the God of history. But God's history with the Jewish people has meant, for the last two thousand years, an existence as sojourners among the nations of the world. Returning to God means for the Jews to say an obedient "yes" to this history with God: the misery of being scattered, the pain of obedient acceptance of Israel's forced exile. Assimilation and Zionism are both equally manifestations of disobedience, of a Judaism that resists God. *Real Judaism remains true to its symbolic being as a restless and homeless sojourner wandering the earth.*

So for the best of the Jews today the problem is: whether it will be possible *to awaken a living religion within a Judaism that affirms its stranger-status.* It would need to have the strength to overcome both the superficiality of liberalism and the petrification of orthodoxy; but it would have to draw that strength from the ancestral religion. It may be that in Martin Buber the Jews have been given a leader for such a path, even though he was previously identified quite strongly with the Zionist ideal. His life-work on behalf of a revival of the ancestral religion and his struggle for the soul of his people can and should be greeted by Germans also, and especially by German Christians, with respect and esteem.

The situation is, indeed, analogous to that of the Christian nations [*Völker*]. They, too, are beginning to awaken from the fever of homogenized religion. We are all learning again that the ultimate questions of the peoples cannot be answered by civilization and cultural philosophy, as has been the doctrine since the end of the eighteenth century, but only where culture and common life are sustained by a living faith in God that grows out of the *Volkstum.*

We are beginning again to understand how deceptive and hostile to the people [*Volk*] is the slogan, "religion is a private matter." The fateful question for our German Christianity is also whether we can overcome the orthodox petrification and liberal superficiality arising out of the spirit of the nineteenth century; whether we can build a church that can sustain the current common life of all classes with the message about the living God. The same is true of Judaism: if Buber and those like him succeed in opening for those who are Jews and must remain Jews, and who nevertheless, as twentieth-century people, cannot return to the frozen, dead ghetto-religion of laws and yet are sickened and stunted by the emptiness and flatness of the modern notion of religion—if they succeed in showing these people once again the spiritual homeland of Judaism, the living God of its history and that God's sacred revelation—if they succeed in that, they will have made the most important and conclusive contribution to the resolution of the Jewish question.

In this sense the Jewish question is ultimately a religious question, and all its political and social sides must somehow be brought into the light of this way of thinking. If that way of thinking about religion is pursued consistently, a final distinction becomes necessary. We have spoken of a solution to the Jewish question. Religiously speaking, in the course of history there can only be relative solutions. The absolute solution lies elsewhere. Devout Judaism awaits a fulfillment of its history and its destiny; it is that fulfillment that is awaited by those touching figures at the Wailing Wall in Jerusalem when they pray for an end to the life of exile, for God's one final coming to Zion, which is so altogether different from "Zionism." *Even that genuine Judaism of the future about which I have been speaking will only acquire the strength for obedience in its state of sojourning from its hope and expectation of God's day.*

Jewish Christianity

At this point the faithful Jew and the faithful Christian part ways.

Even from a genuine Christian perspective, one cannot say: What do I care about the Jews; they belong to a different religion. But one dare not think that a Christian perspective on the Jewish question would be to advocate softer or milder measures and to hinder a necessary and substantively correct struggle. If the struggle is right in its substance, then the Christian's place is in its front lines. Certainly he may and should—as he would in any war—do what he can to see to it that the battle is fought fairly and not barbarically; by the same token it is his privilege, never to be relinquished, to bind up wounds that must be inflicted. But that does not exhaust the Jewish question for the Christian. *The Christian also knows of a fulfillment of Judaism; that fulfillment is called Christ.*

Now I do not think I have to defend myself from the idea that I am talking about the sort of *external, Godless conversion* from Judaism to Christianity based only on social or economic motives. On the contrary, it should be said openly for once: not only Jews but the church bears *massive guilt* that for a hundred years the baptism of Jews could be the object of humor magazines; that such an external sign of conversion was condoned to the point that a Jew's conversion to Christianity out of serious conviction appeared to be the exception rather than the rule. The "German Christian" Faith Movement has raised the question of what position non-Aryans should have in the future German church. It was certainly not contrary to the thinking of the German Christian Faith Movement to be asked for a clear formulation, and to have it pointed out that schematic state norms could not simply be adopted in formulating church law, since internal laws in one and the other case are quite different. Nor, on the Christian side or in the German Christian Faith Movement could there be a moment's doubt about the right and duty of Christians to proclaim the message of the Gospel to the Jews. Jesus Christ's command to evangelize the nations, which also includes the duty of a mission to the Jews, remains irrevocable and indispensable for every Christian church.

But we cannot obscure the fact that the question raised by the German Christian Faith Movement makes a great deal of sense and cannot be dismissed with platitudes. If, at the point of Jewish conversion, the church had held the sacrament of their baptism to be as holy as it was their duty to hold it; if the church had not made itself the lead horse for the sin of assimilation; and if it had not allowed baptism to be misused for social and mercantile purposes, then the Aryan question would not need to be raised in the church. A church that has permitted this misuse for a hundred years has thrown away its right to deal with this question as such. *It must rather be the first to insist, with full and complete clarity, that the baptism of a Jew does not affect his Jewishness, that becoming a Christian does not mean becoming a German. The converted Jew does not become a German, but rather a Jewish Christian,* just as the Jews of whom the New Testament reports that they accepted baptism did not become part of a different ethnic culture [*Volkstum*], but were and remained Jewish Christians and members of the Jewish people. This is exactly what the missionaries have learned: that their task with the Chinese and the Indians to whom they proclaim the Gospel is not to make them into cosmopolitan Central Europeans, but into Chinese and Indian Christians.

But there is more. The missions have also learned that Chinese and Indian Christianity is not simply a copy of Central European Christianity. Rather, the one Gospel is born anew in each people and manifests itself in new forms and languages and practices just as, even in the beginnings of Christianity, the Jewish Christian Matthew and the Hellenistic Christian Luke recounted the same Gospel differently. Just as we must say to the Jews that in cultural matters they must become Jews again, so also Jewish Christians must know that the German theology they have appropriated will not so readily express the experience of faith that has been given to them. They need a *Jewish Christian theology*, a set of *Jewish Christian customs* that give shape to the life of the Jewish Christian.

If these things are clear, then countless questions will resolve themselves, even though they seem very difficult at the moment. On the one hand the conclusion is that in these circumstances *Jewish Christians in general will no longer be assigned as pastors or church elders in a German congregation*, no more than an Anglican living in Germany or a Negro in a white American congregation or a white man in a Negro congregation. The duty of a Jewish Christian who wants to be a preacher will be first to his own people, to Jewish Christians: as a Jewish missionary or a Jewish Christian pastor, he will himself be drawn to proclaim the Gospel to his own people. The goal and the ideal would be a *Jewish Christian church*. Outside of the large cities, simply on logistical grounds—that is, because of the small number of Jewish Christians—it will be impossible to establish separate Jewish Christian congregations. But it would be good if at least a beginning could be made to establish an organic union of Jewish Christians within Germany.

On the other hand, it is equally clear that making such observations does not in any way detract from *the Christian community given in Christ*. The Christian Jew is obviously, like every believer in the whole world, entirely my brother in Christ; among Christians there can be absolutely no doubt or discussion about this. This in no way absolves us from the necessity of some clear political decisions, which Christians will also applaud. This brotherhood among Christians has nothing at all to do with the political position of Jews as foreigners. This is the point, above all, that the church must insist upon: that civil norms are not simply identical with the church's norms. Wherever and whenever Jewish Christian individuals live and have no Jewish Christian congregation of their own, it should be a matter of course that they should be able to participate in the proclamation of the Word, in pastoral care, in prayer, in baptism, and in the Lord's Supper in German Christian congregations. The church can never deny its right and the duty to serve its Jewish Christian brothers, too, when they have need of it. Moreover, it must also be a clear and inviolable fact that if we had an independent Jewish Christian church, such a church would be our brother-church, for it would be a member of the body of Christ and a part of what we confess and will always confess in the Third Article [of the Apostles Creed]: "One holy universal Christian church."

But let me repeat that all these questions become all the more simple and clear and all the less embarrassing the more clearly *the fatal union of baptism and assimilation is abolished, radically and in principle.* The clearer this is, the greater the conviction with which the church can bring the message even to the Jews: the message of the Messiah Jesus of Nazareth, who is the goal of this people's history with God, and whom Israel rejected and crucified. All the more clearly will the Christian church then be able to speak about what the blessing and the curse of Judaism are, *in the deepest biblical and salvation-historical sense.* The Christian community can and must not forget that this people was once "God's people," that the one who became the savior of the world and also the savior of the Germans came from this people. No German Christianity, so long as it remains Christianity, will be able to erase from its Bible the New Testament word that salvation comes from the Jews [John 4:22].

Of course, a true Jewish Christian is especially aware of why this people became homeless, and why its destiny has been dispersion and foreignness. Here the discussion of the Jewish question is clearly related to the *specifically Christian* shaping of the question, which draws its meaning from a Christian understanding of history and also the history of the Jewish people. It seems clear that this reading of the question is accessible only to a faith drawn from the New Testament. For it, the ultimate solution to the puzzle of this most puzzling of all peoples is this: that this people became homeless because it crucified the one who was the fulfillment of its own history with God. Jesus wept over Jerusalem because he saw the destruction of the city and the curse on his people, but his words were: "Jerusalem, Jerusalem, the city that kills the prophets and stones those who are sent to it! How often have I desired to gather your children together as a hen gathers her brood under her wings, and you were not willing!" [Luke 13:34]

A faithful Jewish Christian understood the essence of his Jewish Christianity when, on the evening of April 1, 1933, the day of the boycott, he said to a friend: "Now I know what God wanted to teach me today. I am to learn that I, too, as a Jewish Christian, must bear the shame of my people and the judgment against my people."

Conclusion

Thus most important points of view according to which the Jewish question can be resolved by Christian Germans or by German Christians have been presented. Here, too, we must attain a clear and meaningful stance. It must not be that the German man within me battles against the Christian man in me; the commandments that apply to one must be brought into harmony with those that apply to the other. I would not be acting in a Christian manner if I weakened my people's justified struggle for its existence by a hair's breadth on

225

purportedly Christian grounds. But equally, as a German, I would be doing my people an utter disservice, if I silenced God's voice. Even if it cost me my life, I must testify to it. For my people cannot and must not proceed, even in the struggle over the Jewish question, without attending to God's voice.

Incomplete knowledge leads to incomplete solutions, and incomplete solutions are always worse than no solutions at all. The most pressing danger for anyone who would master the Jewish question is to imagine that it is not subject to a solution, because any solution would bring injustice and errors and new difficulties with it. This is true of any solution that is only political or only economic or only racial. There is only one solution that can claim to make sense in all of its parts and therefore to get at the deepest roots of the problem, but consequently can also stand up to every crippling counter-argument. This is the solution that touches the Jewish question at its innermost core, as a *religious* matter. Oddly enough, this solution is completely confirmed by the historical circumstances that constitute the Jewish question today.

What is remarkable, however, is that it can touch the deepest and most genuine currents of Judaism itself. It shows itself hostile only to assimilationist Judaism, depraved and untrue to its own mission, to the history of genuine Judaism. Ultimately it is allied with true and devout Judaism, to the extent that it still exists in the world. It appears as if Judaism must be forced by its supposed adversaries to attend to itself and find its way back to the path laid out for it according to the history and tradition it has itself acknowledged as sacred.

At the beginning of April, during the days after the boycott, the following sentences were written by a Jew: "One knows who is a Jew. It is no longer possible to evade or to hide it. The Jewish response is clear. It is the short sentence Moses spoke to the

Egyptians: *Iwri anochi*; yes, I am a Jew. To say yes to being Jewish, that is the moral sense of today's events."[16]

---

16. *Jüdische Rundschau* 3, March–April 1933, p. 2. [Footnote in German original.]

8

Our Struggle

Joachim Hossenfelder

Introduction

Joachim Hossenfelder (1899–1976) was a German Lutheran pastor and one of the founders and first national leader of the German Christian Faith Movement, whose members he called "the storm troopers of Christ."[1] Hossenfelder served in the First World War, studied theology thereafter, and was ordained to the ministry; in 1929 he joined the Nazi Party. He was one of the founding members of the German Christian Faith Movement, which in 1932 brought together several like-minded groups. In May of that year he drew up

---

1. Much of his life story is recounted in Arnold Dannenmann's *The History of the German Christian Faith Movement*, which also appears in this volume.

the original "guidelines" for the movement, guidelines that reflected its founders' Nazi—and Christian—commitments.[2]

Hossenfelder was known as an effective organizer and orator; for many he became one of the most easily recognizable faces of the German Christian cause. Following their victory in the church election on July 23, 1933, the synod of the Prussian church—Germany's largest Protestant body—named him Bishop of Brandenburg. Months later, at the Berlin Sports Palace on November 13, 1933, he was on the platform when Reinhold Krause gave his incendiary speech, which included references to "rabbi Paul's scapegoat- and inferiority-theology" and called for the excision of "Israelite-isms" from Christian worship.[3] The Sports Palace "scandal" led many German Christian pastors to leave the movement; it also signaled a diminution of the movement's public influence. National bishop Ludwig Müller relinquished his "patronage" of the movement, Krause was removed from his post, and Hossenfelder was forced to give up his position as national leader of the German Christians. In 1935 he founded another group with essentially the same commitments, but it never achieved the public status the German Christian Faith Movement had gained in 1933.

Hossenfelder's narrative reflects a number of the pro-Nazi commitments and beliefs of the German Christians, among them the theme of life as a struggle for survival; an allusion to Nordic myths—the Word of God as "faith's Siegfried"; the conviction that 1933 is "a turning point in history"; the alliance between National Socialism and German Christianity in the fight against Marxism; and a long exposition of race as one of the "orders of God."

Our Struggle contains the text of a sermon Hossenfelder delivered at a "Thanksgiving Service" in the Marienkirche in Berlin on February

---

2. See these original 1932 guidelines on pp. 48–51 in this book.
3. This speech appears on pp. 251–262 in this volume.

3, just a few days after President Hindenburg had named Hitler chancellor. The sermon's theme is that, as in other historic moments of need, so too in this one God has provided Germany with the man of the hour: Adolf Hitler.

Unſer Kampf

Von

Joachim Hoſſenfelder
Reichsleiter der Glaubensbewegung „Deutſche Chriſten"

Verlag
Max Grevemeyer („Deutſche Chriſten")
Berlin-Charlottenburg 4, Wilmersdorfer Straße 95
1933

Figure 8. Title page for *Our Struggle* by Joachim Hossenfelder.

Our Struggle[4]

Joachim Hossenfelder

Foreword

At the beginning of 1932 the German Christian Faith Movement published guidelines that would become the basic program for the church elections that took place in the fall of 1932.

This second edition [of *Our Struggle*] has been expanded to include programmatic remarks by the National Leader [*Reichsleiter*], as well as some of the movement's essential documents. It appears as a publication in the "German Christian" Series.

Our movement has today become a powerful force in the life of the church.

We hope that this publication will encourage many to find in their faith the courage to join our ranks as companions in the struggle.

The German Christian Faith Movement

Our Struggle[5]

Struggle is the father of life. That is the law of God that our time bears on its brow. The new Germany and the people of the new Germany have learned together that struggle is part of their life. Wherever people live who are no longer willing to struggle and then, ultimately, are no longer capable of fighting, life fades, and with it the good of the nation. Such people are not able to hold on to the inheritance of their fathers and to hand it on intact to their children. But where a people [*Volk*] still contains individuals who are resolved to see their life as an ongoing struggle, life continues.

---

4. From Joachim Hossenfelder, *Our Struggle* [*Unser Kampf*] (Berlin-Charlottenburg: Verlag Max Grevemeyer ["Deutsche Christen"], 1933).
5. The title "Our Struggle" is an obvious allusion to Hitler's *Mein Kampf* ["My Struggle."]

Many alive today have known nothing but struggle. One may envy or curse them, but they knew nothing else, nor did they want it otherwise. They did not put their weapons down in 1918; they did not belong to those who marched shamefully through the Brandenburg Gate in 1918 to the howls of the Berlin mob. Rather, they belonged to those who, gritting their teeth and balling their fists, committed themselves in that hour, without wasting words, from that point on to dedicate their lives to the reawakening of their nation, and not to rest until a triumphal army marched through that same Brandenburg Gate with discipline and with honor. They have held to this commitment. They carried the destiny of Germany in their hearts. Year in and year out, they struggled; they were mocked and ridiculed. The citizen who thought the most important duty was peace and quiet reckoned them a gang of lost souls. But they bore it all, because they carried within themselves both trust in the living God and a sense of responsibility toward their people.

When we as Christians speak about struggle, though, we know that in the end all struggle is a wrestling between day and night, light and darkness, faith and unfaith, Christ and Anti-Christ. We who belong to Germany-in-struggle have somehow sensed that what has been at stake during the last fourteen years is not just about the sheer existence of a people, not just about economics and politics, but ultimately about the faith and the soul of our nation. . . .

It was all about German faith. Faith lives from the Word of God. The Word of God is [faith's] Siegfried, which stands invisible behind the believer and shields him. Where faith no longer stands beneath the Word's shield, it is dead. The Word of God cannot be imagined or described by human beings; it is a daughter of Heaven, revealed and of divine power. But precisely because the Word comes from Heaven, it must reckon with the world's opposition; the world has always contradicted the Word of God. The Bible calls this opposition "sin." We all know something about this from the history of nations and religions and our own lives. We all know of the human longing to bridge this distance between God and humanity from our side. Peoples and individuals, through their religious cults, their prayers and fasting, have always tried to do this. So it was even more traumatic for the young Germany to see a godless ruling class idealize this opposition to God and lift up sin as the ideal way to live. This was the way of godlessness, and godlessness began to organize, to become warlike and active. It drove a breach into the life of the church. The broad masses of the people were especially vulnerable to the propaganda of godlessness. But it must be said that the cradle of this godlessness was not among the broad masses of German working people, but rather in the camp of the educated, in the German university, where it was taught that faith and knowledge are incompatible. But no matter how conventional the scholar, and no matter how much he showed an outwardly friendly face toward the church, no matter how many people still brought their children to be baptized and did not want to do without church weddings and having the pastor present at their parents' burials, the German worker in all his naturalness and genuineness was forced to take seriously whatever German science whispered in his ear. He severed the tie between himself and the church.

But godlessness succeeded for another reason, too. It appeared in the guise of a prophecy. It proclaimed the classless society, the collective of the godless, as the ultimate goal. Karl Marx deliberately gave his worldview the appearance of religion and spoke of an unholy Trinity. God the Father was the economic relationships that have created everything and are constantly recreating them; the Son was the development that saves, that becomes the redeemer especially of the worker who has lost all rights. And God the Holy Spirit is the compulsive, impersonal will of the masses that shapes the unholy society of a communistic collective. That artist who portrays the people of this time of salvation, the communist people, as a body with a thousand feet but no head, storming around without purpose—he got it right.

The bourgeois world was not capable of dealing with this warlike and prophetic godlessness. It could not do battle with it because it did not understand it. And the front that knows nothing about the other side is always lost.

Two antagonists arose to do battle with Marxism: Adolf Hitler's popular movement and the "German Christian" Faith Movement. Both were determined to fight to the death against unbelief and to wrestle for the soul of the nation. Both National Socialism and a faith movement were an embarrassment to bourgeois people; they were militant, active, and straightforward in their ways and their speech. But that was precisely why they were capable of facing the Marxist underworld, and they were determined to be victorious in the most unheard-of battle in the history of our people.

Because of this the struggle acquired yet another very special character, namely, that God placed this militant generation at a turning point in history. God had brought one era to an end and brought a new one into being. God alone makes history, assigning to periods of time their content and their tasks. God makes history. But He makes it through men, whom He calls out of the darkness of the present and who sense in themselves something of the mystery of God and recognize the will of God for their time. . . .

. . .

Two worldviews are in conflict. One says: Death has the last word in the world. The other says: Life has the last word.

The message that death is the final truth has a seductive power. When the tired, apathetic proletariat hears that with death, it is all over, it seems to them something like redemption. That was the message of materialism, shouted in everyone's face: after your death there is no more life, and beyond your grave no land awaits you. This message had to be not only seductive but also pernicious. A person who hears this lives his life, knowing now that there is only this pathetic existence and no eternal life like what the priests say. He knows now that he has only these sixty or seventy years, and that once he is dead, the game is up. All he has to cling to is this short lifespan. For if this is really all there is, then at least he wants to savor it to the last dregs and call the material goods of this world his own. Knowing that there is only one existence also makes him think only about himself. For him it makes sense to think, "There's nothing more important to me than me." All the consequences of materialism necessarily follow.

If death is the final truth, then any responsibility for the Fatherland dies. Someone with this outlook—that this life is all there is—has to remain indifferent, even in years of destiny like those of the world war, to what the Fatherland is and requires of one. And that was the case. Whether or not the German soldier marched through the Brandenburg Gate as a victor or not, such people wanted only one thing, and that was to stay alive and see home again. And so they welcomed any forces that would bring the wretched war to an end.

If death is the final truth, any responsibility toward the *Volk* [nation] is also dead. People cease to see that the *Volk* is one of God's orders [of creation]⁶, and that people of one blood, one language, one

---

6. "Orders of creation" is a theological construct referring to certain structures or institutions God is said to have established in the earthly realm to order human life; marriage, family, the economy, the state, and the church might all be counted among them. For the German Christians, race—as they understood it—and *Volk* or *Volkstum* were "orders of creation," too, and, because they were established by God, were utterly sanctified.

history form a unity of life and feeling. One withdraws all the more easily from the destiny of one's *Volk* if one lives in the delusion that one could live better and more securely as part of another *Volk*, on another front. Some think others fortunate if they believe they see in the opponent and the enemy of their *Volk* a fellow human being; they are more likely to begin to hate their *Volksgenossen*, those who gladly did their duty in the war. . . .

If death is the final truth, then courage, honor, faith, love, and work all die; then the soul of a *Volk* dies. And indeed this is how Germans' inner life died.

. . .

All of that died, for the message of death as the last truth was seductive and sure in its effect. Over against this message of death we set the Christian proclamation, that the final truth is life itself, that a kingdom awaits us, and beyond our death a life, that the Lord of this kingdom and this life is the almighty God, and that there is a redeemer who has opened our way to this God.

If life is the final truth, then there is also responsibility to Fatherland and *Volk*, wife and child, and then courage, honor, discipline and truth, faith and love, come to life in us again. If life is the final truth, then we can forget the saying, "There's nothing more important to me than me." Then one may live out the truth of the Bible's word: "Christ lives in me."

. . . The creative person . . . gives a face to this new era . . . placing himself under the God-given, creative life-forces of race and Gospel.

Race creates the *Volk*. *Volk* is not the sum of individuals who happen to live in the same area, but rather the community of those who are of the same blood and have the same history. That has been perhaps the greatest experience of our time, that God has caused the *Volk* to come into being. To the state once ruled by Frederick the Great and to the Reich once ruled by of Otto von Bismarck, he gave the most precious gift: the *Volk*. And God has done this through Adolf Hitler, whom we can therefore confidently call the greatest man since Dr. Martin Luther. Now we have a German *Volk*, and out of our faith we say that this German *Volk* is God's will and order. We say that race has a particular claim to validity. This claim rejects the concept of humankind as utopian, as set against God. We recognize the creative will of God anew: God wants race and peoples [*Völker*], wants people to remain with their kind, to grow there, and to take their worth from it. In blood and in ethnicity [*Volkstum*], God speaks a powerful language, more powerful than in the concept of humankind. God places greater beauty and greater value in diversity and manifoldness than in monotony and sameness. We certainly know that our *Volk* is not racially pure, just as it is not without sin and because it is not without sin. But we know that it is God's will that we generate and struggle to maintain race and kind [*Art*]. It is not, as the Jew maintains, that because of sin the unity of humankind was destroyed and various peoples arose. Just the reverse is true. Where there is sin, a *Volk* forgets and loses its own original nobility, which it has from creation. Even the Germanic peoples are guilty of this sin. Race and *Volkstum* are part of creation. We do not divinize them; they are given to us through God's holy will. On the morning of the new day we face the challenge, that is, to recognize race and *Volkstum* as unconditional values. To serve them is the calling of the new man, and only this service carries the promise of a new life and a future. In relation to God each race has the value that God, not men, establishes. Our pride in our race and our love for our *Volkstum* do not carry with them contempt for other races. We respect those races that respect themselves, and all peoples who want nothing more, in face of the creative will of God, than to be who they are, are a blessing to other peoples.

Where the same blood is found, there, according to God's order, is a *Volk* . . . [along with] the same language, the same history, and the same home. The sacredness of language is demonstrated by the fact that we can pray only in our own language. In the languages of other peoples we can accomplish a great deal, even pursue the highest and most successful policies, but we can speak to God only in our own language. To this we can add the pride we have in our history and the love for our home. We want to be nothing more than a German *Volk*. . . .

The *Volk* gives today's faith its real meaning. Christ wants to encounter the German *Volk*, the structured ordering of all German people in which one loses oneself for others.

If race and *Volkstum* shape the *Volk*, then the Gospel shapes the community [*Gemeinde*]. This is the goal of the German Christian Faith Movement, to create the church as community by recognizing the creative power of life. "Church" is not the sum of Christian individuals, but rather the community of those who have been grasped by the Gospel. In the Gospel God does not speak to us only as he does through blood and *Volkstum*; in the Gospel he reveals himself to us.

To have God is to have something over one to which one is simply bound (Luther, *Large Catechism*). Power and sovereignty are fundamental to God. He is our Lord, who stands over us, over all our thinking, over all our searching, over all our theology. He is therefore the invisible God. A visible God would be the servant of our thoughts and our mind. We cannot come to him; he comes to us. His coming is revelation. Christianity is wholly a matter of revelation. God reveals himself to us in the Gospel, in Jesus Christ. The Gospel is therefore not "religion"; it is more than religion—it is a response to religion. Religion is a particular, human way of living and believing, a longing and seeking after God and salvation, a glimpse of another, better world. Human religion is the proof that a human being knows in his deepest recesses about a lost life that is bound to God, about time and the land of Paradise, and that he has not forgotten this life during his thousands of years of wandering, but rather continues to dream of it, search for it, and fight for it. We do not know the religion of the individual man, nor that of humankind. But we do know the religions of the nations [*Völker*] and therefore we know that they are closely bound up with race and *Volkstum*, that is, they are type-specific. Attitudes toward God and the quest for God differ from one particular people to another and remain different. The religious disposition of Indians is different, as is that of the Chinese, as is that of the Negroes, as is that of the Semites, as is that of the Nordic people. This is what was intended in the order of creation, and any attempt at homogenization contradicts the will of God and results in a *Volk*'s loss of its soul. Even though the quest for God is different from one *Volk* to another, God's response is unique and absolute. God speaks to all peoples [*Völker*] in the Gospel. Jesus commands his disciples to take the Gospel to all nations [*Völker*], and his great apostle knew, as he preached the Gospel, that he must not destroy the *Volkstum* of the particular *Volk* and that he must start with the religious disposition of each *Volk*. How can a *Volk* understand God's answer if it is taught to forget its own question about God and abandon its attitude toward God? What is tragic among our *Volk* is that in our proclamation of the Gospel, the power of all powers of life, in German schools and churches, we always start with the religious quest of the Jews. We introduce our children and our people in the pews to the foreign Jewish attitudes toward life and faith, and we should not be surprised when our people, alienated from their own proper questions and faith-attitudes, do not understand God's response or take the Gospel seriously. We see, and we demand, that a distinction be made between the Old and the New Testament. What is [Jewish] *Volk*-religion and [Jewish] *Volk*-history in the Old Testament does not belong in our Protestant churches and in our German schools, but what is prophecy and God's response [in the Old Testament] is the eternal inheritance of all peoples, including ours. We must learn to forget the culture and way of life of a people that is in this respect far below the level of our [German] *Volk*, a people whose worship is bound up with the physical and the sexual. The Jewish covenantal sign and taking of oaths are associated with sexuality.[7]

The Gospel's power of life carries within itself its claim to validity. Liberalism and intellectualism criticize this claim, subvert the Gospel, and empty it of its value. We demand pure preaching of the Gospel. The visible sign of the Gospel is the cross of Golgotha, which has always been the sign of victory for Christians. Under this sign German Christianity, too, will overcome the demonic powers of liberalism and Marxism and sanctify itself in both custom and ethnicity [*Volkstum*]. Against everything that is artificial, against all theology, we set the divine, the unimaginable: the Gospel. The Gospel is revealed in Word and Sacrament. That we are permitted to be preachers and hearers of this Word is something we cannot comprehend, but it is essential to the life of the new man. Just as our politics is Germany, and our culture is race, so also our religion is Christ. Without him we can do nothing, with him everything. With him we will wrench our *Volk* up out of the abyss. We want to

7. The reference is to male circumcision (the covenantal sign), and probably to the oath in Gen. 24:2-3; cf. also Numbers 5.

be German Christians who seek God and fight for God in our own God-given way, who as people of this world want to be grasped by the Gospel and sanctified by their *Volkstum*, and who as people whom God has declared righteous await another heaven and another earth.

We call upon the German people in this last hour to submit itself to the will of God, who speaks to us in our *Volkstum* and reveals himself in the Gospel.

You people of Luther, hear the Word of the Lord, be devout and German, and the living God will provide your children their daily bread for this and the next world!

When Germany can no longer survive, then Luther must arise.

Service of Thanksgiving, February 3, 1933, Marienkirche, Berlin

Text: I Corinthians 15:57

"What a turn of events through God's providence!" This was the telegram the old king sent his wife after the *victory at Sedan*. This was the deep conviction of the whole German people during the war of 1870–71 and after its glorious ending: God has helped us. This was the faithful conviction of German preachers in German chancels, and this is what they preached: God has given us the victory through our Lord Jesus Christ. . . . It was harvest time then, and the duty to give thanks for the harvest lived in the hearts of all.

In the lives of nations there are times to sow and times to reap. Sixty-two years ago such times of sowing and reaping arose for us Germans, times that could not have been more joyful, prouder, or brighter. The whole of the German people was behind the German empire ruled by the Kaiser. . . . It was a day of fulfillment . . . and sovereign and *Volk* both confessed: God has given this to us through our Lord Jesus Christ.

243

Christ was the Lord of this history and is the Lord of all history. Wherever God deals with nations and peoples, he acts through Christ. Christ makes history through men he calls. In times of need he has always given our German people men who appeared to them as miraculously sent, and who themselves sensed something of the mystery of God that was within them and acted through them.

We remember another moment in our German history: late summer of 1914, and a murmur went through the forests of East Prussia, a groaning sprang from the soul of the Masurian lakes.[8]

A nation in crisis; a people in crisis. . . .

. . . Great God, help us! The borderlands are in flames!

God sent the man who became for East Prussia a Saint Michael . . . and the Kaiser sent him to the bloody-red border. For ten days the more-than-human battle continued. In inexpressible anxiety, the heart of East Prussia waited, but after ten days the jubilant news rang out: the Russian army had been defeated at Tannenberg.[9]

Tannenberg was defeated, the Russian dragon shot in the heart, driven back into the Masurian lakes and swamps. And with the name Tannenberg, the name of the man who had made Tannenberg possible also rang out. This man was Hindenburg.

Confidence in him built a spiritual wall around Germany: from the coasts of Flanders as far as the blue Adriatic, from the hot sands of Asia Minor to the icy Daugava.[10] A Siegfried Line such as the world had never seen: the Hindenburg Front.[11]

---

8. The Masurian Lakes Plateau, with more than 4,000 lakes, is located in the northern part of Poland. From September 9 to 14, Germany and Russia fought each other in the First Battle of the Masurian Lakes; the Germans won this battle.

9. This battle actually took place close to Allenstein; an aide to General Erich Ludendorff suggested naming it after Tannenberg, in the interest of Pan-German ideology, to counter the defeat of the Teutonic Knights at the Battle of Grünwald (Tannenberg) in 1410.

10. The Daugava River (in German: Düna) flows through present-day Russia, Belarus, and Latvia, and drains into the Gulf of Riga, an arm of the Baltic Sea.

From this recollection our gaze turns to the last fourteen years. All there is to say about these years can be said quite simply: *Of the Reich that Bismarck forged, the Reich for which Hindenburg wielded his sword for four long years, all glory has faded and been trodden underfoot.*

Once again a groan goes through the forests of Germany, and the wounded soul of the German people murmurs aloud. Heavily armed enemies on our borders, a pestilential cloud of lies, meanness, and alien rudeness upon the land, a swamp that breathes out a thousand death-dealing bacteria. A crisis like no other reigns in our land, and our faith in German life threatens to collapse. But when a people's faith in life collapses, all is lost; then faith in death reigns; then there is death. Faith in death is a seductive power. It robs life of all seriousness and all sense of responsibility, a people of any future. If death is the last word . . . then it makes no more sense to stand up with all you have for what should be and what endures. If death is the last word, then the fate of the other and of the neighbor become a matter of indifference, then one thinks only of oneself . . . .

Faith in death has lorded it over us, and the international powers that up to now have ruled in Prussia and in Germany have proclaimed it, since they themselves can live only as long as Germany languishes. Faith in death has created godlessness, infamy, joblessness.

In this time of crisis—when what has been at stake is not just bare existence but much more, the soul of the German people—*God fashioned for himself a man, one of the millions who fought in the world war, and gave him the greatest mission in our history*: to draw the German people up out of despair and to give them faith in life again. . . . In his sense of mission he dares great things, and he turns those who have despaired and those who have failed into believers again. He gathers

11. The original Siegfried line, a line of defensive forts and tank defenses, was built by Germany in northern France during World War I; it should be distinguished from the defensive line Adolf Hitler built between 1938 and 1940.

around himself an army of millions who know only one thing about him: God has sent you to us. Because you believe, we also want to believe again; because you struggle, we also want to struggle, so that the sun may rise over Germany.

Wasn't it foolishness to keep on believing? Weren't the vultures already circling over the once-so-royal body called Germany, preparing to devour it? Hadn't the thirty pieces of silver, the Judas-bribe to betray the German soul, been cast down a hundred times and picked up a hundred times? . . . Was the German soil still capable of bearing a leader sent and blessed by God? . . .

. . .

. . . Even just a few days ago one could hear the anxious question, "When will Germany's time of trial be over; when will God intervene?" And with this question, the prayer, "Lord, help us!" Then at last, on January 30, came the hour: *the old Marshal Hindenburg called the leader of the young, struggling Germany to take the reins of government.* Just as the Kaiser called him during a time of greatest crisis, so in this moment he called the best man imaginable, a man shaped in a mold made of purity, piety, energy, and strength of character: *our Adolf Hitler.* It was a day of fulfillment, an auspicious hour, as the battalions of the brown army, together with the old front-line soldiers, marched through the Brandenburg Gate to greet the Marshal of the World War and the *architect of the Third Reich.* Faith in life has triumphed.

. . . Once again God gives us the opportunity to build a stately house; once again, God calls the German people into its history. God grant that we all hear his call and obey it! . . .

. . .

This is the heroism that the Führer has required of us during the struggle of the last thirteen years, and this is the heroism that as Chancellor he now requires of every German man and every German woman. If the war we fought was sacred, so also is the hour God has given us. He is worthy of honor, blessing, and praise. We can only thank him and ask him to watch over us.

It is the Prussian and German spirit to receive the victory from God's hand, and this victory, too—over the powers of death—we receive from God's hand, and give him thanks in the words of our text: "But thanks be to God who gives us the victory through our Lord Jesus Christ!"

The Fundamentals

Why the German Christian Faith Movement?

1. We strive for the unification of all regional churches [Landeskirchen] in one German National Protestant Church [Reichskirche] with strong leadership, a uniform administration, and a uniform order of worship.
2. In this church the eternal truth of God, which Christ brought, should be preached in a language and a style that are intelligible to the German soul.
3. The Savior shall be the leader and shaper of the awakening German will to freedom, as its heroic soldier, helper, and champion, even unto death.
4. Reliance on God, consciousness of responsibility, a will to freedom that rejoices in victory: these are to be taught and preached by a pastorate that fights on the front line under energetic leadership.

5. The battle is being waged for the unconditional truth of the Savior against all subversive powers, especially at this time against Marxism, Bolshevism, and Judaism.

6. To fight on behalf of race and *Volkstum* is a newly recognized duty and a serious task.

7. The church should be the state's strong helper in internalizing and in strengthening the legacy of German *Volkstum* in the spirit of truth and the love of Christ.

We want no new "party"; the age of parliamentarianism is over, in the church as well [as in the civic realm].

We want a strong movement that renews the people of the church and its leadership with the power of life.

The current church leadership is too soft and not aggressive enough; it was wrong to make a deal with the Marxist-Ultramontanist government of Prussia.

We want a combative church, courageous in faith, that brings strength and comfort, joy and freedom to the German people of this new era,

that has decisive influence on the whole spiritual disposition of our *völkisch* experience,

that is tightly bound together with our *Volkstum*, with all of its spirituality,

that we love, and that loves us.

Protestant men and women, join the German Christians.

Build the congregation, and you build the church.

9

Speech at the Sports Palace in Berlin

Reinhold Krause

Introduction

On Nov. 13, 1933, Dr. Reinhold Krause (1893–1980), a high school teacher, a committed Nazi Party member, and the forty-year-old *Gauobmann,* or [Berlin] district leader of the German Christian Faith Movement, spoke to an audience of 20,000 packed into the huge Sports Palace in Berlin. The stenographers who transcribed the speech noted in parentheses the audience's frequent and enthusiastic responses to Krause's performance. Detailed newspaper reports subsequently informed millions more within Germany and abroad.

Krause begins by calling for the "completion of the German Reformation in the Third Reich"; Luther, he claims, "[strove to] . . . altogether [abolish] the institutional church as mediator between

God and humanity." The creation of a genuine "people's church" [*Volkskirche*] can occur only now that National Socialism has come to power in Germany; this new church's one mission is "to reshape our German people without exception and to the depths of their souls into German National Socialists." This requires that the church "liberat[e itself] from the Old Testament with its Jewish reward-and-punishment morality [and] its stories of cattle-dealers and pimps"; it must reject "the rabbi Paul's scapegoat- and inferiority-theology." German Christians must "return to the heroic Jesus" and lift him up as the "fearless combatant" rather than the "Crucified One."

Krause himself was not a very important figure in the German Christian movement, but the Sports Palace rally, and his speech, had important consequences for the movement. Doris Bergen writes that it "sparked a wave of departures from German Christian ranks . . . [and] precipitated a shake-up of the group's leadership."[1] Krause was forced out of his leadership post in Berlin; he soon founded a neo-pagan group, the Faith Movement of the German People's Church [*Glaubensbewegung Deutsche Volkskirche*]. Reich Bishop Ludwig Müller withdrew his membership from the movement and spoke out sharply against Krause's attacks on Scripture and the creeds.[2] The movement's forward momentum throughout 1933 halted, its apparent unity fragmented by the dismayed reaction many within and outside its ranks had to Krause's crude attacks on Christianity.

---

1. Bergen, 17.
2. See "Declaration of the National Bishop Regarding the Events in the Sports Palace," on pp. 265-266 in this volume.

Speech at the Sports Palace in Berlin[3]

Reinhold Krause

Fellow Germans! [*Volksgenosse*] The tremendous experience we had yesterday[4] brought out into the open what [our] enemies and betrayers feared most and what the yearning souls of old and young fighters for a new Germany fervently hoped for: *Germans have become one people* [*Volk*]. (Applause.) What a thousand years of German history could not accomplish, what even Bismarck could not achieve, God—through the strength of our Führer Adolf Hitler—has brought to pass. Our hearts are proud and filled with gratitude that we have not only witnessed the emergence of this *Volk*, but that we have also been able, as combatants during the long years of disgrace, to be part of designing it. "*One Volk, one Führer*," shines from the banners above the streets and the faces of our fellow Germans, and we German Christians would like to have added these words: *one God and one Church!*

But the path there is still a long one, and the Führer has always refused to accept the role of Reformer. Does this mean that we should not follow this path? Absolutely not! Precisely during these days, isn't the figure of the man from Wittenberg standing before us—not a perfect saint, whose accomplishments one regards only as past history, but rather the living Luther who wants to lead the way to the German God and the German Church, who has left us a precious legacy: *the completion of the German Reformation in the*

---

3. From Reinhold Krause, *Speech of Dr. Krause, the regional district leader of the German Christian Faith Movement in Greater Berlin (according to two stenographic reports)* [*Rede des Gauobmannes der Glaubensbewegung "Deutsche Christen" in Gross-Berlin Dr. Krause (nach doppeltem stenographischen Bericht]* (n.p., n.d.).

4. Parliamentary elections took place on November 12, 1933. They were the second under Nazi rule and the first since the passage of the Enabling Act. All opposition parties had been banned or had disbanded; the ballot consisted of a single list containing Nazis and 22 non-party "guests" of the Nazi Party who supported Hitler.

Third Reich! (Very loud applause.) Though Luther's followers, in their limited and confession-bound "churchliness," did not understand that his life's work was a *mission* for his Germans, one he could not accomplish because he did not at that point have a German *Volk*, today, as we become a *Volk*, we are living out the Reformer's ethno-national [*völkische*] *mission*. Today it isn't the theologian Luther, and even less the professor of theology Luther, who interests us, but rather *Luther the German popular preacher* who stands before us (applause), who from the depths of his soul cried out, "*I was born for my dear Germans, them will I serve,*"[5] the man of God who strove to close the profound chasm the medieval church had opened up between God and the German, by returning to the unadorned Good News of Jesus, and *by altogether abolishing the institutional church as mediator between God and humanity.*

Starting from the work of the German mystic Meister Eckhart, Luther came to a personal, inner experience of God, out of the God-forsakenness of an alienating "monkery" into the deep attachment to God characteristic of the Nordic God-seeker. It is true that at first his religious struggle was a personal matter. But like Adolf Hitler, he was not satisfied to have found the path to freedom only *for himself*. He had also to become the leader [*Führer*] for his fellow Germans, a liberator of the German soul who saw, beyond anything written or taught, the ultimate connection with God only in *conscience*, in the God *within us*. The German fighter Luther was always on the side of *the values of German ethno-national identity [deutsche Volkstum]* in language and customs, in home and family, in poetry and music. *All of this*, my fellow Germans, was to him, exactly as *Nature* was, *God's work* and *God's gift*.

---

5. Quoted from Luther's *Table Talk*.

But Luther could not complete this *völkische* mission. His liberating action assumed the law of *Volkstum*. But in those days—as in the Middle Ages—that was still unknown. Protestantism as a movement died quickly, hardening into an emerging Lutheran or Reformed "churchliness." And because Luther found no *Volk*, he tied his church to the power of the princes and the state they sustained. Hence this church was caught up in every state crisis, dragged in each time the state became corrupt, and in the end, with the dissolution of all sense of community, sank into an existence as a mere *"religious association"* in the liberalistic state. Marxism had already set itself, under the camouflage of the notion that "religion is private" to eradicate from the German people, root and branch, all feeling of connection with God, until the day when Adolf Hitler came and swept away this rubbish of alienation, soullessness, and degeneracy. (Strong applause)

Nor has the stormy course of the National Socialist revolution halted at the doors of the church. There was rottenness in Luther's church as well. The emerging *Volk* wants to shape a new church, and so we cry out in these times to the fiery spirit of Dr. Martinus, asking that he help us to complete his work, to create not a Lutheran, not a Reformed, not a unified, not a synodical or consistorial, not a bishops' or a General Superintendents' church, but rather *a powerful, new, all-encompassing German people's church* [*Volkskirche*]. (Very strong applause)

This task could not be undertaken until National Socialism no longer had to fight for the power to lead Germany, but could fight instead *for the soul of the German Volk.* (Applause) Since this soul belongs utterly to the new state, the National Socialist state's claim to total loyalty cannot stop at the church (applause), the church that the state does not want to smash but rather to renew and reshape in its spirit. And if Adolf Hitler is the liberator and savior whom God has sent, then *this spirit is the Spirit of God. The new church can never grow alongside the state, but only within it, and all of the same laws of life apply to the church.* (Applause)

Of course the uneducable and the half-hearted are still standing aside, and while we may see our struggle for external power, in the church also, as concluded and behind us, we see before us a much more difficult struggle against these uneducable and half-hearted people. (Applause)

More than a year ago, my fellow Germans, as we entered into the church-political fight, we very consciously left all confessional matters in the background. Let us be very clear about this: if we had begun by unleashing the argument over confessional forms, we would not be sitting here tonight. (Very loud applause)

So it was right that, in our *Guidelines,*[6] we indicated the *direction* to follow, but created *no new dogma.* Now we have set the direction in which this new church should march. And in this old program there are some things that at this very moment shine forth and can be the torch that leads us on our way to this new church. I am thinking here of only two things that must be brought into this church: *a heroic piety* in the spirit of Luther, and *a Christianity specific to us* [as Germans].

This church now awaits its fulfillment, its actualization in the National Church [*Reichskirche*]. We all know—those of us who were there—what difficulties, what labor pains accompanied the emergence of this National Church, how the parliamentary-legal path that was originally followed turned out to be such an endlessly tedious one, and how the initiatives toward getting rid of it more quickly, which were already in motion when the state intervened during the summer, collapsed as a result. Today we know that this national church is only beginning its work, that it has not done

---

6. See the *Guidelines of the German Christian Faith Movement* on pp. 48-51 in this volume.

what is essential by creating *a national bishop and a national church administration*; instead, it must now clearly, and plainly show the way the internal structure of the church must take. (Shouts of "absolutely right.") We also know, however, that for us Protestant Christians this national church can never create ultimate and binding dogma, but can only be the capacious space, the great organization and facility that sets forth major guidelines. We know, too, that its constitution has its weaknesses. We have already spoken of the concern the *Volk* has expressed regarding a new church constitution. The guidelines have not yet been made public, but I would like here in the name of our Berlin [contingent] to articulate one thing very clearly to the national church: we have no use for a church run by pastors. (Very strong applause.) *We can only have a church that, from first to last, follows the ancient rule: the church builds itself out of the congregations.* (Very strong applause.) And in the midst of this congregation stands the pastor, as a fellow fighter, a comrade in the struggle. *We cannot acknowledge any power in the church to command.* (Applause.)

There are real difficulties in this national church, both small and large. Here and there the thought arises that it is doubtful to derive such a power to command from the basic principles of Protestantism. But I may surely say that the greatest concern has been inspired by the first announcement from the national church: the Peace Decree issued by the national bishop. (That's right.) He provoked in us German Christians a terrible insecurity, and in our adversaries a sense of triumph (That's right! Strong applause.), a triumph, my fellow Germans, expressed in the fact that these people have a new burst of energy (Very true!) and think that when peace is offered them they can respond with aggression. This is what their newspaper, "The Young Church" [*Junge Kirche*], says: "Our defensive church-political struggle must have as its focus that the law for the reform of the civil service, including the Aryan paragraph, which the national synod has approved, shall not be implemented." This is the thanks they give us for the offer of peace. (Shouts from the audience: We don't need any white Jews!) We don't need any Jews at all in the church. (Loud applause.)

We see very clearly the potential danger at present in implementing the leadership ideal of the unconditional submission of the congregation to the pastor, who runs the show. *They cannot—I want to say this very clearly—impose people on us as leaders whom we must inwardly reject* (Very loud applause), *because we do not have enough confidence in either their National Socialism or their German faith. The ultimate ground of Protestant freedom is freedom of conscience. My fellow Germans, this is not a relapse into liberalism, for we consider ourselves, we National Socialist fighters, bound to our Volk and to our Führer.* (Loud applause.) *And if it comes to who rules: we need only one regime, the regime of Adolf Hitler and his advisers.* (Very loud applause.) *We need only one program for our youth, an education in the spirit of Adolf Hitler.* (Applause.) *And most important of all: we now need but one mission: to remold our German people—without exception and to the depths of their souls—into German National Socialists.* (Very loud applause.) *Our struggle has to do with nothing less than the spiritual awakening of our Volk. Our religion is the honor of the nation in the spirit of a combative, heroic Christianity.*

The German Christian leadership in the high offices of the church will have to decide whether they will accompany us through this struggle—and I hope they will—or whether they will allow themselves to be restrained by their offices. The air up there in the consistories[7] (I'd make exceptions of all the gentlemen here

7. A consistory is a court appointed to regulate ecclesiastical affairs in Lutheran regional churches [*Landeskirchen*].

present)—(Chuckles all around)—seems at times to carry some germs from the old days. (Very good! Loud applause.) When they tell us, "Not so fast," then it looks as if the old bureaucratic mold has reappeared (chuckles). Perhaps things would go a bit faster if one could *see past the objections* and recognize that it's really five minutes to midnight. We find ourselves at this time in such a crisis of church renewal that only one thing is of use to us: *absolutely goal-directed work and utterly drastic measures.* (Very strong applause) Sometimes—and here I am in complete agreement with our national leader—it becomes necessary during a time of struggle for the movement to part company with the church leadership. And I say to those who continually reproach us on this account: *our movement is no pastoral association whose members, once they've become bishops, deans, and consistorial counselors, forget their responsibilities in the struggle; on the contrary, [its members] will all stand their ground in our struggle!*

For the Protestant Volk the key issue was not [to write] a new constitution for the church, nor was it [to elect] new Church officials, but rather to complete the völkisch mission of Martin Luther in a second German Reformation, whose fruit is not an authoritarian pastors' church with confessional ties, but simply a German Volkskirche that leaves room for the whole range of the truly German [artgemäss] experience of God, and that is also in its external form as utterly German as one would expect it to be in the Third Reich. (Very strong applause.)

Is this something our national church, our regional churches, can fulfill? Only, my Protestant *Volksgenossen*, if it renounces any mutilation of the religious life, if it rejects any kind of "Christianity on command." The host of those who are coming back to the church must first be won over. Indispensable to this is a feeling of coming home, and the first step in this direction is liberation from everything in the worship service and our confession of faith that is not German, liberation from the Old Testament with its Jewish reward-and-punishment morality, with its stories of cattle-dealers and pimps. It's completely understandable that this book is considered one of the most dubious in the history of the world. It is not acceptable for German Christian pastors to maintain, "We continue to stand on the ground of the Old Testament," while their Guiding Principles say, "Christianity suited to Germans [*artgemässes Christentum*]." For all practical purposes, the one excludes the other.

A week ago the Bavarian Minister of Culture, Hans Schemm, stood up here and said: "For art only one thing is true: remain in the land of your own German soul!" and "Spiritual desolation enters when art and *Volk* are alienated from each other." My fellow Germans, this statement applies a hundred times more when religion and *Volk* are alienated from each other. If we conjure today the spirit of Martin Luther, we should not suppress Luther's position on the Old Testament and the Jews, when he writes: "Therefore let Moses be the law book for the Jews, and let us heathens not be confused by it. The law of Moses applies only to the Jews. The Old Testament is not of God's grace, but the result of human effort."[8] *The Jews are certainly not God's people.* (Hearty applause.)

If we National Socialists are ashamed to buy a necktie from a Jew, then we should really be ashamed to accept from a Jew anything that speaks to our soul, the most intimate matters of religion. (Sustained applause.)

It should also be said here that our churches must accept no more people of Jewish blood into their ranks. We have not only fought against the mission to the Jews, but have also emphasized repeatedly that *people of Jewish blood do not belong in the German people's church* (strong applause), *either in the pulpit or in front of it.* Wherever they are

---

8. Allegedly quoted from Luther's *Table Talk*, but in fact pasted together from unrelated snippets or wholly made up.

now standing in the pulpit they must vanish as quickly as possible. (Shouts of Bravo, applause.)

Our state church must also get busy removing all the apparently misplaced and superstitious stories in the New Testament, and there must be a thoroughgoing and outspoken rejection of the rabbi Paul's scapegoat- and inferiority-theology, which falsified what was a plain and joyful message, namely, "Love your neighbor as yourself," treat the neighbor as your brother and God as your father. It makes sense that the whole line of development of dialectical theology from Paul through Barth has made a brain-teaser out of God our Father. Theology has always sought to separate God and humanity, has repeatedly tried to justify its own existence by claiming that humanity is burdened by original sin, fallen, and must therefore be saved by the church. *We recognize no separation between God and humanity as long as the human does not separate from God of his own free will.* The Redeemer showed us this quite clearly in his Parable of the Prodigal Son. If we depart from the Father, only then do we fall, and if we have the will and make the decision, "I will return to my Father," then we are saved. Kant is entirely correct: a human being must take responsibility for himself; no one else can remove his sins. And it is un–National Socialist to cling to a kind of salvation-egotism, since the National Socialist says: "You, individual, you are nothing, your *Volk* is everything, it's not about your well-being, but about the well-being of your *Volk.*"

The pure teaching of Jesus must again become the foundation of the church. If we take from the gospels what speaks to our German hearts, then what is at the heart of Jesus' teaching comes clearly and brilliantly to light and coincides—and we can take pride in this—completely with the demands of National Socialism. Just think for a moment—to take one example—of the story of the Feeding of the Five Thousand, which for Jewish historians is a miracle, because they cannot grasp that, through the commandment "Love your neighbor," everything that is godly in humanity is redeemed and freed, and that in this way capacities emerge that seem miraculous in their results. When National Socialism issues the challenge, "If each person gives something, each person will have something," we experience in our own time the miracle of the feeding of five, ten thousand, one hundred thousand—yes, of millions—apparently from nothing. (Very hearty applause.)

We must demand a return to the heroic Jesus, whose life possesses exemplary meaning for us, and whose death is the seal upon this life, the resolution of a heroic and combative life in service to the mission his Father gave him. This is also why we must avoid exalting the Crucified One too much. We do not need as our leader a distant, enthroned God; rather we need only the fearless combatant. Our church needs leaders [Führer]; it has a leader [Führer] in our Redeemer. It needs leaders for here and now, not chairmen—a word that was also spoken here some weeks ago—nor "haves," but rather someone who knows himself to be poor, and who out of this same misery can be a leader who leads to God. Honoring heroes must become honoring God.

Sacred sites must be designated in our land. Our sacred sites, enriched by our blood, must be more to us than distant sites in Palestine, for the victims of the struggle for German freedom have soaked this homeland with their blood. For this we want to praise God, feel ourselves bound together with our God. (Applause.) And this is why as children of God we do not want a doctrine of slavery. This is something that the old fighters in the Party have always emphasized to me: we do not want slavish people, but rather proud people, people who feel themselves bound and obligated to what is godly. And when the Führer says the individual needs to trust himself, then we want to understand that in this sense: that when we as God's children feel ourselves obligated to the Father and to our people, we are offering proper worship to God.

So we call for a return to this plain and simple childlike faith as Jesus' joyful message proclaims it, without all of the extras human beings have attached to it. We want our *worship* to be service to the *Volk* in daily life, and we want to have our *worship service* in God's house, within the community, hearing the Word in German and in a German spirit. We want to sing songs that are free from any Israelite-isms. We want to free ourselves from the language of Canaan and return to the German mother-tongue, for only in the German mother-tongue can a person express himself most profoundly in prayer, praise, and thanksgiving. (loud applause)

In this way the National Church and our state church can fulfill the duties we have a right to expect from a *völkisch* church. And the National Church will have to clarify for itself how it will meet this challenge. This will show whether the future church is to be built with or against the present ecclesiastical regime. For the faith movement [that is, the German Christian Faith Movement], the existing church cannot signify fulfillment [of our expectations] as long as it does not earn the trust of the German *Volk* through its actions. Until then the faith movement will remain a National Socialist community in struggle, even if its leading men have become church officials! (Very good! Strong applause.)

We want peace; just as Adolf Hitler wants peace with the world, so too do we want peace among our *Volk*, but only when our goal has been reached, when the struggle for the German soul has found a resolution in a German *Volks*-religion that can give all German people, in the words of Lagarde,[9] the great German man of God, "the air of home even abroad, the guarantee of eternal life in time, indestructible community among the children of God in the midst of hate and vanity, a life on intimate terms with the almighty Creator, King of Kings and Ruling Power, over against all that is not of the divine race."

If Luther were alive today, we may be sure that he would be in the vanguard of this German people's church. In the *Volks*-community of the Third Reich, the community of faith, that is, the community of those who feel themselves bound to God, will grow unstoppably.

Millions of German people reach out their arms in search of a German church, pressing toward the same goal by a multitude of different paths. For us too it is important not to break down bridges, but to build them; not, like Pharisees, to see in others only sinners, but rather to open wide the gates of the emerging *Volkskirche* to all the seeking and all the striving, as long as it arises out of a genuine German spirit.

Then we will experience just how close the relationship is between the Nordic German spirit and the heroic spirit of Jesus. It will then become evident that the fulfillment of the Reformation of Martin Luther means the definitive triumph of the Nordic spirit over oriental materialism. *Heil!* (Long-sustained applause.)

9. Paul Anton Lagarde (1827–1891), German biblical scholar and orientalist, probably the best-known nineteenth-century scholar of the Septuagint, and a violent antisemite whose views underpinned National Socialist ideology, particularly that of Alfred Rosenberg.

10

Declaration of the National Bishop Regarding the Events in the Sports Palace

Ludwig Müller

Introduction

Ludwig Müller (1883–1945) served as a chaplain in the German Marines during World War I, joined the Nazi Party in the early 1920s, and met Hitler in 1926. In April 1933 Hitler designated him Representative of the Reich Chancellor for Protestant Church Affairs, with "particular responsibility for furthering all endeavors to create an Evangelical [Protestant] Reich Church."[1] Both Hitler and the

---

1. From the document appointing Müller, quoted in Peter Matheson, *The Third Reich and the Christian Churches: A Documentary Account of Christian Resistance and Complicity During the Nazi Era* (Edinburgh: T & T Clark, 1981), 12.

German Christians wanted to unite the twenty-nine regional churches [*Landeskirchen*] in one national, or Reich Church. The results of the church elections on July 23—achieved with decisive help from the Nazi Party organization and an election-eve radio address by Hitler himself[2]—brought German Christians into decision-making positions in most of the regional churches. In August, Müller, himself a member of the German Christian Faith Movement, was elected State Bishop of Prussia, by far the largest regional church. After an intense struggle over the position of Reich [or National] bishop, the German Christians succeeded in electing Müller to that position. The national synod at which he was confirmed was called the "Brown Synod" because so many delegates were wearing brown S.A. uniforms. He was officially installed as Reich bishop in a service at the Berlin Cathedral on September 23, 1934.

The declaration below was made on November 14, 1933, the day after Reinhold Krause's incendiary speech to 20,000 German Christians at the Sports Palace in Berlin.[3] Leaders of the Pastors' Emergency League (established in September 1933) and other pastors, including Karl Barth, who were opposed to the German Christians, confronted Müller with a set of demands, among them that he dissociate himself from the German Christian movement and see to it that Krause and several other German Christian leaders were removed from their positions. Müller's opponents assured him that if he did not accede to their demands there would be a split in the church on the following day. Müller agreed to the demands and issued the statement that appears below. (The text of this statement was taken from a 1934 publication.)

2. See Dannenmann's *History of the German Christian Faith Movement* in this volume for an excerpt from Hitler's radio address.
3. See previous document in this volume.

Declaration of the National Bishop Regarding the Events in the Sports Palace[4]

Ludwig Müller

At a rally of the Greater Berlin District of the German Christian Faith Movement the district leader gave a speech and succeeded in getting a resolution passed that quite rightly have caused the most profound dismay and outrage throughout our church.

At this moment I will not go into the speaker's demands with regard to constitutional reform of the regional churches, many of which I agree with and will take note of. I will also leave it to the national leadership of the German Christians to deal with the accusations made against its members. I am speaking here as the leader of the church who is responsible before God for safeguarding the confession, and therefore in opposition to the attacks on the substance of our Protestant church.

The speech included an unheard-of, aggressive attack against the Old Testament, and even the New Testament was subjected to a critique that is not acceptable to the church. It signifies nothing less than removing the Bible from its position as the unique and immovable foundation of the church.

Other views that were aired amounted to a rejection of the Reformation teaching of justification by faith alone, and revived a rationalist depiction of Jesus drawn from the bygone days of liberalism. It was even suggested—which I find almost impossible to believe—that the crucifix be rejected.

---

4. Ludwig Müller, "Declaration of the National Bishop Regarding the Events in the Sports Palace," ["Kundgebung des Reichsbischofs zu den Vorgängen im Sportpalast"], in Constantin Grossmann, *German Christians: A Book for the People: A Guide Through Today's Faith Movement* [*Deutsche Christen: Ein Volksbuch: Wegweiser durch die Glaubensbewegung unserer Zeit*] (Dresden: Verlag E. am Ende, 1934), 95.

I declare that such views and demands are nothing but an unacceptable attack on the confession of the church. The leadership and administration of the German Protestant Church utterly rejects such attacks, just as I am convinced that the active members of our congregations desire to have nothing to do with such a spirit.

I will never, ever allow this kind of heresy to be spread about in the Protestant Church.

I ask the authorities of the German Protestant regional churches, by means of a special decree, to inform their clergy and church councils of my remarks. Moreover, especially in light of the upcoming celebration of Luther Day, I ask that they recall very vividly their ordination vows and official promises, which obligate them to an emphatic defense of the purity of church teaching.

Only a church that practices a living proclamation the true and unadulterated gospel can serve the national community [*Volksgemeinschaft*] of the Third Reich as is pleasing to God.

11

Outline of German Theology

Friedrich Wieneke

Introduction

Friedrich Wieneke (1892–1957) served in World War I, joined the Nazi Party in 1929, and was active in local Nazi politics in Soldin, Brandenburg, where he was also cathedral pastor. He was an early member of the Christian-German Movement [*Christlich-Deutsche Bewegung*], then switched in 1932 to the German Christian Faith Movement [*Glaubensbewegung Deutsche Christen*], with its more profound racialism.[1] Wieneke, as he recounts in the excerpt below, became that group's "national advisor for theology and higher education," its self-styled chief theologian, and one of its chroniclers.

---

1. According to Doris Bergen, for the German Christians, "race" was "the fundamental reality of human existence" and "at the heart of creation." Bergen, 34.

Outline of German Theology was published in the fall of 1933, a year Wieneke calls "a turning point in the destiny of Germany," requiring "a *rebirth of the church*" that can occur "only on the basis of a truly *German* theology." While university professors have now joined the ranks of the German Christians' movement, "what is new and decisive about our movement is precisely that here a people's theology comes to expression." He sees what he calls a "people's theology" [*Volkstheologie*] as a challenge to "scholarly theology"; the contrast helps to document Doris Bergen's observation that the German Christians were antidoctrinal.[2]

The excerpts begin with Wieneke's introduction to his account of this new "people's theology," which in his judgment is well on its way to full articulation. A brief account of the emergence of the German Christian Faith Movement follows, in which Wieneke argues that—far from being "an ecclesiastical sideshow of the NSDAP" (the Nazi Party)—the movement has multiple and deep roots in German history, going back as far as Martin Luther's attempt "to create a German Christianity."

The second excerpt included here comes from Wieneke's treatment of biblical theology. "For us Germans," Wieneke claims—thanks to Martin Luther's translation—the Bible has brought about *"linguistic unity and with it one of the most important preconditions for the creation of the German nation."* Unfortunately, since the Enlightenment, the combined influences of liberalism and "Jewish Marxism" have worked to "tear . . . the nation's biblical faith out of its heart." In the end, Wieneke contends, only "the book that 'preaches Christ'"—Luther's description of the Bible—can liberate "the nation from liberalism and Marxism."

2. Bergen, 44ff.

The last excerpt focuses on the Old Testament, and specifically its "value and . . . binding authority . . . for German faith." This question, Wieneke argues, arises chiefly because of the "tension between the Jewish and the German races," as well as the laity's lack of familiarity with the Bible. Wieneke proposes three reasons "to hold on to the Old Testament": (a) we can see in it an essential part of "God's great story"; (b) those who complain that the God of the Old Testament "has all the deficiencies of the Jewish race" are being short-sighted; the persecution of the Old Testament prophets by "the Jewish people" makes clear that the God of the Old Testament ought not to be confused with the "*view* of God" in the Old Testament, which reflects the anthropomorphizing of God by Jewish writers; and (c) we "read and study the Old Testament because . . . it was the religious book of the Lord Jesus Christ" and "the starting point for the proclamation of Jesus. . . ."

Deutsche Theologie
im Umriß

von

Friedrich Wieneke, Dr. phil.

Oberkonsistorialrat im Evangelischen Oberkirchenrat, Berlin
Reichsreferent der Glaubensbewegung „Deutsche Christen"
für Theologie und Hochschule

1933

Druck und Verlag: H. Madrasch, Soldin

Figure 9. Title page of *Outline of German Theology* by Friedrich
Wieneke.

Outline of German Theology[3]

Friedrich Wieneke

Foreword

"German theology"—*theologia theutsch*—was the title of a book once written at a historical turning point and that helped prepare the way for the reformer Dr. Luther. In contrast to the dogmatic works of the international Roman church, this book was intended for German theologians [*Theologen deutscher Art*].[4] It was perhaps audacious for the writer of this present book to appropriate the same title. But the point of this work could not have been signaled more clearly than by the use of this title.

In this year 1933, a turning point in the destiny of Germany—which has blessed us with a rebirth of the *Volk* [people][5] and aims to cleanse us from all things adulterated and alien—we need a *rebirth of the church*. And this reshaping, which the German Christian Faith Movement is today striving and struggling to bring about, can be accomplished only on the basis of a truly *German* theology.

A few months ago the General Superintendent of the Kurmark, Dr. [Otto] Dibelius, wrote . . . the following: "The National Socialist movement within the Protestant church, as well as the movement called 'German Christians,' still has no theological leadership." The national assembly of the German Christians, held in the spring, should have proved otherwise, as demonstrated in its proceedings and

---

3. From Friedrich Wieneke, *Outline of German Theology* [*Deutsche Theologie im Umriss*] (Soldin: H. Madrasch, 1933), 4–6, 30–36, 39–53.
4. Wieneke's use of "*deutscher Art*"—literally, "of the German kind"—has distinctly and intentionally racial overtones.
5. In its nazified meaning, which excluded everyone and everything the Nazis considered "un-German," especially the Jews, *Volk* could mean "race" or "nation."

its powerful impact. As the national advisor for theology and higher education, I can assert that, despite the participation of innumerable scholars from all parts of the Reich, a really astonishing unanimity emerged in the theological position of those who attended. It is not the impact of individual personalities, but rather the tremendous work of God that all these men felt and that compelled them, whatever their past church-political or theological limits, to enter into a great stream of development. And this stream is called "German theology."

As the leader of the theological work being done within the faith movement, I recognized long ago the necessity of setting down in a treatise the theological wealth we share. I am fully aware that this is but a *beginning* and that future discussions will improve and deepen many things, the more so since many topics in our field are more ably treated by specialists. But we must dare to begin, if the work is to progress.

This work rests on a foundation involving three years' accumulation of documents. It began with the theological discussion of the National Socialist worldview. . . . The honest and serious communications from those who are deeply concerned about the questions having to do with "German theology" have been richly fruitful for our movement. Everyone knows how all manner of lectures and publications have most fruitfully advanced the discussion from year to year. It is a remarkable fact that, over time, many of those who originally opposed us gradually began to take up our cause. And it is not the worst thing about German theology that it has moved forward, step by step, only after scholarly testing. I am thinking here especially of men like [Emanuel] Hirsch, [Karl] Fezer,[6] and others, who are presently promoting our movement in

---

6. Karl Fezer (1891–1960), professor of Practical Theology in Tübingen and from 1933 to 1935 Rector of the University, joined the "German Christian" movement briefly in 1933, but,

very valuable ways, though at the beginning they were quite hesitant. For this reason it should not bother us that in [Leopold Klotz's] collection *The Church and the Third Reich* (Gotha: L. Klotz, 1932, 2 vols.),[7] so many theologians still take their positions on the other side of the [historical] turning point. Most of them are under the misapprehension that the German Christians want to promote a "party-political" theology. Events since the beginning of 1933 will no doubt have taught them a great deal, namely, that what is at stake is the awakening of Germany and therefore the innermost recasting of German theology.

Under the leadership of Berlin pastor Joachim Hossenfelder, the movement of the German Christians has grown by leaps and bounds in just a few months. The call for a deepening of our collective work becomes louder from one day to the next. Here the theologian must work quietly to do his best. Therefore *this text* is structured in such a way as to follow the tradition of our field. It serves a double purpose: First, it is meant to provide the many spiritual and other speakers in our land the theological underpinnings they need, especially those that are essential for purposes of discussion. On the other hand, it is also designed to offer the youngest theologians in the universities an introduction to their subject area based on the experience of our time. For this reason also the structure of the text follows the traditional divisions of theology.

From time to time it has been said that the German Christians have no professors of theology behind them. By now this accusation has become invalid; significant university instructors have joined our ranks. But let us not forget: what is new and decisive about our

despite his association with National Socialism, he cooperated with the Landesbischof for Württemberg to protect the university from being controlled either by the National Socialists or the German Christians.

7. Leopold Klotz (1878–1956) was a publisher and a proponent of "liberal theology." He was active in ecumenical theology and in the peace movement.

movement is precisely that here a people's theology [*Volkstheologie*] comes to expression, one that poses important questions and tasks for scholarly theology. In this regard Richard Wagner's words are also relevant:

> and whether you are still
> on the right track of Nature
> will only be told you by someone
> who knows nothing of the table of rules.[8]

If the work of the professors is added to this people's theology, then the German nation of today will have received the richest and newest of gifts, one that will guide the common spiritual life of the coming generations on their path to their goal.

German theology—may it help to shape German destiny at this turning point according to the will of the One who gave us form and calling and being as a nation, and who alone can make us truly free and sustain us!

Berlin-Charlottenburg, September 1933

Dr. W.

4. The German Faith Movement

[At a recent church conference] there was a talk about how to negotiate the relationship between church and politics. In the context of the discussion a Christian Socialist claimed that the German Christians were actually nothing more than an ecclesiastical sideshow of the NSDAP. Our long-time comrade in the struggle, Pastor Sylvester-Blumberg, gave a noteworthy response, saying that was not the case, for our main idea was much older than the whole Hitler party. He pointed out that since *Luther's* time the attempt had been made to create a particularly German Christianity. In the nineteenth

---

8. From *Die Meistersinger von Nürnberg*, Act 1, Scene 3.

century it was the court preacher *Stöcker*[9] who with great decisiveness raised this call to conscience. A man like *Maurenbrecher*[10] moved in the same direction. The *Bund für Deutschkirche*[11] made the first church-political advance; though it was small, it was far-seeing. We must also mention *Friedrich Naumann*,[12] who, despite his liberalism, made an effort toward a serious German "national-socialist" Christianity. We should also add what are in my judgment the misguided efforts of an *Artur Dinter*[13] to create a German "Spirit-Christianity," or *Alfred Rosenberg's*[14] proposals for a new mystical Christianity in the manner of Meister Eckhart, and let us consider also the serious and profound research of [Houston Stewart] *Chamberlain*.[15] [The work of these men] appears long before the emergence of the [German Christian] faith movement. Finally, the Christianity of the *wars of liberation*, as presented by *Ernst M. Arndt*[16] and *Theodor Körner*,[17] belongs in this series; their "German faith" is more than just an idealistic phrase, but rather a Christianity that never died out and in fact awakened to new,

---

9. Adolf Stöcker (1835–1909), court preacher and pastor, fanatic antisemite, especially influential in late-nineteenth-century Germany.

10. Max Maurenbrecher (1874–1929), pastor and politician.

11. League for a German Church, founded after World War I by Pastor Friedrich Anderson, which sought to build an "Aryanized," Germanic church from within the Protestant churches.

12. 1860–1919. German politician, journalist, and Protestant parish pastor.

13. Artur Dinter (1876–1948), author of *Sin Against the Blood* [*Die Sünde Wider das Blut*], a deeply antisemitic, best-selling novel published in 1917, was an early member of the Nazi Party, later expelled by Hitler, in part because he tried to turn Nazism into a religious movement, which Hitler utterly opposed. Dinter founded an organization in the 1920s that in 1934 became known as the German People's Church [*Deutsche Volkskirche*], which aimed to de-judaize Christianity. See, among other sources, Richard Steigmann-Gall, *The Holy Reich: Nazi Conceptions of Christianity, 1919–1945* (Cambridge, U.K.: Cambridge University Press, 2003).

14. Alfred Rosenberg (1893–1946), a leading Nazi intellectual, wrote *Der Mythus des Zwanzigsten Jahrhundert* [*The Myth of the Twentieth Century*], published in 1930, which was very influential in Nazi thinking.

15. Houston Stewart Chamberlain (1855–1927) was a British Germanophile writer who argued for the racial and cultural superiority of the so-called Aryan element in European culture. His two-volume *The Foundations of the 19th Century* (1899) became a standard reference work for European and particularly Nazi antisemites.

16. Arndt (1769–1860) was an antisemitic German nationalist author and poet.

17. Körner (1791–1813) was a German soldier and poet.

great, and profound life in the World War. We must also mention the work of *Guida Diehl*[18] in the New Land League [*Neulandbund*] of Eisenach, who for eighteen years has pursued in a highly commendable manner a line of thought that in many ways anticipated that of the German Christians. All these efforts go back before the time of National Socialism and allow us to recognize that for a very long time there has been a longing for a Christianity appropriate [*artgemäss*] to us [as Germans].

In any case, it is clear that there was already a "movement" before our church-political group came to be. This occurred quite recently: under the guidance of the then *märkischen*[19] provincial youth pastor [Werner] Wilm,[20] the court preacher [Bruno] Doehring,[21] and most recently the Mecklenburg bishop [Heinrich] Rendtorff, the so-called *Christian German Movement* [*Christlich-Deutsche Bewegung*] emerged. This circle gathered together the first community determined to do battle against Marxism, pacifism, and weak church leadership, and for a positive Christianity. For a period of time the author of this text also belonged to this group.

The German Christians established themselves as a wholly new group, without direct connections to the above-named men and communities of struggle, because of the following circumstances:

1. This was a very large *movement to gather* church people and had to be led by the best men from all parts of the Reich.

---

18. Diehl (1868–1961) founded the nationalist New Land League in 1919 to help mobilize Christian energies in the war effort. She became a prominent leader among Protestant women; after joining the Nazi Party in 1930, she played an important role in the National Socialist Women's Organization. In the early 1930s she endorsed the German Christian cause, calling for a "renewal of faith" based on race, family, people [*Volk*], and Fatherland.

19. The Mark was a portion of Brandenburg that (now) extends from the outskirts of Berlin in the west to the Oder river and the Polish border in the east.

20. Wilm was a youth pastor for the province of Brandenburg and founder, in 1930, of the Christian German Movement [*Christlich-Deutsche Bewegung*].

21. Döhring was pastor at the Berlin Cathedral [*Dom*] and a leading member of the Christian German Movement.

The "Christian-German Movement" had excellent materials, but possessed very little connection to the broad masses and limited itself mainly to winning over prominent circles that had little to do with the contemporary ethno-national [*völkisch*]movement.

2. The League for a German Church [*Bund für Deutschkirche*] certainly bore within itself a deep sense of *völkisch*-ness. But even from the time of its founding it was still influenced by the liberal theology of the history-of-religions school. After overcoming the Enlightenment, however, our church people again want a simple and pious Christianity that avoids liberal experiments and stands on the foundation established by Martin Luther.

3. The Christian German Movement had bound itself too closely to the conservative ecclesial worldview and, in its honorable effort to remain "purely" Christian, did not dare to boldly assume the strengths that demanded to be expressed *politically*. In particular, out of faith considerations it could not decide on a clear theological support for the idea of *race*. Most of those in its south German branch, which had a different view of this matter, went over to the German Christians.

4. During this historical moment of *völkisch* awakening, the lack of one great and self-consciously German church movement of struggle [*Kampfbewegung*] would necessarily lead to religious distortion, which would surely do great harm to Christianity. One thinks here of the influence exercised by the Ludendorffs,[22] Dinter, Hermann Wirth,[23] and so forth, and of the opposition of a Rosenberg and a Reventlow![24] When it comes to them, defense

---

22. Erich Ludendorff (1865–1937) was one of the most important military commanders of the German forces in World War I. He was an early member of the Nazi Party (though he was later expelled from it by Hitler), which he tried to turn into a religious movement. With his wife Mathilde he founded the Tannenberg League [*Tannenbergbund*], a pagan, anti-Christian mystical religious sect that embraced what they called German faith in God.

is not enough; only a complete reawakening of the truth that has been hidden will help.

It must, quite honestly, be admitted that the first truly decisive inspiration to establish a movement of struggle for the reshaping of the church in contemporary Germany came from the *National Socialist German Workers Party*. If anyone takes offense at this, it should be noted that God is also capable of working his miracles in politics. I was also able to provide a modest stimulus by means of several essays and a piece on "Christianity and National Socialism" (1930). They grew out of a question of conscience as to whether I could unite the exercise of my theological office with my concern to be politically effective as part of the NSDAP [Nazi party]. These initial publications unleashed a tremendous battle of opinions among German theologians. Gradually, through subsequent exchanges of letters, I came to know the names of many persons who had views similar to mine: [Julius] Kuptsch[25] from Riesenburg, [Friedrich] Peter[26] from Berlin, [Wolf] Meyer[27] from Aurich, Guida Diehl, and many others. Among the political leaders to whom I had in 1929

23. Hermann Wirth (1885–1981) was a Dutch-German scholar of ancient religions. He co-founded (with Heinrich Himmler and Richard Walther Darré) the SS-organization *Ahnenerbe* [Inheritance of the Forefathers] to research the archaeology and cultural history of the Aryan race. Wirth tried to reinterpret Christianity in terms of ethnic Nordic original monotheism. Ultimately he was forced into exile along with other German mystics who did not support (as he formerly had) National Socialism.

24. Ernst Graf zu Reventlow (1869–1943), publisher of *Der Reichswart*, was a cultural, not a racial, antisemite; he was involved early on with the German Faith Movement and was its deputy chairman from 1934 to 1936. Its anti-Christian direction disillusioned him and he returned to Christianity even before the movement was suppressed in 1937.

25. Julius Kuptsch, a pastor from Riesenburg in East Prussia, was the author of a number of books, including *Christentum im Nationalsozialismus* [*Christianity in National Socialism*] (Munich: Eher, 1932) and *Nationalsozialismus und Positives Christentum* [*National Socialism and Positive Christianity*] (Weimar: Verlag Deutsche Christen, 1937). In 1927 he had also published a book critical of biblical scholars. According to Arnold Dannenberg, author of *History of the German Christian Faith Movement*, he was also at one time Latvian Minister of Culture (see p. XX).

26. Friedrich Peter (1892–1960), an early member of the "German Christians" and bishop of Saxony for a short period in 1936.

27. The reference is to Wolf Meyer-Erlach, who added the suffix to his name in 1935 in order that no one should mistake him for a Jew. One of his radio talks is excerpted in this volume.

presented my personal suggestions, however, there was one who with clarity of purpose, despite his hectic schedule, always and consistently supported them, and does to this day: the leader of the Prussian NSDAP parliamentary delegation, Wilhelm Kube. His name must be mentioned here with the greatest emphasis, for he has become very controversial in church circles. . . . Kube, who himself comes from a church background and who, as he once said to me in a letter, knows how to honor the church for its true worth, did not hesitate to speak the unvarnished truth to the church leadership. So, for example, he appeared at the national conference of the German Christians to criticize sharply the bloodless theology of General Superintendent [Otto] Dibelius, but did not refrain—something the opposition press was silent about—from connecting it with a forthright declaration of belief in Martin Luther's cause. Kube combines in his person the distinctive, basically conservative attitude of a Prussian with National Socialism. He demonstrated his love for the church, which he has always cherished, not only during the time he advised the NSDAP on church matters, but also later, when he worked with the German Christians and became a candidate for the local synod assembly. Among those surrounding Kube, parliamentary representative Pastor Karl Eckert should be mentioned; a long-time National Socialist, he took up the cause of the German Christians energetically and in particular displayed his organizational capabilities when it was crucial to advance the empowerment of the faith movement.

On June 6, 1932, in Berlin, a group of Prussian churchmen called together by Kube founded the "German Christian Faith Movement." At Hitler's request, the name that had been suggested by some, "Protestant National Socialists," was rejected, in order to avoid the impression that this act was driven by party-political interests. From the outset the intention was to use church resources to promote something genuinely of and for the church. The name "German Christians" was first suggested by Hitler. The designation "Faith Movement" came from an article I had published. It is meant to express that this has to do with a call from God and not with a party-political matter.

For a short time the group was led by . . . [Hanno] Konopath of Berlin, who was joined as theological advisor by another Berliner, the young Pastor Joachim Hossenfelder from Silesia . . . . The two men worked together with other theologians to prepare the ten guidelines for which I prepared a commentary [*Die Glaubensbewegung "Deutsche Christen,"* 1932]. In these guidelines one finds the real ancient treasure of the faith movement to which it owes its growth and its drive.[28]

After Konopath retired, Hossenfelder took over sole leadership and chose a staff of fifteen to twenty coworkers. . . . Pastor Fritz Loerzer, one of two brothers who had made a name for themselves as combat pilots, became his representative. I myself was given the position of national advisor for theology and higher education, and with it the task of working out and setting forth the fundamental tenets of the movement. This was not always easy, for many theologians opposed to us, no longer able to obstruct the church-political triumph of the faith movement, attempted to water down our spiritual treasure by introducing a theology that was fundamentally antagonistic, and from that position attacking the "radical" national leadership. The basic position of our militant movement [*Kampfbewegung*] had to be kept pure from the center outward. The national leadership remained unified. Each and every *Gau* [district] of the German Reich was in the hands of a similarly equipped working staff. . . .

If the faith movement wanted to reach the masses of the people [*Volk*] . . . a special press organ had to be created. The national

---

28. See the 1932 *Guidelines*, on pp. 48–51 in this volume.

leadership decided to publish a Sunday newspaper, to which in 1932 they gave the bold title *Gospel in the Third Reich* [*Evangelium im Dritten Reich*]. The paper displayed the swastika and the cross of Christ; initially an unheard-of undertaking, it has become today one of the most important church-political publications, its content dedicated primarily to serving the spiritual rebuilding of the people of the church.

In Berlin from April 3–5, 1933 . . . the first national conference took place—a profoundly significant event in the development of the German church. Around 1,500 men and women, theologians and laypersons, streamed in from the whole Fatherland. There was a tremendous response to . . . all aspects of the gathering. National and international broadcast and press media ensured the widest possible coverage. Individual speeches and the contents of the working group discussions were published as a collection.

The impact of the national conference was not long in coming. In the church elections [of July 23, 1933] the faith movement made an impressive showing. It was absolutely not just the collaboration of the National Socialist district leaders that made the victory possible, but the deep longing that church people have felt for such a long time and pressed for action. . . .

5: The Bible as a German People's Book [*Volksbuch*]

The basis for all Protestant theology is sacred Scripture, and every church and theological movement should begin with a serious examination of conscience with regard to the Bible. Christianity is not just a worldview, nor is it comparable to a philosophy; rather, it is a life-force based on biblical faith. Small minds concern themselves with the question of how one could get along totally or partially without the Bible, or to what extent one ought to remove this or that from the Bible; great and important people, however, have seriously and humbly searched this book of books until out of the richness of its contents they been assured of the wonderful gift of the eternal Word. The Bible has become a global book [*Weltbuch*] whose significance surpasses all the creations of human wisdom and, beyond all cultures throughout world history, reveals that which is most profound and most holy. But—and this is a kind of miracle—for us Germans it became a "people's book" in the true sense of the word at a particular time, certainly at a unique summit of spiritual development. This was the work of *Dr. Martin Luther.*

Before the days of the Reformation the Bible was a reference book for Roman Catholic scholars; it never had a direct impact on the masses of the people, but was always mediated by theological learning. Through Luther this changed. It is no accident that it was precisely in his translation of the Bible that a new high-German *language* [*Volkssprache*] was created for the people both inside and outside the Reich. This language laid the groundwork for popular unity and, in a sense, even bound Catholics and Protestants to one another. *Only a book with this sort of holy content could effect this linguistic unity and with it one of the most important preconditions for the creation of the German nation.*

For this reason the Luther translation of the Bible—even though, in terms of correctness, it may have been overtaken by more modern translations—will always remain the truly *volkstümliche*[29] translation, especially since over the centuries it has become engraved in German hearts through preaching, literature, poetry, music, and science. Without Luther and his rendering of the Bible, subsequent German intellectual life would be unthinkable. Christians of all sorts, intellectuals, masters of the art of sound, poets, idealists, even

---

29. Reflective of the ethnicity of the German *Volk.*

nationalists drew out of Luther's Bible the most profound thoughts and values. Without Luther and his Bible, Lessing, Kant, Schiller, Goethe, and Bismarck would be unthinkable; indeed, it is quite obvious that the present German liberation movement, which has been so severely attacked and opposed until quite recently by Rome in particular, must gain its deepest and firmest hold through the power of the Reformation and the Luther Bible. Even if only a few still understand it today, it must be said that *the Bible is the book of destiny for German Christians.*

At the German hearth the holiest things have always been honored and cared for. This is why the German citizen and farmer have reached lovingly for the Luther Bible and, reading it at family devotions, practiced their own common priesthood. The fact that until the emergence of Marxism—that is, until around 1871—most German families actually read the Holy Scriptures is attested everywhere by copies of the Bible that have come to us from the grandparents' generation, which reveal in an absolutely amazing way traces of enduring use. One need only think of the well-worn old copies of the Bible, especially in the rural areas, that, filled with names, dates, and life-events, have at the same time served as priceless chronicles of family history. Precisely in this regard, we ought to resume a regular recording of family history in the Bible.

How did it happen that this book began to lose its unique character as a people's book? And how is it that, outside of school and church, it is now read seriously in fewer and fewer homes, with the exception of community and sectarian circles? Here we come face to face again with the phenomena that have also distorted and alienated the German character in other cultural fields, namely, liberalism and Marxism.

Liberalism is a foreign weed. England and France may be said to be its home, the place where it emerged as a philosophy of the

"Enlightenment." The fact that some individual German leaders of the past, among them Frederick the Great, Lessing, and others were deeply influenced by it created a spiritual crisis. Gradually it became a part of "proper etiquette." But what had been a meaningful worldview for brilliant minds was trivialized by others. Gradually people came to take childish pleasure in somehow "explaining" the eternal truths, mysteries, and miracles of the Bible. Enlightenment theology sought in an utterly tasteless way to set up "sound human reason" as the center and guiding star of all wisdom. For its part, the Bible—where it even continued to be read—became the object of more or less clever bourgeois critique. Of course, the upper crust continued to have a certain awareness of the power of this book to sustain the people. Therefore responsible people emphasized that the Bible should be kept, at least for *them*. But this people sensed instinctively that those in high places no longer had a heart for education in biblical faith. So in the end they decided not to allow themselves be "dumbed down" any more and demanded that they, too, be included in the all-sanctifying Enlightenment. *This is how the intellectual upper class freed itself from the feelings of the nation*, believing that it would actually be possible to educate the people according to a standard that it did not itself recognize. From this point on, the bourgeois intelligentsia acted in religious matters like a captain who sends his company out to battle, while himself staying behind the lines with his staff. In the end he surely discovers that his soldiers despise his leadership.

. . .

The one thing that bourgeois liberalism gave the people in the theological arena—and which has been of unmistakable value—is modern biblical criticism. The liberal school around the turn of the [twentieth] century accomplished something tremendously valuable, which has also illuminated the truth of the Word. People learned to read much in the Bible with new eyes and to recognize connections that had previously been hidden. At the same time, because this biblical criticism essentially emerged more from speculative than from religious impulses it could not bring blessing, but instead did a great deal of damage, insofar as it filled churchgoers with mistrust of what had once been regarded as a sacred book. Not surprisingly, many people backed away from Bible study, leaving it to the erudition of the theologians. Unfortunately, we must say that during the time of its blossoming, liberal theology—with some exceptions—was not adequately conscious of its responsibility to the people. One sensed that its representatives were insufficiently aware that biblical criticism requires great humility. Moreover, practical theologians were perplexed about how to bring the newly discovered scientific insights to the faithful churchgoer. Liberal theologians too often took on this task too blithely; conservatives simply distanced themselves from the task of transmitting these insights to the people.

Nevertheless, it would be unfair—and it happens all too often nowadays—to cast all the blame for the biblical famine among the people on bourgeois liberalism and its theological representatives, since spiritual piety and reverence for the tradition were too deeply rooted in the mass of the people. There must have been another agent at work in tearing the nation's biblical faith out of its heart; that agent was the emergence of Jewish Marxism.

At the same time that its leader Karl Marx (Mardochai)[30] was, with unbelievable skill, dragging the sins of bourgeois capitalism into the light, mercilessly playing the judge as he did, he also suggested to the masses an awareness of their own perfection and sinlessness. The doctrine of the substructure of sensual-creaturely being, out of

30. A variation on the Hebrew name Mordechai; in the Hebrew Bible, in the book of Esther, Mordechai is Esther's cousin and foster-father. The name of Karl Marx's father, Heinrich Marx, was originally Hirschl Mordechai.

which the superstructure of spirit rises only as a poisonous haze or a fog of romanticism, became the materialist foundation of this way of thinking. The negation of the independent existence of spiritual realities and truths followed as a matter of course. Therefore religion had to be an "opium of the people" and the Bible a book to stupefy the masses. Social Democracy was a bit more careful in its judgments, especially during the time of its unnatural political marriage with the Center [Party]. It wanted to let religion continue as a "private matter." But precisely that word "private" expresses their intention: to "separate" the believing person, and thereby biblical faith, from the people. In practice the Social Democrats stood perilously close to the godless Communist movement, and their leaders were almost all dissidents or Jews. The difference between Social Democrats and Communists, as Doehring once said, was only in tempo.

In its last stages, the German people's political struggle for liberation was increasingly a battle against *godlessness*, its absolute opposite pole. Particularly in the Third Reich that should not be forgotten, given that today Marxism appears to have been defeated. Politically it has been conquered; it can be eliminated only through the Spirit of the living Christ and the Word of the Bible.

Of course, this kind of restoration of biblical authority can be both genuine and a blessing can occur only if beforehand not only theologians but also the people make a break with their acceptance of so-called *verbal inspiration*. Theologians, even the conservative ones, have already outgrown this assumption on the part of our forefathers. But the people still have the sense that what is spiritual is bound up not with the Word but with the individual words. It is imperative that the results of all respectable theological research be shared openly and honestly with the people. But despite all the freedom accorded to scholarship, the German theologian must get beyond the negative and proclaim to simple people what is eternally *positive* in the great book of faith. He will have to tell them that the Bible is really and truly the expression of the divine Word and the eternal Will, under which we temporal beings stand. Positive Christianity is and will ever remain a *biblical Christianity.* "Positive" means nothing other than "fundamental." What is at stake here is the spiritual liberation of the nation from liberalism and Marxism, and this liberation is possible only through the book that "preaches Christ." In any case, this much is true: "no one can lay any foundation other than the one that has been laid; that foundation is Jesus Christ" (1 Cor. 3:11).

6. The Old Testament

Despite what has already been said, the German Christian who has heard and knows from his own experience about the particular nature of race will not be able to free himself from his doubts. When he opens his Bible a question arises that during centuries past never concerned him: that of the value and the binding authority of the Old Testament for German faith. Before the war only a few people recognized the tension between the Jewish and the German races, though many instinctively sensed it; after the collapse this tension produced the most extreme degree of cultural, economic, and political conflict. It also presented a theological problematic that had never been experienced before and is still hardly understood by the older generation. *The binding authority of the Old Testament was disputed in many respects.* Indeed, many described this portion of the Bible as a serious threat to the German sense of morality.

As we think about the wide-ranging battle being waged against the Old Testament, it is worth noting that it is not the theologians, but rather the so-called laity who, for the most part with honest concern about preserving the German character, are therefore raising this issue most urgently. The fact that these people are for the most part unfamiliar with either the church or the Bible makes the discussion with them all the more challenging. Understandably, the specifically Jewish components of the Old Testament, and the interpretations of them that are for us Germans strange and intolerable, have become more widely known through popular compilations and indictments. In the antisemitic literature the positive, worthwhile sections and testimonies of a deeper religious sensibility are seldom referenced, and so they are scarcely noticed by those who have not really read the Bible. Thus the lay critic of the Old Testament knows practically nothing about the prophets and the Psalms, while he has more than enough of the story of Jacob in his head. If we as Germans wish to decide the question of whether to hold on to the Old Testament, we must take these facts into account.

. . .

. . . As long as we consider the Old Testament only in terms of individual stories, we will not understand its meaning. We will feel pressured to leave out the old, questionable stories of Jacob and Joseph and many others as without value, even as morally damaging. It will all be quite different, however, if we start by looking at the *whole*, at *God's great story*, revealed in this book and in the whole Bible. In this way we will recognize how in the Old Testament two threads are spun from the outset: the black thread of sin, which becomes darker and darker the more the legalistic morality of Israel unfolds, until it reaches its darkest depth in the figures of the Pharisees and the scribes—to the extent that here sin itself is made into a religion. But on the other side we observe a golden thread that also begins to be spun even in the first stories and that, despite all the aberrations of the patriarchs, never disappears, but rather becomes brighter and brighter, that later shines forth in the work and proclamation of the prophets, until in Christ it becomes for us the light of the world. These threads, of sin on the one hand and of *grace* on the other, come together and become tangled on Good Friday, in the cross of the Lord, who through grace takes all our sins away.

So it must be said: each story in the Old Testament has its purpose, if we are willing to understand sin and grace in the context of God's revelation to humankind. And the darkest sections must surely be present, for they are the ground from which the divine light must shine brightest. . . .

[Among] . . . the best-known objections of lay groups against the authority of the Old Testament . . . [is this] complaint: . . . The God of the Old Testament has all the deficiencies of the Jewish race and is therefore utterly different from the God of the New Covenant and the Father of Jesus Christ. . . .

When someone today maintains that the God of the Old Testament has all the shortcomings of the Jewish race, it is less a mean-spirited than a short-sighted opinion. A logical error is being made here: "God" is being confused with a "view of God." The latter is, for most people, anthropomorphic. Just think of the ancient Greeks! In this sense it is understandable that Jews would for the most part integrate their Jewish nature into their view of God, and that they would think of the Lord God as legislating and acting in a Jewish way [nach jüdischer Art]. Even the old Germanic peoples, in their pious, pagan songs, gave the deity their own human character.

But we observe that the great men of God of the Old Covenant—Moses, the prophets, the Psalmist, and the greatest kings—learned from their dealings with God to enter into judgment in a way that contradicted the Jewish nature and to emphasize that God is other than what humans imagine him to be. One need think only of the words of the later Isaiah (Isa. 55:8-9): "For my thoughts are not your thoughts, nor are your ways my ways, says the Lord. For as the heavens are higher than the earth, so are my ways higher than your ways and my thoughts than your thoughts."

This is the great experience of the Old Testament prophets, and here lies their meaning for all peoples [*Völker*] who seek God. God does not want to be a plaything of human peculiarities and the highest degree of human virtues; rather, he remains in his solitary holiness as Creator, Redeemer, Lord, and Judge of all the nations. Consider what, for the sake of this proclamation, God's Old Testament messengers had to endure: mockery, persecution, and torment of every kind, simply because they didn't want to hand over the Most Holy God to this Jewish people and its this-worldly ways! This may explain why a university professor once aptly remarked, "Whoever is not yet an antisemite will become one as soon as he reads the Old Testament." I think that [Julius] Kuptsch, despite all his many outstanding explanations of the Old Testament, did not comprehend at depth this significance of the prophetic warriors for God.

Finally . . . one more observation: We read and study the Old Testament because, with all its faults and weaknesses, it was the religious book of the Lord Jesus Christ. During a discussion on this subject among some young people, a young National Socialist once said, "If you want to understand Hitler, you have to know Marxism; if you want to come to Christ, you must first study the Old Testament." In this formulation there is an unmistakable truth. In the Old Testament we have the starting point for the proclamation of Jesus to the people of Israel and the world. Whoever wants to grasp the Lord of all lords and the Redeemer of humankind in his whole becoming and being must be familiar with this book; this was the book to which the boy Jesus owed his first exposure to God's message, whose contents revealed to him as a youngster the deepest need of his people, and whose promises allowed him to recognize that the heavenly Father would send the people of Israel and thereby all humankind a new, immeasurable gift of grace through a Savior, who as his beloved child must live, testify, suffer, and die. *Thus upon the foundation of the Old Testament, the New is lifted up.*

12

German Christians: A People's Book

A Guide to Today's Faith Movement

Constantin Grossmann

Introduction

The technically correct English word for *Volksbuch*, here translated "people's book," is "chapbook." Historically, chapbooks, an early type of popular literature, were a medium of entertainment, information, and (generally unreliable) history, especially during the seventeenth and eighteenth centuries. Popular or folk literature, such as pamphlets, political and religious tracts, nursery rhymes, poetry, folk tales, children's literature, and almanacs were published in the form of chapbooks, mainly to disseminate popular culture to the common people, especially in rural areas. By giving his publication the name *Volksbuch*, or chapbook, Grossmann is calling to mind a romantic medium of centuries past.

Grossmann's *Volksbuch* is divided into sections that deal respectively with the current situation (including the need for and emergence of the German Christians, their positions on the Old Testament and the Gospel, as well as their competitors and antagonists); the most significant documents pertaining to the movement; and what the author calls "German Christianity in the mirror of history"—interpreted as very early Germanic history through the Reformation. These are bracketed by the foreword and introduction, at the beginning, and two brief closing pieces, one on race and one on how to read the gospels. The excerpts that appear below are from the foreword, the introduction, the section on the Old Testament, and the author's reflections on race.

The author contends that the German Christian Faith Movement stands "at the center of the ecclesiastical and religious stirring"—the National Socialist revolution—that is sweeping Germany. Its goal is the integration of Christianity and Germanness, or—what is for all practical purposes the same, from the author's viewpoint—Christianity and National Socialism. Its antagonists are those who "want to leave everything as it was"—the establishment Protestant church, on the one hand, and the German Faith Movement, who "believe that Germanness and Christianity are incompatible," on the other. The audience for this book is "the people," not academic theologians, whose language, the author claims, is unintelligible to ordinary people. German Christians' deep mistrust of the intellect—a mistrust they seem to cultivate precisely on behalf of "the people"—is evident here. "The great experience"—the accession of Hitler to power—is far more persuasive than any argument could possibly be. The author claims that "the Führer . . . the most German man, is also the most faithful, a believing Christian [who] begins and ends . . . his day with prayer."

In the section "The German Christian and the Old Testament," the author provides guidance on how to read the Old Testament. He underscores what he believes are contrasting pieties in the Old and New Testaments. Wherever he finds something in the Old Testament that he as a German Christian can embrace, he denies its supposed Hebrew or Jewish roots, ascribing it instead to Persian influences. "Christianity," he observes, "is the opposite pole from the Jewish religion." While "Nordic" or "Germanic" morality is based on doing what is right for its own sake, "the joy [the Jew] gets from working is connected, in a way that is alien to us, with his obsession with rewards, in this case with the delight in profit." It is crucial, he advises, to read the Old Testament "with a New Testament sensibility and a German heart." And, he concludes, "[T]here can be only one motto: Clear distinctions and goal-conscious de-Judaization of Christianity!"

As may be clear from Grossmann's use of the phrase "a German heart," he is very concerned that the reader "who wants to participate in a conversation about religion today must be thoroughly informed about the science relating race and spiritual matters." So his reflection on race begins with the physical aspect—"What does the German look like?" Racial science, he explains, "has taught us that there are four to six shapes or forms that distinguish those settled in Germany." Thinking perhaps of some of the leaders of the Nazi Party, he assures the reader that what is important "is not that we should all have blond hair and blue eyes; it is rather that we all allow ourselves to be molded . . . by the Nordic spirit of the German culture. . . . Someone can appear really 'non-German,' and still possess the nobility of the German soul because he has decided in favor of the Nordic type."

Grossmann concludes: "There is a Germanic, Nordic perspective for everything—marriage, family, community, the law, the state—morality, art, faith!" While it is "a shame to waste time" on discussion between different types of people, discussion between those "who have made the same kind of commitment is beautiful and congenial." In a Germany whose Nazi government was seeking to "purify" the population by eliminating all who were "different," Grossmann's words must have resonated widely.

Deutsche Christen

Ein Volksbuch

Wegweiser durch die Glaubensbewegung unserer Zeit von

Pfarrer Constantin Großmann

Mit Illustrationen aus der Zeitgeschichte

1934

Verlag E. am Ende, Dresden-U.6

Figure 10. Title page for Constantin Grossmann's *German Christians: A People's Book.*

German Christians: A People's Book: A Guide Through Today's Faith Movement[1]

Constantin Grossmann

Foreword

In my memory there has never been so much to read in the daily press about the Protestant church as there has been during the last weeks and months. The powerful event of the National Socialist revolution has affected all areas of life, and—how could it be otherwise?— it has also grasped the church of the Reformation, German Protestantism, as a structure within society and as the bearer of a faith; it has put an end to the ecclesiastical sectionalism in our Fatherland, and evoked a great discussion about the relationship between Christianity and Germanness [*Germanentum*].

At the center of the ecclesiastical and religious stirring stands the German Christian Faith Movement. "German National Church!" is this movement's motto, and thanks to its determination, it has in a short time made this old German Protestant dream a reality. It appeals and struggles on the foundation of the Bible and the confessions to integrate Christianity and Germanness, Christianity and National Socialism. It seeks to persuade our dear Germans that this bond is both possible and necessary. It likewise rejects both the Christians who see no work to be done here and want to leave everything as it was, on the one hand, and the men and associations who believe that Germanness and Christianity are incompatible and who proclaim a pure Nordic worldview and piety of blood and race, on the other.

---

1. From Constantin Grossmann, *German Christians: A People's Book: A Guide Through Today's Faith Movement* [*Deutsche Christen: Ein Volksbuch: Wegweiser durch die Glaubensbewegung unserer Zeit*] (Dresden: Verlag E. am Ende, 1934), 4–5, 7–9, 46–55, 153–57.

The more intensely the conflict of opinions among these three groups rages, the more difficult it becomes for the non-expert to gain an overview and form an opinion. Consequently we pastors—and not least we NSDAP [Nazi Party] officials, advisors on church matters, and leaders in the German Christian Faith Movement—are continuously bombarded with questions about these things.

"What exactly is happening in the Protestant church?" "What do the German Christians want?" or, more naïvely, "Why 'German' Christians? Isn't that self-evident? Haven't we always been that?" or, "Isn't this a dangerous, heretical movement?" And so on!

When the E. am Ende Publishing House proposed that I write a book called "German Christians" that would provide the requested overview and deal with questions about the faith movement in an accessible way, I saw it as a timely assignment. . . .

I have titled it "A People's Book [*Volksbuch*]." The people, not the theologians, are the audience. Wherever possible, the book avoids the professional language of theologians and contains no discussions with recent forms of theology that are unintelligible to laypeople, so-called "dialectical theology."[2] It deliberately limits itself so that anyone can read it who is moved by today's faith questions and is looking for guidance.

. . .

Dresden, January 1934

The Author

Introduction: The Great Experience

The great experience from which radiates everything we think and do today is

---

2. This is the name given to the theology championed by Karl Barth, one of German Christians' arch-enemies. See his *Theological Existence Today!*, pp. 81ff in this volume.

Adolf Hitler and the National Socialist revolution.

The influence of this great experience touches all areas of life. Everything is transformed, arises with new strength for living to new forms of living. And in a book about religion and church in the Third Reich, too—in the reborn German Fatherland—the first word must be

The Great Experience!

Struck by the internal enemy, betrayed, destroyed, in servitude and shame, we lay upon the ground. There, in the moment of our deepest misery, we suddenly heard a voice: "Germany, awake!"—the voice of a German prophet. "My German people," it cried, "you are not as weak as it seems, and you are not as powerless as you think you are! Within you wonderful powers are sleeping, powers of mind and spirit that you need only awaken in order to find your way out of the abyss—the way I will show you!"

And that one voice of the German future became many, became millions. They swelled to a powerful chorus; high above that choir a clear young boy's voice sounded: "The flag on high, the lines tightly closed!"[3]

In those dark years, as we walked among the monuments to those who had fallen in the world war, to decorate them love's greeting, how heavy were our hearts! No kind thought lightened the gloom of this celebration of the dead, for after all we had experienced, the millions sacrificed in the war seemed in vain; in vain the tears of German men, women, and children who wept for the son, husband, father, brother, bridegroom, and friend who had sunk into the grave.

---

3. First two lines of the Nazi song, *"Die Fahne hoch, die Reihen fest geschlossen!,"* known as the Horst-Wessel-Lied. For all practical purposes, this song became the German national anthem during Nazi times.

But even worse: it looked as if the German people were no longer worthy of such a sacrifice.

But when we experienced how once again: German men and youth were prepared to sacrifice their lives for the Führer and for the freedom and honor of their Fatherland, we recognized: No, it is not dead, the heroic spirit and noble soul of Germany! And as the rhythmic march of the brown battalions[4] rang through the streets, and defiant voices sang out the Horst-Wessel-Lied, which echoed from the walls, and when they came to the prophetic words—"Millions are looking on the swastika full of hope, the day of freedom and of bread dawns!"—we knew with a blessed certainty: They did not fall in vain, the heroes of the Great War and the National Socialist movement. The day will come when these blood-stained seeds will rise in a glorious harvest in the morning light of German freedom!

The Great Experience!

We sink once more into the depths of German misery and shame, the death of nation, morality, and religion. How empty were the churches then! And in those days no Christian song was as timely and true as the heartfelt groan and cry of misery of Johann Philipp Spitta[5]:

> Unbelief and folly boast
> More cheeky than before.
> Therefore you must equip us
> With weapons from above.

In those days to be German and to be pious in the German Fatherland invited ridicule and slander; that was considered laughably old-fashioned, like a bunch of old rags, worth nothing. . . . In those

---

4. The S.A., or *Sturmabteilung*, the paramilitary force of the Nazi Party, whose uniforms were brown.
5. Spitta was a nineteenth-century German pastor and hymn writer (1801–1859).

days any immigrant lad of a foreign race among us could deny Germanness and piety the very right to exist. In those days the community of the German people [*Volk*] and the community of German believers were being rent asunder and scattered to the four winds. In those days millions of German men and women no longer knew what they should think and believe.

And today they know again. The German people has found itself again. In unforgettably exalted hours, under the waving flags of the Third Reich, the flags with the swastika, hearing the words of the Führer—God bless him!—it happened: millions of hearts beat together, illumined and glowing with one spirit, one will, one thought: We want to be what we are in our innermost feeling, what God has made us to be: German to the core, German and faithful!

Whoever has experienced this not just externally but internally knows that behind this experience stood God with his almighty power and his goodness! He has sent us the leader we needed to become a people once again. He has given him a great spirit and a great soul. In his heart he has kept the faith—faith in his people and in the triumphant power of the good. And because of him this faith has seized us too, so that with Adolf Hitler we believe, will, and dare.

This is the Great Experience!

And now it is our responsibility, with the strength and enthusiasm this great experience gives us, to build up our spiritual world, with all our hearts to be both German and Christian, to be German Christians.

This is what the Führer wants. He, the most German man, is also the most faithful, a believing Christian. We know that he begins and ends the course of his day with prayer, that he has found in the Gospel the deepest source of his strength. On the eve of the National Socialist ascendancy, in Königsberg, and repeatedly since then, he has confessed his faith and admonished the German people: "Everything rests in God's blessing," and "If the Lord does not build the house, the builders work in vain."

National Socialism and Christianity are deeply related to one another. "The common good before the private good." [and] "You are nothing, your people is everything": these are mottos that breathe the Christian spirit of brotherly love, the willingness to sacrifice, the spirit of the Lord's Prayer.

No wonder, then, that never since the time of the Reformation has the German people seen such a powerful faith movement—part of an all-encompassing spiritual movement—as the one within our ranks today. But we are also reminded of the time of the Reformation because conflicts are arising within the faith movement, now as they did then, and spiritual struggles are aflame. In the midst of these struggles, embattled on the right and the left, stand the German Christians.

Our task will be to provide the reader with an overview and an evaluation of what is happening.

. . .

The German Christian and the Old Testament

According to an old proverb, "Just try to take the first step correctly; the remaining steps will happen by themselves." The correct first step in the question of German faith is beyond all doubt . . . the de-Judaization of Christianity. "In the year 1847," according to Chamberlain,[6] "Prince Bismarck demanded emancipation from the Jews. Only religious emancipation would be definitive . . . If we were

---

6. Houston Stewart Chamberlain (1855–1927) was a British Germanophile writer who argued for the racial and cultural superiority of the so-called Aryan element in European culture. His two-volume *The Foundations of the 19th Century* (1899) became a standard reference work for European and particularly Nazi antisemites. Grossmann's supposed "quotation" from Chamberlain is, rather, a very loose paraphrase of his ideas.

to succeed in removing the Semitic element from our religious life, we would be born anew."

Here the German raises the strongest objections, and in this matter . . . all the earlier champions of German piety are united, both the moderates and the radicals. . . . This is the point at which the lever must be applied. Everything else can be dealt with later.

So we must dedicate a special section to the position of the Christian in relation to the Old Testament.

The foundations of religion for the Semites and their half-brothers, the Jews, are unique historical events. For Israel that event is the making of the covenant at Sinai. Religion is a contract between YHWH and his "chosen people"—and indirectly with the individual members of this people, somewhat like a business contract.

Both parties commit themselves to certain contractual duties. The human party binds himself to obey a series of cultic and moral commandments. In return, YHWH promises the people of Israel that they will have earthly success, good fortune, world domination, an image that is not exactly philanthropic. Psalm 2 [vv. 8-9]: "Ask of me, and I will make the nations your heritage, and the ends of the earth your possession. You shall break them with a rod of iron, and dash them in pieces like a potter's vessel." And he likewise promises the individual Jew who follows the commandments that he will supply him with earthly good fortune and give him a long life, wealth, the blessing of children, and that sort of thing.

In keeping with this Jewish understanding, misfortune is always a just punishment for disobeying the commandments, violation of the contract. Otherwise all would go well for the individual or the people.

As the battered Job sits in deepest misery, his friends come to visit, "to show their sympathy and to comfort him." They sit down with him, weep, tear their clothes, and throw dust toward heaven

304

and upon their own heads. But their consolation is imbued with a search for secret sin; and insofar as they overcome this common Jewish viewpoint—Job is, after all, the book that focuses on this—their wisdom tells them that the evil situation will necessarily take a turn for the better.

> Think now, who that was innocent ever perished?
> Or where were the upright cut off?
> As I have seen, those who plow iniquity
> And sow trouble reap the same.
> By the breath of God they perish,
> And by the blast of his anger they are consumed. [Job 4:7-9]

The tragic destruction of an innocent, which happens thousands of times, is for them unthinkable.

This is not a New Testament point of view. In response to the very Jewish question of the disciples about the man born blind (John 9:2), "Master, who sinned, this man or his parents, that he was born blind?" the Lord says, "Neither this man nor his parents sinned."

Misfortune can be the result of sin, and often the connection between guilt and suffering is obvious. The folk wisdom is right: . . . "You've made your bed, now you must lie in it." "As a man sins, so will he be punished." But misfortune need not be punishment. . . . To seek refuge in God when one suffers; to feel protected in him; to have the experience that "all things work together for good for those who love God" [Rom 8:28]: this, and all that flows from this knowledge, is Christianity.

But during these fateful years since 1914, how many people have gone astray in their faith because through the traditional use of the Old Testament as something of equal value with the New Testament a kind of "double religion," a dismal mixture of Old Testament and New Testament perspectives, has made its home in their heads and hearts—because they have been responding to destiny's call out of a sense of the Old Testament that is both sub-Christian and not Nordic, a sense not yet expunged from their souls!

Love of destiny is Nordic because in its storms, as nowhere else, one can prove one's heroic character. Defiance is Nordic: defiance, which with gritted teeth fights to the last breath before allowing destiny to crush it.

And when misfortune becomes too much to bear, so that despite heroic efforts we are on the brink of defeat? Then the Old Testament does not help at all, but only Christianity in its purest form, the religion that according to Master Goethe's description knows how to blend "powerlessness and poverty, mockery and contempt, slander and misery, suffering and death" into the unity of divine necessity, that teaches one how to bear and overcome these things in God and, as Goethe writes in *Wilhelm Meister* . . .[7]

We see that in relation to this question—the question of destiny—Christian and Nordic character are not one and the same. But there is a bridge between them. In contrast, Nordic and Jewish characters are utterly incompatible.

The approach to this goal is not absent even from the Old Testament. Psalm 73:

And there is nothing on earth that I desire other than you.
My flesh and my heart may fail,
but God is the strength of my heart and my portion forever. [Ps 73:25-26]

But this is an isolated trace and, as Friedrich Delitzsch[8] has rightly shown, this psalm has been subjected to non-Jewish influence. . . .

---

7. The reference is to Johann Wolfgang von Goethe, *Wilhelm Meisters Lehrjahre*, Book II, Chapter 1.

8. Franz Delitzsch (1813–1890), a Lutheran theologian, was a noted Hebraist who made what is still the standard translation of the New Testament into Hebrew, a book originally intended for proselytizing among Jews. However, Delitzsch was a defender of the Jewish community in Leipzig against anti-Jewish attacks.

. . . Delitzsch points at the same time to another deficiency in Jewish–Old Testament piety: it knows of earthly goods, but not the eternal good, immortality, involving the union of natures between God and the soul.

With a sweet naïvete Luther read his Christian faith into the Old Testament. "I know that my redeemer lives, and that at the last he will raise me from the earth; and thereafter, clothed in this my skin, in my flesh I shall see God." (Job 19:25-26). In reality that is not what the text says. (Given the struggle over the Hebrew language at the time of the Reformation, this error in translation of a passage that remains in dispute is of course understandable.) But what does it really say? Nothing about the church teaching of the "resurrection of the body," but rather this: "I know that my redeemer lives, and in the end he will rise from the dust. And after this my skin has been destroyed, I will see God without my flesh." So: a fearfully broken man's vision of an appearance of God! Even if it were translated somewhat differently, it would remain very much within the bounds of the here and now!

Likewise, some passages in the Psalms in which one might find the dawning of the concept of immortality are of uncertain meaning or are clearly already under the influence of Iranian intellectual culture—for example, Psalm 16:10: "For you do not give me up to Sheol, or let your faithful one see the Pit"—or Psalm 49:16: "But God will ransom my soul from the power of Sheol."[9] That influence is first fully obvious in Daniel 12.

In the Old Testament writings that came into being before the Israelites became more closely acquainted with the Persian religion, there is no mention of immortality. They know only the joyless shadow existence of the underworld (Sheol). That is where one goes when one is "gathered to his fathers," and one is removed, for good or ill, from the influence of YHWH, who can take revenge only on

9. Ps 49:15 NRSV.

the descendants. Psalm 6:6: "For in death there is no remembrance of you; in Sheol who can give you praise?"[10]

We make note again of the contrast with New Testament piety, culminating in the words at the raising of Lazarus: "Those who believe in me, even though they die, will live, and everyone who lives and believes in me will never die" [John 11:25b-26a]. Death is only an illusion, like the setting of the sun, reflected on the screen of mortality. The metaphysical ("supernatural") in us does not know death. Like the sun it lives and shines on and on.

Here, too, Christianity is the opposite pole from the Jewish religion. Arthur Schopenhauer[11] explains that Judaism, because its most basic teaching is creation out of nothing, cannot logically teach immortality, and for this reason cannot be included among the higher religions.

A third shortcoming in Jewish piety: crass addiction to rewards! Those who know nothing of immortality must concentrate on the here and now. Eastern spirituality strengthens this understandable drive toward a sense of religious relationship as a kind of business deal, which necessarily poisons piety altogether.

And, as everyone knows, this is precisely what the Savior combats repeatedly and in the sharpest terms: in the story of the prayer of the Pharisee and the tax collector in the Temple; in the parable of the workers in the vineyard; in the parable of the attentive servant. "Do you thank the slave for doing what was commanded? I do not think so. So you also, when you have done all that you were ordered to do, say, 'We are worthless slaves; we have done only what we ought to have done!'" [Luke 17:9-10] This runs through Jesus' preaching like a scarlet thread.

---

10. Ps 6:5 NRSV.
11. Schopenhauer (1788–1860) was a German philosopher.

This Jewish addiction to rewards clings even to the most beautiful old Hebrew poetry. We need think only of Psalm 23, the glorious song of God's faithfulness as a shepherd: "The Lord is my shepherd; I shall not want." Even here we find a trace of addiction to rewards, and ultimately an attachment to scorn and spitefulness: "You prepare a table before me in the presence of my enemies (or: against my enemies)"—that is, so that they see it and are annoyed.

We don't think about it this way if we read this psalm with a New Testament sensibility and a German heart. The Christian preacher associates these words with the table of the Lord's Supper, and the enemies are the evil powers in the world and in human hearts. But this is a Christian reinterpretation. The historically correct clarification of this saying is a passage like Psalm 112:10: "The wicked see it and are angry; they gnash their teeth and melt away." Here again speaks a man who knows of nothing more lovely than—as is said in Psalms 37, 54, 92, and many others—to "look in triumph on his enemies" and who is thinking of religion as a business relationship: "You prepare a table before me . . . you anoint my head with oil and my cup runs over" [Ps 23:5], as for an honored guest; in other words: you keep the bargain. And I keep it, too: "And I will live in the house of the Lord forever" [Ps 23:6].

That such an addiction to rewards is altogether un-Nordic needs no proof. What is Germanic is this: to do what is right for its own sake, without concern for success, reward, or fear of punishment.

> To do the good for pure love of the good,
> Leave that to your blood!
> And if it doesn't benefit your children,
> It will be good for your grandchildren. (Goethe)

Which is to say: When a Nordic person considers the consequences of a good act he thinks about its blessings for his race; it is an expression of awareness of the moral meaning of life and his duty to those who come after, free from any attachment to reward.

This is also how Luther understood life: "Yes, if they (the faithful) did what is right in order to gain the kingdom, they would never gain the kingdom; they would belong instead to the godless, who with malicious and greedy eyes seek what is theirs even from God. But the children of God do what is right because they want to and without expecting anything; they seek no reward, but simply for the sake of the glory and the will of God they are prepared to do what is right, even if—and this is impossible—there were no heaven or hell." Here the Reformer appeals to Jesus' Gospel against Roman works-righteousness.

As we evaluate the Old Testament, let us consider a fourth point: the Jewish and the Germanic valuation of work.

Here Luther's translation of Psalm 90 [:10] is revealing. This psalm is again a pearl of Jewish Scripture, worthy to be included in a selection of the very finest poetry of all times and places. Luther writes:

> The days of our life are seventy years,
> or perhaps eighty at most;
> and even if it has been delightful,
> still it is only toil and trouble.

He writes this way because this is what his heart tells him it means, and because it does not even occur to him that the psalmist could have another viewpoint.

But if we translate the verse literally, it says, "And if it has been out of the ordinary, it was still only hardship and vanity." Or in another reading, "And if it seemed as if there were something to it, it was still only toil and nuisance."

Where the one recognizes great worth and says "delightful," the other sees worthlessness. For Lutherans this psalm becomes a poetic celebration of the work of creation that makes life worth living and gives it its real meaning and content. To the Eastern poet the fleeting succession of generations and the striving of conscientious people is a bitter necessity and the working out of divine wrath, a punishment for sin. Think about Genesis 3[:17, 19]: ". . . Cursed is the ground because of you. . . . By the sweat of your face you shall eat your bread." A paradise of doing nothing! That is in any case not German. Certainly the Jew can also be terribly hardworking. But if he is, then again, the joy he gets from working is connected, in a way that is alien to us, with his obsession with rewards, in this case the delight in profit. And if he begins to philosophize about work, then he ends up always at Psalm 90, verse 10.

Now, finally, to the fifth and sixth points: The two thought-pictures according to which a people values itself and sees itself mirrored in cultural terms are their gods, or their God, and their heroes.

The tribal heroes of Israel are the patriarchs. The older custom, until recently, was to discuss these men in Bible history classes in the first several years of school—though they have not been used in children's worship for some time now. And it is especially these that arouse the most serious concern about them among those who are thinking about Germanness. These men—Abraham, Isaac, and Jacob—are as Jewish, which is to say, as sub-Christian [unterchristlich] and as un-German as it is possible to be.

We only need to indicate a few details! Abraham, who pretends that his wife is his sister and sells her off to Pharaoh's harem, for which—remarkably—not he, but the utterly unaware, innocent king, is punished by YHWH. Isaac, about whom the same story and some other even less savory tales are told. Jacob, who betrays father, brother, and uncle, and never repents, remaining to the end the same cunning son of the desert and deal-maker: these are no treasure troves for illustrating great, moral personalities. One has to apply a lot of makeup and rearrange a lot of things in order to use these stories.

. . .

For these reasons many people today are demanding the total banning of the Old Testament from religious instruction classes.

I think, from every point of view, that is going too far. A course of instruction that doesn't want to put blinders on people has to take all religious perspectives into account, and in particular, [understanding] Jesus' conflicts with Judaism requires some special knowledge of Israel's religious development. But the Old Testament should be reserved for the later school years, when the time has come to offer . . . some instruction in discernment. . . .

As Schiller writes, "In *his gods, man paints* a picture of *himself.*" "As a man is, so is his God"—more accurately, his conception of God.

A few words should be said about the Jewish conception of God . . . in the form of some quotations from the Old Testament! This is how YHWH speaks through his "mouthpieces," the prophets:

- Isaiah 60:16: "You shall suck the milk of nations, you shall suck the breasts of kings."
- Isaiah 61:6: "You shall enjoy the wealth of the nations, and in their riches you shall glory."
- Deut 7:16: "You shall devour all the peoples that the Lord your God is giving over to you, showing them no pity."
- Deut 7:21: "Have no dread of them, for the Lord your God, who is present with you, is a great and awesome God. The Lord your God will clear away these nations before you little by little."
- Deut 7:24: "He will hand their kings over to you and you shall blot out their name from under heaven; no one will be able to stand against you, until you have destroyed them."

- Deut 6:10[-11]: "[He will give you] fine, large cities that you did not build, houses filled with all sorts of goods that you did not fill, hewn cisterns that you did not hew, vineyards and olive groves that you did not plant—and [you will eat] your fill. . . ."

Even the Psalms are not free of the pestilence of Bedouin-Jewish greed and hatred for all other peoples—for example, Psalm 137 against hated Babylon: "Happy shall they be who take your little ones and dash them against the rock!"

These examples can suffice. . . .

If one looks at it correctly, there is therefore nothing at all to the claim one sometimes hears that the Old Testament is so "*völkisch*," a real treasure trove for nationalistic thinking. Our "nationalism" is not aimed at stealing land and destruction, but rather seeks peace among the peoples. It does not begrudge others their pleasure in existing. With what is Jewish it has only a name in common.

On the other hand, it is particularly apt to point out the obfuscation of Christianity in the church before and after the Reformation because of the use of Old Testament examples, especially the nasty example of Deuteronomy, and to show how, during the Middle Ages, "the insane claims to power of the Old Testament turned the heads of the priests," how the Old Testament became the source of religious intolerance, the Inquisition, and the elimination of heretics.

"[Even as late as the Thirty Years' War] the indiscriminate slaughter of whole populations was justified by a reference to the [Old Testament; stealing and plundering, for example, with reference to how the Jews robbed the Egyptians;] torture and mutilation of enemies was sanctioned by the conduct of Samuel against Agag[12] . . . even the slaughter of babes in arms was supported by a passage from the Psalms . . . Treachery and assassination were supported by a

12. See 1 Sam. 15:32.

reference to the divinely appointed Phinehas, Ehud, Judith, and Jael, and Judith; and murdering the ministers of unapproved religions, by Elijah's slaughter of the priests of Baal."[13] Only in this way can events like the Paris Reign of Terror and similar horrors be explained. Over against these horrific influences, everything else that we could mention regarding the side-effects of the Jewish spirit flowing from the Old Testament is harmless.

It is known that [in 732] Charlemagne commanded that 4500 Saxon nobles be executed at the Aller River. Why exactly this many? It seems clear that he was following the example of Elijah[14] at the Kishon brook, multiplying the number by ten for emphasis.

Between the Semitic intolerance that breaks out here and the Germanic tolerance in matters of faith, which our forbears had in common with all Aryans—and between the contrast between the ludicrous egomania, the greed, and the misanthropy the Jews "project into" their concept of God, on the one hand, and the "highest and best nature of the Aryans," which is also that of the heavenly Father of Jesus Christ, lies an unbridgeable chasm. Putting the two together is clearly ridiculous, not to say an insult to our Lord Jesus Christ.

. . .

With regard to a number of Hebrew names and phrases used by the church, like "Hallelujah," I don't think one need be concerned in the least. "To thee, Jehovah, will I sing." No Christian hears Jewish overtones in this old name. . . . My suggestion? "To thee, my Father (God the Father), will I sing." We are taking pains these days to eliminate everything alien, in our speech as well; we say "church office" [*Kirchenamt*] instead of "consistorium," and so forth. This kind

---

13. Here Grossmann references the 1913 German edition, published by Reinhardt of Munich, of Andrew Dickson White's 1910 book *Seven Great Statesmen in the Warfare of Humanity with Unreason*. His quotation of the German has been modified by direct quotation from the English original, 85–86.
14. See 1 Kings 18:17-40.

of cleansing can never hurt, as long as it remains tasteful and does not cloud the spirit of the poetry.

Conclusion! Besides what we described in a preceding section as eternal, one can honor individual sayings, passages, and stories in the Old Testament, just as they really read, and sometimes as we interpret them for ourselves. One can interpret these details in a German manner. But one cannot now or ever speak of a German interpretation of the Old Testament in its totality. Here there can be only one motto: Clear distinctions and goal-conscious de-Judaization of Christianity! Not "the dismal mixing of Old and New Testament piety," but rather "the pure Christ," the unadulterated gospel. Between this and the German sensibility there is no contradiction. . . .

A Final Note: What is German?

The position we take on the question "Germanness and Christianity" will be decided, first and last, by our essential racial background [*Rasseprägung*]. Someone revealed as a half-breed [*Mischling*][15] will find this question fairly pointless; a person of distinctively Eastern blood will have a different viewpoint than a Nordic person. In my experience, the people who ask—not out of a naïve ignorance, but petulantly—"German Christian: what exactly does that mean?" are usually for the most part Eastern people. For them religion is "a structured set of rules, which, when followed correctly, pacify all the bothersome upsets of their Eastern life experience." (Ludwig Ferdinand Clauss, *Rasse und Seele*, Munich: Lehmann, 1926). "Problems" bother them, and how Christianity relates to Germanness is for them no problem. While we are deeply engaged in presenting what is distinctive about the Germanic consciousness of sin—which

---

15. *Mischlinge* were hybrids, or of mixed blood, defining the degree of Jewishness based on a system codified in the Nuremberg Laws of 1935.

is to state the crucial point—they simply equate this with the Oriental consciousness of sin and moan about heresy if it is questioned.

Consequently, the attitude the reader will take toward our whole book depends in the end on racial assumptions. And so it is appropriate to conclude our observations once more by paying attention to the question: What is German?—German character, German nature, German lifestyle, and especially, German piety!

If things were simple for Germans, the discussion would be superfluous. For then we would be so well-defined and unanimous in a particular orientation that we would only need to look at one another to know: that is German! With a wonderful certainty we would think, feel, and act German. And we would all do it together with self-awareness and quiet reserve over against alien ways of life.

When was this self-confidence and deep respect for our inborn German nature lost? In the storms of the Thirty Years' War, because of the terrible impoverishment, extermination, and race mixing of that awful time! At that time—at least, mainly at that time and in a decisive way—the German learned to forget and despise himself and to admire and privilege what was alien. What took the South, with its alien culture, and Rome, with its Latin teachings, hundreds of years of effort to accomplish—and then not completely—the horrors of this war accomplished in three decades: German self-awareness was shattered.

. . .

. . . German self-awareness did not recover from this degeneration completely until well into the twentieth century. . . . We have learned to write German; but many have not learned to truly feel German again, at least not in an unconfused and unerring way. . . . This is why it has been terribly important that, through the great national revolution, our whole people learn to ask again: What is German?—that we become aware of ourselves once again and clear the rubbish out of our souls, so that the buried springs of our nature may bubble up again.

What is German? First: physically! What does the German look like? We all know: this is not at all easy to say. We Germans look very different from one another. But racial science has brought us clarity. It has taught us that there are four to six shapes or forms that distinguish those settled in Germany:

the blond, blue-eyed, tall, long-skulled Nordic type
the dark-haired, brown-eyed, stocky, round-skulled Eastern type
the tall, short-skulled, *dinarisch*[16] type, in short, the "Defregger[17] type" (after the artist's robust farmer-figures, for example in his pictures of the Tyrolian revolt in the Napoleonic era)
the agile, delicate, dark-haired and -eyed *westisch* type—generally characterized by laypeople as "Roman."

In addition to these, there is an additional Nordic type

the *fälisch* type, or let us say, the heavy "Hindenburg"-type

and, as noted earlier, another *ostisch* type

the East Baltic type, very much like the *ostisch* type, but heavier-set and with striking special features, differently characterized.

Knowledge of these things is becoming more widespread. Many people have read Hans Günther's *Racial Science of the German People* . . . or at least his *Little [Book of] Racial Science*. Members of the Hitler Youth are admirably knowledgeable in racial science.

Which of these races is distinctively German?

---

16. "One of the six races that allegedly comprise the Germans. Characteristics are large nose, high small face, dark hair, and slender, as well as loving the homeland and being heroic." Robert Michael and Karin Doerr, *Nazi-Deutsch/Nazi German: An English Lexicon of the Language of the Third Reich* (Westport, CT: Greenwood Press, 2002), 129. (All the other German "races" are described in the dictionary in the same terms.)
17. Franz Defregger (1835–1921) was an Austrian genre artist.

We can answer this question on the bases of feeling and history. If we try to imagine a truly distinctive German girl, our imagination will not show us a small, stout, Black or something else, but inevitably "a blond Gretchen." We ask: How did the Roman writers depict our ancestors, who marched over the Alps to the South and against whom they battled in the forests of our Fatherland? As terrifying, powerful blond heroes, representatives of the Nordic race!

As we now know from prehistoric research, the great stone-age settlements, and other archaeological finds, this race emerged from the far North; from there the Nords spread out through land migrations and sea voyages. In all the lands they conquered, they created high cultures. In particular they remained settled in those regions where even today most blond people live: on the western edges of the Baltic Sea basin, in southern Sweden, northern Germany, and the Danish islands. They also conquered Norway and England, settled Iceland, and established themselves solidly in all of these places. They also formed the kernel of the German people.

We are all familiar with Herman "the liberator," Herman "the German." In fact, it makes no sense to speak of Germans [Deutschen] at that time. They were rather "Germanic peoples," from the North, the East, the West, and—for us—the South. This was the time when all these tribes still formed a closed, unified Germanic-Nordic unity.

We became "Germans" [Deutsche] out of the "Germanic peoples" [Germanen] through our cohabitation with the other races we have listed, as we advanced progressively over what then came to be called "German" territory. These peoples of other races were in part the original or previous inhabitants of Germany—those who were first conquered by the Nordic peoples and gradually gained equality with them—and in part, those who "seeped in" later from the East.

Naturally, these latter have influenced the development of Germanness, both physically and spiritually, through intermarriage with the blond people. And by no means can we say without reservation that their influence has been detrimental! God has not given any race everything that is good. In bringing with them their inner resources, these other races have enriched and enhanced our own spiritual nature.

. . .

But there is also surely a danger in disturbing a uniform, well-balanced spiritual structure! And seen from the perspective of the whole people, there is no doubt that if such a flowing together of races is not to have a fragmenting, destructive impact, one race must take charge. In the creative and successful periods of our history, the Northern race did this. Our culture is Germanic. And if we do not want to go into decline, it must remain so in the future—or, to put it more exactly, it must become so once again. This is one of the great goals of National Socialism.

The point is not that we should all have blond hair and blue eyes; it is rather that we all allow ourselves to be molded by the great German past, by the Nordic spirit of the German culture. *What matters is the decision to be Nordic.* Someone can appear very "non-German," and still possess the nobility of the German soul because he has decided in favor of the Nordic type. By the same token, someone can have all the physical traits of genetically Nordic-racial nobility, and still be internally alienated from his Nordic forebears—"easternized," in a manner of speaking, or worse yet, completely fragmented racially, without the strength to choose, and therefore an awful pest among his people.

. . .

And now we will spell out the implications for our subject. This information has great significance for religion as for all areas of life. There is a Germanic, Nordic perspective for everything—marriage, family, community, the law, the state—morality, art, faith! Anyone who wants to participate in a conversation about religion today must be thoroughly informed about the science relating race and spiritual matters. And one cannot truly understand any of this unless one has made a serious racial commitment [*Willensentscheidung*], consciously or unconsciously. And no one can understand anything about the shape of a German, Germanic faith unless that person possess a Germanic soul.

Someone who in his encounter with God feels, questions, and responds in an "eastern" [*ostisch*] or "western" [*westisch*] fashion, cannot understand someone who feels, questions, and responds in a Nordic fashion. He can perhaps "empathize hypothetically" to some degree, but the two will never truly understand each other—in such a way that their souls harmonize and they need few words, that a few indications are enough, and they nod to each other, "Yes, my brother!"

This is why, in the end, discussion between different types of people never succeeds. It is a shame to waste time on it! But discussion between "kindred souls," between people who have made the same kind of commitment, is beautiful and congenial.

My presentation has been intended as that kind of conversation.

13

The German Community of Christ

The Path to the German National Church

Julius Leutheuser

Introduction

Julius Leutheuser (1900–1942) was a German Lutheran pastor. A teenager during the First World War, he was a standard bearer by 1918. After the war he studied theology and, shortly after its founding, joined the Nazi Party, becoming an orator in its cause. Both he and his good friend Siegfried Leffler[1] were ordained and took positions in Bavarian churches. In part because of their political views, and their enthusiasm in promoting them, the two young pastors came into conflict with the Bavarian Lutheran church authorities. They moved to Thuringia and founded the German Christian Church Movement [*Kirchenbewegung Deutsche Christen*]

---

1. See excerpts from Leffler's *Christ in Germany's Third Reich,* and the Godesberg Declaration, which he also wrote, elsewhere in this volume.

among other pastors and teachers in the Wiera Valley. After 1933, Leutheuser became a leader in the Thuringian regional church and a nationally recognized German Christian speaker who specialized in ideas having to do with God's direct intervention in modern German history. Leutheuser was called into the German military and was killed at Stalingrad in November 1942.

Leutheuser's *The German Community of Christ* is a stunning example of the German Christian wedding of German history with salvation history. The crisis that occasions this piece is a "struggle over the religious foundations of the Third Reich," he writes. The churches themselves are to blame for the failure of Germans' faith in God—but even more important, their faith in Germany. The churches trap the "stream of eternal life in rigid theories, doctrines, and formulas," and theologians supplant "militant believers" in the churches. Leutheuser still yearns to unify German churches into one national institution, a *Reichskirche*—a goal he and all German Christians tried to realize in 1933 as part of the National Socialist *Gleichschaltung*, or coordination of German life within the Nazi project. He praises Hitler as the one who unified all Germans and exhorts them now to follow him.

For Leutheuser, Germany is "the land and the people decisive for the continued existence of the world," and "[o]ur obedience to the National Socialist state . . . a demonstration of our obedience to a commanding and demanding God. . . ."

Figure 11. German Christian logo from the title page of *Der Deutschen Christen Reichs-Kalender*, published in the same year (1935).

The German Community of Christ: The Path to the German National Church[2]

Julius Leutheuser

Foreword

What follows testifies to the inner urgency that animates my comrades and me—an urgency that has brought us together in the National Socialist struggle to prepare for the contest over the homecoming of the German soul to the Savior. It is my hope that this little book will help clarify for Germans the origins of the idea of German Christianity, which has been so distorted by church politics.

---

2. From Julius Leutheuser, *The German Community of Christ: The Path to the German National Church* [*Die deutsche Christusgemeinde: Der Weg zur deutschen Nationalkirche*] (Weimar [Thüringen]: Verlag Deutsche Christen, 1935), 2–16.

◆◆◆

"National church." This phrase carries with it the holiest longings of the awakened Germans of the Third Reich. We want to be united, united to the marrow, united until all eternity. Throughout history the voice of God has seldom rung out as it does every day in today's Germany. Day after day it reminds us: "Germans, become one people [*Volk*], one in body and soul!" Relentlessly this voice implores us: "Listen to me, and I will show you the way to a united people! Do not excuse yourselves by saying you are weak. I will give you strength. I shine through your thoughts. I give you clarity in your confusion. I drive out doubt. I will make you torchbearers for those who fumble in the darkness, so that none of them—no German—will be lost, but will see the light of life. I am the light of the world. Let it shine among you at least, you Germans! Even if other peoples hate me, you will lift me up. I want to make my home in you. I do not seek what is mine, but what is yours. I am selflessness, I am love, I am life for all the world. I am the only one united within myself. I am the origin of all things; for I am God."

God, who loves his world, has been speaking to us Germans loudly and clearly since the wars of liberation: "Become one people!" "As a people you shall be the temple of my holy Spirit." "Become my people." To you I give the mission to carry the banner of my kingdom in the world. Show the world that it is not hatred that built the world, but love; not injustice, but justice; not the ambition of a man or a people, but rather respect by men, races, and peoples [*Völker*] for the worth of every creature. Germans, fight for your freedom, and know that your freedom guarantees the freedom of the world. Germans, fight for your homeland and you will bring it about that other peoples will retrieve their little piece of earth as their own homeland. Germans, love your homeland until death and show the world that this world will be a blessing only to those who love it with the sacrifice of their sweat, their love, and their life. Love is the seed of God that makes all the world blossom. Love alone contains within itself eternal life. This is what our fathers and mothers sensed a hundred years ago: "You divine being, long ago you chose for yourself the German kind [*Art*]." Since then world events have shown that responsibility for Germany and responsibility for the whole world are intertwined. Whoever does not love Germany, does not love the world either. Whoever despairs of Germany, despairs of the meaning of the world. Whoever is not prepared to die for Germany knows nothing of God's way of the cross in the world. Whoever does not believe in the resurrection of Germany, does not believe in the resurrection of God, despite the night and might of this world.

Yes, a hundred years ago, a few at first, then more and more German men and women heard God's clear voice: "Germany, I have called you. Construct a parable of my eternal kingdom [*Reich*] in this world, which has become like a hell in which heaven no longer shines." And Germany, hearing the eternal voice, stood up . . . with one idea in [its] heart: *the freedom of Germans and through them the freedom of humankind.* They shed their German blood upon the battlefields for the freedom of the children of God from the power of the children of evil. . . . God's kingdom [*Reich*] and the German Reich made a covenant: "I will be your God and you will be my people."[3] . . . Since then the honor of the German Reich has been to set the praise of God above the fame and ambition of a king or a people, to believe more in the triumph of righteousness than in the apparent victories of the violent, and more in community among the people and between peoples than in the insane destructiveness of self-seeking individuals, and to fear God more than all the enemies of

---

3. An allusion to a host of biblical passages, most of them in the Old Testament, that articulate God's covenant with the people. There are a few in the New Testament, including Rev. 21:7.

God in the world. Loyalty to God and loyalty to Germany, faith in God and faith in Germany, love for our eternal home and love for our German home, love for our German brother and Christian love of neighbor, striving for the kingdom [*Reich*] of God and striving for the German Reich, being a German and being a Christian—these notions are indissolubly linked with one another. *God and his kingdom are the source of German strength, Jesus' world-conquering faith is the core of German faith.* Germany's life is dedicated to the triumph of eternal life over the power of death, to the struggle to save the world by conquering the eternal powers, to giving one's life out of love for the resurrection of the world, to the triumph of the glory of God over the satanic powers of sin, death, and the devil. Humility before God and defiance of the world are the traits of the German soul. If you ask this German where he gets his strength, he will confess with thanks: "*Christ and his faith in the victory of the kingdom of God.*" If you ask him about his duty in the world, he will cry out enthusiastically and bravely: "*Germany and its Reich.*"

Soon enough the evil enemy marched across Germany and drowned out the voice of God among the Germans. . . .

How was it possible . . . that the battle for the holy German Reich was debased, made into a struggle among Germans about whether to have a democratic or a monarchical form of government?

In misery and want, faith in Germany was reborn: it had to fight through much suffering and hatred in German hearts, until, through Bismarck, it again found a home in the German Reich. Then came a glorious time, a time of work and of peace, of life in the beloved family circle, of friendly relations with neighbors. The child, "holy Germany," grew and became a man. Then God, who had created this child, called it to the way of the cross in the world. Germany moved out—out of its Fatherland, the Germany of old and young, of boys and men, of wives and mothers, of girls and grandmothers.

The German Reich was on the march. The thought of Germany sang out above railroad lines and marching columns. A people prepared to sacrifice for the victory of justice, reconciliation, truth, love, and fidelity to earth and heaven; a people prepared to carry the cross that led to the resurrection of a new world through God's triumph: those were the watchwords that strengthened our hearts on our way to Golgotha. Yes, the World War became the Golgotha of the German Reich. During those August days in 1914 we heard God's voice: "Your faith alone is your victory. They may take your body, your goods, your honor, your child, your wife: let them take them, they have won nothing; the Empire will remain ours."[4] But the path of suffering had begun even before 1914. They had all come, those who hungered and thirsted for life. They sought healing from German physicians, revelation of the deepest mysteries of technology from German inventors, the elevation of their spirits from German thinkers and poets, models of a sense of duty from German civil servants, lessons about unconditional obedience from German soldiers. Even so, those who hated and despised us crept through the hordes of peoples around us and accused us of being barbarians or defilers of culture and civilization, or mocked Germans as dreamers, enthusiasts, short-sighted idealists. Our enemies used slogans—"To save culture, in the name of civilization"—to impose their judgment on us after the war. Germany took up the gauntlet. It took it up in the name of God. Submitting itself to a baptism of fire and sword, it went its way. We thought we could control the outcome of the war. But the day came when we had nothing more—no bread, no ammunition, no faithful young men who could keep watch and make sure the evil enemy did not do his work inside Germany.

4. An allusion to several lines from Martin Luther's Reformation hymn, "A Mighty Fortress."

Then we stopped believing. We threw away faith in Germany's eternal mission. We no longer believed in a God who strode from Gethsemane to Easter Day. Why did we not recognize him? Because all too often during the glorious time of peace of the German nation—between 1870 and 1914—we had thoughtlessly overlooked the suffering and the cross of Germany's youngest son, the working class, who had become homeless. We made good use of the manpower of millions of German workers, but we did not notice that all the wealth of our people had been erected on the cross of these millions. The "haves" did not see their cross as a call for them to offer some relief by taking some of that cross onto their own shoulders. When it came time for precisely these working people to raise the German flag, they could not do it, and they despaired because for decades the German bourgeoisie had worshipped their own "I" as the path to the good life, but had forgotten all about the collective responsibility to "carry of the cross." The idol "money" had poisoned the ruling class of old Germany. We could not throw ourselves blindly into the arms of God. We allowed ourselves to be led as far as Gethsemane by our belief in the triumph of a just cause. There, however, some went to sleep and the others became a Judas to the sacred empire of the Germans. Silver coins and peace at any price were their worldview, masked as love for the people, and so they handed Germany over to the Pharisees and Sadducees among other peoples, delivering it to the knife with the world-kiss [*Weltkuss*] of reconciliation among the world's peoples. The betrayer's kiss in Gethsemane and the peace treaty of Versailles are the signs of the lie. "Truly, the devil is a liar from the start."[5] This saying of Jesus was true two thousand years ago, and it is true today.

5. Compare John 8:44.

And Germany scattered in all directions. Every man sought his own home. A few, more daring, made protest speeches. But silent, holy Germany had been betrayed. Only one man tossed and turned in his cot in the military hospital at Pasewalk, and could not escape the will of God: the simple, unknown front-line soldier Adolf Hitler. He let himself be made the instrument of faith in Germany. He could not let go of his love for Germany, for the people he had been called to lead, for the holy German Reich. "Whoever abides in love abides in God, and God in him."[6] Because of Adolf Hitler's faith, the Germans' road of suffering and death could be transformed into resurrection. And so, through Adolf Hitler's faith, the Golgotha of the World War became the path to resurrection for the German nation. All those who had weakened but could not let go of the empire that was their joy—the holy Reich of the Germans—gathered around the bearer of faith. And the day of Pentecost, too, came for the German nation. Let us never forget March of 1933! Then we were community in body and soul, one Reich, one community of faith and destiny, one people. The God of love dwelt among us as Holy Spirit and gave us the strength to believe in freedom and glory of the German nation, the willingness to serve blood and soil, to be faithful to the Third Reich. Yes, it was so: we saw his glory, the glory of the kingdom of God among the Germans.

We must not lose that which was our salvation. We must make sure that our people is reborn daily as God's community. For history's warning can already be heard: "Now that the victory is won, Satan is up to new tricks." The old, evil foe had to relinquish the leadership of the state. But now he is starting to tear up our soul again. It happens wherever he foments struggle over the religious foundations of the Third Reich. He knows that a people can only become and remain

---

6. Compare I John 4:16.

a people when it is united in the one God who has called it, when it drinks again and again from the springs of the kingdom of God. Satan knows that he can destroy the world in two ways. One means is the state, the other the church. He loses only if both are torn from his hands by a single community of faith in the victory of the kingdom of God. This is why the decisive question for Germany today is this: How are we to form such a community of faith among the German churches? How shall we form a German national church?

The watchword is this: "Change your way of thinking!" Turn toward home, to the nature of Jesus and his original community! From there come the resources that strengthen faith in the victory of the kingdom of God. From there the streams of eternal life have flowed again into the world. There we can see the worlds that even now are wrestling for our hearts: heaven and hell, good and evil, the kingdom of God and the kingdom of Satan. There our longing for God's assurance can be replenished by the force of the message of God's triumph over sin, death, and the devil. There you see a man who has fought your battle and suffered your want and carried your cross, who suffered death, just as you must suffer it, who came to know hell, just as you know it, who wanted to bring the fragmented world together, just as you do, who called for community, just as you do, but who could believe with certainty, as you cannot without him, who could forgive out of divine nobility, as you cannot without him, who could love without selfish second thoughts, as you cannot without him, who could hate evil with the omnipotence of the Good, as you cannot without him, who could have courage without ambition, as you cannot without him, who did not despair as you do, did not sin as you do, who was joyful in all simplicity, as you never are, who bore the kingdom of God within himself, as you never bear it without him, who conquered hell, as you never can conquer it without him, who was the Son of God, which you will never be without him, who was perfect, as you will never be without him, who knew the eternal Father, whom you will never know without him, who went to the Father, to whom you cannot come without him, who rose from the dead, which you will never do without him, who created a community, as you will never manage to do without him, who gives the Holy Spirit, which you never have without him, who makes heaven shine throughout the world, as you cannot do without him, who makes the world free, as you can never do without him, who makes your people a community of God, as you cannot without him, who helps you to build, from the German Reich, a parable of the Reich of God.

But millions of our German people say: *We hear the words, but we lack faith.* For this these millions are not to blame, but rather the institutions that claim for themselves the task of being guides to Jesus: the churches. A people like ours, one that over the centuries and the millennia has given enough evidence of its faithfulness and its willingness to sacrifice, is not so stubborn that it has given up searching for the figure of Jesus in all his grandeur and divinity. But one thing this *Volk* has never been able to bear for long: to hear the teaching but forego its realization in the present. Even when the teaching is correct, a bad example can confuse a people and drive them to despair.

. . . *Ordinary men, women, ordinary people cry out, not for the knowledge of sin, but for the kind of faith that can move mountains.* The people cry out eternally for shepherds who have more courage than they themselves have, who love them, who sacrifice themselves, who throw themselves into the trenches for the sake of the lost. . . .

Powerless, the churches—those called to care for the souls of the people—stood and watched the godless unfolding [of the World War]. They went out to battle for the souls of the nations and humanity with weapons that might have been useful in centuries past. Hundreds and thousands of times they sounded their cry: "Back to the church! Back to the church!" But fewer and fewer heard, or could hear, their shouting as a call to eternal life. Death had already taken over the churches, had trapped the stream of eternal life in rigid theories, doctrines, and formulas. In the churches, the theologian had taken the place of the militant believer. . . .

. . . Christ's cross loomed throughout the world: atop church steeples, in private rooms, on the altars, it announced the victory of Christ over sin, death, and the devil, the victory of faith in the kingdom of God over the demons of death, hell, and destruction. *But so many fences had been built around these signs of God's triumph.* People who were searching could no longer make their way through the confusion of formulas and teachings to reach the sanctuary, could no longer find faith in the victory of God's kingdom . . . the victory of eternal life over the apparently victorious machinery of this world, faith in the Christ of the world and the victory of his kingdom over all the false kingdoms of this world.

And then, over the world's gloomy night, filled with lies, hate, and corruption, there broke, like a cleansing thunderstorm, the storm-movement [Sturmbewegung] of National Socialism. In the musty parlors of bourgeois idleness the words of Adolf Hitler flashed like lightning and thunder.

They awakened a holy unease in those for whom life had become nothing more than a quiet deathbed. They called forth a blazing hatred in the hearts of those who, disappointed too often by life, dreamed only of vengeance and destruction. All the enemies of life felt challenged by Adolf Hitler; year by year they huddled closer together, hoping ultimately to use their collective power to defeat the young Siegfried of our time. Between 1929 and 1932 we could clearly see the two fronts. One saw in Adolf Hitler the herald of its most sacred longing, the message of the Reich of the German people's community [*Volksgemeinde*] and its leader [*Führer*] in the fight against the enemies of this kingdom; the other was without a leader or a spokesman, a shimmering monster, a horde without a leader and without a sense of community, driven together like the dust on the road by the voice of faith that rang from Adolf Hitler's movement.

When we examine the masses of adversaries of National Socialism those years churned out, we find in them a remarkable mixture of hypocritical politicians, bloodthirsty criminals, affluent money-worshipers, and effeminate literati. A spiritual cross-section would have yielded a collection of all the world-destroying character traits. Over against a newly-risen world of valor, selflessness, camaraderie, truthfulness, love, and the courage of faith stood a world of cowardice, lies, hatred, egotism, and vulgarity. *If the German who truly believed in Jesus could find the Spirit of the kingdom of God anywhere, he could find it in Adolf Hitler's movement.* Millions of Germans who despite the churches had lost their connection with the forces of eternity, learned through Adolf Hitler to believe again in God and his kingdom [*Reich*]. Faith in the victory of good over evil again filled the hearts of our people. A cheerful disposition replaced the mood of a dying age. A new spirit of life turned enervated youngsters into death-defying fighters, turned tired men into defiant combatants, turned despairing women into mothers of the people who radiated faith, turned old men into fathers who gave their blessing.

The Spirit of Jesus strode through Germany: faith in the victory of the kingdom of God over the powers of hell. We sensed that the battle to be fought in Germany will be global in scope. We felt that the battle for the rebirth of Germany was a battle for the rebirth of the whole world. We could believe again that Germany is the heart of the world and that the destruction of Germany would mean the destruction of the world, and the salvation of Germany, the salvation of the world. Germany, wedged between Western mammonism and Eastern anarchy, the plaything of Jewish high finance and the destructive lust of Asiatic bestiality, was the land and the people decisive for the continued existence of the world. If Soviet flags had first flown in Germany, no people in the West could have prevented the conflagration from spreading across the world; what is bestial in human beings could have raged unhindered until it destroyed all the institutions and laws that, in the name of a higher world, have been set in place to guard the divine order of things. The state as the protector of the divine law and the church as the protectress of the fire of divine love would have fallen victims to the rule of the forces of hell. Therefore the Christian, more than anyone, should thank God that at last the Spirit of God has again fallen like fire from heaven and has come to rest on at least one people of the earth, our German people.

May we finally recognize in this reality our calling: to take responsibility for the working out of the notion of the kingdom of God throughout the whole world. Other peoples may be satisfied with halfway commitments, and the Jews in their wealth may worship the princes of this world, but we Germans may be neither halfway-people nor those who care only about this-worldly matters. *We Germans can live only as people of faith in the triumph of the eternal world within the transitory world and over what is transitory.* The Lord of providence has given us a stingy land, so that we are not too easily satisfied. He has given us open borders in East and West, so that we do not become cowards. He has poured cold and hot blood, thick and thin blood, into our veins, so that we are never at rest within ourselves and are always striving. As varied as our landscape is, just as varied is our soul. The Creator of the whole world has not made things easy for us. He has placed in our hearts both the inclination to solitude and the sacred longing for community. *There is no people in the world in which the tension is so great between an interiority estranged from the world and an urgent desire to shape the world.* The German hates a community that exists only for the sake of community. His community has a deeper source than just the good life on this earth. For him a community without freedom is no great thing. Since time immemorial, innumerable men—for the sake of the freedom of their souls or their lives—have left their houses and fields and exchanged the external good fortune of a secure life for a life of adversity, struggle, and suffering, but also inner and outer freedom. Jesus' words apply more to us Germans than to any other people: "For what will it profit them to gain the whole world and forfeit their life?" [Mark 8:36] The Lord of the nations has fashioned our people out of soil, blood, and destiny, to mature and become the people of the revelation of the triumph of his kingdom on earth. God does not want another Judas-people to arise in this world—a people who will destroy his world because they betray God for money. No, a salvation-people shall arise that will carry on his Son's struggle, the struggle of the eternal Christ, the struggle of light, the struggle for the rebirth of the world out of faith in the Heavenly Father and his kingdom, until the end of the world.

. . .

The German Reich is established in the stars. . . . Our belief in Germany is only the touchstone of our belief in God. Our love for Germany is the measure of our love for the eternal. Our love for our fellow Germans [Volksgenossen] is the confirmation of our faith in the fact that we are all children of God. Our obedience to the National Socialist state is a demonstration of our obedience to a commanding and demanding God.

. . .

14

Christ in Germany's Third Reich

The Nature, the Path, and the Goal of the German Christian Church Movement

Siegfried Leffler

Introduction

Siegfried Leffler (1900–1983) was a German Lutheran pastor. He was a good friend of Julius Leutheuser[1]; in 1927 both left their parishes in Bavaria, where they believed their National Socialist political views were bringing them into conflict with church authorities, and moved to Thuringia. There they organized a German Christian group comprising pastors and teachers—a group whose chief aim was the establishment of a unified, supraconfessional national Protestant church structured along National Socialist lines and closely coordinated with the Nazi organization. For young pastors like

1. See Leutheuser's *The German Community of Christ*, also in this volume.

Leffler and Leutheuser, "there was no longer any distinction between church, cultural and political work, because everything was done in the same spirit and served the same goal: the Christian-*völkisch* renewal of the German nation."[2] The Thuringian organization Leffler and Leutheuser founded kept its independence even through the crisis in the larger German Christian movement at the end of 1933 and after. A prolific writer—he published a book a year for the German Christian press between 1935 and 1939—Leffler was also one of the driving forces behind the establishment in 1939 of the Institute for the Study and Eradication of Jewish Influence in German Religious Life.

The excerpts from *Christ in Germany's Third Reich* exemplify the convictions around which Leffler and his coworkers organized their efforts. "In the person of the Führer we see the one God has sent," he writes; Hitler is the one who "calls us to . . . holy service." Germans have been "selected to become the counter-people [*Gegenvolk*] to the Jews, to remove the veil of night from the cross, and to perform for the world a truly redemptive service, a service no people on earth has done until this day." Jesus "became the greatest anti-Jew—*yes, through his act of love, the most positive antisemite of all time.*" Leffler draws this connection between the great reformer, Martin Luther, whom the German Christians as well as the Nazis claimed as a national hero: ". . . [W]e cannot imagine Adolf Hitler without Martin Luther. *And vice versa: without the appearance of Adolf Hitler four hundred years later, Martin Luther's act would not have fulfilled its total significance for Germany.*"

Leffler's text also suggests the German Christians' anti-intellectual tendencies. For example: "While the smart-aleck is surrounded by a cloud of pride, reason, and wit, and he irreverently imagines himself

2. Scholder, 194.

capable of figuring out the world and all its secrets, the farmer who has grown up on the soil piously and with holy wisdom folds his hands in quiet, blessed knowledge of the greatest, the eternal events." Finally, the excerpts translated here also mention the "two antagonists" the German Christians face: "Jewish Christianity" in the form of those Christians who opposed the German Christians, especially the Confessing Church, and "modern paganism" in the form of the German Faith Movement.

Christ in Germany's Third Reich: The Nature, the Path, and the Goal of the German Christian Church Movement[3]

Siegfried Leffler

Foreword

The text before you presents explanations of German Christian thought in compact form. My concern is to report briefly on the nature, the path, and the goals of our movement, not for the sake of publishing something of my own but rather to put an end, once and for all, to a variety of baseless rumors, so that we do not waste our valuable work time defending ourselves against falsehoods and correcting misunderstandings.

Nothing is farther from my intention than to provide finely tuned theological grounds for what we do. That will be done by others whose assignment it is, coworkers and fellow fighters who also have time for it. We know we have people like that, and that they will continue to help consolidate the movement. So those who are

---

3. From Siegfried Leffler, *Christ in Germany's Third Reich: The Nature, the Path, and the Goal of the German Christian Church Movement* [*Christus im Dritten Reich der Deutschen: Wesen, Weg und Ziel der Kirchenbewegung "Deutsche Christen"*] (Weimar [Thüringen]: Verlag Deutsche Christen, 1935), 7–9, 13–18, 26–29, 31–34, 46–48, 69–77, 98–99, 119–20, 124–25.

expecting to find here a theological, scholarly commentary on which they as theologians can take this or that position, according to their interests, will be disappointed. I would advise them not even to begin reading this text, because their preconceived opinions make them blind to what this is really all about. It is high time, in the church just as everywhere else, to make a simple life in God our focus and to give reverence to God.

It was out of this concern that I wrote this little book about the German Christians, we who have for many years committed ourselves as National Socialists and Germans. The open-hearted Germans who know nothing but love for their people [*Volk*], the genuine seekers after God, they will understand us. Someday we will and must gather with them, whatever the situation they find themselves in today. We believe this. In this sense and toward this end I wanted for my part to help bring some clarity, in written form, to the great confusion of religious opinions and movements.

From time to time people talk about the Thuringian German Christians in contrast to the German Christians in the Reich. This makes sense. It must be said clearly that we are not limited to Thuringia, but rather that quietly, steadily, and continuously, we want to and we will gain ground throughout the Reich because we believe that we have the right and the duty to do so. What has not grown will not be able to endure. German Christianity is a truth that has to do with the whole German people, that remains dormant, so to speak, within the German people. If that were not the case, then all of our striving and sacrifice would be for nothing. The victory will ultimately belong, however, to the movement that is about this truth, and about those people who stand brave and tall when this truth is crucified, ridiculed, and laughed at through clumsiness, stupidity, and sin.

Names, symbols, practices, and goals that have gained significance through our congregations have been appropriated by others. It wasn't long before they did not know what to do with them. They faked their own views into things that had acquired form and character and life only after years of devotion to the cause, after long struggles together, traveling together, and comradeship. One cannot cut the twigs and branches off a sapling and claim that they are the tree. It must be said that they are just parts of the whole. Whoever is a German Christian will enter selflessly into the community of German Christians, without any kind of personal ambition and claims to power. Our only ambition must be that each of us serves the cause with the gifts he has. This is why I would like to prevent others from decking themselves in foreign garb and thus pretending that the ideas so laboriously worked out in the community are their own and acting as if they had originated with them.

Finally, I don't want to leave it unsaid that we German Christians did not appear on the church scene by accident after January 30, 1933. As older comrades will recognize from my description, we have stood for the last decade, deeply loyal to our people and its glorious Führer, and today we are and will remain Hitler's loyal followers on the church front. Some who are part of the German Faith Movement[4] have sharpened their arrows against us and chided us that Christianity is something un-German; they should ask themselves whether, in the difficult moments of our struggle as followers of the Führer, they could have acted in a more German way than we had to, with no thought for our own interests. We will let no one outdo us in our faithfulness to Germany and to our Führer, for out of this faithfulness we are and remain Christians.

Weimar, Easter Season 1935
Siegfried Leffler

4. The neo-pagan movement.

Part I: The Essence of German Christianity

Christ means the dawning of a new day; he won for old humanity a new youth, and so he also became the God of the young, vital Indo-Europeans (Aryans), and under the sign of his cross, on the ruins of the ancient world, a new culture was slowly built, one on which we must continue to work for a long time if it is at some point in the distant future to earn the name "Christian."

—H. St. Chamberlain[5]

The German Homeland

Anyone who, out of love for his people, has felt the urge to become a National Socialist during the past decade has been able to see that National Socialism in its deepest essence was and is calling the German people to return to their homeland. So it is that today, after the seizure of power [*Machtergreifung*], this return to Germany is being fulfilled in National Socialism in every region through its prophetic Führer. The concept and content of "homeland" [*Heimat*] is being revealed to us anew.

For many years the German wandered about as if in a foreign land. No matter his profession or calling, he asked himself, what was the sense of his existence, his work, his struggle, his sacrifice. Nowhere could he find an answer, not even in religion. . . . In times past only one goal remained, one that people sought to attain by effort, slaving away, employing the most brutal methods: money. Money was the watchword, the reason the worker went to work day after day, the reason the farmer plowed, the scholar sat and thought, the

---

5. Houston Stewart Chamberlain (1855–1927) was a British Germanophile writer who argued for the racial and cultural superiority of the so-called Aryan element in European culture. His two-volume *The Foundations of the 19th Century* (1899) became a standard reference work for European and particularly Nazi antisemites. This is a much-garbled quotation, not from Chamberlain, but from Lord Redesdale's introduction to the first volume of Chamberlain's *magnum opus*.

businessman seized the earth for himself. Even among those who proclaimed the holy sacrifice, all our thinking turned to money. . . .

In countless songs the German people have praised their homeland, have expressed their longing for it. Mother, father, children, love and faithfulness, devotion—this little word "homeland" embraces them all. In it a man works, sows, and reaps without getting tired. In it he lives and gathers around him his circle of loved ones. In it he loves, suffers, and prays. In their folksongs the German people have recounted, in childlike simplicity, what their country, their land, their homeland means to them. . . .

People of the same blood spent years, even centuries, in their valleys, on a small piece of German earth. They went out to their fields when the sun came up. They toiled by the sweat of their brow and fought for the existence of their farms. On the paths and on the fields, spring brought green growth and blooming flowers. How the stars shone at night! How close heaven seemed! . . . [And then] suddenly, the sun overhead darkened. Shadows upon shadows fell on German soil. The songs were silenced. No one could sing them any more. They were no longer true. Perhaps a person sensed what he had once had, what he had lost. . . . The farmer still went out, as his fathers had, to his fields and turned the soil, but how seldom could he rejoice in his blessings. . . . He had to calculate when he got up early, calculate when he came back home, calculate when he sank exhausted into his bed. Who will get the farm? What will the second, third, fourth child receive? Money challenged and filled his thoughts. The farm, the village, the soil of his fathers, all became a burden to him. Is it any surprise that the enervating scent of an alien city life wafted into the farmer's living room and rendered this caretaker and protector of the German homeland spiritually homeless? Service to the land was no longer a service to God. . . .

But the farmer's experience was visited even more crudely on other classes within the *Volk*. Like a sinister disease it ate away at the mass of German workers. One or another sunny farming village, surrounded by forests and fields, full of snug, trusted places: that was once the homeland for all of us. There a German mother rocked us, there was our fathers' land. There we had once heard the harmony of God, blood, and soil. Then the field became too small to sustain us. The son tore himself away from the father, the daughter from the mother, brother from brother—and they moved into the alienation of the city. Far away, they had to establish build a new home for themselves.

They found work in mines and factories. The farmers' children and their families took shelter in rented tenements, building upon building, without even a little land, without air and sun. In the morning they went to work—work that offered no advancement. The work used them up, crippled them. . . . Into this wasteland of stone they had brought with them all the memories of home, and they had told their children about them, in songs and words and morals and customs. But they were only memories, fainter every day. . . . Money became their homeland. . . . What was God to them now, the God who is goodness, love, righteousness? No prayer now crossed their lips. In their hearts the longing for God died. There was no longer either an earthly or a heavenly Fatherland. . . .

Why didn't the scholar, the artist, the priest—the man who still wanted, still could be a man with a living soul—why didn't he give these German workers back their lost homeland? Why didn't he, who still had something? Why did they all stand by and watch, while their youngest brothers went downhill? Why didn't they help? Why did leaders come from other races, from other places, from other homelands, and rob them and us of heaven and earth and Fatherland? The spirit of alienation had already crept in and destroyed the soul and the roots of even the well-educated. . . .

There were, in fact, many professions that might have sustained and comforted the people's soul, that could have raised and built up their innermost homeland, but they had become mechanical, transformed into techniques. Everything had frozen into teaching, dogma, book-learning. A cry for living people, familiar with life and homeland, sounded through the age. There were experts in law in every city, yet the people sought and hungered for true justice. Thousands of doctors plied their services, and the people became sick and sicker. There was scarcely a village in Germany in which pastor, teachers, and educators were not at work, and yet the people became poor, impoverished in soul and faith. God was lost. Many books were written to help, but how few had enduring value! How rarely did they even touch on the deep crisis of the times! Those who do not have peace in themselves cannot pass it along to others. Those who have no homeland cannot lead others home. . . .

How We Saw and Must See Adolf Hitler!

In the course of a conversation with a member of the National Socialist Pastors' League in Bavaria, I was asked whether I could endorse the oath of service[6] for pastors of the German Protestant Church as proposed by the national church leadership. I responded that I could understand that this oath could cause some internal conflicts for pastors who have not had the National Socialist experience. I had hardly spoken the words "National Socialist experience" when he interrupted me: "Get out of here with your

---

6. After President Hindenburg's death on August 2, 1934, Hitler became both head of state and commander in chief of the armed forces. The Reich cabinet decreed the "Law on the Allegiance of Civil Servants and Soldiers of the Armed Forces," requiring members of the military and the civil service to swear an oath of personal loyalty to Hitler. After the national synod of the German Protestant Church met on August 8, 1934, the church leadership called on pastors, who were technically civil servants, to follow suit. The oath read: "I swear: I will be true and obedient to the Führer of the German Reich and nation Adolf Hitler, observe the laws, and conscientiously fulfill my official duties, so help me God."

National Socialist experience; I don't want to hear any more about it. It has nothing to say to theology." I answered, "Only someone who has never been a National Socialist, has never in his heart of hearts felt compelled to be, who has never had to make any existential decisions out of loyalty to Hitler, who has never had to risk his calling and his living, wife and children, out of a sense of this inner necessity. . . ." There may be some who, young and sheltered, got to know National Socialism, decided to join, but who never investigated it to its marrow and ultimate core, and who therefore have always remained utterly superficial representatives of the Party. Their actual being and life remain untouched. Such people will never find a bridge between National Socialism and Christianity. . . .

No one can force himself to love and to a living, daring faith. These are gifts. Anyone who can treat this experience with indifference or ignore it, anyone who says it could just as easily have been otherwise, will never understand German Christianity or find his way to it. It is simply foolishness to believe that one can and must grasp everything through reason or by being taught about God. Whatever is not understood will be branded godless or demonic, anti-Christian. For such a person the deepest ground of being, the basis of all that happens, is often contrary to reason, unimaginable. Here the only way forward is through a heart filled with reverence and faith.

. . .

In the person of the Führer we see the one God has sent, who sets Germany before the Lord of history, who calls us from the worship of words, from the cult of the Pharisees and the Levites, to the holy service of the Samaritan. This is why we who are and wanted to be pastors chose him. His struggle, his triumph, were just as decisive for the church as for all other areas of German life. People have often criticized us, accusing us of idolizing Hitler, saying that for us "he has taken the place of Christ." That has never crossed our minds, for the simple reason that the community of German people, one people in every detail, in life and death, had already been revealed to us through the spirit of Christ and been made our obligation. But the fact is that in the pitch-black night of Christian church history, Hitler became like a wonderful transparency for our time, a window through which light fell upon the history of Christianity. Through him we were able to see the Savior in the history of the Germans. Hitler stood there like a rock in a broad wilderness, like an island in an endless sea. Whoever wanted to live into the future had to align with him. Through him the historical current of life poured into Germany. He is the instrument through whom the little word "German" has been filled with life, yes, with eternal value. . . .

One God, One People!

. . .

In the whole history of humankind only one people experienced itself as a people down to its blood, that spoke of God as its own God who was with them, who knew and spoke of the meaning of their existence, their mission for the world. That is the people Israel. As a people it became a Satanic curse for the world when it decided against the God of heaven and earth and crucified him in Christ his Son. . . .

. . . Wherever they live—whether in Japan, in Germany, or in America—whether they were the most liberal Jews in Western Europe or the most orthodox Zionists in Tel Aviv or Bethany, they remained one people with one pulse, one will, one world-goal. They forced virtually the whole world to obey the laws of their way of thinking and acting; their spirit infected the thinking of all other peoples and in this way destroyed their cohesion. They became a "ferment of decomposition" (Mommsen).[7] Because of them the world teetered on the edge of the abyss. Didn't it have to be this way?

Anyone who surveys human life and the events of the world from a religious point of view falls silent and recognizes that remarkable "necessity" that underlies all development over the years and the centuries. Such a person bows humbly before eternal, omniscient Wisdom. Doesn't the cross on Golgotha, shrouded by night and tragedy, stand in the background of the past two millennia? Doesn't the world, with countless tortured voices, cry out to it, "The Savior has lost the struggle, the Jews have won"? Don't we hear, from books and writings of the past, out of human suffering, misery, and despair, complaint on complaint against heaven at the victories and the orgies celebrated by evil?

From of old, one people refused to serve the eternal Creator, refused to open itself to his kingdom on earth. One people once turned against the Redeemer. Today, should not one people, prepared by its disposition and its history, and equipped for this calling, set an example of freedom for the world, by in its best members clearly choosing God and his Savior? Today, should not one people be selected to become the counter-people [*Gegenvolk*] to the Jews, to remove the veil of night from the cross, and to perform for the world a truly redemptive service, a service no people on earth has done until this day?

---

7. The reference is to Theodor Mommsen, *Römische Geschichte*, vol. 3 (1856), 550 [*The History of Rome*, trans. William P. Dickson (New York: Scribners, 1885), 4:643; the translation there is "leaven" rather than "ferment"]; in fact, in contrast to his associate Heinrich von Treitschke, Mommsen thought that the process of "decomposition," that is, of dissolving the various German ethnic groups into a German nationality not conformed to a single regional group, was a positive outcome, if painful while in process. Treitschke saw it as leading to "only a homeless cosmopolitanism" destructive of German nationality and pride. The Nazis, taking Treitschke's point of view, twisted Mommsen's words to their own purpose and made them a part of their anti-Jewish vocabulary. See Alex Bein, *The Jewish Question: Biography of a World Problem* (Madison, NJ: Fairleigh Dickinson University Press, 1990), 619.

This is our belief, from which we cannot release ourselves: that after 2,000 years the Eternal One has called the German people to the mission that he has been nurturing for them since time began. . . .

The world must choose between Israel and Germany, between a people with a law that looses destructive, ruinous forces everywhere and binds the creative spirit, that struck the Lord dead, and a people with the will and the gift to bring heaven and earth into a mysterious and creative relationship, and thereby to exorcise the forces of destruction. Germany's destiny is the world's destiny. . . .

The Savior

Never has a man of greater clarity, simplicity, and greatness than the Savior walked the earth. The learned men of every age will never be able to understand completely what the world was given in him. And yet little children in their lack of sophistication are closer to him than anyone else. Two paths lead to this holy life two thousand years ago: the one, taken by the spiritual sphere's cleverest thinkers, leads to heights so dizzying that a human being is shaken and falls apart in recognizing his own powerlessness and sin and guilt, letting out a Faustian cry: "And see, we can know—nothing. It almost breaks my heart."[8] Reverence grasps the heart and the "humble, divine madness of faith"[9] in the Son of God. The other path leads through the midst of the people, through their villages, cities, and markets. There walk the people who are close to the earth, who in their relationship with nature have retained that heavenly gift of intuition unspoiled. While the smart-aleck is surrounded by a cloud of pride, reason, and wit, and he irreverently imagines himself capable of figuring out the world and all its secrets, the farmer who has grown up on the

8. A line from Goethe's *Faust*.
9. A phrase loosely taken from Søren Kierkegaard, the Danish theologian.

soil piously and with holy wisdom folds his hands in quiet, blessed knowledge of the greatest, the eternal events.

Today the German Christian must defend his faith in the Savior against two antagonists. One is Jewish Christianity, the other, modern paganism. The Jewish Christian charges that the Savior hardly matters to us: we place so much emphasis on blood, race, and soil that as a consequence we must be opposed to Christ as a manifestation of the Jewish people. *Now of course it is true that God and the fact of our being children of God stand far beyond all categories of race and uniqueness of blood and nation [Volk].* The question is whether one should necessarily regard Jesus as belonging to the Jewish nation [*Staatsvolk*] or the Jewish race. We will never be able to solve this problem conclusively. In any case, it is irrelevant for faith itself and the reality of salvation that he embodies. Everyone can think as he likes on this matter. In any case, I can imagine that this noble and greatest revelation of God to humankind was fulfilled in a body, in flesh and blood, that bore the laws of its own kind within it. But when the Spirit [of Jesus] enters into all of heaven and earth, however, when he returns to the Father's kingdom and frees himself again from earth, blood, and *Volk*, he breaks through the barriers of time, space, and race, and then it becomes true that "the Savior pastures all peoples alike." At this point we must respond to the serious concern with which race researchers and German pagans confront us as Christians. They hit the nerve of the thing.

On the one hand, they maintain that Christ was, after all, a Jew. Whoever embraces Christianity therefore is more an adherent and representative of a Jewish spirituality than of a German [*deutsch*], Germanic [*germanisch*] religious concept. Christianity is Semitic; it functions in the Nordic, Western world only as something alien, like an alien skin we have pulled on, under which we slowly suffocate and must necessarily lose everything that makes us who we are. It is sacrilegious presumption and a wild fanaticism of faith to confess that he is the Son of God. He was a man like every other, and of course should be included among the great spiritual heroes. We respond by asking: "Would the idea of God [Gottesgedanke] ever in the history of the world have been illuminated if it had not been preached, lived, and presented to us by the sacred passion, in the very place where human darkness lay most fully over everything we know as soul?" For there the contradiction between light and darkness was captured most powerfully and revealed to the whole world. "The light shines in the darkness, and the darkness did not overcome it" (John 1:5). Why it had to be that way we leave to wisdom that we will never fathom.

Where else in the world was there a people to whom God vouchsafed such knowledge, revealing to them the kind [Art], race, blood, meaning, and mission of their ethnic culture [Volkstum]? A people that in its racial and religious cohesiveness could have taken up a global task, embraced the Savior? In the midst of the Jewish people, Jesus became the greatest anti-Jew—*yes, through his act of love, the most positive antisemite of all time.* Anyone who has felt compelled to join the German struggle out of love for his people and every worthy value will understand this. As Dr. Goebbels writes:

Christ is the genius of love, as such the most diametrical opposite of Judaism, which is the incarnation of hate. . . . Christ is the first great enemy of the Jews. "You should devour all nations!" He declared war against that. That is why Judaism had to get rid of him. For he was shaking the very foundations of its future international power. The Jew is the lie personified. When he crucified Christ, he crucified eternal truth. The idea of sacrifice first gained visible shape in Christ. . . . The struggle we are now waging today until victory or the bitter end is, in its deepest sense, a struggle between Christ and Marx. Christ: the principle of love. Marx: the principle of hatred.[10]

Whoever takes the social questions of our time seriously—those that touch our people—knows that what is at stake today is maintaining Christian principles against Jewish ones. . . .

Martin Luther

Not long ago German scholarly circles earnestly discussed whether the reformer Martin Luther had completed an old era or begun a new one. Neither side could give a clear and definitive answer. Two sides confronted one another in him, in his heart, in his struggle and work. He was the bridge that brought the West, and the German people, over into the new era. "His spirit is the battleground of two epochs." He was the source of renewal for the whole history of the West—in politics, economics, and religion. It would be a mistake for us to isolate this German prophet from his world and the events of his time and evaluate his stature and significance only in light of conventional theology. Because in his time Luther had to work in the field of theology, had to accomplish his breakthrough as a man of the cloth, we have mistakenly inferred that he belongs only to the church, only to the theologians. He was very quickly snatched away from the German people, out of whose womb he had been born; no wonder, then, that today his name is more a cause of division than of unification of the German people. This is why it is of the utmost importance that we should see and acknowledge Martin Luther not only as a theologian, but also as a German beyond the limits of theology. We must insist that without him, progress in either the history of Germany or that of the West would have been unthinkable.

Since the eighth century German minds and souls had never been wedded to the Christian message in such a powerful and liberating

10. Joseph Goebbels, *Michael* (Verlag Franz Eher, 1934), 82 [English: *Michael: A Novel*, trans. Joachim Neugroschel (New York: Amok Press, 1987)].

manner by anyone as they were by this simple miner's son. *In Martin Luther we received the spiritual foundations of German Christianity.* We should have eyes to see this and—in the hour of grace that the eternal Lord has granted us through Adolf Hitler—to meet the challenge Luther's redemptive act presents, but that could not be met during his own time: to become a community of German Christians. It is amazing how today the Protestant churches of Germany shut themselves off from daily life, as if God were permitted to reveal himself as helper only on theological or ecclesiastical soil. They say that Hitler has come on behalf of and been sent only to those involved in politics and economics. That is true. And it is also false. For the Guide of history does not send a particular angel from heaven to every unrepentant person in every class and in every single field. He usually speaks urgently and mercifully to everyone—even to the church and the scribes—through one man. Therefore it behooves us to enter deeply into the inexhaustible spiritual mine of a Luther and hear the message that now is the time, in the Spirit of the Savior—toward whom, after all, Martin Luther pointed all Germans—to build up simple, living congregations of pious German people.

Life's breakthrough, the gracious and kind-hearted mercy of God usually happens in contradiction to all human understanding and recognition. As is written, "What is man, that Thou art mindful of him?" [Psalm 8:4] When God is pleased to speak to people through a politician, those in the rigid, supposedly religious circles see that as a worldly concern. People like that believe that God's voice can make itself heard only according to the letter, the concepts, the voice of the Bible and religious language. When God used a monk to free Germans spiritually from the utter insanity of the Middle Ages, then the politician, the scientist, the engineer, thought that this was something only the church, only the parsons, should be concerned about. It had nothing to do with them otherwise. When the Almighty addresses a time and a people through a marvelous individual, it means for everyone: have faith, choose, follow—even if it appears to have nothing to do with my calling, even when it rubs me the wrong way. The Savior himself associated "following after"[11] with "carrying one's cross," and, tragically for us humans, he linked them by the little word "and." This is how it is, and this is probably how it will always be. Just as with Hitler today, so also it was clear with Martin Luther in the sixteenth century that a man sent by God has an impact on all areas and all people.

The centuries before the appearance of the Reformer were characterized by arduous attempts and struggles to find certainty about God and faith—to find a sure and direct alignment for the German soul. A stupefying spell lay over any development, any progress. The medieval church held spiritual life captive and passed it on only sparingly. It laid claim to power and influence wherever life appeared and took form. Life, sustained through the church, should likewise take its shape from Christianity. A powerful thought, practically impossible to conceive of!

But when the church is made into something human, when what is Christian is made into something worldly, then the doors to the quiet, mysterious, eternal Kingdom [*Reich*] of Life, the Kingdom of God, are barred and locked by priests, who hold the keys to the heavenly kingdom in their hands. *Priestly rule, the kingdom of the priests, has nothing to do with the Kingdom of God.*

The priest's job is not to rule. Quietly and selflessly, he is to lead human beings to the wellspring of eternal life and to shed light on the heaven above the earth, the homeland of our souls. Rome held the keys to the Kingdom of God and did not hand them over.

---

11. The German word *Nachfolgen,* or "following after," also suggests "discipleship."

The freedom of the human race, of the human will, of conscience, was thus endangered. History lost its meaning; everywhere people became aware that the threads of life were being broken, or that things had gotten to such a point that life simply could not go on in the same way any more. In the cities, misery cowered in every corner and alleyway. The upper classes had many different views and opinions about life, but life itself had slipped away from them; the whole earth was in upheaval. The seas and the continents were being explored. The experience of the monk Martin Luther—a tiny step into the dark, invisible chamber of the human soul—was the experience of an entire world, searching, exploring: a world filled with longing. . . .

And then through Martin Luther, through the tumultuous struggle of this monk, God gave the answer to the whole German people. Luther, German by nature and blood and history; Luther, the son of the German people, is guided into the Holy of Holies as priest and theologian and speaks there with God, in order to experience the sanctification of this faith. And God pointed the seeker to his Son, the Crucified and Risen One. He spoke deep into his heart: "This is my beloved Son, in whom I have revealed myself and my mercy to the world. He is the place where my Kingdom and the kingdom of the world and humanity meet and encounter one another. Through him and in him faith becomes certitude about God, the narrow but sure path to me and the Kingdom of all life." Luther dared to trust the God who had called him, to trust his eternal word. This is how the German people and all humankind received the explanation of the phrase, "*sola fide*!" By faith alone! "The righteous shall live by faith." [Romans 1:17]

. . . Luther discovered Christ anew—the embodiment of the eternal Creator-God and Creator-Spirit—for Germans and so for the whole world. The bravest and most conscientious man of his time was also the humblest and most reverent. Thus everything that the struggling, God-seeking human race has ever said and written about God regained its significance and its weight through him. This is why people understood him when he cried: "Without any merit or value of my own!"[12] Luther could and would do nothing other than be a preacher of God's word. . . . The individual must become something different, completely different—*totaliter aliter*[13]—in order to be able to understand the risk of faith in the cross, human powerlessness, weakness, sinfulness, death and the Devil, and beyond all that, the Holy God and Father, and eternal life. Here the "Whore Reason" breaks down. There is no path to God based on one's own strength and one's own reason. . . . Through this German prophet the Savior's mission and the Savior's Word burst forth like a bud in springtime, clear for every eye to see. People understood once again that without him, without this holy creating and redeeming Word, without Christ, this divine breath of life in human form, you can do nothing! It was no wonder then that everywhere a Spirit of spring-like power began to blow through the old ways, that storms rushed through the world, blowing away withered leaves and stiff branches, that the earth became pregnant with life and began to stir. And what were the fruits of this redeeming Spirit? To what purpose were people being redeemed?

The forces of blood and emotion, of spirit and of speech, shook off their chains. Humanity stood up, as it was created to stand, and stripped off the old outer garments. The German returned home to himself, to his home, his task, his nature. . . . Once again, as it had happened before, the temple fell, the external dome, the artificial walls built by an alien spirit. They collapsed upon each other. Life, work,

---

12. From Luther's *Small Catechism*.

13. Karl Barth's expression *totaliter aliter* ("wholly other"), refers to God. This is a dig at Barth, chief theological antagonist of the German Christians.

struggle, need were no longer sanctified by the church and the priest, but by the Gospel. The human person knew what he should be and become. And he heard that in faith, no power of earth or hell could hold him back.

Jewish Christianity, Roman, Oriental Christianity, was decisively defeated. The German does not have first to become a priest or a theologian to get closer to God than other people, laypeople. He serves God wherever he does his duty in faith. Be a worker by God's grace, be a German according to the will of your Creator! Be a statesman, a soldier, a teacher, a priest, a servant, a maidservant, a mother and housewife, a farmer—be whatever you are in faith and you are so by God's grace! How could the German do otherwise than to speak German, how could he do otherwise than, out of his history, to produce one thinker and poet and inventor after another, from Jacob Böhme to Goethe to Kant to Nietzsche. How could Germans—spiritually redeemed and freed—do otherwise than to build a nation . . . a German empire of the Germanic nation from Bismarck to its present-day creator, Adolf Hitler. So we cannot imagine Adolf Hitler without Martin Luther. *And vice versa: without the appearance of Adolf Hitler four hundred years later, Martin Luther's act would not have fulfilled its total significance for Germany.* Despite its positive effect, it would have been for Germans simply the destruction and splitting up of confessions, rather than German unification.

What Luther actually did not want or seek—what, according to his own words, was not his interest—came to life and significance through him: the state. The national state is the practical, visible fruit of the Reformation. . . . Could it be that Hitler, the prophet, must as a statesman become the midwife at the birth of the church in Germany? . . . How Luther would rejoice today to find the unified German state he did not see in his own time! . . .

It is high time that German theologians recognize that they no longer live in the sixteenth and seventeenth centuries, but rather in the twentieth; that God has once again raised his voice in a singular individual. It makes no sense always to call on Luther, to want to lead us back to Luther. It is a cheap escape to say "we are Lutheran, we have Luther as our authority, we defend Luther." That is nothing more than adorning his grave. We never get beyond theological formulas and formulations and perspectives. This does not bring his spirit to life again; at the most it raises up the false spirit of the theological bickerers and dogmatists who in the decades after Luther tormented and divided the German people.

Luther research is important. Luther is without doubt a mine with immeasurable treasures and spiritual wealth that must be extracted. But it is even more important, in the spirit of Luther, to seize this day, to allow the spirit of the eternal Lord and Redeemer to work and in us. We must embrace our common bond and our common work, and on this German soil in this German Reich, on the foundation of the Gospel, build a dwelling place for the Spirit of God in the form of a community of faithful German people. In this dwelling place the people will come before God. Here it will be gathered, enlightened, and sanctified. Because of it God will again become a certainty for the world, for other peoples. Martin Luther is its forefather and prophet; in it Luther's mighty work becomes—in German form and in a German way—church and cathedral for the German soul. The signs of the times point to it! Recognize them and, with perseverance and clarity, get to work!

Part II: The Way of the German Christians

Is the Church Still Relevant?

. . .

. . . It is senseless and foolish to say, "Leave the Catholic church! Leave the Protestant church! The denominations are obsolete!" No! Everyone should remain in his church; the denominations are a reality. But they will be transformed by the lives and the entry into them of living Christians, and they can only come to where the German people gather, beyond denominations, as one praying, Christian people. The denominations are like two arms on one body. The arms can be useful, the hands can be folded, if they are moved and guided by one heart with one Savior, one God. Just as they are still two arms and two hands, there will always be two and perhaps even more streams, but for the sake of God and the people they can and must become one will, one desire, one holy order. Is not every serious man, every German woman who reverently folds his or her hands and prays a parable and a real possibility along the way to this goal?

The Old Testament

Throughout the history of the church, the Old Testament has sometimes been at the center of religious and theological discussions. What is the German Christian position on this matter? The Old Testament is the religious book [*Volksbuch*] of the Jewish people. It contains the history the Savior studied during his lifetime, that he relied upon. Doesn't it say that at the end of his life on earth ". . . he began to interpret to them Moses and the prophets"? [Luke 24:27] Do we as Germans have anything to seek in this book? For the old church, and for ecclesial and religious history, it will have and retain its value and meaning. We cannot simply say that it has no value for religious life; it contains insights and words of lasting value that will be respected by all peoples at all times. I think only of a verse from Psalm 23, ". . . and though I walk through the valley of the shadow, I will fear no evil, for you are with me!" or the opening verses of the 90th Psalm: "Lord, you have been our dwelling place in all generations; before the mountains were brought forth, or ever you had formed the earth and the world, from everlasting to everlasting you are God." Whether such passages have Nordic origins, whether Nordic wisdom is expressed in the writings of the prophets, is not the first question for religious life in general. What matters is that this book tells about religious life, and that in their need, countless people have been edified and uplifted by it.

However, it also understandable that serious *völkisch*– and German-minded people reject the Old Testament. They say, we are doing political battle with Judaism, and at the same time we are allowing their influence to affect our people's religious life through the Old Testament. We also think that German history and faithful German people and seers are more important for the instruction and edification of German children's souls than pious Jewish history. To mature fellow Germans [*Volksgenossen*] we would advise the following: Dear friend, if you are happy without the Old Testament, by all means leave it aside! But don't take away from your fellow German—especially if you want to be tolerant—the words and insights that they have found comforting in their hour of need. Anna Schieber[14] has written that one should not leave the revelation of the Bible for retirement. She is right. As long as it is revelation to a single German, it can never be set aside for retirement. The judgments of a Herder, a Goethe, or a Kant, to name just these, show us how much

14. Scheiber (1867–1945) was a German poet.

one can learn here, with gratitude, for one's spiritual enrichment, without thereby ceasing to be a good German.

The "German Christian" Church Movement

Isn't the German Christian Faith Movement superfluous? Must this special organization exist? Is it necessary to have two organizations, the church and German Christians? What tasks are German Christians supposed to fulfill?

Most Germans do not attend church these days. For this the churches, not the people are to blame. The church must be renewed. But it doesn't allow itself to experiment, to risk anything. Hence it needs a free movement that is willing to risk starting something new from the ground up, without being dogmatically harnessed, a movement that is flexible enough to enter all the diverse religious streams to seek out people who have gotten lost or gone astray. This is one of the reasons this movement does not have a fixed, planned program. It needs short, clear guidelines; it needs only to equip itself for battles and storms. It must say clearly where it is going, and for what purpose it wants to gather the German people together. This is why its confession is simply: Christ! Its task is to unlock the Kingdom of God for the German people.

If the movement worked out a clear-cut religious—that is, dogmatic—program that individuals who join the movement would be obligated to follow, then it would not serve the awakening of the heart or promote true religion. It would resonate with the intellectuals; only those who go to church would listen to it; it would lose its reason for being for those it wants to gather together. Vibrant people are not won over to religion through a thought process or a program, but rather through the heart, through the power of faith. . . . For this reason the German Christians offer no world-shattering commentary about Christ, but instead have to demonstrate to the world that Christ is the power out of which it lives.

So we don't ask you, "My friend, what is your position on the Old Testament, on Paul? Are you a member of the German church? Do you belong to this or that denomination?" That would not help overcome the diversity of religious opinions and chaos in the churches. We could just be creating one more sect, one more movement alongside all the others. But then we would not be acting out of love for our people. . . .

If people who opposed each other for dogmatic reasons and could no longer understand each other come together in one community; if the eternal Lord lives among them as faith, as forgiveness, as the Revealer of God, then clarity and resolution of differences will happen by itself, and the community will not fall apart over them. . . . Church can take the shape of a community [*Gemeinschaftsform*] of German people only in and through the community [*Gemeinde*].

This is the guarantee that the living Christ is working among and shaping the German people. He falls like the eternal divine seed, as faith and strength, into German hearts, German blood, German soil. So we will at some point, without our own effort, arrive at the forms of religion that God desires among the German people. Without meddling with the dogma and the confession of one particular church or another, we will go our way and build a community of German men and women in which the peace of God dwells and is felt, the peace that passes all human understanding and wisdom.

The Congregation of German Christians and Its Task

The old church is concerned that German Christians may tear apart and destroy congregations. They are said to threaten the church's peace. Couldn't a pastor, teacher, farmer, or worker who is fully committed to German Christianity bring the Christian body of thought to life without becoming a member of the German Christian Faith Movement, without having to pay—besides the church tax—a small contribution [to the movement], without having to belong to the organization? This ideal possibility would exist if the church were a church of Christ for German people. This is not the case. And our whole effort is aimed at this goal. But I cannot hand over anything on earth unless I have a structure, a vessel, living people. If I want to scoop up water to drink, I have to use at least a cupped hand. . . .

If two men are truly grasped by the German Christian cause, filled with this cause, then they will form the first cell of the congregation of German Christians. They will not first establish an association or a club. They know that they are there for everyone, for their whole village, for their whole city, for the whole people. They see that very often their compatriots are separated from one another by organizations, clubs, ways of thinking, different currents. They feel within themselves the passionate will to become the bridge, the way, the path from one German to another. For them Christianity is a new disposition to love one's neighbor and one's brother. This is why they can and may organize only as much and as widely as is necessary to gather the German people [*Volksgenossen*] together. At first they will find each other and come together by the simplest means. In the process their gaze will never be fixed on themselves but rather on the larger project. But they must gather, for it is characteristic of Christians to carry within themselves this one ability: to form communities. They cannot ignore the neighbor. They cannot be egoists, separatists, or sectarians. They may and must necessarily, as Christians in Germany, be the most German of Germans—Germans to the hilt—the people who recognize the task that God has given their people and devote themselves to it selflessly. Hence the congregation emerges not from outside, but from inside, from the kernel, from the thing itself, from the ground up. It beams its strength into all the lifeless bodies of the community and its associations, peacefully and surely, just as life does, always and everywhere. There is no need to keep careful statistics. No one will start by worrying about how many show up. . . . In the end religion knows only a quiet way into a person's heart. "God drops his anchor only in a quiet place." One person after another will be embraced, just as with the tree in springtime, when one branch after another is quietly rejuvenated and made to bloom again by life's power. . . .

Soon the two men will become four, and the four eight, until in the end all who belong to the people by blood and history will be unable to do otherwise than to think, act, and work in this direction. It may even be necessary for the congregation to adopt strict forms, military in a spiritual sense, for its most committed and decisive supporters, the better to be able to overcome all those who stand in the way of a true people's congregation [*Volksgemeinschaft*].

15

Political Christianity

On the Thuringian "German Christians"

Paul Althaus

Introduction

Paul Althaus (1888–1966) was a German Lutheran pastor, theologian, and professor. He lectured at the University of Göttingen and then served as a hospital chaplain in World War I. After the war he taught at the University of Rostock until the mid-1920s, and then was called to a position in systematic and New Testament theology at the University of Erlangen. There he also served as University Preacher for more than three decades. Althaus greeted the Nazi *Machtergreifung* (seizure of power) in 1933 as "a gift and miracle of God" and an "Easter moment."

Althaus developed a theological concept he called *Ur-Offenbarung*, or "natural revelation," according to which God's revelation occurs not only through Christ (who is revealed through the Bible) but also through creation, i.e., nature and natural events such as history. "Natural revelation" is not enough by itself; what is revealed through nature cannot be fully understood without knowledge of the message of God in Christ. In *Theologie der Ordnungen*, or "theology of orders," Althaus spells out what he argues are the "orders of creation" given by God, which he defines as "the forms of social life of people, which are the indispensable conditions for the historical life of humanity."[1] For Althaus the most important of these orders is the *Volk*, or the (German) people. What these theological notions allow us to discern more clearly must also be understood to be imperfect because of human sin; nonetheless, the consequence of Althaus's categories is the embracing of the status quo under National Socialism as sanctioned by God. Althaus was also an authority on Martin Luther; his *The Theology of Martin Luther* (1966) and *The Ethics of Martin Luther* (1972) are still standard works in the field.

In 1933 Althaus, a member of the Erlangen theological faculty, co-authored the professional opinion of that faculty on the question of whether the Aryan paragraph should be implemented in the churches—an opinion that could be characterized as equivocal: Althaus and Werner Elert wrote, among other things, that since the church had always recognized restrictions on admitting people to the ministry based on age, gender, and physical ability, adding

---

1. Quoted in Ericksen, 100. Dietrich Bonhoeffer argued against this theological notion in the sense in which Althaus defined it: "In fallen creation," Bonhoeffer wrote, "we must speak of *order of preservation* rather than *order of creation*. The concept of order of preservation differs from that of order of creation in that historical orders as such do not possess ontological validity in an absolute sense but are only preserved by God . . . for the hope of new creation." [Emphasis added.] In *Dietrich Bonhoeffer Works*, Vol. 11: *Ecumenical, Academic, and Pastoral Work: 1931–1932*, ed. Victoria J. Barnett, Mark S. Brocker, and Michael B. Lukens (Minneapolis: Fortress Press, 2012), 267. In this same volume, editor Victoria Barnett writes, "One of the central elements of this debate was the distinction between 'fixed orders of creation,' which provided a theological foundation for drawing permanent and racialized distinctions between different peoples and ethnic groups, and 'orders of preservation,' which viewed such distinctions as transitory in anticipation of the redemption of the world" (351–52, n. 23).

the category of race should not be a problem. On the other hand, Christians of Jewish background who were already serving in pastorates should not be dismissed, and exceptions should be made, for example, for those who had served on the front in World War I.[2]

At least at the outset of the Third Reich, Althaus shared with the German Christians a genuine enthusiasm for National Socialism and for an ethno-national [völkisch] Christianity. Like the German Christians, he attacked the neo-pagan (and anti-Christian) German Faith Movement. Despite these areas of resonance—and they were significant, both politically and theologically—he never joined a German Christian organization. Moreover, as the text below demonstrates, he was deeply critical of the German Christians. For Althaus they went too far when they claimed that God's salvation history was being played out in Germany's history. "The attempt to appoint the German people as the people of God of the new covenant," he writes, "is a bald-faced theological heresy." He chides the German Christians: "A messianic ideology erases the real worldliness of political events and political will, the dignity of a simple German necessity of life. . . . For the national movement [the National Socialist project] what matters is the life of Germany, and nothing else. We are not a world-savior. . . ." Althaus's antisemitism—which he shares with the German Christians—is also evident in this text, which is a direct response to several publications by two key leaders of the Thuringian German Christians:[3] "It is not the German people"—as the German Christians claim—"but the church that is the 'counter-people to the Jews.'"

---

2. This document is also included in this volume on p. 57.
3. Excerpts from these documents, by Siegfried Leffler and Julius Leutheuser, immediately precede this document.

Political Christianity: On the Thuringian "German Christians"[4]

Paul Althaus

Foreword

On the following pages the main ideas of the Thuringian "German Christians"[5] will be theologically scrutinized. They demand this, and they must submit to it. In the church of Luther an appeal to "experience," no matter whose it might be, cannot excuse anyone from theological responsibility and critique.[6] What the Thuringians represent is simply a theology of a particular sort, namely, a religio-national dogmatic, an obvious antithesis to the religio-social teaching of the postwar period.

Our examination is based on the Thuringians' own writings, in particular the most characteristic and definitive volumes by [Siegfried] Leffler and [Julius] Leutheuser. The strongly rhetorical strain in Leutheuser's writings makes any discussion more difficult: the careless amplitude and momentum of his speech often leaves his thoughts unclear and enigmatic. That is probably not just a personal idiosyncrasy; it accords with his message's confusion between the Gospel and a national faith.

Nevertheless, several things do bind me to the men I am criticizing here. In their own way they have seriously engaged the relationship between the national popular movement [*Volksbewegung*] and the Christian faith. This is also a theme of mine, since my involvement,

---

4. From Paul Althaus, *Political Christianity: On the Thuringian "German Christians"* [*Politisches Christentum: Ein Wort über die Thüringer "Deutsche Christen"*], 2nd ed. (Leipzig: A. Deichertsche Verlagsbuchhandlung, 1935), 2–3, 5–16.

5. That part of the German Christian movement gathered around Julius Leutheuser and Siegfried Leffler, two German Lutheran pastors active in Thuringia. See excerpts of their work also included in this volume.

6. In this case the "experience" would have been the experience of the rise of Hitler and National Socialism to power in Germany.

starting in 1915, in the German people's movement in Poland. Their question confronts all of us. Lutheran Christianity knows itself responsible for both the people and the nation—not just for the spiritual well-being of individual souls, but rather for the people and the state in general, for the preservation of God's creation and order. In this sense political commitment does follow from our faith, and our Christianity is political. But the Thuringians *wrongly* join Christian faith to political faith and commitment in a "political Christianity" that misjudges both the Gospel and the political. Our critique is intended to clarify what the genuine, Lutheran connection is between faith in Christ and political conduct, and which is the false one, that is, false political claims to the Gospel and false "Christianizing" of political events.

May this document assist in the theological cleansing and thereby in the unifying of our church in the unvarnished Protestant truth!

Erlangen, St. Michael's Day 1933

Paul Althaus

Reference is made to the following writings by Leutheuser and Leffler:

Julius Leutheuser, *The German Community of Christ*, 3rd ed., 1933 (cited as I).[7]

———, *The German Community of Christ and Its Adversaries*, n.d. (= II).

Siegfried Leffler, *Christ in Germany's Third Reich*, 1933 (= III).[8]

Julius Leutheuser, *The Savior in the History of the Germans*, 1933 (= IV).

---

7. Excerpted in this volume.
8. Excerpted in this volume.

German History as Salvation History

The Thuringians turn German history into salvation history.[9] God has chosen the German people [*Volk*] to be the people of salvation for the whole world, the people of the kingdom of God. "The Lord of the nations [*Völker*] has fashioned our people out of soil, blood, and destiny to mature and become the people of the revelation of the triumph of his kingdom on earth."[10] The German people is thus a second Israel. Israel has decided against God, has failed to carry out the vocation God gave it. Now God has selected the German people to "become the counter-people to the Jews . . . to perform for the world a truly redemptive service, a service no people on earth has done until this day."[11]

Jesus says in Matthew 21:43: "Therefore I tell you, the kingdom of God will be taken away from you and given to a people that produces the fruits of the kingdom." This passage can be taken to refer to the German people. Germans should pick up and carry forward the banner of Jesus Christ, "carry the banner of [his] kingdom in the world."[12] "A salvation-people shall arise that will carry on his Son's struggle, the struggle of the eternal Christ, the struggle of light, the struggle for the rebirth of the world out of faith in the Heavenly Father and his kingdom, until the end of the world."[13] Germany is to be a "parable," to construct a reminder to the peoples of the eternal kingdom of God.[14] The German Reich is this "parable" of the eternal

---

9. In Christian theology, the term "salvation history" [*Heilsgeschichte*] refers to the redemptive activity of God in human history.

10. Throughout this document Althaus quotes directly from the four documents he lists at the end of his Foreword (see above). He refers to them by the numbers he has provided in that list, and here also provides the page numbers. In this case, for example, he is quoting from Julius Leutheuser, *The German Community of Christ* [*Die deutsche Christusgemeinde*], 15–16.

11. III, 31ff. (See p. 348 in this volume.)

12. I, 3. (See p. 324 in this volume.)

13. I, 16. (See p. 335 in this volume.)

14. I, 4. (See p. 325 in this volume.)

kingdom of God, and it should be built up as such.[15] This is the eternal purpose of the German mission.

Because the mission given by Christ to the German people is for the whole world, it must first suffer Christ's fate. Germany's recent history is interpreted in that sense. As was the case with Christ, the recognition of the mission precedes the Passion. In Leutheuser's view,[16] Germany, beginning with the wars of liberation, has recognized and taken up its God-given calling, to fight God's battle in the world against the powers of death and for the Reich, the German Empire, in which God's Reich [kingdom] will take historical form. "God's kingdom and the German Empire made a covenant." But now, according to God's will, the chosen people must walk the "way of the cross," the path of suffering and death. "The World War became the Golgotha of the German Empire." God did not want Germany's death. We threw away our faith in Germany's eternal mission, but God made Adolf Hitler his "instrument of faith in Germany." "Because of Adolf Hitler's faith, the Germans' road of suffering and death could be transformed into resurrection. And so, through Adolf Hitler's faith, the Golgotha of the World War became the path to resurrection for the German nation."[17] This is the German Easter and at the same time its Pentecost. "The Spirit of God has again fallen like fire from heaven, and has come to rest on at least one people of the earth, our German people."[18] This is German salvation history. "It is written over Germany: 'A crucified people, a people resurrected.'"[19]

This German salvation history has worldwide significance, because it has given the chosen people a rebirth for its redemptive mission.

15. I, 9, 16.
16. I, 4ff. (See p. 324 in this volume)
17. I, 7. (See p. 327 in this volume)
18. I, 15. (See p. 334 in this volume)
19. III, 51. (Not in the present volume.)

On Germany's fate depends the salvation of the world. "Whoever despairs of Germany, despairs of the meaning of the world. Whoever does not believe in the resurrection of Germany, does not believe in the resurrection of God, despite the night and might [*Nacht und Macht*] of this world."[20] "Germany is the heart of the world, and the destruction of Germany would mean the destruction of the world, and the salvation of Germany, the salvation of the world."[21]

Everything that the New Testament describes as the mission of the community of Christ becomes here the task of the German people: it should be a people "that brings the world the Redeemer, redeemed people and a redeemed nation, for peace, blessing, and healing for the nations!"[22] "The mystery of the German mission is this, that the Germanic blood-instinct [*Blut-instinkt*], together with the figure of the Savior, brought forth the German, *who took upon himself the mission of redemption* as a people secure in a kingdom of faith within and a strong Reich without, to preserve the purpose of life."[23] The redeemed people redeems the world. The world awaits this people, "a people that will show the path of peace and redemption."[24] "The world must choose between Israel and Germany!" Germany as such, and no longer the church, is now the agent of salvation. "In place of the body of the church appears the body of the Germans, which finds its symbol in the state." "People of Germany, recognize yourselves as the people of Christ, that is, in the 'person' of your *Volk* become the agents of revelation of the Gospel; be for all peoples the way home to the heavenly Father."[25]

---

20. I, 4. (See p. 325 in this volume.)
21. I, 14. (See p. 333 in this volume.)
22. III, 51. (Not in the present volume.)
23. I, 27. (Not in the present volume.)
24. III, 34. (Not in the present volume.)
25. IV, 14ff. (Not in the present volume)

Enough, for the moment, of the Thuringian message! Is it not criticism enough simply to bring such key statements to light, to repeat, to read aloud, to put them in print? Need one say anything more? There is a time for everything: to be sober and to be drunk. Because there is a time for everything, we must be patient. But in order that no one else should sink under this rapturous spell, a few things should be said. . . .

The thoughts repeated here signify an intolerably religious, namely a *messianic, inflation of political events*, and at the same time an intolerable secularization—namely, a *nationalizing of the reality of the kingdom of God*. Both politics and theology are being violated here.

. . .

Leutheuser wants to see the "German mission" in light of eternity. So do we. Every Christian understands his everyday work, whether it is great or small, modest or significant, as the fulfillment of the calling God has given him. To recognize one's own striving and action as a calling from God—we need not attach more meaning to it than that. Leutheuser wants to understand "the meaning of the Third Reich in the framework of eternity"; without this, he believes, one could not fight on. But is it not a sufficient sense of eternity that we people of the Third Reich obey God's will that has commanded us to struggle for the unity, honor, and freedom of our people? The Third Reich has grasped the German mission that God has set before us—to know this is enough. Anyone who needs to see a world mission in addition to this, a *Kingdom-of-God* significance, in order to fight devotedly and untiringly—well, for that person, God's will for us, in all its sober definitiveness and limited nature, is not enough to give us meaning; such a person substitutes devotion to a self-selected historico-philosophical abstraction for simple obedience to God.

A messianic ideology erases the actual worldliness of political events and political will, the dignity of a simple German necessity of life. What might the leaders of our state say to the exhilarating words of the Thuringian German Christians? For the national movement what matters is the life of Germany, and nothing else. We are not a world-savior; we are not dreaming of our destiny's messianic meaning for the whole world. Other peoples, too, have claimed to be saving the world and to be the chosen people. The Anglo-Saxons believed they were fighting the World War as a crusade for the cause of humanity, of freedom and justice. Over and over again, people imagine that it is necessary to dress up the mundane necessities of political action, the simple national content of the history of one's own people, with high-flown messianic significance. But that is a misrepresentation of political events. The followers of Luther will oppose it to the bloody end, here among us Germans just as much as among the Anglo-Saxons.

The messianic self-concept of political movements has always, and necessarily, led to scrupulous moralizing of political opposition. Then, as in the distorted Jewish text of the Dutch thanksgiving prayer, the "bad ones" and the "good ones" stand in opposition: the children of God and the children of evil, the fighters for the light and the warriors of Satan. One sees in the camp of one's political opponent only "a world of cowardice, lies, hatred, egoism, and vulgarity," while one's own camp is "a world of valor, selflessness, camaraderie, truthfulness, love, and the courage of faith."[26] None of us will deny that political oppositions are often also contraries in their moral character. But whether and when this is the case with regard to persons, only those schooled in matters of the heart can know. We have no right to trace even the most passionate antagonisms in the political world to the absolute contrast between good and evil. The fight against Germany has nothing to do with the "raging of the peoples against the anointed of the Lord."[27] The misery of Germany

---

26. I, 14. (See p. 333 in this volume.)

during and after the war should not be mentioned in the same breath with the passion of Christ and the suffering of his community. That is actually the Jewish view of history. Why plant it in the soil of German Lutheranism?

German history is not messianic salvation history. Of course it is filled with God's activity. God works not only through individuals and through his communities; he also acts through peoples. He calls them mysteriously and ineluctably into being, gives them gifts and strengths, gives them their place in history, space, and time. They can take up their historical task or ignore it. As their destiny unfolds, they should try to hear both God's question to them and also God's answer. There are divine, historical judgments in the life of peoples, but also renewal and rebirth, experienced as a miracle of the Lord of history. It is God who awakens great leaders in times of crisis and through them rescues and offers a new beginning. Luther spoke about these "miracle-men" [*Wundermänner*] in his interpretation of Psalm 101:[28] "Some have a special star before God; these He teaches Himself and raises them up as He would have them. They are also the ones who have smooth sailing on earth and so-called good luck and success. Whatever they undertake prospers; and even if all the world were to work against it, it would still be accomplished without hindrance. For God, who puts it into their heart and stimulates their intelligence and courage, also puts it into their hands that it must come to pass and must be carried out." "It is a great gift if God gives an extraordinary leader [*Wundermann*] whom He Himself rules. This person may honorably be called king, prince, and lord." Luther also emphasizes that God gives such individuals not only to

27. See Ps. 2:1-2. Note Althaus's use of irony.
28. Althaus provides the reference to the complete and authoritative works of Luther in German and Latin, the so-called *Weimar Ausgabe*, or Weimar edition. The citation is *WA* 51, 207ff. The passage is quoted here from Martin Luther, *Works*, ed. Jaroslav Pelikan, et al. (St. Louis: Concordia, 1955–86), 13:154–55, 165, 199.

his own people, but also to "the heathen and godless." "I do not call such people trained or made but rather created; they are princes and lords directed by God." Luther's remark that God awakens such "miracle-men" also among the godless and the heathen shows how little he thinks of them as instruments of salvation history. The story of God's acts and salvation history are two different things. National rebirth, which happens also among the heathen and Turks, and rebirth through the resurrection of Jesus Christ are two different things. The grace of a historical renewal by means of a leader raised up by God and the grace of the Gospel are two different things. That first kind of grace does not break through the law of sin and death, under which all that is temporal must live; the grace of the Gospel explodes it. National renewal is part of God's governance, which is the subject of the First Article [of the Apostle's Creed]; we should also recognize this governance as God's grace and thank him from our hearts. But it is different from his saving and sanctifying activity, which we confess in the Second and Third Articles [of the Creed]. To be "directed by God," as Luther puts it in the above-quoted passages concerning "miracle-men," and to be moved by the Holy Spirit are in Luther's sense two different things. Leffler does use what he obviously intends to be taken as a quotation from Luther, according to which heroes "accomplish their miraculous deeds through special inspiration by the Holy Spirit." He associates it with an unquestionable passage in [Luther's] Table Talk, but unlike the latter, he gives no source for the former. The quotation does not come from Luther; I do not know where Leffler got it. Political leaders, according to Luther, are God's instruments; moved and driven by him, they carry out their careers and their work, even among "the heathen and godless." But at this point Luther does not speak of the Holy Spirit. God gives the Holy Spirit only to his people, that is, to those he has led to faith in his holy love in Jesus Christ. A high spirit of national idealism and the Holy Spirit are not the same. The rebirth of the national ethos, a new and fervent will to freedom and community among the people is also God's activity, but it is the work of the Creator, not of the Savior and the Holy Spirit. It is also a miracle of God, before which we stand in awe, but it is not the miracle of Pentecost.

To make Germany into a second Israel, into the chosen people of salvation, is an embarrassing piece of religious presumption. Who gives us the right to do so? Israel did not assert its own salvation-historical calling as God's people; God sent them prophets into whose mouths he placed his word to issue that call. They proclaimed to the people what their calling was to be. Have such prophets arisen among us? I don't see any....

Every competent people, the German people surely more than many others, lives for all humanity. There is no question but that some of the battles over ideas that are occurring in Germany are representative for the whole world. God has given us a special place among the peoples, in that he permitted the Reformation of the church to begin on German soil; since then German Christians have had their own mission in the world. And our most recent national history has something to say to other peoples in their own circumstances. National Socialism is of course not an article for export, but many peoples find themselves in a political and social crisis, similar to what we have lived through over the last generation. The great work of defense and renewal undertaken by National Socialism will also be meaningful for them.

But why must one so gratuitously inflate the real and potential meaning of Germany for other peoples into a messianic mission of salvation? Why must one speak in biblical tones about the "way of freedom and salvation" we are to show the world; why speak of Germany as the "peoples' way home to the eternal Father"?[29] ...

The attempt to appoint the German people as the people of God
of the new covenant is a bald-faced theological heresy. When Israel
as a whole turned against God, and failed to recognize its calling
and threw it aside, God's people and the calling remained intact only
in the holy remnant. This remnant was "the Israel of God." That
remnant no longer lives in a particular people, but rather in the
community of Jesus Christ among all peoples. This community—the
people of God—is certainly not just a platonic idea . . . nor simply
a spiritual reality "otherworldly and distant from the whole world."[30]
We experience it as the powerful "embodied" reality of a communion
of saints within our people and among all peoples. The church
militant of today has learned that "church" is not a bloodless idea,
but rather a sustaining and community committed to Christ and to
each other, a community with obligations, as real and tangible as
any natural relationship or community in our lives. The idea, then,
that it is necessary for a people to be chosen so that the truth of
the Kingdom and the people of God will be realized "in blood and
reality" is absurd.

It is true that the church strives to enter into all historical peoples
and take them up completely into itself, so that the natural and
the spiritual communities are completely integrated: the people as
entirely the community of God, and the community completely
incorporated in the natural order. In young mission churches this
is a shining reality for a time. It is a goal for all those who want
to serve their whole people by preaching the Gospel. But only in
eternity will it be fully realized. That is when the duality of natural
and spiritual orders will cease. Then God's people will be completely
incorporated into humankind, into the peoples. To turn the notion of
this designation and duty for all peoples into a special election of the

29. IV, 15. (not in the present volume)
30. III, 37. (Not in the present volume.)

German people to be the new body of Christ, is wicked nationalist-religious hubris. Such a belief [*Glaube*] about Germany is superstition [*Aberglaube*]. It is wild speculation, not obedience to the clear Word of God that has been given to us.

. . . The church of Christ aspires to take shape in every people. But no people dare confuse its mission with that of the people of God, Christ's church. It is not a people that brings "the Savior and those who are saved" to the world, but rather the community of Jesus Christ, by its witness to Jesus Christ. It is not the German people but the church that is the "counter-people to the Jews."

The Reich [Empire] as a Symbol of God's Kingdom [*Reich*]

From the beginning—from Luther's struggles on—the Lutheran church has had to battle for the biblical truth about the kingdom of God: against Rome, against the Reformed, against the Anabaptists [*Schwärmer*]. It is a thankless struggle, for the opponents' version of the kingdom of God is easier to accept than the rigor and majesty of the pure evangelical understanding. But it is a necessary struggle, one we are commanded to fight again today. It is for the sake of the glory of Christ, the seriousness of eternity, the purity of Christian faith—and political thought.

This is the basic biblical-Lutheran perspective on the Kingdom:

Christ is the Kingdom. Where he is present, there is the Kingdom. For that reason it *has* come and comes today, just as he *came* and comes today. Where he leads people into the judgment and mercy of his death, there the spell of this world of guilt and nothingness is broken; the kingdom is present in the receiving of the Word and Christ's sacraments.

But since Christ ascended to heaven and is hidden in God and will only come again in glory, just so also the Kingdom will come "in power" (Mark 9:1) only at the end of the world. Only then will the promise of forgiveness and adoption as children of God be fulfilled; only then will the law of sin and the judgment of death that lie upon all humankind and upon the whole cosmos be publicly abolished. The kingdom will come "on earth." It is not another world beyond the created world of God, but rather its renewal, its redemption. It is a new world, the city of God, the nation of God.

. . .

The kingdom that is already here is present in our national, political history to the extent that people serve their brothers, their people, in the peace of Jesus Christ, with faith, love, hope in the sense of the New Testament. . . . They are bound to time and to the earth, but are not enslaved to them; they are deeply involved but not sunk in them. This is how the kingdom is present in our national political history, namely, in the people who participate in this history as Christ's redeemed ones, encouraging and restraining.

However, our history is also not unrelated to the Kingdom in that the Kingdom is still to come.[31]

The future kingdom is "worldly," "political." It is not a kingdom of inwardness, but rather a new *world*, redemption not only from our hard hearts, but also from the disorder and evil order of this epoch into the true, just order; redemption from sickness and wars into eternal health and peace among all creatures. The kingdom will be just that broad, that all-embracing, that real. . . . In God's kingdom, which is to come, not only the church but also the state will be fulfilled; not just our prayers, our theology, and our worship, bur also our political institutions in that things as they now are will be put away like childish things (1 Cor. 13:11). God's new world is not just

---

31. Here Althaus refers readers to his *Die deutsche Stunde der Kirche* [*The Church's German Hour*], 3rd ed. (Göttingen: Vandenhoeck & Ruprecht, 1934), 24–33.

temple, but also city—the city in which there will be no temple with walls (Rev. 21:22), because it is itself temple.

This is why a just political regime can also be experienced as a parable of the coming Kingdom. . . . Political, "princely" peace is a model of the peace of God in his kingdom, and the same applies to true discipline, honor, the spirit of community. If the Thuringians want to say only this, then they can call on Luther [to warrant what they say]. But unfortunately the Thuringians neglect to add that even the best historical form of state can be a parable of the kingdom only in its *elements of dissimilarity* [to that kingdom]. They have taken the parable-relationship and made it an equation, as when Leutheuser says of March 1933:

> Then we were a community in body and soul, one *Reich*, one community of faith and destiny, one people. The God of love dwelt among us as Holy Spirit and gave us the strength to believe in the freedom and glory of the German nation. . . .Yes, it was so: we saw his glory, the glory of the kingdom of God among the Germans.[32]

For biblical and Lutheran thinking, such declarations are impossible and intolerable. National renewal, breaking through a time of disintegration to a just order for the people and a renewed national community—the heathen have had and continue to have these, too. The glory of such great national moments is something different from the "glory of the Kingdom of God" . . . .

. . .

32. I, 7. (See p. 329 in this volume)

16

God's Word in German

The Sermon on the Mount, Germanized

Ludwig Müller

Introduction

By 1936, when *God's Word in German* was published, National Bishop Ludwig Müller had lost most of whatever authority he had enjoyed in the early days of the German Christian faith movement. Like most German Christians, however, he continued to support Hitler and the National Socialist project with great enthusiasm. Like many of his coworkers, Müller believed their movement could serve the German people by helping "to make the Bible more understandable to modern Germans by putting its messages into modern terms."[1] For someone as devoted to the Nazi renewal of Germany as he was, doing so would inevitably involve the use of

---

1. James A. Zabel, *Nazism and the Pastors: A Study of the Ideas of Three* Deutsche Christen *Groups* (Missoula, MT: Scholars Press, 1976), 206. Through the centuries countless efforts have been

a vocabulary intelligible to others—most but not all of them Christians—who shared his devotion.

In an article published in the German Christian newsletter *Letters to German Christians* [*Briefe an deutsche Christen*], Müller explained his motivation in "Germanizing" Luther's sixteenth-century translation of the New Testament:

> I have permitted myself to present [Christ's] challenges as they really are: the simplest challenges of camaraderie [*Kameradschaft*], of *Volk* community [*Volksgemeinschaft*] . . . with the result that S.A.-men and Hitler-Youth admitted [with astonishment] that . . . these were the elementary challenges the fulfillment of which they struggled for in their own circles. . . . Our people [*Volk*] has said "yes" to the great venture of faith in a politics . . . characterized by the spirit of the Sermon on the Mount . . . with which the Führer is trying to save Europe from the edge of the precipice.[2]

Setting Müller's version next to, say, the New Revised Standard Version of the text of the Sermon on the Mount reveals the extent to which Müller's "Germanization" changes the meaning of the text to serve the purposes and needs of the German Christian movement in its dedication to the ongoing Nazi project.

made, and continue to be made, to "update" the language of the Bible for new generations; each effort no doubt has reflected the cultural, political, and social circumstances of its milieu.

2. Quoted in Zabel, 207.

Reichsbischof Müller spricht vor Studenten der Berliner Universität über die Aufgaben der Kirche

Figure 12. Reich bishop Müller speaking to students at the University of Berlin about the responsibilities of the church. [Original caption.]

God's Word in German: The Sermon on the Mount, Germanized[3]

Ludwig Müller

Foreword

For whom is the "Sermon on the Mount" rendered into the kind of German we think and speak today?

For those to whom biblical language has become alien.

For those who believe that something isn't quite right about the Christian churches and Christianity itself, but who would like to make their own judgments about Christ and about what he wants.

For you, my fellow Germans [*Volksgenosse*] in the Third Reich, I have "Germanized"—not "translated"—the Sermon on the Mount;

For you who have become estranged from Christianity, so that you might understand and grasp anew God's Word in German.

Your National Bishop [Reichsbischof]

The eternal Christ speaks:

Happy the man [*Wohl dem*] who trusts God in childlike innocence. He has communion with God.

Happy the man who bears his suffering like a man. He will find the strength never to sink into despair.

Happy the man who is always sociable. He will amount to something in the world.

Happy the man who hungers and thirsts to be pure with the help of God. He will find God's peace.

Happy the man who is merciful. He will experience God's mercy.

---

3. From Ludwig Müller, *God's Word in German: The Sermon on the Mount, Germanized* [*Deutsche Gottesworte: Aus der Bergpredigt verdeutscht*] (Weimar/Thüringen: Verlag Deutsche Christen, 1936), 7–13, 16–17, 33–40. See pp. 263-264 in this volume for biographical information about Ludwig Müller.

Happy the man who is pure in heart. He has communion with God.

Happy are those who are at peace with their fellow Germans [*Volksgenosse*]; they do God's will.

Happy are those who live and work honestly and faithfully, and yet are persecuted and slandered—they will have communion with God.

Happy are you when you are mocked and persecuted for the sake of God and your faithfulness to him, or when people say evil and disparaging things about you falsely. Be joyful and unbowed, for this is what the world that is alienated from God has always done; your own faithful fathers were also persecuted in this way.

What salt is for food, this is what God's children should be in the world. But when salt loses its strength, it has no more value and becomes completely useless.

Just so, the children of God should be like a shining light, or like a city on the hill, which can be seen from far away.

When one lights a light, one does not hide it in a corner, but rather places it on a lampstand, so that the whole room is filled with light.

In the same way, the children of God will shine like a light because of their whole way of being and their good behavior; by these people will recognize what is good and godly and will learn to trust God with thanksgiving.

You should not think that I want to change or cancel the divine truths and commandments that have been passed down to you by your fathers. I actually intend to fulfill them. For even if heaven and earth pass away, the eternal and the true will remain, even to the smallest details.

Now if anyone teaches and interprets one of the smallest demands of the eternal truth, he will be the least in the Kingdom of God; but the one who does not simply teach it, but also lives it out will be called great in the Kingdom of God.

Therefore I say to you:

If you want to have a part in the Kingdom of God, then your behavior must be better than that of the teachers and preachers whose lives do not match their teachings.

You carry this in your blood and your fathers also taught you:

You shall not commit a cowardly murder. Such a murderer is guilty and must be sentenced to death.

But you must recognize and be clear that committing a murder is the consequence of an internal process that begins with resentment, envy, and hate.

Whoever allows such an attitude to develop within himself has already made himself guilty.

But whoever, out of such an attitude, willfully curses and persecutes his fellow Germans [*Volksgenosse*] really makes himself guilty.

But whoever tries to destroy him morally, or physically threatens him, that person destroys community among his people [*Volksgemeinschaft*] and makes himself worthy of the severest punishment before God and man.

Do not remain unreconciled to the fellow member of your own people [*Volksgenosse*] with whom you are on bad terms. Do not allow your dispute to go so far that it becomes impossible to come to terms and be reconciled.

If you are on your way to church services and it occurs to you that you are estranged from your comrade [*Volksgenosse*], then it is better to go first and work things out with him, and then go to church.

One single act of comradely reconciliation counts before God far more than going to church out of habit.

. . .

The saying goes, "What you do to me, I'll do to you," or "An eye for an eye, a tooth for a tooth." That is also just part of our human nature.

I tell you:

It is better to get along with your *Volksgenossen*.

Volksgemeinschaft is a great and holy good, for which you must sacrifice something.

Therefore, if at all possible, meet the one who is speaking ill of you halfway before you are completely alienated from him.

If your comrade, in his anger, should hit you in the face, it is not always right to hit him back. It is more manly to preserve a superior calm. Then your comrade will probably be ashamed of himself.

. . .

In the olden days they used to say, "Love your friend and hate your adversary."

I say to you:

If you want to be God's children, you must have a different attitude toward your *Volksgenossen* and your comrades.

Be comradely not just to your friend, but also to your adversary. Be calm and relaxed with the person who at the moment is hateful; make an effort to maintain a noble and calm disposition toward someone who slanders or otherwise persecutes you.

The children of God should try to be different from those who are egotistical. God lets his sun shine on the bad and the good, on the just and the unjust.

If you are willing to love only those who love you, there's no trick to that.

And if you do good only to those who are good to you, what's so special about that?

If you want to do God's will, then in your struggle for the good you must set your goal as high as possible. The highest goal, though, is to strive to be perfect, as God, your eternal father, is perfect.

. . .

Afterword

Why is it necessary to make another German rendering of Christ's words available, in addition to the Luther Bible?

Because most people in today's Germany no longer understand the language of the Luther Bible.

The following should also be noted:

In assessing the religious life of our time it is critically important to recognize that a very significant portion of our people [*Volk*] is entirely alienated from the church.

This alienation is especially marked in the younger generation, so much so that one must speak of an overt antagonism against Christianity.

Sometimes, though, one has the feeling that the enemies of Christianity are less interested in targeting pure Christianity with their critique than they are in a particular posture that one ought to call "churchiness" [*Kirchentum*] instead of Christianity [*Christentum*].

But the alienation of people from Christianity and the church is occurring not only in Germany; it is occurring among all the so-called Christian peoples.

The opposition to the church is especially evident in Germany because National Socialism, by its nature as a "worldview," deeply moves the spiritual lives of individuals, and because the religious problem has always been of crucial significance for the German soul and will remain so.

The alienation between the people and the church is traceable chiefly to the fact that the people no longer "understand" the church, that is, the doctrines, the rigid dogmas of the church, have become fundamentally foreign to people today.

At the center of religious conflicts stands, as it has for ages, the person of Christ.

In that regard, two basic things must be said:

1. One does not change in one's innermost being—become a "new man"—simply by embracing or rejecting a particular dogma about Christ.

2. Christ was not in the world mainly in order to put himself and his own person at center stage, *but rather to win human beings for God.*

Further to the first point: The era of church dogmatism is on its way out; for most people it is already over. All signs indicate that we are growing into a time in which each individual people will grasp and shape its religious values and truths according to its most proper sense of itself as a people, in a way that is appropriate to its own special character.

For example, it is quite a matter of course that the English see and shape their outer and inner lives in an English way.

We Germans, who have gained a new German vision of our lives through National Socialism, make the same claim for ourselves.

When, however, the spiritual life of a people—even more so a people like the Germans—is reshaped in a new way, such a change is going to be accompanied by powerful upheavals.

The way in which the people of the Reformation, in this religious renewal, fashion and grasp the Christian values and truths that have come down to them from their ancestors depends on how much and with what degree of inner commitment the individual person is willing again to listen to God.

In any case, one thing seems certain: if every German would make the effort to live, to think, and to act according to the Sermon on the Mount, all religious separation caused by church dogma and propositions would be overcome, and a truly, spiritually faithful German *Volksgemeinschaft* of real Christians would emerge!

Further to the second point: What Christ said about God and his Kingdom was not spoken to our reason, to our intellect, but rather to our soul or, as we say, to our heart.

So God's workshop is our heart, our soul.

From the beginning Christ's proclamation of God and his Kingdom has been called "Gospel," that is, "good news."

What is joyful and liberating about this message is the proclamation that we human beings should relate to God as a child to its father.

The upshot of this is:

We should not live our lives in slavish fear of avenging punishment, but rather with childlike trust in God and an honest sense of responsibility.

This obligates us to work on ourselves and to struggle.

To struggle for what is good, in that we continually vanquish what in us is not good, what is self-serving.

To serve our *Volk*, making the effort to practice true and faithful comradeship.

The whole Sermon on the Mount is a single, powerful call from God to serve God and to practice comradeship within the Volk.

The Sermon on the Mount without doubt goes back to Christ. There are no two ways about it.

In this connection we should say a brief word about Christianity and Judaism. Today one frequently hears people say, "Christ was a Jew. Christianity is so steeped in the Jewish spirit that it should be rejected because of it."

In response to this it must be said with great decisiveness that Christianity did not grow out of Judaism as a tree grows out of its roots. On the contrary, Christianity arose out of a struggle against Judaism, so that Christian and the Jew stand over against each other, like fire and water.

In any case the Jew is the oldest and bitterest enemy of Christian sensibility and morality, and so he will remain until the end of days.

We must certainly admit that some so-called Judaisms—Jewish words and expressions—remain embedded in the tradition of the church, in the liturgy, and in some chorales.

But in this regard we have the National Socialist experience to thank for the fact that our eyes have been opened to see how unacceptable these fundamentally alien words and expressions are for us; with the renewal of the life of our German *Volk* what is strange and un-German will disappear from "church-speak" and cease on its own.

Now, as far as the Sermon on the Mount itself is concerned, we may note merely in terms of form that it is in no way a "sermon" in today's sense; rather, it is a direct, written collection of the words of Christ.

Christ himself left no written records; very likely he spoke Aramaic, and perhaps he understood Greek.

In any case, the words of Christ directly handed down to us are written in Greek.

The most important thing for which we must thank our Reformation fathers, and in particular the German Dr. Martin Luther, is, as we know, the translation of the Bible.

The most valuable part of the Bible is without doubt the New Testament, and here again, that which stands decisively above all the rest is the Word of Christ.

Now Dr. Luther did not "translate" the Holy Scriptures literally; rather he "Germanized" them—or, as he himself expressed it, he "interpreted" them for Germans.

Luther's German rendition of the Bible was such a powerful historical accomplishment that it cannot be surpassed.

But Luther's German is in many respects no longer intelligible to our *Volksgenossen* because today we think and speak differently than our fathers did four hundred years ago.

The present attempt to create a new German version more appropriate to our time arose out of a single desire: to present the words of the Sermon on the Mount in our own current way of thinking and speaking to my National Socialist comrades and my *Volksgenossen,* so that they may be "understand" anew, that is, grasped by German hearts.

. . .

17

What Do the German Christians Want?

118 Questions and Answers

Otto Brökelschen

Introduction

This pamphlet, sixteen pages in the original German, was prepared by a German Christian pastor from the Rhineland town of Oberhausen. With its simple question-and-answer format, it is clearly meant for a popular audience.

What Do the German Christians Want? offers responses to questions the reader may have about German Christian beliefs in what its author acknowledges as brief, "almost slogan-like terms." (For more information he refers the reader to other publications listed toward the end of the pamphlet.) Among the topics covered are a host of standard German Christian themes and convictions, among them these: that the state—in this case, the National Socialist state—and the people, or *Volk*, are "God-given orders"; that the organization and structure of the church come from these "God-given orders," not from the Bible; that the church exists to serve the German people; that God is revealed not only in Scripture but "in all of life—in nature, history, [and] the nature of the *Volk*"; that the New Testament of the Christian Bible supersedes the Old Testament; that Christ was not a Jew; that "Jews are our misfortune"; that National Socialism makes a demand like the one God makes: a demand of "the whole of one's life"; and that "Adolf Hitler . . . [is today] the instrument of God's revelation."

The pamphlet also includes the nine-point program of the group responsible for its publication, the National Church Union of German Christians [*Nationalkirchliche Einung der Deutsche Christen*],[1] one of the multitude of splinter groups created even after the German Christians lost favor with Hitler and the Nazi Party in 1934. The platform, which "professes without reservation the National Socialist worldview," includes the following plank: "The National Church Union of German Christians stands for the defeat and removal of all church teachings and practices that are Jewish or otherwise foreign, and pledges itself to German Christianity as the religion ideally suited to the German people. Christ is not the fulfiller of Judaism, but rather its mortal enemy and conqueror."

---

1. The National Church Union of German Christians [*Deutsche Christen (Nationalkirchliche Einung)*] was the 1937 incarnation of what had previously been called the National Church Movement of German Christians [*Deutsche Christen (Nationalkirchliche Bewegung)*]. The name change occurred because the Nazi Party had just decided to restrict the use of the term "movement" [*Bewegung*] to the National Socialist German Workers Party. See Ernst Christian Helmreich, *The German Churches Under Hitler: Background, Struggle, and Epilogue* (Detroit: Wayne State University Press, 1979), 209–10.

What Do the German Christians Want?
118 Questions and Answers[2]

Otto Brökelschen

Introduction

It is no accident that this decisive question about the aims of the German Christians [What do the German Christians want?] is raised anew in the first pamphlet published by the press department on behalf of the leader of the National Church [*Reichsgemeinde*], as part of its new ten-penny series, "*Volks*-publications of the National Church Union of German Christians." The question is raised again and again. Despite five years of struggle and work, the question continues to meet with astonishing ignorance, and responses to it are often mean-spirited misrepresentations.

In order to clear the air, we have therefore intentionally chosen the form of questions and answers, which we think will not only provide the necessary popular tone for a clear presentation. It will also surely give many comrades who are on the front lines the practical tool they need to provide urgently needed explanations to all those among our people who are still out of the loop with respect to the matter of German Christianity, or who reject or oppose it.

It should be noted that when such an attempt is made, especially when the available space is so limited, some connections can be laid out only very briefly, in almost slogan-like terms.

Those who seek greater depth are therefore urged to examine the periodicals listed on pages 13 and 14 [of this publication]. There they will find ongoing discussions, exhaustive and thorough, of all the

---

2. Otto Brökelschen, *What Do the German Christians Want? 118 Questions and Answers* [*Was wollen die Deutschen Christen? 118 Fragen und Antworten*] (Weimar [Thüringen]: Verlag Deutsche Christen, 1937).

questions the present publication has raised and answered with the brevity that limited space has allowed.

Otto Brökelschen, Oberhausen (Rhineland)

Our Genesis and Path

1. *Who are the German Christians?*

The German Christians (GC) are not a church-political group, but rather the *religious renewal- and unification movement of the German Volk*, rooted in German Christianity.

2. *Where do the German Christians come from?*

The German Christians emerge from the *revolution inspired by National Socialism*. Their original cell was in the National Socialist Circle of Pastors and Teachers of Wiertal in Thuringia (1927). Siegfried Leffler and Julius Leutheuser are the founders.

3. *What has the German Christian path been like?*

Their path has had many ups and downs, as, on the one hand, the idea of a German Christian movement awakened throughout the country, and, on the other, because of its *struggle against the [forces of] reaction in the existing church system* (since 1932).

. . .

6. *What generated the church struggle?*

a. The question of the pastors' oath of loyalty to the Führer.[3]

---

3. After President Hindenburg's death on August 2, 1934, Hitler became both head of state and commander in chief of the armed forces. The Reich cabinet decreed the "Law on the Allegiance of Civil Servants and Soldiers of the Armed Forces," requiring members of the military and the civil service to swear an oath of personal loyalty to Hitler. After the national synod of the German Protestant Church met on August 8, 1934, the church leadership called on pastors, who were technically civil servants, to follow suit. The oath read: "I swear: I will be true and obedient to the Führer of the German Reich and nation Adolf Hitler, observe the laws, and conscientiously fulfill my official duties, so help me God."

b. The question of the introduction of the Aryan paragraph in the church.[4]

c. The question of the reordering of the church in line with the reorganization of society [*Volksordnung*] in the German Reich. (Bringing together the regional churches [*Landeskirchen*]; the principle of leadership [*Führerprinzip*] in the church; the National Bishop [*Reichsbischof*].)

7. *What are adversaries of the German Christians called?*

At first they called themselves "Gospel and Church," "Pastors' Emergency League." Later: Confessing Church, Confessing Front, Council of Brethren of the Confessing Church, Provisional Leadership of the German Protestant Church, the Lutheran Council, and so forth.

8. *What was the state's position on the church struggle?*

It repeatedly offered its help for the introduction of an order that would make it possible for the church to settle its faith issues and confessional questions in complete freedom.

9. *How was this done?*

By establishing *regional commissioners* (June 1933). Conducting a *church election* on July 23, 1933. Establishing a *control office* in the Interior Ministry of the Reich, as well as *Finance Departments* in the church's offices (July 1, 1935). Appointing *Reichsminister Kerrl* as national Minister for Church Affairs (July 18, 1935). Creation of national *Church Committees* by Reich Minister Kerrl (October 3, 1935).

10. *Have these measures taken by the state actually helped?*

---

4. See pp. 53ff in this volume.

The Confessing front fought against each individual measure, mostly without success. The GC [German Christians] accepted these measures as helpful and cooperated.

. . .

12. *Which regional churches presently have German Christian church governance?*

Thuringia, Mecklenburg, Anhalt, Lübeck, Bremen.

13. *What about the rest of the regional churches?*

In Bavaria, Baden, Württemberg, and Hannover there is a CC [Confessing church] regime; in Prussia, the largest regional church, the state has appointed the church leadership. . . . The situation is similar in Saxony.

14. *What is the primary issue today?*

Equal rights for the German Christians in all churches with respect to freedom of belief and action.

15. *What important law was passed in most regional churches in the spring of 1938?*

The law that *requires pastors to swear an oath of loyalty* to the Führer, which caused the church struggle to break out in the first place, and which the GC have always supported.

16. *Which law must follow immediately?*

The *introduction of the Aryan paragraph into the church.* Even today there are still pastors of Jewish blood working in the church!

. . .

Church, State, and People [*Volk*]

19. *How do we define "the church"?*

The Church is:

1. perceived from within, *a home* for German piety in belief and love, joy and strength;
2. perceived from the outside, *an earthly organization* that must align itself with the ethnic-national [*völkisch*] order.

20. *Do we still need the church?*

True piety requires community. The church's job is to build community through word and deed.

21. *What risk did and does the church run?*

The risk of *becoming an end in itself*, an order in itself, isolating itself from the God-given orders of state and *Volk*.

22. *What should be the relationship of church and state?*

A relationship of trust. Not church over state (Roman power-church), *not church under* the state (state church), *not church alongside* the state (separate), but instead *church within* the state (Father State, Mother Church).

23. *That is what Luther thought. How did he understand the governing authority and the church?*

According to Luther, the governing authority and the church are necessary, *equally valuable functions* within the body of the *Volk*.

24. *What is the precondition for a relationship of trust between church and state?*

The church must relinquish all *claims to power*.

. . .

28. *We oppose every claim to power. Why?*

Because the duty of the church is not to rule, but rather to serve.

29. *Whom is it the church's duty to serve?*

The German church's duty is to serve *the German Volk* with the power of the Gospel. *Service to the Volk is service to God.*

30. *What do we want, so as to ensure that the church will be free to serve and set aside all desire for power?*

We want the entire structure and administration of the church to be turned over to the *regulating agencies of the Volk.*

31. *But aren't the structure and administration of the church established in the Bible?*

No, these matters are *neither established in the Bible* nor are they *the object of faith.* They are governed by the orders of life [*Lebensordnungen*] of the *Volk* and the state.

32. *Which principle must be clearly implemented here?*

The principle that *the order of the Volk takes priority over the order of the church.*

33. *What do we understand by the term "Volk"?*

"*Volk*" is the *divinely willed community* of German people based on the created orders of race, blood, and soil [*Rasse, Blut und Boden*].

34. *What does this mean for the church's service to the German Volk?*

All the church's service must be directed to *the community that is the German Volk*; its core is the heartfelt unification of Germans before God.

35. *Who still stands in the way of this heartfelt unification of Germans?*

The *Confessing churches*, which must not be smashed from without, but rather conquered *from within*.

36. *How did the confessional churches come about?*

Confessional churches are a consequence of the political splintering of Germany before and after the Reformation. They are not, as "the confessors" say, ordained by God, but are the *ecclesial manifestation of the political formulation* of 1530: *cuius regio, eius religio* (as is the ruler, so is the religion of the state).

37. *On what legal and faith grounds may we set aside the denominations?*

On the grounds of Adolf Hitler's political, economic, and cultural *unification of the German Volk*, and on the basis of Jesus' command to struggle "that all may be one."

38. *Which is the only church that can realize the unification of the German Volk?*

The National Church [Reichskirche]. It is the church of the community of the German *Volk*, Christ's congregation of Germans in service and faith.

39. *Wouldn't it be better to just walk out of the Confessing churches?*

It is a law of religious life that separation from a religious community brings with it spiritual impoverishment. We have a *right to the church*, and we cannot conquer it by walking out, but only by faithful *saturation and conquest*.

40. *Do we still need pastors?*

• *Pastors* must be separated from *parsons [Pfaffen]*, that is, from those "churchmen" who misuse their spiritual influence.

- *Pastors* must be delivered from *false priests*, who claim to be mediators between God and the people.

- The *pastor* should be *the one the Volk designates* to work as a spiritual counselor in the sanctuary of its soul.

Theology and Confession

41. *What does "theology" mean?*

Theology is the thoughtful and conceptual understanding of the truths of the Christian faith.

42. *Do we need theology?*

Yes, because the church has a *teaching office*, and that requires knowledge of the faith.

43. *What risks does theology run?*

It is in danger of placing teachings above life, and concepts above the reality of faith, and so becoming abstract, that is, alienated from both life and *Volk*. (*Book learning*.)

44. *Which theology manifests this especially?*

The so-called *dialectical theology* of the Social Democrat professor Karl Barth, previously of Bonn and Münster, who after refusing to take the oath of loyalty to the Führer is now again in Switzerland: the Confessing Church calls this fellow its "dear teacher"—honorary doctorate from Oxford!

45. *Barthian theology has miseducated a whole new generation of theologians. What effect has this had?*

The effect has been that a large number of German pastors have *not been able to establish a positive relationship* to German life today.

46. *What is German theology about?*

German theology has to do with the relationship to God of the *German* in his character as a *member of the Volk*. Starting point: the created human being. *Ethno-national* [*Völkisch*] *theology*.

47. *What battle cry has been used in the church struggle to mobilize congregations against the GC?*

The cry has been, "The German Christians are attacking the church's very substance!" "*Our creed is in danger!*"

48. *Are we German Christians rejecting the creed?*

No. As the state must have a constitution, so the church must have a creed.

49. *So what needs to be said about the church's creeds?*

The creeds are *human words* and *human work*. They are therefore *time-bound*. They are only *contours for faith* that, as expressions of God's eternal truth, must change in keeping with changes in the thought and speech of different times; given the revolutionary change that is occurring these days, the creeds also require an expression appropriate to this historic moment.

50. *In light of this, is the oft-used formula "Bible and Creed" correct?*

As has already been said, Bible and the creed lie on *different levels*. A creed is a human word, while in the Bible we have God's word in the form of the eternal truths of faith.

51. *For what purpose have creed and dogma often been used in the course of the church's history?*

Both have often been subjects of dispute and used to dissociate [the church] from the German struggle for freedom and faith, as well as to undergird clerical authority.

52. What is our position on church dogma?

Church dogma must *never* lead to coerced belief. *Belief that is coerced is un-German and un-Christian.*

53. What must be and remain the unconditional principle of the life of any authentic church based on German Christianity?

The fundamental principle of freedom of conscience, set on the lampstand by Luther, won in the struggle for the freedom of the German soul, realized in National Socialism, is the only thing that provides the breadth and depth that can embrace and express the religious life of the nation. . . .

God's Word and Revelation

54. Is the Bible the word of God?

The Bible is not altogether God's Word, *but we have God's word in the Bible.*

. . .

57. Luther knew nothing about this teaching. What was Luther's position on Scripture?

Luther had a *"free" position in regard to the Bible.* For example, he calls the Ten Commandments the "Jewish law book" and the Epistle of James a "straw epistle." In translating the Bible he actually "Germanized" some texts, for example, Exodus 20, Exodus 8–11; Psalm 19:10.

58. Does anyone still hold to the doctrine of biblical inspiration?

Even though science *disproved* it a long time ago, it is still defended by power-hungry priests and is therefore widely considered part of the true faith by pious congregations.

59. *What are we to think of the Old Testament?*

If one could attain salvation through the O.T. [Old Testament], there would be no need for a N.T. [New Testament]. *The N.T. supersedes the O.T.*

60. *Shouldn't the O.T. be removed from the Bible?*

No. In the O.T., as in many other ancient religious scriptures, there is real piety.

61. *What do we reject in the O.T.?*

We reject the materials that are marked as *clearly Jewish*, whose purpose is to present the Jews as the *chosen people*.

. . .

63. *What do we understand by God's revelation?*

Revelation is the unveiling, the proclamation of the living God.

64. *Where does God's revelation take place?*

The Confessing front asserts that it takes place only in the Bible.

65. *What are we to make of that?*

If that were true, then the living God would be locked into the book that is the Bible and its letters.

66. *God is Spirit, that is, he works eternally. What follows from this?*

This means that God's revelation takes place *in all of life*: in nature, history, the nature of the *Volk*, and the destiny of individual lives, as has also come to light in the holy books of our German forefathers.

67. *What do we believe, specifically, about the present history of our Volk?*

We believe that God reveals himself today in the history of the German *Volk through Adolf Hitler*. The Führer, who calls Germans to faith and unifies them in love, *is the instrument of God's revelation, the German prophet.*

Christ

68. *We have been criticized for wanting to take Christ away from the Germans. Is that true?*

This is a *church-political* lie. There is no Christianity, nor is there German Christianity, without Christ. "He is for us the indissoluble union of faith and love. In him the German soul finds its way home to God and to itself." (¶3 of "The Will and Aim of the National Church Union of German Christians," July 14, 1937.)

69. *Some claim that we want to get rid of the cross. Is that true?*

This is yet another *church-political lie.* For us the cross is an eternal *symbol of a love that frees one from the self,* a symbol of the victory of God, and therefore God's strength for struggle and service.

70. *Why does the German of today, in general, no longer have a relationship with Christ?*

Because the real Christ is hidden from him by the dogmatic Christ of the church, and falsified by an *image of Christ* as weak and inferior.

71. *In light of this, what is our duty?*

Our duty is to break through to the *actual Christ* of the gospels and to free his image from all the Jewish-Roman-Catholic-dogmatic *overpainting.*

72. *Was Christ a Jew?*

No. Even if his Aryan descent cannot be established, his whole life's struggle proves that he was *"the first significant adversary of the Jews."*[5]

73. *What is the proof of Jesus' anti-Jewish posture?*

In Jesus' struggle against *faith in the letter*, against Jewish *legalistic piety*, against Jewish *materialism*, against Jewish *self-centeredness*, against the Jewish *concept of the Messiah* and the *Jewish view of God*.

74. *As proof of Jesus' Jewish ties, Jewish-Christians and adversaries of Christ like to quote Jesus' saying: "Salvation comes from the Jews." (John 4:22) How do we respond?*

It is significant that both Christ *and opponents of the Bible* appeal to a biblical saying. It is significant that there are still Christians who encourage the Jews. As is clear from the context, the passage being quoted has is a falsehood apparently inserted into the text by a Jew or a Jewish-Christian writer. For Jesus' words—"God is Spirit and those who worship him must worship him in spirit and in truth"—have lost their meaning because of what was interpolated.

75. *What is the content of Jesus' message?*

The message of Jesus consists of *two central truths*:

1. *God the Father is love.*
2. *The kingdom of God is within you*!

76. *What follows from the proclamation of God's fatherly love?*

If God is love, then *He does not calculate* like the Jews' God Jehovah. The Father *forgives* those who *trust* in His love. This obviates the whole *Jewish concept of sacrifice and judgment*. The way to God's fatherly heart is *free*. Hence, Jewish-Roman *priestly mediation* is condemned.

77. *What follows from Jesus' proclamation of the kingdom within us?*

---

5. This quotation comes from a 1934 novel written by Josef Goebbels: *Michael* (Verlag Franz), 82. [English: *Michael: A Novel*, trans. Joachim Neugroschel (New York: Amok Press, 1987)].

It destroys the Jewish concept of a political *messianic kingdom*. The kingdom of God is *communion with God*, being one of *God's children*.

78. *Who has falsified the message of the kingdom of God?*

The *Roman Church*, with its teaching of the unity of the kingdom of God and the organization of the Catholic Church. (Political nature of the church.) The *Confessing Church*, which claims to be the "Church of Christ," teaches fundamentally the same thing, in that it condemns all who do not belong to it. (Barmen Confession)

79. *What should we think of sin?*

Sin consists not only in morally bad individual acts, but also in the *self-seeking condition* of the human, because of which he rejects God's claim of love.

Germanness and Christianity, Politics and Religion

80. *Why does the relationship between Germanness and Christianity seem to have become such a problem?*

Because of foreign theologians who are alienated from the land and the *Volk* (K. Barth!) and also because of a democratic-pacifist church government that does not consider the German people's bond in race, blood, and soil [*Rasse, Blut, und Boden*] as obligatory for faith.

81. *What does Christianity have to do with Germanness?*

We are not just human beings, but *according to God's will* we are Germans, and we can be Christians *only as Germans*.

82. *Are we then rejecting the transnational mission of Christianity?*

Not at all. We respect the religious and ecclesiastical individuality of other nations, but we believe that German Christianity is the *religion that is ideally suited* for Germans.

83. *What does it mean to speak of a Christianity "ideally suited to the German character"?*

A Christianity that in its proclamation, character, and form does not distort or tear apart the German character, *but rather fulfills it.*

84. *Who rejects this ideally suited [German] Christianity?*

1. The *Confessing Church*, because it knows only a *generic* Christianity.
2. The members of the *German Faith Movement* [*Deutschgläubigen*], because they regard Christianity as a *foreign religion.*

85. *Is Christianity a foreign religion?*

If Christianity were Near Eastern-Oriental, it would *never* have gained a foothold in the West. As a matter of fact, Christianity has *shaped the German people* and has created a 1,000-year-old *German culture.* The NSDAP [Nazi Party] would never (see Point 24 of its program) have been able to establish itself on the foundation of positive Christianity if Christianity were a foreign religion.[6]

86. *Is National Socialism a religion?*

This has been repeatedly rejected by the men in leadership positions. National Socialism is a *worldview and way of life.*

87. *What have we been able to learn anew through National Socialism?*

We have learned again to have *faith* that can move mountains, and *love* that through sacrifice and self-giving builds community.

. . .

89. *What is the position of National Socialism in relation to Christianity?*

---

6. A "positive Christianity" was understood to be beyond denominations and emphasized an "active," heroic Christ. That Hitler included this in the platform signaled his sense that he would need the support of the churches as he embarked on his National Socialist project.

According to the party platform, it is based on a *positive Christianity* (Point 24), but does not associate itself with a specific denomination.

90. *What does positive Christianity mean?*

A positive Christianity, in contrast to a negative Christianity of the word, means a *Christianity of action.*

91. *The Savior also demands a positive Christianity ("What you have done . . ."; "By their fruits you shall know them,"; "Not all who say, Lord, Lord . . ."). How does this positive Christianity come to expression in our program?*

Germany is our duty, Christ is our strength. (Will and Goal, ¶3, July 14, 1937.)

92. *Doesn't this really confuse politics and religion?*

Anyone who thinks that is still thinking in terms of *dividing up life* into a lot of different areas.

93. *What is the relationship between politics and religion?*

They are not two different spheres: politics and religion are *two directions* [of our thought and action]. What is religious has to do with the *way home to God*, what is political, with *marching out* to shape the world. Only those who know the way home can march out into the world.

94. *What does National Socialism demand of the human being?*

It demands *totality*, that is, the whole of one's life. In this sense it is like the demand of God, which is directed to the whole human being.

95. *How might we summarize our worldview?*

For a Christian whom God has created a German, the only worldview that counts is his German—that is to say, National Socialist—worldview. (Siegfried Leffler.)

Judaism and Jewish-Christianity

96. *What position do we German Christians take in relation to Judaism?*

The Jews are the element of *decay* in our *Volk*, therefore we stand against them in an uncompromising struggle. *The Jews are our misfortune.*

97. *Where does the Confessing Church stand on the Jewish question?*

To this day they have *rejected* the introduction of the Aryan paragraph into the church.

98. *What is the basis for this position?*

They maintain that the Aryan paragraph would violate the confessional stance of the church. In reality, they are caught up in a *Jewish Christianity* or a Christian Judaism.

99. *What do we understand by Jewish Christianity?*

A Christianity that values Jewish religion and Jewish-rabbinical theology above the *God-given law of German life.*

100. *What important duty do we German Christians have in this area?*

To *break down and remove* every spirit that is Jewish and foreign to our *Volk* from church teachings and practices. . . .

101. *In which teachings can we recognize this Jewish disguise?*

1. In the equating of Christ's *Father-God* with the Jew-God *Jehovah.*

2. In a faith bound up with *law and its letter.*

3. In *the notion of reward.*

4. In a *theology of punishment.*

5. In a theology of *atonement.*

6. In the teaching of *election,* etc.

102. *What special duty do we have in breaking down the Jewish spirit in the church's teaching and life?*

The duty of reshaping our worship services as *celebrations of God* [*Gottesfeier*] along German Christian lines.

103. *What is the significance of our celebrations of God?*

To gather German people together, to edify and activate them: this is the sense of our celebrations. This is where we get the *strength* for actual service to God [*Gottesdienst*] in everyday life.

104. *What about baptism and communion?*

The celebrations of the sacraments, as well as the rites of marriage and burial, must be structurally *freed* from the Jewish spirit and placed within the divine law of German life.

105. *What do we think of the hymnal?*

We will hold fast to the tried and true songs of our forefathers. The many *Judaisms* must be Germanized. The new song of our movement has already *gained its place* in the hearts of German Christians.

The "German Faith" Group

106. *Which organized groups advocate the "German Faith"?*

1. The *Fighting Circle of German Faith* (formerly German Faith Movement)

2. *German Knowledge of God* (Ludendorff).

107. *What can we say in principle about the "German Faith"?*

In principle, we are delighted that after years of living without faith or with an impoverished faith, the German people are once again confessing their faith.

108. *What can be said about the content of the "German Faith"?*

1. The German Faith *opposes Christianity* and asserts that it is antithetical to the sense of what is essential to Germanness [*Wesensgefühl*].
2. The German Faith asserts that God *becomes incarnate* in the values of race, blood, and soil [*Rasse, Blut, und Boden*].

109. *Wheredo we stand in relation to those who profess the "German Faith"?*

We must never forget that they are our comrades within the *Volk*, and we want to contend with them honestly for the truth.

110. *At the same time, what should we watch out for?*

We note:

1. that their critique of Christianity has to a large degree turned into a general *hatred* of Christianity that reminds us painfully of the times of the *freethinkers*;
2. that, much like the Confessing Church with its dogmatism, the German-faith people practice their own kind of German-faith dogmatism, and in doing so, disturb free German people;
3. that the German-faith adherents are trying to make their faith viewpoint the *criterion* for National Socialist authenticity.

4. that by their struggle against Christ, those who profess the "German Faith" are actually doing a service for the Confessing front and the Jews.

. . .

Appendix

112. *Is the National Church Union still necessary, along with the church?*

The church needs a movement that can dare to build something new from the ground up, without being dogmatically bound (S. Leffler). Moreover, the National Church Union is *not tied to a church*; in setting its goals it extends much further than the confessional churches.

113. *Can those who have left the church participate?*

Of course. We invite *every* comrade of the *Volk* without regard to class, church, or confession.

114. *How is our National Church Union organized?*

a. The *leader* of the national [*Reichs-*] community, Senior Counselor Siegfried Leffler, Weimar (P.O.B. Weimar 443).

b. Leadership of the national community

c. Department leaders for individual divisions, for example, organization, race [*Rasse*], propaganda, press, publishing, arrangements for social events, theology, etc. Associated with the organization is also the German Christian pastors and deacons, "The German Pastoral Community."

d. National congregational leadership. The infrastructure of the organization is broken up into provincial teams, provincial communities, borderland communities, and local communities.

115. *What periodicals and newspapers do we publish?*

a. *The National Church*, the weekly, twelve-page newsletter, with a two-page regional district supplement.

b. *German Christianity*, the weekly newspaper.

c. *The Church of the German Volk*, the weekly community newspaper.

d. *German Piety*, the monthly periodical; there are also newsletters for communities in several regions [*Länder*], for example, *The German Christian* (Baden), *German Sunday* (Württemberg), and local community newsletters.

The Future

116. *To whom do we German Christians pledge ourselves as we carry out our duty and work?*

. . . *solely to God and the German Volk*, as *unconditional* followers of Adolf Hitler.

117. *What is the only way to our goal?*

Our struggle and the steady growth of our movement have convinced us that the path to our goal is a *heartfelt and faithful saturation of the German people with our vision.*

118. *When will we reach our goal?*

We have *already established* the National Church as a German community of Christ where, in our German Christian communities, German comrades within the *Volk* can live beyond all confessional boundaries, in faith and love.

It is our will, our service and our prayer,
that the National Church become and grow
as a place of peace and worship,
a refuge of German piety,

an outpost of faith and strength.

All for Germany!

The Desire and the Goal of the National Church Union of German Christians

1. The National Church Union of German Christians supports the national church vision. It appeals to every German person without regard to class, background, or creed. Its goal is the religious renewal and unification of the German people.

2. The National Church Union of German Christians sees the division of the German people into religious groups, denominations, and sects as a renunciation of God, according to whose creative will all Germans are one people. The confessional churches and their transnational striving endanger the unity and strength of the nation. The German Christian National Church Union fights to overcome the denominations under the banner:

One People – One Faith!

3. The German Christian National Church Union is based on its struggle for the religious unification of the German people in Christ. He embodies for us the indissoluble unity of belief and love. In him, the German soul finds its way home to God and to itself. On the basis of his message of God the eternal Father and human beings as children of God, Germans grow together into a community unto life and death:

Germany is our Duty, Christ is our Strength

4. The National Church Union of German Christians engages for the defeat and removal of everything having a Jewish or foreign spirit in church teachings and practices, and pledges itself to German Christianity as the religion ideally suited to the German

people. Christ is not the perfecter of Judaism, but rather its mortal enemy and conqueror.

The National Church Union of German Christians respects the individual religious and ecclesial realities of other nations, just as it may expect to be shown the same respect by the religious communities and churches of other nations. It is certain that, on this basis, it can contribute to greater understanding among Christian peoples and fruitful collaboration among their churches.

5. The National Church Union of German Christians rejects every ecclesiastical claim to power and to the coercion of conscience as un-German and un-Christian. It identifies itself with the more-than-one-thousand-year-long struggle for the freedom of the German soul against a power-mongering church system. It fulfills the legacy of those the church has condemned as heretics because they struggled for a free German Christianity. German faith in Christ, rooted in conscience and freedom, produces both breadth and depth to embrace and to shape the religious life of the whole nation.

6. The National Church Union of German Christians follows the Führer and the Reich unconditionally. It professes without reservation the National Socialist worldview and dedicates itself to the totality of German life as demanded by National Socialism:

Service to the People is Service to God

7. The National Church Union of German Christians demands that the church be integrated into the community of the German people. It rejects any special political position and legal independence for the church, and urges that the structure of the

entire church be transferred into the governing structures of the German people.

8. The National Church Union of German Christians advocates a radical renewal of the German pastoral office and works toward the organic integration of pastoral ministry into the common life of the German people. The introduction of German laws regarding civil servants (loyalty oath to the Führer, Aryan paragraph) is, as far as the national church is concerned, self-evident.

9. The national church is the fulfillment of an eternal desire of the German people: *A place of peace and worship, a refuge of German piety, an outpost of faith and strength.*

German Christians, National Church Union, Inc.

Signed by Siegfried Leffler[7]

Declared on July 14, 1937

---

7. See more about and by Leffler elsewhere in this volume.

18

Freedom of Conscience

Wolf Meyer-Erlach

Introduction

Wolf Meyer–Erlach (1899–1982) was a German Lutheran pastor and professor. He studied theology at the universities of Erlangen and Tübingen, served in the military during World War I, and was ordained to the ministry thereafter. Early in the 1920s he became a speaker for the National Socialist German Workers Party. In 1931 he became a radio "broadcast pastor" for the Bavarian state radio system. He joined the Nazi Party in 1933; during the same year he became a leader of the German Christians in Bavaria.

Despite his lack of the academic credentials needed to assume a university teaching position, he was appointed later in 1933 to a position in practical theology at the University of Jena, a stronghold of German Christian academics. He also served as university preacher. In 1934–35 he became dean of the theological faculty, and in 1935—contravening a vote of the faculty—the Reich Ministry of Education in Berlin appointed him rector of the university, a position he held until 1937. His position as rector enabled him to facilitate the appointment of professors with German Christian sympathies.

According to several scholars, in 1935 he changed his name from Wolfgang Meyer to Wolf Meyer-Erlach to avoid the possibility he would be mistakenly identified as a Jew.[1] Meyer-Erlach was an active member of the Institute for the Study and Eradication of Jewish Influence in German Religious Life, beginning with its establishment in 1939.[2]

Meyer-Erlach published several collections of radio talks during the 1930s. "Freedom of Conscience" is one of eight such talks that make up *Defiant Faith,* which appeared in 1937. In language and imagery aimed to captivate a radio audience Meyer-Erlach weaves together several key German Christian themes. One is deep suspicion of, even antagonism toward, the "establishment" church (or, to use Meyer-Erlach's words, "the visible church"), with its traditions and its doctrines, its insistence on self-administration (in contrast to German Christians' desires for a unified—and nazified—national church), and its "priests and scribes," who are tied to the intellectually oppressive history of the church. "Is it not true that," he asks rhetorically, "except for very brief periods, freedom has never found a home in the church?" He continues, "[T]his same disposition . . . pervades every denomination and church to this day."

---

1. Wolfgang Schenk, "Der Jenaer Jesus. Zu Werk und Wirken des völkischen Theologen Walter Grundmann und seiner Kollegen," in *Das missbrauchte Evangelium. Studien zu Theologie und Praxis der Thüringer Deutschen Christen,* ed. Peter von der Osten-Sacken (Berlin: Institut Kirche und Judentum, 2002), 167–279.

2. After the war he fled the German Democratic Republic, resumed his work as a pastor, and was awarded the Federal Service Cross [*Bundesverdienstkreuz*] by the Federal Republic of Germany for his anti-Communist work.

We must look "beyond the visible church," he says. We must "look upon . . . Christ," who "lives by an entirely different Spirit . . . than do most of those who call themselves his servants." He "moves through the land like a king or a free lord." Christ is like a leader [*Führer*] with whom one has a direct, emotional connection; there is no need for the "apparatus" of the church establishment. And this is no suffering messiah; for German Christians, this Christ is powerful and heroic, like a king or a free lord, striding across the German countryside.

Alternating between "priests," "scribes," and "temple," terms that refer to Jews and Judaism, and "church," "dogmas," and "ecclesiastical," terms that refer to Christians and Christianity, Meyer-Erlach's radio talk conflates the Christian establishment he is criticizing with Judaism and Jews, who "reject and crucify the Son of God as a blasphemer." He claims both the apostle Paul and the reformer Luther as allies in "the good fight for Christian freedom against all Jewish oppression." Associating his Christian antagonists in the church struggle with the Jews puts them even more on the defensive.

God's friends, he concludes, are not found "in the narrow 'church space,' but in the world in which the farmer, the soldier, the laborer, the scholar, the S.A.-man, the official, father and mother, do their work in fidelity and faith day in and day out." The "God-given orders of marriage, the family, the German ethnic culture [*Volkstum*], the Fatherland" are the framework for "true Christianity": for Meyer-Erlach, the German Christian, this means a faith oriented toward the realization of the Nazi project.

Freedom of Conscience[3]

Wolf Meyer-Erlach

> For freedom Christ has set us free.
> Stand firm, therefore,
> and do not submit again to a yoke of slavery. (Gal. 5:1)

Church and freedom: how do they go together? So inquire the well-informed as they scrutinize the last two thousand years. Is it not true that, except for very brief periods, freedom has never found a home in the church? They point to the leaves of church history [books], filled with violent intellectual and spiritual oppression. It is precisely those nations in which the church has become the ruling power that have suffered the most from the enslavement of conscience. The history of the humanities and the natural sciences, men like Kepler, Giordano Bruno, Galileo, and Fichte and nearly all great scholars and path-breakers in the realm of the intellect bear witness that the visible church has never vouchsafed freedom, that it has almost always been the greatest obstacle in the way of progress both forward and upward. And this same disposition—which we identify with the word "medieval"—pervades every denomination and church to this day.

Despite this we dare to speak of the church of freedom. It is not that we do not see the awful reality of this spiritual oppression. But we are looking beyond the visible church with all its dubious aspects. We leave behind all idolatry, whether of persons or of the letter, and look upon him who is greater than all churchdoms and Christendoms put together: upon Christ. We speak of the church of freedom because we know that the Lord of the church lives by an entirely different Spirit, a completely different teaching, an utterly different life than do most of those who call themselves his servants. It

---

3. From Wolf Meyer-Erlach, *Defiant Faith: Eight Radio Talks* [*Glaubenstrotz: Acht Rundfunkreden*] (Weimar [Thüringen]: Verlag Deutsche Christen, 1937), 3–9.

is to this Lord, to His Word and His will, that we must give account, not to the self-destructive Christian powers that be. In the face of the invisible church and in light of the eternity of our people [*Volk*] everything that swells the church with such self-importance means nothing. There only truth reigns, not lunacy. There only the actual [*Sein*], not the appearance [*Schein*], counts. And from there the word rings out: Only the one whom the Son liberates is truly free.

In all the millennia that have come before, no one has ever walked the earth more freely than Christ. Looking at his life, what he did, we find again and again the testimony of the greatest men who came under his influence: that he emanated a worthiness, a purity and nobility, a strength, the likes of which has never been seen since in any religion. We understand how he could ask, "Which of you convicts me of sin?" [John 8:46].

From this inner freedom flows his external freedom. He moves through the land like a king. He observes the thousand ecclesial laws of his time that have to do with fasting, with contact with sinners and tax collectors. He sees how the people around him labor under the delusion that they will gain God's mercy by obeying these laws. Through the whole thorny underbrush of these soul-wounding ecclesiastical laws he strides like a free lord. He sees the snares of pious observance with which the priests and scribes continually seek to imprison a life lived in God. This is why he flings these words at the poisoners of life: "The Sabbath was made for humankind, not humankind for the Sabbath." [Mark 2:27] To uncover all the loveless mendacity, the fratricidal godlessness of the priests' piety, he defies the prohibitions and heals the sick on the Sabbath. He sees how the priests do violence to divinely-created human souls by their commandments and dogmas. So he rips apart these nets fashioned to capture both life and God, by setting his reckless "but I say to you" against it [see Matthew 5]. He sees how the pious, led astray by their spiritual teachers, idolize the Temple, how they worship stone and wood instead of the living God, and so he says, "Tear down this temple. A day is coming and an hour, in which no stone will remain upon another." For God, who directs the destiny of each person, the history of the peoples, is more than stone and wood, more than towers and walls, more than dogmas and printer's ink and paper. It is not where the temple is that God is. Where God, the living One is: only there is the church—even if it were a stable, as Luther says.

For Christ, the human being is the temple of God. This is why he reaches even into the human heart. Of what use are holy walls, or the whole enchanting magnificence of the priesthood, if the heart is filled with wild demons? The people—the simple, faithful people—look at the robes and imagine that putting on the robes means putting on a new, consecrated person. But God sees the heart, and with the penetrating eyes of God Jesus sees into the scribes' innermost being. With his insight into the depths of all priesthood, he cries woe on the scribes and Pharisees, who wear long robes and pray long prayers.[4] With the courage that only the truth of God can give, he calls them the great hypocrites, whitewashed graves.[5]

We can understand why the priests, exposed in all their wretchedness, hate the Lord of Truth. We can understand why the servants of God, in their concern for their worldly power, reject and crucify the Son of God as a blasphemer. Across the centuries his melancholic words ring out: If they have called me Satan, how much more will they treat you this way, my disciples. If they have persecuted me in the name of their God, how much more will they persecute you.

But we can also understand why those who in their innermost selves hunger for the truth, for freedom, feel themselves drawn

4. See Matt. 23:1-36; Mark 12:37-40; Luke 20:45-47.
5. Matthew 23:27.

irresistibly to Christ. We know from centuries of history and from our own experience, that it is precisely the unspoiled who are most often drawn to him. A shout rises up out of the hearts of those who have been touched by his words, as if by a ray of light. The storm of freedom that rushes through the life of Christ breaks into their souls and transforms them in heart and attitude and behavior. They sense that where the spirit of the scribes rules, there is servitude and death. But where the Spirit of Christ, the Spirit of God blows, there is freedom.

Let us look at the Gospel according to John. This supreme gospel is one long song of praise to the liberating power of Christ. Turning eternally, like the vault of stars, this freedom of the Spirit and the soul shines through all his speeches. All the wonderful words that have moved the human heart for millennia, that quiet the deepest longing of our souls, in whose truthfulness lie happiness and blessedness, John pours out before us like shining gold: Christ is love, light that shines in the darkness and drives it out. He is joy and peace that flow through our souls like a stream of water. He is truth and life, in whose depths we can submerge ourselves, soothed from all the bitterness and puzzlement of our existence, enabled to walk like victors through our daily lives. Only those who receive these words deep into their hearts, in faith, in those quiet hours of solitude that are destiny, will sense something of the full glory of Christ, of that freedom of faith that lifts human beings to divine nature.

Thousands have experienced it. They come to Jesus filled with tribulation and misery and go forth from him upright and strong. What pours out of the mouth of the greatest evangelist, the most eloquent and greatest apostle attests. God's kindness and geniality, the liberating power that shatters all demons and lifts the soul out of the constriction of anxiety and sets it in a spacious, free place, where there is no more distress: these entered his life and broke it in two. Behind

427

him lay the night of his time of scribal learning, and before him lay the day, the bright light of the freedom of the Christian.

Because this apostle[6] had himself been freed from the deadly noose of a thousand laws, of dogmas and moral prohibitions, he fought the good fight for Christian freedom against all Jewish oppression. This is why he implores the faithful: Stand firm [in the freedom for which Christ has set us free], and do not submit again to a yoke of slavery![7] As one who is free he faces down the apostles who wanted to make the Gentiles into Jews before they would be permitted to become Christians.[8] He fights to establish that only the Spirit of Christ—but never, ever, Jewish law—can make a person into a Christian. He fights because God has placed his law and his will in the hearts of the peoples whom the scribes of every era scornfully call heathens. Into the theological quarrels that are tearing apart the congregation in Corinth he speaks the liberating word that all the heretic-chasers forget: Here not Paul, not Apollos, not Peter is Lord, but only Christ.

The visible church forgot this gospel of freedom. But it could never be completely suppressed. Again and again a lone believer has arisen, someone who dares to live his life in the freedom of faith. Among the Germans, the song of the freedom of a Christian was sung most powerfully and thrillingly by Luther, the Thuringian miner's son. Like a swift-racing storm, redeeming power burst forth from his German awareness of God and Christ. In a period of upheaval Luther hurled his great apostolic discovery into our people: dogmas and doctrines, priests and scribes, ecclesiastical commandments and prohibitions are nothing. Christ alone is everything; no slavish obedience to the all-too-human commands of the priests, no bowing and scraping to the scribes' claims to authority,

---

6. Now Meyer-Erlach is referring to the apostle Paul.

7. Gal. 5:1.

8. He is referring to the controversy in the early church about whether Gentile men had to be circumcised first—following the Jewish law—before they could become members of the church.

but rather community with Christ, living, active, and bustling faith[9] alone is what is decisive, both in time and in eternity: "It matters not at all to the soul"—as he says across the centuries—"whether the body is dressed in holy garments, as the priests and clerics do, whether one is in church or in holy places, or whether one goes around with holy objects or prays outwardly, fasts, and makes pilgrimages. An evil person, dissembler, or hypocrite may also do this. And it does the soul no harm to wear clothing that is not holy, or to be in a place that is not holy, or not to eat, drink, make pilgrimages, or pray, and leave aside all the things that hypocrites do as well."

Truth be told, every day of the last few years has confirmed the truth of this. Not the appearance, but what is inside; not the teaching, but the living out of faith; not the pious garment, but the believing heart is what is decisive. This faith glows in the soul of a person like a fire and transforms him. Christ is like a wedding ring: he encloses God in himself and gives humans a share in the divine nature. In this faith each individual becomes a priest, requiring no mediator between himself and God. Today we must hear once again the Reformation message about the priesthood of all believers, and precisely in the so-called Lutheran church: "Injustice has been done to the words 'priest,' 'pastor,' 'cleric,' in that it has been withdrawn from the great heap of all Christians and placed on the one heap that is now called clerical status. The truth is that all who do their daily work in faith and love are priests." Today Luther's words must be proclaimed with a prophetic voice again: "One stroke of the thresher in the barn is worth as much before God as a whole Psalter sung by a Carthusian [monk]." And further: "Justification will not be experienced by the people in the cloisters, the priests, and the saints, but rather by the mothers who wash their children's diapers, the maids who sweep the house, the artisan and the farmer who pursue

9. This is a phrase directly from Luther.

their vocations, the authorities who carry out their offices." Not in the narrow "church space," but in the world in which the farmer, the soldier, the laborer, the scholar, the S.A.-man, the official, father and mother, do their work in fidelity and faith day in and day out—in this wide space of everyday life—here God's friends and coworkers live.

This is why Luther breaks out of the depth and solitude of his Christianity, through the walls of the cloisters, and takes up residence among his people, with all their needs and struggles and concerns. As the free lord of all through faith he becomes, in love, the servant of his people.[10] True Christianity always stands in the midst of this world, in the God-given orders of marriage, the family, the *Volkstum*, the Fatherland. True faith always breaks open the deadly constriction that priests and scribes cast around life. We are all priests; we are, as Luther says, all bishops.[11] How can any group of people dare to condemn others because they are led on another path by God, by the Lord of the church? The Spirit of God always blows where and how it will. And this would surely not be the first time that God's spring storm blew outside the church, while inside it cold death and the moldy air of graves reign. The Spirit of God is as free as God himself, free as the Lord who bypassed all the demands of law and commandment by which the church wishes to enslave humanity. And as free as God's Spirit, as free as the eternal Lord, is the one who lives his life in faith and love.

Because God's Spirit does its work in human souls in divine freedom; because we know that this God is a God of the living and not of the dead: this is why, with the authority of faith and in defiance of all the constraints on conscience and faith imposed by the visible church, we speak of the only true, invisible church of freedom. We

10. An allusion to Luther's 1520 Reformation tract, *The Freedom of a Christian*.
11. An allusion to two other 1520 tracts by Luther, *To the Christian Nobility of the German Nation* and *On the Babylonian Captivity of the Church*; in both, Luther refers to what is now known as "the priesthood of all believers."

are free through our faith; we are strong through the night and in any danger. We will never again be the slaves of the human, all-too-human.

19

Jesus and the Jews!

Organization for German Christianity

Introduction

The Organization for German Christianity [*Bund für deutsches Christentum*], which issued the pamphlet from which the excerpt below is taken, came into being in November 1936 when "leaders of German-Christian-controlled regional churches . . . met in the Wartburg Castle outside Eisenach."[1] Their goal, writes Susannah Heschel, was "creating a judenrein [Jew-free] Christianity for a judenrein Nazi Reich," that is, a thorough de-judaizing of Christian

---

1. Susannah Heschel, *The Aryan Jesus: Christian Theologians and the Bible in Nazi Germany* (Princeton, NJ: Princeton University Press, 2008), 70. The Wartburg Castle, renowned as the place where Luther translated the New Testament into German, was also the setting for the inauguration of Walter Grundmann's Institute for the Study and Eradication of Jewish Influence on German Religious Life in May 1939.

scriptures, worship, music, theology, and anything else related to the church.[2]

The fragmentation of the German Christian movement from early 1934 onward, and its failure, in any case, to unify the Protestant churches as part of Hitler's *Gleichschaltung*, had cooled Hitler's interest in the movement's practical usefulness. The Bund's plan was to show its continuing devotion to the National Socialist cause, as well as to convince the regime that its members were still effective coworkers in the Nazi project, which displayed increasing militancy in its treatment of the Jews. Their publications disseminated a passionate Christian brand of antisemitism that relied on many of the same sources non-Christian Nazi propagandists used: Houston Stewart Chamberlain,[3] Alfred Rosenberg,[4] and others like them.

The excerpt below begins by explaining why publications like this are necessary: "Many people are troubled by the question of whether the church is not once again giving the Jews and the Jewish spirit the opportunity to influence the people on the sly, even after National Socialism has fought so successfully against their influence." The centrality of "the Jewish question" to the Nazi worldview made it imperative that the Bund, devoted as it was to National Socialism, add its voice to the conversation.

The pamphlet adduces "evidence" from both the New Testament, where it depends heavily on Jesus' arguments with other Jews, and "scholarly" sources that include Chamberlain and Rosenberg. "Racial distinctions," another Nazi theme, play a key role in emphasizing

---

2. Ibid., 72.

3. Houston Stewart Chamberlain (1855–1927) was a British Germanophile writer who argued for the racial and cultural superiority of the so-called Aryan element in European culture. His two-volume *The Foundations of the 19th Century* (1899) became a standard reference work for European and particularly Nazi antisemites.

4. Alfred Rosenberg (1893–1946), a leading Nazi intellectual, wrote *Der Mythus des Zwanzigsten Jahrhundert* [*The Myth of the Twentieth Century*], published in 1930, which was very influential in Nazi thinking.

what the author of the pamphlet calls the "contrast between Jesus and the Jews of his time and every century since then." Finally, the pamphlet compares Jesus and Hitler: "Just as once the Redeemer tore the mask from the face of the 'pious Judaism of the high priests,' in the same way the Führer has unmasked the terrifying face of godless Judaism, Marxism and Bolshevism, liberalism and Free Thought." The triumph of National Socialism, the author declares, has insured the survival of Christianity in Germany. Both National Socialists and German Christians "support the struggle against [Jewish] murder and lies and for the brotherhood and the truth that God desires."

Deutsche Christen im Kampf

Schriften zur allgemeinen Unterrichtung
Herausgegeben vom Bund für Deutsches Christentum.

Heft 1: „Jesus und die Juden" . . . . RM. —.10
Heft 2: „Gegen den jüdischen Geist in der Kirche" . . . . . RM. —.10
Heft 3: „Man muß Gott mehr gehorchen als den Menschen" . RM. —.10
Heft 4: „Ein Volk — ein Glaube" . . . . RM. —.10
Heft 5: „Das Ringen der deutschen Christen um die Kirche" . RM. —.10

Weitere billige Aufklärungsschriften:

Generalsuperintendent i. R. Hans Schöttler:
Der Heilandsglaube in der Geschichte der Völker . . . . . . RM. —.10
Hans Paulin:
Bekennende Kirche oder Deutsche Christusgemeinde? (14. Aufl.) RM. —.10
Hugo Rönck: Deutsche Helden oder Deutsche Christen? (11. Aufl.) RM. —.10
Deutsche Pfarrergemeinde: Die evangelische Kirche im Kampf RM. —.10
Wolf Meyer-Erlach: Entscheidet sich die Kirche? . . . . . RM. —.15
Heinrich Meyer-Aurich: Für Klarheit, Recht und Wahrheit! . RM. —.15
Dokumente aus dem Kirchenkampf (5. erweiterte Aufl.)
Dr. Walter Grundmann:
Deutsches Christentum oder Konfessionalismus? . . . . RM. —.20

Wichtige Broschüren und Bücher:

Siegfried Leffler: Christus im Dritten Reich der Deutschen geb. RM. 3.—
Jul. Leutheuser: Der Weg zur deutschen christl. Nationalkirche RM. —.50
(6. und 7. erweiterte Aufl.)
Prof. Dr. Rich. Karth: Die Krisis im evangelischen Religions-
unterricht im Lichte deutschen Christentums RM. 2.40
Wolf Meyer-Erlach: Verrat an Luther (3. Aufl.) . . . . . . RM. 1.—
ders.: Die Kirche der Freiheit Fünf Rundfunkpredigten (2. Aufl.) RM. —.50

Diese Schriften muß jeder von Hand zu Hand weitergeben!

Verlag Deutsche Christen, Weimar/Thür., Postfach 443

Figure 13. Advertisement for German Christian publications, among them *Jesus and the Jews!*

Jesus and the Jews![5]

Organization for German Christianity

Some will ask in astonishment, "What on earth does this subject have to do with the present hour in the German Protestant church?" It has precisely to do with bringing peace to the Protestant church, with pastors' learning to integrate themselves into the community of the German people [*Volksgemeinde*] as it is being shaped by the National Socialist movement. It has to do with the church no longer setting itself apart from the people [*Volk*] as a whole, demanding special rights, and instead deciding, during this time of creation of a total national consciousness, in favor of selfless pastoral service to its fellow Germans. What does Judaism have to do with this? What does Jesus' attitude toward the Jews have to do with it?

A great deal! Many people are troubled by the question of whether the church is not once again giving the Jews and the Jewish spirit the opportunity to influence the people on the sly, even after National Socialism has fought so successfully against their influence. The question must be taken seriously: Is Christianity putting us in spiritual bondage to Judaism? Listening carefully to what the people are saying, one perceives clashing viewpoints. One can sense the tensions and the contradictions. And because the Jewish question is so fundamental to the National Socialist worldview, we can neither skip over it nor resolve it in traditional ways.

Some shout, "*Salvation comes from the Jews!*" Others fight under the banner, "*The Jews are our misfortune!*"

---

5. From Bund für deutsches Christentum. *Jesus and the Jews!* [*Jesus und die* Juden!] Weimar: Verlag Deutsche Christen, 1937.

Some glorify the Jewish people, since Jesus was supposedly a son of that people; others see in them a people of Satan who killed the Savior!

Some see in Jesus the spiritual forerunner of a secret Jewish dominion over the nations; others recognize him as the "first great enemy of the Jews" (Goebbels).[6]

Some speak of him as the "Son of David" and the second person of the Triune God (as if the second person of the Triune God were a Jew, that is to say, that God himself were Jewish!); others see in him the heroic Aryan Savior.

Some declare that the religious question in Germany can be resolved only by ignoring Christianity and bypassing Jesus; others are of the opinion that for Germans, the God-question cannot ignore Christ.

Some denounce Christianity in all its forms as a Jewish sect and see in every Christian a spiritual companion of the Jews; others recognize in the Gospel the all-out assault on every Jewish-pharisaic conceit!

For many Germans, therefore, the question of Jesus and the Jews is the point of departure regarding whether they should have anything more to do with the church or with positive Christianity.[7] A people like ours, which has suffered so unspeakably from the negative influence of the Jewish race, is rightfully cautious about anything that originates with Judah. Many will therefore begin to pay attention again to the message and the person of Jesus only when they have been convinced that if they do so, they will not wind up again in "Abraham's bosom."

6. The quotation comes from Joseph Goebbels, *Michael* (Verlag Franz Eher, 1934), 82 [English: *Michael: A Novel*, trans. Joachim Neugroschel (New York: Amok Press, 1987).].

7. The phrase "positive Christianity" references Point 24 of the 1920 platform of the Nazi Party, which declared itself in favor of a "positive Christianity," understood to be beyond denominations and emphasizing an "active," heroic Christ. That Hitler included this in the platform signaled his sense that he would need the support of the churches as he embarked on his National Socialist project.

Can Jesus possibly be detached from Judaism?

Conventional wisdom says No. Some people say that he is in fact a Jew; that he is David's descendant, and that on his radiant likeness there are actually some disgusting blemishes: he just feels Jewish. If that were so, all efforts would be for naught. Whoever examines these matters seriously, however, will find such a wealth of evidence to the contrary that the resulting judgment differs completely.

1.

In light of the Nuremberg Laws of 1935,[8] we are deeply interested in the question of *whether Jesus was a Jew by blood*; for we are convinced that for any judgment regarding racial superiority, infinite importance must be ascribed to the matter of blood.

Is Jesus the Son of David?

Many statements in the Bible attest to this, but none of them originates with Jesus himself! In his christological teaching, Paul writes that "Christ according to the flesh" descends from David; Jesus himself, however, laughingly rejects this interpretation in a verbal sparring match with the scribes. "How can Christ be David's *son?*" he asks (Matt 22:45; Mark 12:35ff; Luke 20:41ff). When the sick address Jesus as "Son of David," this expression should not be understood in the genealogical or genetic sense, but rather as a title that the sick (or perhaps also the gospel writers?) apply to him.

---

8. The Nuremberg Laws, introduced at the annual Nazi Party Day rally in Nuremberg in 1935, legally defined who was a Jew and thereby made it easier to enforce legislation restricting the rights of German Jews. Individuals with four German grandparents were classified as German; individuals with three or four Jewish grandparents were classified as Jews. A person with one or two Jewish grandparents was a *Mischling*—of "mixed blood." According to the Nuremberg Laws, all non-Jewish white Europeans counted as "Aryans." The laws deprived Jews and other non-Aryans of German citizenship and prohibited sexual relations and marriages between Germans and Jews. In November 1935 the laws were extended to "gypsies, negroes, or their bastard offspring."

Little need be said about the genealogical *value of the family trees* (Matthew 1 and Luke 3); *they do not prove Jesus' Jewish origin.* Their complete unreliability is demonstrated in that (1) they differ from one another; and (2) they clearly bear the stamp of clumsy theological work (three or four epochs of 14 Matthean or 20 Lukan generations between Abraham, David, Zerubbabel, and Joseph). (3) If Joseph was not even Jesus' father, we no longer understand for what purpose the family trees were even written.

Within the limits of a short piece like this it is not possible to lay out all the details: for example, how on the basis of the so-called *Galilean hypothesis*[9] one can show with the highest degree of probability that Jesus was not a Jew by blood at all. It is true that Galilee, a "Gentile province," was won over to the synagogue through Jewish mission work about a hundred years before Christ, but religious mission work does not change the nature of the blood![10] Together with the vast majority of his followers, he was rejected precisely because he was a Galilean. "Can anything good come out of Nazareth?" asked the arrogant Jew (John 1:46). "No prophet comes out of Galilee," declare the rabbis, and therefore they reject Jesus (John 7:41 and 7:52). Jesus' contemporaries knew him only as a "Galilean." On the other hand, when Jesus speaks to the Jews, he says *"Abraham, your father"* (John 8:57), and he repeatedly shows signs of a completely un-Jewish sympathy for the "Gentiles" (Matt 8:10ff.).

We agree with the point of view expressed by *H. S. Chamberlain* and shared by [Alfred] Rosenberg and others: *"The likelihood that*

9. This hypothesis was first popularized by Houston Stewart Chamberlain. According to Susannah Heschel, "the argument received enormous prestige in the world of New Testament scholarship through the work of the distinguished scholar of early Christianity, Walter Bauer, professor of New Testament at the University of Göttingen." *The Aryan Jesus,* 60.
10. Jewish converts to Christianity—or whose Jewish parents or grandparents had converted—were nonetheless defined as Jews, for the same "reason": baptism, according to German Christians, could not change the blood. Few non-Jewish Christians questioned this obvious contradiction of Christian doctrine.

Christ was not a Jew, that he had not a drop of real Jewish blood in his veins, is so great that it is almost a certainty."

2.

These results of a critical review of the information about Jesus' racial membership in Judaism are further strengthened if one also considers *Jesus' own judgments about Judaism*, about Jewish traits, and his attitude toward non-Jews, the so-called "pagans." The contrast between Jesus and the Jews of his time and every century since then can only be understood against the background of the racial distinctions intended by the Almighty. That Jesus clashed most sharply with the Pharisees, the "best and most pious Jews" of his time, resulted from their profound differences.

Read, for example, [Jesus'] words in John 8:44ff. Even Martin Luther or *Der Stürmer*,[11] whose anti-Jewish attitudes are known to everyone, have never come at Judaism with such a merciless edge as Jesus did that day. He really is "the first great enemy of the Jews" when he says to them: "*You are from your father the devil, and you choose to do your father's desires. He was a murderer from the beginning and does not stand in the truth, because there is no truth in him.*" Jesus recognized that "next to the devil there is no more dangerous enemy" of humanity than the Jew (Luther). He, who was himself murdered by the Jews for the sake of the truth to which he knew himself sent to testify, recognized the *two essential traits of the satanic Jews* in their Godforsaken cruelty: *murder and lies!* Our time also knows something of this spirit of lies, which tears apart the brotherhood of peoples through hate and demagoguery and villainy, which poisons the community of peoples with reports generated by a venal press.[12]

---

11. *Der Stürmer* was a viciously anti-Jewish Nazi weekly newspaper, published by Julius Streicher.
12. The Nazis believed that the foreign press, which was often critical of Nazi policies and actions, and to whose criticism the Nazi regime was quite sensitive, was controlled by Jews.

And we know that murderous spirit that threw thousands out of work and then drove them into darkness and despair; the spirit that is constructing the "Soviet paradise" in Russia, driving millions into hunger and death or letting them perish like animals; that murderous spirit whose bloodthirsty sadism is perpetrating the gruesome horror in Spain. Just as once the Redeemer tore the mask from the face of the "pious Judaism of the high priests," in the same way the Führer has unmasked the terrifying face of godless Judaism, Marxism and Bolshevism, liberalism and Free Thought. And we intuit the deep connections between the Christian cross [*Christenkreuz*] and the swastika [*Hackenkreuz*]! It is not only that the Christian crosses in Germany would have been toppled, if the swastika had not triumphed! No, both support the struggle against [Jewish] murder and lies and for the brotherhood and the truth that God desires. This why the "Germanic race's sense of morality and decency" and a "positive Christianity" must encounter one another anew.

. . .

20

The Godesberg Declaration and Responses

Various Authors

Introduction

The Godesberg Declaration was drafted in March 1939 by Thuringian pastor Siegfried Leffler[1] and other German Christian leaders meeting in the Bonn suburb of Bad Godesberg. They met and composed the statement as the Nazi regime intensified its anti-Jewish policies; *Kristallnacht*, the vicious pogrom directed at Jewish businesses, synagogues, and homes, had occurred only four months earlier, in November 1938. At its core, one sentence—"The Christian faith is the unbridgeable religious opposite of Judaism"—signaled the German Christians' intention to "transform the Protestant church into a tool of racial policy."[2] It also expressed their ongoing

---

1. See excerpts of *Christ in Germany's Third Reich* by Leffler, also in this volume.

conviction that Christians of their stripe had an essential part to play in the implementation of the Nazi project, especially with regard to its vision of a Germany "purified" of the presence and influence of Jews.

Some days later a statement signed by German Christian leaders of eleven regional churches publicly affirmed the Declaration. That statement, published in the Law Gazette [*Gesetzblatt*] of the German Protestant Church, expressed the intention of the Declaration's signers that its principles be carried out through the founding of an Institute for the Study and Eradication of Jewish Influence in German Church Life.[3]

Leaders of the Confessing Church also responded to the Declaration; excerpts from several of their published statements also appear below. While they expressed concern about the possible exclusion of non-Aryans from Christian congregations—the rules promulgated by those who have signed the Declaration "are preventing people [non-Aryan Christians] who have been redeemed by Christ from receiving the comfort of the Word of God in the midst of the Christian community"—they did not mention the broader anti-Jewish implications of the Declaration. Their objections focus instead on their opposition to "the application of political measures to the life of the church" as well as to the German Christians' ongoing influence—at least one of the critiques of the Declaration refers to "the heresy of the German Christians"—in the larger Protestant church.

---

2. Bergen, 24.

3. See the introduction to excerpts of *Who Is Jesus of Nazareth?* by Walter Grundmann, one of the founders of the Institute, the next document in this volume. For a more detailed account of the circumstances surrounding the formulation of the Declaration, its reception by both sympathizers and detractors, and the founding of the Institute, see Susannah Heschel, *The Aryan Jesus: Christian Theologians and the Bible in Nazi Germany* (Princeton, NJ: Princeton University Press, 2008), 70–87.

Godesberg Declaration[4]

With an unwavering determination to lead the church struggle to a resolution in accord with positive Christianity,[5] representatives of the National Church Union of German Christians and men from various groups of Protestant pastors and laymen have come together to consult with one another. The decision was taken to engage in a loosely constituted comradely and cooperative project. The following statements are the basis for our work together:

1. With all the strength of our faith and our active life we serve the man who has led our people [*Volk*] out of servitude and misery to freedom and true greatness.

2. We battle relentlessly against all elements that disguise religion as political freedom. Part of the great religious-political struggle that in our era is coursing through our entire people is evident in the church struggle [*Kirchenkampf*]. The forms of the church struggle are degrading, the struggles for power are reprehensible, but the struggle itself we affirm as a sign of the new growth of religious life.

3. The core questions of this religious debate are the following:

   a. What is the relationship between politics and religion; what is the relationship between the National Socialist worldview and the Christian faith?

   To this question we respond:

4. This and the subsequent extracts from responses to the Declaration are taken from *The Protestant Church in Germany and the Jewish Question: Selected Documents from the Years of the Church Struggle 1933 to 1943* [*Die Evangelische Kirche in Deutschland und die Judenfrage: Ausgewählte Dokumente aus den Jahren des Kirchenkampfes 1933 bis* 1943], compiled and edited by order of the Refugee Service of the Ecumenical Council of Churches (Geneva: Verlag Oikumene, 1945), 168–70, 172–79.

5. "Positive Christianity" refers directly to the same phrase in Point 24 of the 1920 platform of the Nazi Party. A "positive Christianity" was understood to be beyond denominations and emphasized an "active," heroic Christ. That Hitler included this in the platform signaled his sense that he would need the support of the churches as he embarked on his National Socialist project.

In that National Socialism contests any claim on the part of the churches to political authority and makes the National Socialist worldview appropriate to the German people obligatory for everyone, it carries on Martin Luther's work in the political-philosophical realm, and in this way helps us, from a religious point of view, to return to a true understanding of the Christian faith.

b. What is the relationship between Judaism and Christianity? Is Christianity derived from Judaism and therefore its continuation and fulfillment, or does Christianity stand in contradiction to Judaism?

To this question we respond:

The Christian faith is the unbridgeable religious opposite of Judaism.

c. Is Christianity essentially supranational and international?

To this question we respond:

Supranational and international ecclesiasticism of the Roman Catholic or world-Protestant type is a political degeneration of Christianity. Genuine Christian faith develops fruitfully only within the given orders of creation.[6]

4. On the basis of our fundamental knowledge of the tenor of the religious debate, it is self-evident that constructions, constitutions, and legislation will never move things forward. The struggle must rather be carried out internally.

---

6. "Orders of creation" is a theological construct referring to certain structures or institutions God is said to have established in the earthly realm to order human life; marriage, family, the economy, the state, and the church might all be counted among them. For the German Christians, race—as they understood it—and *Volk* or *Volkstum* were "orders of creation," too, and, because they were established by God, were sanctified.

5. The preconditions for such a religious debate are order and tolerance in the church. We applaud as a substantial contribution the regulations of the Protestant Church of the Prussian Union that have just appeared.

6. The stance described by these statements will be the basis for beginning our work together.

The National Church Union of German Christians

by Siegfried Leffler

Signatories: Ellwein, Berlin; Deitenbeck, Frankfurt am Main; Grünagel, Aachen; Hahn, Mannheim; Kittel, Münster; Klein, Bad Freienwalde; Freiherr von Ledebur, Bohmte; Müller, Königsberg; Neumüller, Kaiserslautern; Odenwald, Heidelberg; Pauls, Hirschberg (Silesia); Schomerus, Wittenberg; Seiler, Erlangen; Stapel, Hamburg; Wörmann, Hamburg; Fiebig, Münster; Horn, Duisberg; Bunz, Berlin; Göring, Berlin.

Responses to the Godesberg Declaration from Leaders of the Confessing Church

A group of so-called church leaders has recently published a communiqué that has also found its way into the newspapers. . . . The meaning of this communiqué lies not in its details . . . [but] rather in the fact that [these church leaders] have formally joined the Thuringian German Christians and have made public their agreement with German Christian principles.

. . .

During the weeks around Palm Sunday there was a great uproar in many of the congregations of the Old Prussian Union and other churches about the confirmation services held by German Christians. They altered the creed. They created a new, ethnic [*völkisch*] version of the Lord's Prayer, which Jesus Christ gave to his own and which is something sacred to every Christian. They no longer asked the confirmands whether they would be faithful to the Lord Christ, but instead had them swear to fight against Rome and Judah, or whatever else came to the German-Christian pastor's mind.

These things were brought urgently to the attention of the church council. The response of the council president is that he now declares himself publicly and formally in solidarity with these German Christians. At the same time he issues one regulation after another, through which he arrogates to himself new dictatorial powers. He is forcing confessionally faithful congregations everywhere to open their churches to the Thuringian German Christians—churches our fathers built so that the pure, unadulterated Gospel might be preached there.

The external power is in the hands of those who have issued this communiqué. But wherever the Gospel is preached, pure and unadulterated, there is the Lord Christ. We keep our gaze on him, not on what human beings say or do.

In this time of our church's need, we call on congregations to gather around God's Word and around the confessions of the Reformation. We call on them to join with the pastors and elders who are true to those confessions in the struggle for the authority of the Gospel in our church. We call on them to join with us in the prayer prayed by congregations during the earliest time of persecution: Lord, look upon their threats and grant to your servants to speak your Word with all joy![7]

♦♦♦

. . . For years [these church leaders] have said that they wanted only to establish an external structure for the church; doctrine and

---

7. Cf. Acts 4:29.

confession would "remain undisturbed"; no one would think of embracing one particular ecclesiastical or theological party or other. Now we hear it said quite freely that this "the external structure," is really about something entirely different, namely, that a particular "position," in fact, that of the Thuringian German Christians, should take over in the church. . . .

This is the meaning of that communiqué: the church authorities, in keeping with their official positions, will take charge of the struggle against the biblical Gospel.

That this is really the sense of the communiqué is clear to see, not least in that for a long time all the ecclesiastical conduct of this group of "regional church leaders" has been informed by this same spirit. The regional churches of Thuringia, Saxony, Mecklenburg, and Lübeck have subjected non-Aryan Christians to regulations that have destroyed the unity of the Body of Christ. The president of the church council of the Old Prussian Union has embarked upon a project that again takes up what Ludwig Müller tried and failed to do; he intends to force something on the church that contradicts its very nature.

♦♦♦

[With the announcement of the eleven church leaders,] the struggle for the church of Jesus Christ within the German Protestant Church has entered a new stage. What Ludwig Müller himself hesitated to say is now being said out loud: the leaders of those churches that are supposed to be models for the reform of the whole German Protestant Church have made the heresy of the German Christians their official plan of action. They have accepted principles in which, according to all testimony of Sacred Scripture and the confessions of Christian doctrine, we can only see an apostasy from the gospel of Jesus Christ, which alone saves, and an arbitrary twisting of the truth God has revealed into human wisdom. . . .

[In response to the declaration that international Christianity is a "political degeneration of Christianity," we testify that] . . . the Christian church is the community of those who have been baptized into the death and resurrection of Christ, who are called across all the boundaries of nations [*Völker*] to be citizens of the kingdom over which Christ rules. The fraternal bond to the Body of Christ is given through the unity of faith and cannot be broken by the barriers of state and nationality. To deny this supra-nationality of the church is to destroy the unity of the Body of Christ. . . .

[In response to the declaration that "The Christian faith is the unbridgeable religious opposite of Judaism" we testify that] . . . [i]t pleased God to make Israel the bearer and instrument of divine revelation. That is not revoked because the Jews themselves have become unfaithful to their divine designation. The church as the true Israel is the inheritor of the promise that was given to the people of Israel (see Gal. 4:28-29). The Christian faith stands in unbridgeable religious opposition to Judaism [*Judaismus*]. But this Judaism [*Judaismus*] is alive not only in Judaism [*Judentum*], but also, and just as much, in all attempts to form a national church. It is nothing other than the natural human's attempt to make his religious and moral self-justification invulnerable by confusing it with a *völkisch* sense of mission and so denying Jesus as the Christ of God.

◆◆◆

In the last few months various attempts have been made to come to a resolution of the church question. All have failed. Now eleven church leaders have openly and unmistakably committed themselves to the national-church guidelines. In doing so they have shown themselves to be enemies of the one, holy, catholic [*allgemeinen*] church of Jesus Christ.

The significance of the path the national-church movement has taken has recently become clear in the laws the church administrations of Thuringia, Mecklenburg, Anhalt, Lübeck, and Saxony have promulgated. According to these laws, non-Aryans cannot become members of or belong to these regional churches. For those who were not already members of one of these churches, official acts are impermissible. Pastors in those churches are not required to perform any further official functions for those non-Aryans who were members of these churches when these rules came into effect. If they decide to perform such functions, they may not use church spaces or facilities. With these rules, non-Aryans are excluded from the affected churches.

The above-named church administrations are preventing people who have been redeemed by Christ from receiving the comfort of the Word of God in the midst of the Christian community. They are excluding people in need of salvation from the holy sacraments. They aim to render ineffective what Christ secured by his bitter suffering: For Christ has created, out of Jews and Gentiles, one holy Body, the one Christian church. They are rebuilding the barrier that Christ broke down; in doing so, they are making a Pharisaic sect out of the Christian church.

To this we declare: we protest against the application of political measures to the life of the church.

The men who are responsible for these laws have proven themselves enemies of the cross of Christ. They cannot ban anyone from the Christian church, but through the promulgation of these laws they have separated themselves from the holy Christian church. We ask the pastors and congregations of the affected regional churches not to observe these laws, but instead to relinquish Christian fellowship with all those who bow to this yoke.

We would rather suffer ourselves than be complicit in the guilt of destroying the Body of Christ. We confess the Word of Sacred Scripture, which tells us: ". . . he is our peace; in his flesh he has made both groups into one and has broken down the dividing wall, that is, the hostility between us." (Eph. 2:14)

21.

Who Is Jesus of Nazareth?

Walter Grundmann

Introduction

Walter Grundmann (1906–1976) was a German Lutheran pastor, theologian, and professor. In 1930 he became a member of the Nazi Party, and in 1934 a supporting member of the S.S. Between 1930 and 1932 he served as an assistant to Gerhard Kittel and wrote a score of articles for the *Theological Dictionary of the New* Testament, of which Kittel was the editor.[1] He became active in the German Christian movement in Saxony, and in December 1933 wrote the "Twenty-Eight Theses of the Church of Saxony,"[2] which articulated Protestant statements of faith in Nazi language and using Nazi racial

1. See Kittel's *The Jewish Question* in this volume.
2. This document can be found in the *Handbook of the German Christians* in this volume.

concepts. In 1938 Grundmann became professor of New Testament and *Völkisch* Theology at the nazified University of Jena[3] and, in 1941, Academic Director of the Institute for the Study and Eradication of Jewish Influence on German Religious Life, based in Eisenach.[4] In 1943 he was drafted into military service on the Eastern front.[5]

The pamphlet *Who Is Jesus of Nazareth?* is one of several publications, including a book, *Jesus the Galilean* [*Jesus der Galiläer*], that Grundmann produced on the subject of Jesus during his tenure at Jena and at the Institute. The cover of the pamphlet from which this excerpt was taken indicates it was one of a print run of 11,000 to 20,000 copies, suggesting it had a wide distribution. The pamphlet makes many of the same points the book does, arguing that Jesus was not only not a Jew but was deeply anti-Jewish. His understanding of God and the kingdom of God was diametrically opposed to Jewish ideas: ". . . [T]he Jewish concept of the kingdom of God," Grundmann wrote, was political and "implied Jewish world domination." Jesus' notion of messiahship contradicted Jewish ideas, too: His response to the Pharisees, when they ask him about paying taxes to the Roman emperor, "is a slap in the face to all Jewish messianic expectations." Grundmann also contends that Jesus' teaching was more heavily influenced by Persian or Zoroastrian religion than by Judaism.

---

3. He was appointed by Wolf Meyer-Erlach, the Rector of the University, and also an influential member of the German Christian movement. For more on Meyer-Erlach, see pp. 421.

4. A discussion of the name of the Institute, especially the appearance and disappearance of the words "and Eradication," can be found in Susannah Heschel, *The Aryan Jesus: Christian Theologians and the Bible in Nazi Germany* (Princeton, NJ: Princeton University Press, 2008), 91–94.

5. Grundmann survived the war, living another three decades in what became the German Democratic Republic, where he served as a pastor, published widely-used commentaries on the gospels, and—as became clear after the fall of the Berlin wall in 1989—worked for the Stasi, the GDR secret police, as an informant.

Wer ist Jesus von Nazareth?

Von

Dr. Walter Grundmann

Professor an der Universität Jena

11. bis 20. Tausend

Verlag Deutsche Christen Weimar

Figure 14. Title page of *Who is Jesus of Nazareth?* by Walter Grundmann.

Who Is Jesus of Nazareth?[6]

Walter Grundmann

What is it about Jesus Christ? The question that Jesus of Nazareth himself asked his disciples has not yet been laid to rest. It continues to move people. Both internally and externally, the great and powerful Byzantine Empire fell apart over this question. Its effects reach that far. In our time the question has once again become a vital one and is being discussed with great passion. What is it about Jesus Christ?

Jesus of Nazareth appeared in Palestine. The ancient Christian tradition confesses him as the Messiah, and thus as the fulfillment of the Old Testament. On the basis of the New Testament sources, religious studies research has had to question this traditional confession. This is why the question, "What is it about Jesus Christ?" has occupied German research in the humanities for a century, and does to this day.

Today the question comes from the German people [Volk]. The German people have struggled against the Jews for liberation from [Jewish] subversion of Germany's life and essence. Behind this war that England has forced upon the German people—just as surely as behind the world war—stands the Jew as fomenter.[7] In contrast to Judaism, the German people are aware of their essential nature in every respect. Hence the bitterly earnest and difficult question: Is it possible that at the center of their religion stand the message and the figure of a man who is supposed to be the Jewish Messiah? The

---

6. From Walter Grundmann, *Who Is Jesus of Nazareth?* [*Wer ist Jesus von Nazareth?*] (Weimar: Verlag Deutsche Christen, 1940; published in connection with the Institute for the Study of Jewish Influence on German Religious Life), 3–15.

7. Grundmann is referring to World War II and World War I, respectively.

question becomes a burning one for the spiritual life of Germans: What is it about Jesus Christ?

We can establish three facts: (1) The Jews hated Jesus Christ during his lifetime and brought about his crucifixion. They hated and persecuted the movement that bore his name, and they incited the Roman state to go after Christian congregations. They expelled from their ranks any members of their religion who confessed him. This hatred has continued through the present day. Only as they were integrated into Western society did they change their attitude—purportedly—precisely to make their entry possible. Now they described Jesus of Nazareth as a noble blossom on the tree of Judaism. (2) The message and figure of Jesus of Nazareth were embraced principally in the West, among Romans, Greeks, and Germanic peoples, and became the center of Western religion. Throughout the centuries of German history, German art and poetry have engaged this figure. Here I recall the oldest German paintings on the island of Reichenau in Lake Constance and the oldest German poetry, the *Heliand*; the cathedral at Naumburg and Wolfram's *Parsifal*, Albrecht Dürer and the Isenheimer Altar by Matthias Grünewald, Martin Luther, and Johann Sebastian Bach's *Passion According to Saint Matthew* and the *Christmas Oratorio*. This line continues into present-day Germany, to Paul Ernst's *Der Heiland*[8] and Karl Röttger's *Christuslegenden*.[9] (3) Because of the movement that began with Jesus Christ, a profound and exciting concept of God entered the Western-Aryan world. This conception of God included nature and history, individual personality and society, time and eternity; it has shaped the character of our culture and our life in

---

8. A novel published in 1937.
9. A work of fiction first published in 1914. Neither this book nor Ernst's was translated into English.

a deep and lasting way—even where the name of Jesus Christ is not or is no longer named. These are the facts of history.

What is it about Christ? The greatest variety of answers are given to this question in Germany at present. We will mention only two of the most contradictory ones. Some say "Jesus Christ is the Son of God, born of the Virgin. Therefore it makes no sense to raise the race question in his regard. We don't believe in Jesus the human being, but in the Son of God." Others say, "Jesus of Nazareth was nothing more than a Jewish adventurer. He thought he was the Messiah-King, he called people into a messianic movement, he thought he could occupy Jerusalem and overturn Roman rule with a wave of his hand, and he died in the process. It was his disciples who later made him into the Son of God and took the world by storm." The Jew Robert Eisler attempted to substantiate this position in his two-volume work entitled *Jesus, the King Without a Kingdom*.[10] With his "scientific" work he wanted to undermine the cultural foundations of the West, to toss the flaming torch of religious strife among the peoples of Europe, especially into the midst of the German people, and to justify Judaism regarding the judicial murder of Jesus. Here it is important to be especially alert.

Any serious-minded person can see that the first of the two answers outlined above is not satisfactory. Whatever one's position on the mystery expressed in the words "Son of God," Jesus Christ was a human being. The Fourth Gospel, which speaks most emphatically of the divine Sonship of Jesus, says at the beginning, "And the Logos became flesh. . . ." Thus arises the question of race and type [*Art*], a question that cannot be ignored. Churches of all denominations

---

10. German: *Jesus, der König ohne Königreich.* Robert Eisler (1882–1949) was an Austrian Jewish historian and biblical scholar. Grundmann appears to refer to a work by Eisler entitled *Iesous Basileus ou Basileusas: die messianische Unabhängigkeitsbewegung vom auftreten Johannes des Täufers bis zum Untergang Jakobs des Gerechten, nach der neurschlossenen Eroberung von Jerusalem des Flavius Josephus und den christlichen Quellen* (Heidelberg: Winter, 1930).

confess the full humanity of the Son of God and therefore cannot evade the question of race. They need not discuss it if it is not brought up; but they cannot shove it aside, when it is raised, by referring to the dogma of the Sonship of God and the Virgin Birth.

The other answer has decisive implications, which we would like to make explicit. If Jesus was nothing more than a Jewish adventurer, if it was his disciples—perhaps as deceived deceivers—who made him into the Son of God, then the upshot is this: the whole of Western humanity has fallen prey to a two-thousand-year-old lie. That would be a terrible thought. . . .

The question, "What is it about Jesus Christ?" cannot be avoided and has fateful significance. In this little popular booklet we will try to provide a brief answer. The views articulated here are all based on careful historical research using sources available to us. The present text presents the essential results of this research and omits detail. The reader who wishes to gain greater understanding of these questions will find help in my book, now in its second printing, *Jesus the Galilean and the Jews* [*Jesus der Galiläer und das Judentum*]. . . . There he will find detailed reasoning and the necessary supporting evidence from the sources. . . . We have [also] compiled the essential gospel texts that provide a coherent picture of Jesus in a new translation in the short volume *The Message of God, I. Jesus the Savior* [*Die Botschaft Gottes, I. Jesus der Heiland*] . . . ; a half year after its appearance, 200,000 copies have been distributed among the German people. The present work will provide a brief answer to this question for interested Germans.

1. The Messenger of the Kingdom of God

In Jesus' time, the Jews were awaiting the Messiah with a burning passion. Messianic uprisings repeatedly shook areas of Palestine and caused the Roman authorities to intervene. These uprisings, however, were only expressions of the secret, swelling passion of expectation in the popular mind [*Volksbewusstsein*]. Anticipation of the coming Messiah took many forms. Some thought he would be like King David, the subject of so many popular legends, who would establish a great kingdom and reign in power and glory. Others believed that the Messiah would come like Moses, that he would lead the people into the wilderness, renew them there both spiritually and physically, in order then with the people to retake the land anew. It is highly likely that the figure of John the Baptist, mentioned in the New Testament, whom Christian tradition made into the forerunner of Jesus, was shaped by such ideas. Finally, there were circles—quite small ones—mainly in Galilee, who had the idea of a redeemer coming from heaven, whom they called the Son of Man. This type of messianic expectation was foreign to the Jews; it did not derive from the Old Testament, but was a notion of a savior adopted from the Persians.

The expectation was that this Messiah would bring the kingdom of God. This expression—kingdom of God—is found only in the later writings of the Old Testament, where it appears seldom. It becomes more frequent only in later Judaism, probably under Persian influence. The kingdom of God is understood as the "ideal kingdom" of the end-times, when the world will be renewed in eternal-divine form in which lies and deception, sickness and death are overcome. That, at least, was what the Persians imagined as the triumphant goal of the struggle between light and darkness, good and evil, falsehood and truth. And the kingdom of God, which according to the expectations of small Palestinian (probably primarily Galilean) circles the Son of Man would bring in, was like this Persian "ideal kingdom": a miraculous thing coming from heaven that will renew the earth. The common Jewish expectation surely appropriated this notion of the "ideal kingdom," but transformed it in keeping with Old Testament ideas. The "ideal kingdom" is the religio-political rule of the Messiah-king over Israel and over the peoples of the earth, who must either be destroyed or become Israel's servants. The Messiah comes as a military ruler who destroys the enemies of Israel, and as the prince of peace who establishes an ideal reign of justice, in which Israel rules and the peoples serve Israel—at least insofar as they have not been wiped out. . . .

. . .

John the Baptist's appearance inaugurated a great movement throughout Palestine. He proclaimed the coming end of the world, which would inaugurate the imminent Last Judgment of God. Shockingly, this man destroyed the Jews' comforting claim that God's judgment would not touch them. He spat these words into the faces of the Jewish leaders: "You brood of vipers! Who warned you to flee from the wrath to come? . . . I tell you, God is able from these stones to raise up children to Abraham" (Luke 3:7, 8b). Ancient Christian tradition saw this verbal attack, which made a great impression on the people, as preparation for the movement Jesus of Nazareth initiated. Jesus himself had ties to the movement John led. He was baptized by him, and despite their many differences, agreed with him entirely on one key point: Both emphasized a moral and religious renewal; both therefore criticized any claim Israel made to be "chosen"; and both rejected any political promises. Thus both were essentially different from other messianic expectations and movements.

Jesus of Nazareth brings this message: "The kingdom of God has come near; repent, and believe in the good news" (Matt. 4:17; Mark 1:15) This message, which places the "kingdom of God" at the center, had to have inspired expectations and hopes. Is he the awaited Messiah? Will he lead the people to freedom? The later report about the disciples on the way to Emmaus shows that there were groups in Palestine who were heartbroken when they saw the hopes placed in him collapse at his death. ". . . We had hoped that he was the one to redeem Israel" (Luke 24:21). Even some of the disciples nurtured this hope. Perhaps we should understand Judas's betrayal in light of his disappointed hopes. In any case, Peter said out loud, "You are the Messiah." When Jesus then spoke of the necessity of his suffering, Peter got angry. A Messiah who suffers and dies is no Messiah—not the one Palestine is expecting, in any case. Its Messiah will triumph and rule. But Jesus responds to Peter's anger with these words: ". . . You are setting your mind not on divine things but on human things" (Mark 8:27-33). For Jesus the messianic expectations projected onto him are the human ideas; he counters them with his ideas about God, which include his own suffering.

Apparently he understood something different by the kingdom of God than did his contemporaries. The tradition reports unanimously that Jesus spoke in parables about the mysteries of the kingdom of God. The fact that he spoke in parables suggests that Jesus believed he had first to clarify for the people what he understood the kingdom of God to be, and he could not use their ideas to do so. If he had understood it as they did, he would not have had to use parables. The scholarly comparison between Jesus' parables, especially those he uses to speak of the kingdom of God, and contemporary Jewish parables demonstrates that his parables of the kingdom of God are entirely his own creation. The Gospel of Luke contains an account of Jesus' being asked when the kingdom of God is coming. This old question of expectation touched both Jews and non-Jews in Palestine, and was the reason for the messianic movements we have mentioned. According to this report, Jesus answered the question this way: "The kingdom of God is not coming with things than can be observed, nor will they say, 'Look, here it is!' or 'There it is!' For, in fact, the

kingdom of God is in your midst" (Luke 17:20-21). This answer
is clear. In those circles that expected the kingdom of God, people
tried to figure out when it was coming and what the signs were
that announced its advent. Jesus rejects this kind of observation. . . .
He also argues against their notion that the kingdom of God can be
limited and circumscribed, that it can be compared to a political state
or a human organization that would be here or there. He thus rejects
his contemporaries' notion that the kingdom of God is bound to
Zion and to Jerusalem. Jesus' parables compare the kingdom of God
to seeds thrown on the ground to bear fruit; or crops that grow by
themselves, without any human effort. They thus make it clear that
the kingdom of God is wholly in God's hands and is God's doing and
has its effect in the human heart (Mark 4:3-9, 26-29). These words,
however—"The kingdom of God is in your midst"—mean that this
kingdom of God has come with him and is here in his person and
his message. He is the sower who sows the seeds. He is the one who
carries the battle against the Evil One into the Evil One's territory:
"But if it is by the Spirit of God that I cast our demons, then the
kingdom of God has come to you" (Matt. 12:28). As he understands
it, the power opposed to the kingdom of God is not the earthly-
political authorities of the world's life, but the power of evil. In this
respect Jesus does not stand in the line of Jewish expectation, but
rather in that of the Persian Zarathustra. . . . Jesus stands here in
the line of ancient, foundational Aryan thought, and rejects Jewish
expectations. . . .

Now, how does Jesus understand the nature of the kingdom of
God? As we have already seen, the kingdom of God is nothing that
one could see with one's eyes and recognize without any doubt. It is
God's own act, effected in the message and figure of Jesus; it seizes the
hearts of men and does battle with evil, whose powerbase it destroys.
We can describe its nature from four angles:

1. Where God's kingdom takes hold of someone, a new relationship between God and the human is established. Jesus proclaims to human beings the message that God seeks them and calls them to himself. The call, "Turn toward God"—wrongly translated "Do penance!" by Luther—calls people to make a fundamental change in their lives. They should take God seriously, and do so because God is coming to them. The coming of the kingdom of God is nothing other than the coming of God to human beings. But he does not come as judge, to punish and destroy; rather, he comes as helper, to release people from their guilt and fear and to win them to a trusting faith. Here is the basic difference from the Baptist. He proclaimed the coming of God for a judgment that destroys. Jesus came to people in a different way. He helped people in their physical and emotional need. He went to those who were despised and rejected by the religious leaders, to the "common folk," from whom he himself had come. . . . The anger of the Pharisees and scribes was provoked by his kindness and his love. He wanted only that people turn in trust and faith to God, who wants to be a father who in his innermost being is forgiving and helping Good. The Beatitudes make this just as clear as do a whole series of parables [Jesus uses], just as clear as his calls to faith and his works that awaken faith. When faith is awakened in a person, when he turns trustingly to God, the kingdom of God becomes a reality in him; God has truly come to that person. So the kingdom of God is a new community between God and human.

2. A second point follows directly from this: One cannot have community with God unless community with one's fellow human is also renewed. Whoever accepts God's forgiveness for his overwhelming guilt without himself being ready to forgive

is like the rogue slave whom God condemns (Matt. 18:23ff.). This is why we learn to pray, "And forgive us our trespasses, as we forgive those who trespass against us" (Matt. 6:12). If God offers and renews communion between himself and human beings, they are duty-bound to renew community with others. The great saying of the Sermon on the Mount—"Love your enemies!"—and the examples that illustrate it, in no way demand timorous surrender. Such an interpretation falls apart in the face of Jesus' whole attitude, which reveals something completely different from giving in to injustice and malice. These words are meant to lay a great responsibility upon the human heart—a responsibility to rebuild community that has been torn apart and endangered. The enemy is not the political opponent with whom one crosses swords in war, but rather the person from whom one is alienated but who needs community and aid. This is why the Good Samaritan in the parable (Luke 10:30-35) is the classic representative of love of enemies as Jesus intends it. . . . What Jesus says about loving one's enemies makes us directly responsible to heal and rebuild community. . . . Where this occurs, there God's kingdom is realized between these people, there God has come to them. . . . God encounters humans through other people. And, in the last analysis, what is done to others is done to God. Jesus, according to his word, wants to stand behind others, so that when we see them, we will see him: "Just as you did it to one of the least of these who are members of my family, you did it to me!" (Matt. 25:40). . . .

3. Some of Jesus' sayings have been transmitted in such a way that the words "kingdom of God" and "eternal life" are interchangeable (Mark 9:43-47; 10:17-27). Where the kingdom of God becomes real, there eternal life also becomes real. In the Fourth Gospel, in place of the phrase "kingdom of God"—about

which the historical Jesus spoke—the phrases "eternal life" or "the life" appear. These have the same meaning and the same content as the phrase "kingdom of God." When a person is drawn into a new community with God, and is thereby freed to act in love, eternal life arises in this person, a life that death cannot destroy. . . .

4. The kingdom of God draws humans into community with God, effects a new community among them, and in doing so, is eternal life. Thus it goes far beyond the earthly context. In our earthly life there are realities that militate against the kingdom of God: the community-destroying forces of hatred and envy, malice and lies, but also illness and death, unbelief and contempt for God. Jesus knows evil's sphere of influence, which generates all destruction—of community, of human bodies and lives, of the human soul. When Jesus speaks of demons and of Satan, he is referring to this sphere of influence of evil. People can be bound and trapped there. The kingdom of God as Jesus proclaims it and as it is actualized in his works, penetrates evil's sphere of influence; it is the liberation of human beings from this sphere of influence and beating it back. Part of Jesus' message about the kingdom of God is this proclamation and promise: One day God will decisively overcome and do away with evil's sphere. Then the kingdom of God will be revealed and fulfilled. . . . When this victory will occur, Jesus did not say. His words strike different notes. Sometimes it seems as if he expects it soon. But the "when" is up to the Father alone. The "that" of the victory is for him certain.

Jesus' understanding of the kingdom of God is entirely religious. At its center is only and truly God's reign among humanity, in the human community and in the world. It is clearly distinct from any human organization and political undertaking. The Jewish concept of the kingdom of God, which implies Jewish world domination, is fundamentally rejected. When the Pharisees ask Jesus whether it is right to pay taxes to the emperor, that was a hot topic. If Jesus' message about the kingdom of God is political and he is the Messiah, then he must say No. . . . Jesus' response is a slap in the face to all Jewish messianic expectations: "Give to the emperor the things that are the emperor's, and to God the things that are God's" (Mark 12:17). For the Jews, giving to the emperor denies full devotion to God. The radical Zealot party concluded that a Jew dare not acknowledge any master besides YHWH. Jesus denies any compromise in one's surrender to God; hence his words, "No one can serve two masters" (Matt. 6:24). This indicates his path toward death. He will not flee, but instead consciously goes the way of death because this is the Father's will for him. When these words—"give to the emperor" and "give to God" what belongs to each—are used together, what follows is the idea that the kingdom of God is not a political entity and should not be confused with one. For the same reason it poses no threat to the political order, but instead works within it as a force of faith and love: as a revelation of truth, as the Fourth Evangelist says. When he sets Jesus and Pilate face to face, God's kingdom and the Roman Empire likewise meet, for here each person is representative of something. In their conversation earthly political power is expressly grounded in God (John 19:11). At the same time it is said of the kingdom of God that it is something other than political power. "My kingdom is not from this world. If it were from this world, my followers would be fighting to keep me from being handed over to the Jews. But as it is, my kingdom is not from here" (John 18:36). These words distinguish God's kingdom from political power; they do not refer to the kingdom of God as a dream-world of the dearly departed "on the other side," having nothing to do with this world, as it has often been misunderstood. It means, rather, that the kingdom of God does not grow up out of this earth, but rather that it comes from God and works its way into the world as the power of the illuminating and liberating truth (John 18:37).

So Jesus' understanding of the kingdom of God is fundamentally different from the Jewish understanding. What is marginal to the latter—community with God and justice in common life, Jesus makes the sole focus. And this is not just a hope for the hereafter, but rather God's gift through him and God's command—and both have to do with this world. There is no eternal life that is not realized here in faith and love. What was central for the Jews, that is, the political expectation grounded in their claim to being the chosen people, is for Jesus completely absent. Jesus is actually closer to those small Galilean circles that saw the kingdom of God as a miraculous event coming from heaven to renew the earth. For Jesus the kingdom of God is entirely God's doing; it comes "from heaven" and is God's wondrous work, but it is not in the far future—it is, through him, a richly fulfilled present.

If Jesus has a new understanding of the kingdom of God, then his understanding of the messenger and bringer of the kingdom of God must also change. According to the tradition he wanted to be the messenger of joy who proclaimed peace and healing, brought joy to the poor, freedom to the captives, and help to the sick (compare Luke 4:18ff.). He thus connects with an Old Testament figure—the messenger of good news in Second Isaiah—a figure that probably indicates Persian influence. In making this connection he is rejecting the connection with the actual messianic expectation. This becomes unmistakably clear in the expression that he comes "as a servant," as one who does not come to be served, but rather to serve (Luke 22:26ff.; Mark 10:45). Jesus does not appear as an earthly ruler, but instead as a servant; his mission corresponds to the idea of service, not of rule. . . . The idea that he will be among them as a servant is the negation, the dissolution, and the supersession of the Jewish concept of messiah. . . . [I]n Jesus of Nazareth something utterly un-Jewish appears. The content of his preaching shapes and determines his work. Both emerge from an essential core that cannot be described as Jewish, namely, from his experience of God.

Bibliography

I. Primary Sources

Publications excerpted in this volume appear in boldface.

Althaus, Paul. *Politisches Christentum: Ein Wort über die Thüringer "Deutsche Christen."* 2nd ed. Leipzig: A. Deichertsche Verlagsbuchhandlung, 1935.

Barth, Karl. *Theologische Existenz heute!,* 9th ed. München: Christian Kaiser Verlag, 1934. First published in 1933.

Bauer, Wilhelm. *Im Umbruch der Zeit.* Weimar: Verlag Deutsche Christen, 1935.

Bertram, Georg. *Reichskirche und Bekenntnis.* Darmstadt: Buchdruckerei C. W. Leske, 1933.

Bonhoeffer, Dietrich. *Dietrich Bonhoeffer Works: 1932-1933*, ed. Larry L. Rasmussen, trans. Isabel Best and David Higgins. Minneapolis: Fortress Press, 2009.

Bornhausen, Karl. *Deutscher Volksglaube in der Nordmark: Idealismus und Volksglaube.* Weimar: Verlag Deutsche Christen, 1938.

Brökelschen, Otto. *Was wollen die Deutschen Christen? 118 Fragen und Antworten.* Weimar: Verlag Deutsche Christen, 1937.

Bund für deutsches Christentum. *Jesus und die Juden!* Weimar: Verlag Deutsche Christen, 1937.

———. *Gebet dem Kaiser, was des Kaisers ist, und Gott, was Gottes ist . . . !* Weimar: Verlag Deutsche Christen, 1937.

Dannenmann, Arnold. *Die Geschichte der Glaubensbewegung "Deutsche Christen."* Dresden: Oskar Günther Verlag, 1933.

Deutsche Christen (Nationalkirchliche Einung). *Handbuch der Deutschen Christen.* 2nd ed. [Berlin–Charlottenburg]: Deutsche Christen, 1933[?].

———. *Die Gottesfeier: Entwürfe und Hilfen zur Feiergestaltung in den Gemeinden "Deutscher Christen, Nationalkirchliche Einung."* 5th distribution. Weimar: Verlag Deutsche Christen, 1940[?].

Dungs, Heinz, ed. *Vom Werden deutscher Volkskirche: Grundsätzliche Äusserungen der nationalkirchlichen Bewegung "Deutsche Christen." Zugleich eine Antwort auf die Zeitfrage nach der Zukunft des Protestantismus.* Weimar: Verlag Deutsche Christen, 1937.

Evangelische Kirche in Deutschland und die Judenfrage: Ausgewählte Dokumente aus den Jahren des Kirchenkampfes 1933 bis 1943, compiled and edited by order of the Refugee Service of the Ecumenical Council of Churches. Geneva: Verlag Oikumene, 1945.

Fascher, Erich. *Grosse Deutsche begegnen der Bibel: Eine Wegweisung für deutsche Christen.* 2nd rev. ed. Halle: Akademischer Verlag, 1937.

Grossmann, Constantin. *Deutsche Christen: Ein Volksbuch: Wegweiser durch die Glaubensbewegung unserer Zeit.* Dresden: Verlag E. am Ende, 1934.

Grundmann, Walter. *Wer ist Jesus von Nazareth?* Weimar: Verlag Deutsche Christen, 1937.

Haug, Theodor. *Die völkische Religiosität unserer Tage.* Stuttgart-Zuffenhausen: Evangelischer Weg, 1934.

Hirsch, Emanuel. *Das kirchliche Wollen der Deutschen Christen.* 2nd ed. Berlin–Charlottenburg: Verlag Max Grevemeyer, 1933.

———. *Das Wesen des Christentums.* Weimar: Verlag Deutsche Christen, 1939.

Hossenfelder, Joachim. *Unser Kampf*. Berlin-Charlottenburg: Verlag Max Grevemeyer ["Deutsche Christen"], 1933.

———, ed. *Volk und Kirche: Die amtlichen Berichte der ersten Reichstagung 1933 der Glaubensbewegung "Deutsche Christen."* Berlin-Charlottenburg: Max Grevemeyer, 1933.

Hübener, Friedrich. *Der deutsche Christ und die Judenfrage: Ein offenes Wort an die Deutschen, die sich Christen nennen und an die völkische Bewegung*. 6th ed. Zwickau-Sachsen: J. Hermann, 1932.

Kinder, Christian, ed. *Der Deutschen Christen Reichs-Kalender 1935*. Meissen: Schlimpert & Püschel, 1935.

Krause, Reinhold. *Rede des Gauobmannes der Glaubensbewegung "Deutsche Christen" in Gross-Berlin Dr. Krause (nach doppeltem stenographischen Bericht)*. N.p., n.d.

Kremers, Hermann. *Denkschrift für die Mitglieder und Freunde des Evangelischen Bundes*. Berlin: Christlichen Zeitschriftenvereins, 1934.

Krummacher, Gottfried Adolf. *Weltwirtschaftskrise und Christentum*. Berlin-Charlottenburg: Verlag Max Grevemeyer ["Deutsche Christen"], 1933.

Kuptsch, Julius. *Nationalsozialismus und positives Christentum*. 2nd ed. Weimar: Verlag Deutsche Christen, 1939.

Langmann, Otto. *Deutsche Christenheit in der Zeitenwende*. Hamburg: Agentur des Rauhen Hauses, 1933.

Leffler, Siegfried. *Christus im Dritten Reich der Deutschen: Wesen, Weg und Ziel der Kirchenbewegung "Deutsche Christen."* Weimar: Verlag Deutsche Christen, 1935.

———. *Kirche, Christentum, Bolschewismus*. Weimar: Verlag Deutsche Christen, 1936.

Leutheuser, Julius. *Die deutsche Christusgemeinde: Der Weg zur deutschen Nationalkirche*. 3rd ed. Weimar: Verlag Deutsche Christen, 1935.

——. *Die deutsche Christusgemeinde und ihre Gegner: Eine Antwort an Herrn Pfarrer Ernst Otto und die lutherische Bekenntnisgemeinschaft in Thüringen.* 2nd and 3rd eds. Weimar: Verlag Deutsche Christen, 1935.

——, and Erich Fascher. *Ein theologisches Missverständnis: Unsere Antwort an Paul Althaus.* 2nd ed. Weimar: Verlag Deutsche Christen, 1935.

Lotz, Wilhelm. *Um den deutschen Weg des Glaubens.* Weimar: Verlag Deutsche Christen, 1941.

Meyer-Erlach, Wolf. *Glaubenstrotz: Acht Rundfunkreden.* **Weimar: Verlag Deutsche Christen, 1937.**

——. *Gott in uns: Sechs Rundfunkreden.* Weimar: Verlag Deutsche Christen, 1938.

——. *Kirche oder Sekte: Offener Brief an Herrn Landesbischof D. Meiser (München).* Weimar: Verlag Max Grevemeyer ["Deutsche Christen"], 1934.

——. *Die Kirche der Freiheit: Fünf Rundfunkpredigten.* 2nd ed. Weimar: Verlag Deutsche Christen, 1936.

——. *Verrat an Luther.* 3rd ed. Weimar: Verlag Deutsche Christen, 1936.

Müller, Ludwig. *Deutsche Gottesworte: Aus der Bergpredigt verdeutscht.* **10th ed. Weimar: Verlag Deutsche Christen, 1936.**

—— [Reichsbischof], and Christian Kinder. *Die Deutschen Christen: Die Reden des Reichsbischofs und des Reichleiters der Deutschen Christen, im Berliner Sportpalast am 28. Februar 1934* Berlin: Gesellschaft für Zeitungsdienst, 1934.

Oberheid, Heinrich. *Unpolitisches deutsches Christentum: Ein Wort über das "Politische Christentum" des Professors Paul Althaus.* Bonn: Verlag Gebr. Scheur, 1936.

Pabst, Carl, ed. *Neue Kirche im neuen Staat: Bekenntnis. Gemeindeaufbau. Kirchenleitung. Nationalsocialistischer Staat. "Deutsche Christen."* Gütersloh: C. Bertelsmann, 1933.

Petersmann, Werner. *Die heilige Sache der Deutschen Christen!* Breslau: "Quader" Druckerei u. Verlagsanstalt, 1935[?].

Pohlmann, Hans. *Der Gottesgedanke Jesu: Als Gegensatz gegen den israelitisch-jüdischen Gottesgedanken.* Weimar: Verlag Deutsche Christen, 1939.

Rönk, Hugo. *Ein Reich. Ein Gott. Vom Wesen deutschen Christentums: Handbuch für den Religions- und Konfirmandenunterricht.* Weimar: Verlag Deutsche Christen, 1939.

———. *Nationalkirchliche Einung Deutsche Christen?* 15th and 16th eds. Weimar: Verlag Deutsche Christen, 1939.

Ropp, Friedrich von der. *Die Kirche in der Entscheidung* (Published as a manuscript; also available from Berlin-Tempelhof: Verlag von Edwin Runge, 1933.

Schmidt, Philipp. *Gottestum und Volkstum in der deutschen Zeitenwende: Die Sendung der "Deutschen Christen." Ein Bekenntnis in der deutschen Volk- und Kirchwerdung zum deutschen Menschen und zum ewigen Christ.* Speyer am Rhein: Zechnersche Verlagsbuchhandlung, 1935.

Wagner, Martin. *Die "Deutschen Christen" im Kampf um die innere Erneuerung des deutschen Volkes.* Berlin-Charlottenburg: Verlag Max Grevemeyer ["Deutsche Christen"], 1933.

Weidemann, Heinz. *So sieht die kommende Kirche aus.* Bremen: Kommende Kirche, 1938.

Wieneke, Friedrich. *Deutsche Theologie im Umriss.* Soldin: H. Madrasch, 1933.

———. *Die Glaubensbewegung "Deutsche Christen."* 6th ed. Soldin: H. Madrasch, 1933.

Wolf, Heinrich. *Kulturtragödien der Völker nordischer Rasse: Alttestamentliche Bannungen.* Weimar: Verlag Deutsche Christen, 1939.

II. Secondary Sources in English

Barnett, Victoria J. *For the Soul of the People: Protestant Protest Against Hitler.* New York: Oxford University Press, 1992.

Bergen, Doris L. *Twisted Cross: The German Christian Movement in the Third Reich.* Chapel Hill: University of North Carolina Press, 1996.

Bethge, Eberhard. *Dietrich Bonhoeffer: A Biography.* Revised and edited by Victoria J. Barnett. Minneapolis: Fortress Press, 2000.

Conway, J. S. *The Nazi Persecution of the Churches, 1933–1945.* Vancouver: Regent College Publishing, 1968.

Ericksen, Robert P. *Complicity in the Holocaust: Churches and Universities in Nazi Germany.* Cambridge: Cambridge University Press, 2012.

———. *Theologians Under Hitler: Gerhard Kittel, Paul Althaus and Emanuel Hirsch.* New Haven and London: Yale University Press, 1985.

———, and Susannah Heschel, eds. *Betrayal: German Churches and the Holocaust.* Minneapolis: Fortress Press, 1999.

Friedländer, Saul. *Nazi Germany and the Jews, Vol. 1: The Years of Persecution, 1933–1939.* New York: HarperCollins, 1997.

———. *Nazi Germany and the Jews, Vol. 2: The Years of Extermination, 1939–1945.* New York: HarperCollins, 2007.

Gerlach, Wolfgang. *And the Witnesses Were Silent: The Confessing Church and the Persecution of the Jews.* Translated and edited by Victoria J. Barnett. Lincoln, NE: University of Nebraska Press, 2000.

Helmreich, Ernst Christian. *The German Churches Under Hitler: Background, Struggle, and Epilogue.* Detroit: Wayne State University Press, 1979.

Heschel, Susannah. *The Aryan Jesus: Christian Theologians and the Bible in Nazi Germany.* Princeton, NJ: Princeton University Press, 2008.

Jantzen, Kyle. *Faith and Fatherland: Parish Politics in Hitler's Germany.* Minneapolis: Fortress Press, 2008.

Kershaw, Ian. *Popular Opinion and Political Dissent in the Third Reich: Bavaria 1933–1945*. Oxford: Clarendon Press, 1983.

Matheson, Peter, ed. *The Third Reich and the Christian Churches: A Documentary Account of Christian Resistance and Complicity During the Nazi Era*. Edinburgh: T & T Clark, 1981.

Michael, Robert, and Karin Doerr. *Nazi-Deutsch/Nazi German: An English Lexicon of the Language of the Third Reich*. Westport, CT: Greenwood Press, 2002.

Scholder, Klaus. *The Churches and the Third Reich, Vol. 1: Preliminary History and the Time of Illusions, 1918–1934*. Translated by John Bowden. London: SCM Press, 1987.

———. *The Churches and the Third Reich, Vol. 2: The Year of Disillusionment: 1934 Barmen and Rome*. Translated by John Bowden. London: SCM Press, 1988.

———. *A Requiem for Hitler and Other New Perspectives on the German Church Struggle*. London: SCM Press, 1989; repr. Eugene, OR: Wipf & Stock, 2008.

Steigmann-Gall, Richard. *The Holy Reich: Nazi Conceptions of Christianity, 1919–1945*. Cambridge: Cambridge University Press, 2003.

Zabel, James A. *Nazism and the Pastors: A Study of the Ideas of Three* Deutsche Christen *Groups*. Missoula, MT: Scholars Press, 1976.

Index

298, 303, 313, 327n4, 357, 377,
391, 393, 403, 429, 430n10,
448

Reichsbischof [national (Protestant)
bishop], 16, 32, 39, 45, 88, 89,
91, 102, 151, 152, 153,
154-157, 166, 168, 230, 250n2,
265, 383, 386, 399. *See also*
Müller, Ludwig

Reichskirche [national (Protestant)
church], 16, 48, 51, 152, 168,
171, 247, 254, 322, 403. *See
also* German Protestant Church
[*Deutsche Evangelische Kirche*]

Rendtorff, Heinrich, 132, 276

Reventlow, Ernst Graf zu, 277,
278n24

Roman Catholic (or Catholic),
19n30, 21n32, 26n42, 38,
48n4, 66, 160, 161n37, 168n11,
171, 282, 359, 408, 410, 446.
See also Concordat

Rosenberg, Alfred, 132n11, 262n9,
275, 277, 434, 440

Rust, Bernhard, 159n35, 159n36

S. A. [*Sturmabteilung*], 137, 156,
164, 264, 301n4, 384, 423, 430.
See also Brown battalions

S. S. [*Schutzstaffel*], 102, 137,
278n23, 453

Scholder, Kurt, 16n24, 41, 338n2

Schopenhauer, Arthur, 308

Sermon on the Mount, 383-394,
465

Sports Palace, 15, 16n24, 17, 25,
31n45, 163, 167n8, 230,
249-262. *See also* Krause,
Reinhold

Stahlhelm, 131, 132n8

Stapel, Wilhelm, 112, 447

Steigmann-Gall, Richard, 129n5,
275n13

Twenty-eight Theses of the
Church of Saxony, 163,
171-176, 453

Volkskirche [people's church], 14,
36, 49, 67, 69, 169, 172, 173,
174, 175, 176, 250, 253, 257,
262. *See also* German People's
Church [*Deutsche Volkskirche*]

Wieneke, Friedrich, 15, 29, 37,
122, 130-133, 139, 144, 148,
149, 267-291

Wilm, Werner, 131, 167, 276

Wirth, Hermann, 277, 278n23

World War I, 37, 54, 129n5,
132n8, 135n15, 135n16,
155n30, 245n11, 263, 267,